The Trial of St. Paul

A Juridical Exegesis of the
Second Half of the Acts of the Apostles

by

H. W. Tajra

WIPF & STOCK · Eugene, Oregon

Wipf and Stock Publishers
199 W 8th Ave, Suite 3
Eugene, OR 97401

The Trial of St. Paul
A Juridicial Exegesis of the Second Half of the Acts of the Apostles
By Tajra, Harry W.
Copyright©1989 Mohr Siebeck
ISBN 13: 978-1-61097-005-1
Publication date 10/14/2010
Previously published by Mohr Siebeck, 1989

To my Father
and in Memory of my Mother and Brother

Preface
by Professor François Bovon

A number of years ago, Revd. H.W. Tajra, who had been a student of Professor Maurice Carrez in Paris, came to Geneva to work with me on the Book of Acts. I had been trained in the German tradition of M. Dibelius, E. Haenchen and H. Conzelmann. Revd. Tajra was more influenced by British tradition and especially by the works of F.F. Bruce. Whereas I tried to emphasize to him Luke's literary and theological project, he in turn always called my attention to the evangelist's historical programme and juridical exactitude.

Time passed and today Revd. Tajra is publishing the thesis which he successfully defended at the School of Theology in Geneva in February 1988. The jury which heard the defence was made up of Mr. Bruno Schmidlin, professor of Roman Law, Mr. Adalbert Giovannini, professor of Ancient History and myself as professor of Theology. That experts from three different schools were called in to hear the defence demonstrates the value of this present study. It enriches biblical exegesis through its many references to Roman Law and Ancient History and presents a balanced historical and juridical commentary of that part of the Book of Acts which relates Paul's encounters with Roman justice and especially his appeal to Caesar.

Luke, in my opinion, felt relatively free to reconstruct history in the pursuit of his goals, so I do not always share Mr. Tajra's "historical optimism". I firmly believe, however, that his analyses of legal terminology, his presentation of penal procedure as well as his description of various State and provincial institutions (many of which are complicated or little known) are of great value. They will be of signal service to biblical exegetes who often have trouble coming to grips with such problems. This juridical commentary will take its place, I believe, on library shelves along side H.J. Cadbury's *The Book Of Acts In History* (1955) and A.N. Sherwin-White's *Roman Society And Roman Law In The New Testament* (1963).

In conclusion, the present study puts forth a basically original thesis which theological criticism must henceforth take into account. The appeal to Caesar — a right which had been strengthened in the 1st Century A.D. — would have been lodged by the apostle Paul in order to get Christianity out of its Jewish matrix and to allow it to be heard at the highest Roman legal and political level. This would reflect the apostle's belief that once he had put forth his appeal, his case would no longer be that of a lone man trying to save his life. It would be Christianity itself that the apostle would be putting on trial as well.

School of Theology
University of Genèva
Genèva, August 1988

F. Bovon

Acknowledgements

I owe a profound debt of gratitude to many scholars for their help during the writing of the manuscript. Particular thanks are due to Professor François Bovon of the Faculty of Theology, University of Geneva, for his valuable suggestions and pertinent criticisms of the overall work. Professor Adalbert Giovannini of the Faculty of Letters, University of Geneva, and Professor Bruno Schmidlin of the Faculty of Law, also at the University of Geneva offered most helpful comments and criticisms on the subjects of Roman law, institutions and history. Professor Maurice Carrez of the Faculty of Protestant Theology in Paris read and reviewed the manuscript at an early stage and offered valuable comments on the life and apostleship of St. Paul. Professor Adela Yarbro Collins of Notre Dame University, Indiana, made useful suggestions on the legal and political situation of the Jews in the Diaspora and Professor James S. Ruebel of Iowa State University was particularly helpful in the area of Greek and Latin philology. Many thanks to Professor Martin Hengel for all his help and assistance and to Herr G. Siebeck for his patient attention and care to the technical side of the publication.

Finally I am indebted to Olivier, Beatrice and Thierry Mermod of Chambésy, Geneva for all the moral support they gave during the final stages of the project, as well as to my wife, who gave time so generously from her organ music to offer many interesting and felicitous suggestions during the whole eight years it took to research and write this book.

Genèva, August 1988   H.W. Tajra

Table of Contents

Preface v
Acknowledgements vii
Textual Apparatus xii
Abbreviations xiv
Introduction 1

Chapter I: Philippi: Paul and the Duoviri 3
  I. Paul in the Roman Colony of Philippi. 3
  II. Paul is accused before the *Duoviri*. 8
    1. The Officials: *Principes, Duoviri* and *Lictores* 9
    2. The Accusations 12
  III. Excursus 1: The juridical Situation of Judaism during the
      Early Principate. 14
  IV. Excursus 2: Foreign Cults and the Question of Proselytism 21
  V. Paul proclaims his Roman Citizenship. .24

Chapter II: Thessalonica: Paul, Jason and the Politarchs. 30
  I. The Free City of Thessalonica. 30
  II. Paul is accused of acting *"contra decreta Caesaris"* 31
  III. Excursus: The Emperor: His Authority, Majesty, Cult 36
  IV. Jason gives Security. 43

Chapter III: Corinth: Paul and Gallio 45
  I. The Senatorial Province of Achaia. 45
  II. Paul breaks with the Corinthian Synagogue. 47
  III. Paul before the Proconsul Gallio 51
  IV. *Vos ipsi videritis* 56

Chapter IV: Jerusalem (Part I): Paul and Lysias 63
  I. Paul's last Journey to Jerusalem 63
  II. The Tribune Lysias arrests Paul. 66
  III. The Preliminary Investigation begins. .68
  IV. Excursus: Paul's triple Identity 76
    1. The Concept of Multiple Citizenship. 76

    2. Paul, a Πολίτης of Tarsus 78
    3. Paul, the Pharisaic Jew 81
    4. Paul, the Roman Citizen 81
       a) Aspects of Roman citizenship 81
       b) Was the Apostle Paul indeed a Roman citizen? 86

Chapter V: Jerusalem (Part 2): Paul and the Sanhedrin 90

  I. *Paulus ante Synedrium* 90
    1. The Convening of the Sanhedrin 90
    2. In the Council Chamber 92
  II. Excursus: The Judicial Prerogatives of the Sanhedrin 98
  III. Paul is transferred to Caesarea 103
    1. The Plot to assassinate Paul 103
    2. Lysias' *Dimissoriae Litterae* 106

Chapter VI: Caesarea (Part 1): Paul and Felix 109

  I. The Procuratorship in Judaea: Judicial Competence and
    Exercise of Criminal Jurisdiction 109
  II. Paul is handed over to Felix: the Question of *Forum Domicilii* ... 116
  III. Tertullus the Rhetor presents the Case against Paul 118
  IV. Paul makes his *Apologia* before Felix 125
  V. Felix leaves Paul in Prison 129
    1. Paul in Custody 129
    2. *Biennis Captivitas Caesariensis* 132

Chapter VII: Caesarea (Part 2): Paul and Festus 135

  I. Festus at Jerusalem 135
  II. Festus in Favour of a Change of Jurisdiction 137
  III. Paul appeals to Caesar 142
  IV. Excursus: The Appeal under the early Emperors 144
  V. Festus grants Paul's Appeal 147

Chapter VIII: Caesarea (Part 3): Paul and Agrippa 152

  I. Festus summarizes Paul's Case to Agrippa 152
  II. Festus lays Paul's Case before Agrippa 159
  III. Paul makes his Defence 163
  IV. Agrippa gives his Opinion in Paul's Case 168

Chapter IX: Rome: Paul Spends Two Years Awaiting Trial 172

  I. Paul is transferred from Caesarea to Rome 172
  II. Paul a Prisoner at Rome 176

    1. The Stratopedarch.................................177
    2. *In Custodia Militari*..............................179
  III. Paul and the Roman Jews.............................181
    1. The Jewish Communities at Rome 181
    2. The First Interview: Paul explains his Case 184
    3. The Second Interview: Paul turns to the Gentiles 188
  IV. *Biennis Captivitas Romana* 191

Chapter X: An Afterword — The Lucan Account of Paul's
Legal History..197

Bibliography 202
  1. Reference Works.......................................202
  2. Bibliography of Works cited 203

Index of Passages 209
  1. Holy Scripture...209
  2. Epigraphical and Papyrological Publications 215
  3. Ancient Writers and Sources 216

Index of Names...222

Index of Subjects 224

Textual Apparatus

1. *Codices:*
   - A - Alexandrinus
   - B - Vaticanus
   - C - Ephraemi
   - D - Bezae
   - E - Laudianus
   - H - Mutinensis
   - L - Angelicus
   - P - Porphyrianus
   - S - Athos
   - Ψ - Athos

2. *Versiones Antiquae*
   Vg. - Vulgate
   $Vg.^{codd}$ - Vulgate codices excluding Vg^s, Vg^{cl}
   $Vg.^s$ - Sixtina, 1590
   $Vg.^{cl}$ - Clementina, 1592

   OL - Old Latin
   lat. - Vg + some OL mss.

   d - Codex Bezae, pars latina
   e - Codex Laudianus, pars latina
   g - Codex Gigas
   h - Codex Floriacencis

   sy^h - Syriac Harclean
   sy^p - Syriac Peshitta
   sy^{hmg} - Syriac Harclean marginal readings
   hcl.mg. - Harclean margin
   hcl.* - asterisked additions to the Harclean readings

   sa - Sahidic
   bo - Bohairic
   eth - Ethiopic

   Ambst. - Ambrosiaster

   δ - indicates Western text consensus
   byz. - indicates Byzantine Text
   614 - miniscule (δ - text, Milan)
   p^{48} - Pap. Ital. 1165, Florence, 3rd Century (contains Acts 23).

3. *Alia Signa:*
   R - reading followed in the Revised Version (1881)
   R^m - reading followed in the Revised Version margin
   al - *alii* = a large number of manuscripts
   pc - *pauci* = a few manuscripts
   pl - *plerique* = most witnesses
   pm - *permulti* = the majority
   $\int$ - *Stephanus* = where later manuscripts agree with the *Textus Receptus*.

Abbreviations

Abbott & Johnson	Abbott, Frank Frost & Johnson, Allan Chester, *Municipal Administration In The Roman Empire*, (1926)
AJP	American Journal of Philology
ANRW	*Aufstieg und Niedergang der römischen Welt,* Walter de Gruyter, (Berlin-New York).
Bauer Wb.	Bauer, Walter, Arndt, William & Gingrich, F.W., *A Greek-English Lexicon Of The New Testament,* (E.T.) University of Chicago Press, 10th Impression, 1967.
BC	Foakes-Jackson, F.J. & Lake, Kirsopp (ed.), *The Beginnings Of Christianity,* 5 Volumes, 1920–1933.
BC, Vol. IV.	Lake, Kirsopp & Cadbury, H.J., *The Acts Of The Apostles,* English Translation and Commentary, 1933.
BGU	*Berliner griechische Urkunden* (Agyptische Urkunden aus den Königlichen Museen zu Berlin) Berlin, 1895 –.
BTB	*Biblical Theology Bulletin* (Rome)
Bl. Debr.	Blass, F. & Debrunner, A., *A Greek Grammar Of The New Testament* (E.T.) University of Chicago Press, 3rd Impression, 1967
Bruce,	Bruce, F.F., *The Acts Of The Apostles,* (1975)
Bruns, FIRA	Bruns, Karl Georg, *Fontes Iuris Romani Antiqui,* (1969)
Cadbury, "Roman Law ..."	Cadbury, H.J. "Roman Law and the Trial of Paul", 1933
CJ	Classical Journal
CP	Classical Philology (Chicago)
CIG	*Corpus Inscriptionum Graecarum* Berlin, 1828 –.
CII	*Corpus Inscriptionum Iudaicarum* J.B. Frey, (ed.), Rome: Vol. I, 1936; Vol. II, 1952

CIL	Corpus Inscriptionum Latinarum Berlin, 1863 –.
DAGR	Daremberg, Ch. & Saglio, E. (eds.) Dictionnaire des Antiquités grecques et romaines, Paris, 5 Tomes, 1877–1919.
Diz. Epigr.	de Ruggiero, Ettore, Dizionario Epigrafico di Antichità romane Rome, 1895 –.
Ehrenberg & Jones	Ehrenberg, Victor and Jones, A.H.M., Documents Illustrating The Reigns Of Augustus and Tiberius, 1955.
E.T.	English Translation
F.T.	French Translation
Girard, Textes[4]	Girard, Paul Frédéric, Textes de Droit romain, 4th Edition, 1913.
Haenchen	Haenchen, Ernst, The Acts Of The Apostles (E.T.), 1971
HSCP	Harvard Studies in Classical Philology
HTR	Harvard Theological Review
HDB	Hastings, James (ed.), A Dictionary Of The Bible, Edinburgh, 4 volumes, 1898–1902
IG	Inscriptiones Graecae, Berlin, 1873 – cf. especially Vol. VII, 1892; Vol. XIV, 1890
ILS	Inscriptiones Latinae Selectae, Berlin, Third Edition, 1962
JQR	Jewish Quarterly Review (Philadelphia)
JBL	Journal of Biblical Literature, Philadelphia
JRS	Journal of Roman Studies, London
LS[9]	Liddell, Henry George and Scott, Robert, A Greek-English Lexicon, Clarendon Press, Oxford, 9th Edition, 1940, (reprint 1978).
Loeb	Loeb Classical Library, London/Cambridge, Mass.
Mason, GREEK TERMS	Mason, Hugh, J. Greek Terms For Roman Institutions, Toronto, 1974.
Mommsen, STAATSRECHT	Mommsen, Theodor, Römisches Staatsrecht, 3 Volumes, 1887–1888.
Mommsen, STRAFRECHT	Mommsen, Theodor, Römisches Strafrecht, 1899.
MM	Moulton, James Hope and Milligan, George, The Vocabulary Of The Greek Testament, Hodder and Stoughton, London, 1930, (impression 1963).

Moulton, *PROLEGOMENA*	Moulton, James Hope, *A Grammar Of New Testament Greek,* Volume I = Prolegomena, T. & T. Clark, Edinburgh, 3rd. Edition, 1908 (reprint 1957).
NTS	New Testament Studies (Cambridge)
OGIS	*Orientis Graeci Inscriptiones Selectae,* Leipzig, 1903–1905.
OCD	*The Oxford Classical Dictionary,* Clarendon Press, Oxford, 1949, (reprint, 1957).
P	Papyri
P.Amh.	Amherst Papyri
P.Fay.	Fayûm Towns and their Papyri
P.Flor.	Papiri Fiorentini
P.Hib.	Hibeh Papyri
P.Lille	Papyrus Grecs: Institut Papyrologique de l'Université de Lille
P.Lond.	Greek Papyri in the British Museum
P.Mich.	Michigan Papyri
P.Oxy.	Oxyrhynchus Papyri
P.Petrie	Flinders Petrie Papyri
P.Tebt.	Tebtunis Papyri
PL	Patrologia Latina
PAULYS-WISSOWA-RE	*Paulys Real-Encyclopädie der Classischen Altertumswissenschaft,* 1894 –.
QDAP	Quarterly of the Department of Antiquities in Palestine (Jerusalem)
Ramsay, *SPT*	Ramsay, William M., *St. Paul The Traveller and The Roman Citizen,* 1896.
RSR	Recherches de Science Religieuse (Paris)
RBPH	Revue Belge de Philologie et d'Histoire (Brussels)
RB	Revue Biblique (Paris)
REA	Revue des Etudes Anciennes (Bordeaux)
REG	Revue des Etudes Grecques (Paris)
RHPR	Revue d'Histoire et de Philosophie Religieuses (Strasbourg)
Riccobono, *FIRA*	Riccobono, Salvator, *Fontes Iuris Romani Antejustiniani,* 1941
Sherwin-White	Sherwin-White, A.N., *Roman Society And Roman Law In The New Testament,* Oxford, 1963.
SIG[4]	*Sylloge Inscriptionum Graecarum,* 4th Edition, 1960.

ThWb	Kittel, Gerhard, et al., *Theological Dictionary Of The New Testament,* (E.T.), Eerdmans, Grand Rapids, in nine volumes.
TZ	Theologische Zeitschrift (Basle)
VC	Vigilae Christianae (Amsterdam)
ZNW	Zeitschrift für die Neutestamentliche Wissenschaft, Berlin/New York
Zerwick-GB	Zerwick, Maximilian, *Biblical Greek,* (E.T. from the 4th Latin edition of *Graecitas Biblica*), Rome, 1963 reeditio, 1982.

Introduction

The primary aim of this present study is to cast some light on the legal aspects of the account in Acts of Paul's encounters with the Roman judicial system. To achieve that end, the study not only proceeds with an analysis of the legal data furnished by Acts, but tries to assemble pertinent information on Roman judicial history and practice found in widely disparate sources and apply it to the Acts-narrative. Finally the judicial material thus assembled is examined within the essentially religious setting of Acts.

One of the principal problems in dealing with Paul's legal history is that the sole account one has of its most important developments, e.g. his arrest, appeal to Caesar and transfer to Rome, occurs in Acts alone. As this account is unique, it is impossible to test the narrative's real historical value by comparing its relation of events to the witness of other more or less contemporary writings, the Epistles or early Patristic literature for example. The question thus inevitably arises as to the historical reliability of the Acts-narrative itself. Is there any discernable tension between historical fact on the one hand and the theological and apologetic purposes of Luke on the other? Has Luke distorted the real facts in Paul's case in carrying out his theological and apologetic programme? What is certain is that the narrative's legal dimension cannot be disassociated from its theological dimension; thus Luke's own theological viewpoint and his apologetic strategy play a considerable role in his account of Paul's trial.

The main thesis of the present study is that Luke's account of Paul's legal history in the second half of Acts demonstrates a considerable knowledge of provincial and Roman nomenclature as well as of the intricacies of state and local administration. Luke's writing is characterized by a fine usage of legal terminology. He is well acquainted with legal procedure and with the sundry uses and applications of statutory and customary law. Indeed his account of Paul's appeal to Caesar and its legal consequences is quite in accordance with the little we know of appellate procedure in the middle third of the First Century A.D. In Chapters 16 to 28, Luke pays great attention to the formalities of legal structure; his handling of the judicial material — where it can be checked — is remarkably accurate. Luke's meticulosity would strongly suggest that one is not dealing with fiction here, but with a trustworthy reminiscence of someone who knew Paul quite well in the final years of his apostolic ministry. Concentration on legal terminology and procedure can only lead to the conclusion that Luke has given a *legally realistic* account of Paul's judicial history in Acts.

It is entirely another step, however, to conclude that what is legally realistic is necessarily *historically true*. Luke's narrative of Paul's legal history exhibits a distinctive authorial bias which is intrinsically linked to his overall theological aims. First Luke gives as pronounced a Pharisaic flavour to Paul's discourse as he can. He endeavours throughout his account to place Paul's doctrine and praxis within the mainstream of official Judaism. In Acts, Paul observes ancestral rites and customs, he is never an opponent of the Temple or of the Law. If Paul finds himself in litigation with his nation's authorities in various Roman courts, it is solely because of their violence, injustice and disbelief. He himself remains faithful to his nation and has no griefs against his people to bring forth in a court of law. Thus Luke consistently portrays Paul as being anxious not to become estranged from organized Judaism.

Secondly Luke maintains Paul's innocence on all political charges, and especially on the charge of sedition. In contrast to his portrayal of the Jewish authorities' injustice and unrighteousness, Luke stresses to his essentially Roman audience the sense of justice and the equitable behaviour of the Roman officials whom Paul encounters. This is especially the case at those crucial moments in Paul's legal itinerary when the apostle had to invoke his Roman citizenship. Although Luke does not suppress from his narrative those instances in which Roman officials behave inequitously toward Paul (e.g. the Philippian Duumvirs, Felix), his account is markedly pro-Roman in its overall stance. There is thus a clearly tendentious treatment of both Jews and Romans in the Lucan account of Paul's trial.

It is therefore necessary in studying St. Paul's trial to distinguish between the tendentious and the legally realistic. The method used in the present work consists of examining Paul's encounters with Roman officials sequence by sequence in commentary form:

First of all the Lucan usage of legal terminology is examined and if possible compared to other primary sources, epigraphical, literary or papyrological.

Then, if necessary, the pericope is reviewed from the procedural point of view. Certain points needing more explanation or background information, are developed in an excursus.

Finally, the text is examined from a redactional standpoint to ascertain if Luke did in fact alter the historical facts in Paul's case to suit his theological purposes, and if so, to see whether the historical facts in question can be recovered or reconstructed on the basis of the internal evidence available in Acts.

Chapter I
Philippi: Paul and the Duoviri

I. Paul in the Roman Colony of Philippi

The narrative in Acts records a certain number of judicial encounters which Paul had with local or provincial magistrates prior to his arrest in Jerusalem and subsequent transfer to Rome. Indeed as early as the First Missionary Journey, the apostle had come up against the various local authorities and had fallen foul of them. In Antioch in Pisidia, the Jews stirred up persecution against Paul and Barnabas and had them driven from the city (Acts XIII,50). The two apostles had to flee Iconium lest they be stoned (XIV, 5–6). Luke tells us that at Lystra, Paul was stoned and left for dead (XIV, 19). Jewish hostility towards Paul was already intense and the local Jewish communities spared no effort in inciting the local magistrates to punish and drive away the two missionaries of Jesus Christ.

In the second half of Acts, Luke concentrates almost uniquely on Paul. The apostle becomes the central figure in the narrative and remains so until the end. Luke intertwines the story of Paul's missionary activity and his apologetic discourse with the story of his judicial history, which is related in ever-increasing detail. With the story of the apostle's arrival in Philippi, Luke begins to present Paul's case in a more developed and systematic way. The charges against which Paul would later have to defend himself in Caesarea and Rome were already basically formulated at this early period in his legal history. Luke clearly explicates the indictment against the apostle: it is made up of grave *political* charges which the accusers are unable to substantiate, hence their attempt to offer *theological* evidence as cogent proof. Luke also stresses that the apostle is spared a guilty verdict in the various courts because the examining magistrates consider the case to be nothing other than intra-Jewish theological strife. They consider the political charges as unsubstantiated and irrelevant. As a religious controversy, the matter ought to be judged by the Jewish communal authorities; it is not really cognizable in a Roman or provincial court of law. We also become aware of how vital a factor Paul's Roman citizenship was in his legal history. This is made abundantly clear by Luke in his relation of the proceedings at Philippi. Paul's *civitas* put him into a definite legal status vis-à-vis the authorities and assured him a panoply of rights not available to the peregrine. The final point which Luke makes is that the Jewish communities at Thessalonica and Corinth largely reject the apostle's message. The Jewish leading men are depicted as fierce adversaries of Paul and Silas, men who did not hesitate to resort to violence as a consequence and manifestation of their disbelief. At Corinth especially Paul turns to the Gentiles. The Gentile mission puts into question Paul's status within Judaism and by extension the place the churches born of the Pauline mission had (or did not have) within organized Judaism.

Thus four important aspects of the later trial are already present in Chapters 16 and 18: (a) the mixture of political charges and theological evidence which reflects the basic lack of a well-structured and coherent case against Paul; (b) the importance of Paul's Roman citizenship in his legal history; (c) the reluctance of the magistrates to handle his case; and (d) the discordant relationship between the apostle and the Jewish authorities and the ever-widening rift between the Pauline churches and the synagogue.

The first of the legal encounters which Luke describes at length occurs during Paul's ministry at Philippi (XVI,11–40). Two factors have to be borne in mind when considering the judicial events in that city: (a) Paul's arrest, incarceration and proclamation of his citizenship took place in a Roman colony before the Roman authorities, and (b) the action taken against Paul was formal and official.

Luke relates how Paul and his companions, having left Troas and Samothrace, arrived at the port of Neapolis and went thence to Philippi, "which is the leading city of the district of Macedonia and a Roman colony." (ἥτις ἐστὶν πρώτη τῆς μερίδος Μακεδονίας πόλις, κολωνία). (XVI,12).

A) ἥτις ἐστὶν πρώτη τῆς μερίδος Μακεδονίας πόλις (Vg. = *Quae est prima partis Macedoniae civitas*)

In 167 B.C., Aemilius Paulus, conqueror of Macedonia, divided the vanquished kingdom into four administrative districts (μερίδες/*regiones*)[1]. While this reorganization had the advantage of preserving municipal freedom and self-government, its basic aim was the destruction of the political unity of Macedonia[2]. To prevent any sort of generalized insurrection against Roman rule, the four *regiones* were kept as separate from each other as possible: forming as it were genuine sub-provinces each of which was provided with a separate regional council (συνέδριον)[3]. Luke was correct

---

1 cf. Livy XLV,29.5.
2 C.H. Turner, "Philippi", *HDB*, Edinburgh, 1900, Vol. III,837.
3 Sherwin-White, pg. 93. A.P. Wikgren notes that even after Macedonia was made a Roman pro-

then when he used the term μέρις to describe the geopolitical subdivisions of Macedonia.

Philippi was in the first administrative district. It was however, neither the capital of the province of Macedonia, which was Thessalonica, nor of the first district, which was Amphipolis[4]. It is possible that the word πρώτη refers to the first city in Macedonia in which Paul preached or that Philippi is the first city mentioned in a succession of cities; the rest, Amphipolis, Apollonia and Thessalonica, being mentioned at the beginning of Chapter 17. In the last analysis, however, it seems more likely that the emendation πρώτης (i.e. a city of the first district) is the best reading, all the more so as this solution reflects the precise status of Philippi at the time the Book of Acts was written[5].

B) Κολωνία

This is the only place in which this word appears in the NT. Indeed the transliteration of the Latin *colonia* is found only infrequently in the literary texts of the period; the term ἀποικία being the commoner designation for a colony. The choice of the word κολωνία rather than ἀποικία is clearly part of Luke's literary design. The term κολωνία expresses certain legal and constitutional nuances unlike ἀποικία which gives no indication of the particular and wide judicial privileges enjoyed by a Roman colony as opposed to any other sort of colony which could also be designated by the generic term ἀποικία[6].

Basically *colonia* meant first of all a group of citizens (or allies), regularly organized and sent by a confirmative law in accordance with a *Senatus Consultum*[7] — or still later by imperial decree — to wholly or partially

---

vince (148 B.C.) the fourfold division continued "although the autonomy of each μέρις was modified by the introduction of a supreme administrative body (κοινόν) for Macedonia as a whole". (A.P. Wikgren, "The Problem in Acts 16:12", *NEW TESTAMENT TEXTUAL CRITICISM*, Oxford, 1981, pg. 172.

4 cf. the reading in D, syP: ἥτις ἐστὶν κεφαλὴ τῆς Μακεδονίας πόλις κολωνία / O.L.: *caput*. Certain Vg. codd. read *in prima parte Macedoniae civitas* (also: *primae partis; prima parte*). It is interesting to note that in the Vg. Philippi is referred to here as a *civitas* and in XVI,39 as an *urbs*. Livy XLV,29.9 gives the names of the four capitals: First Region, Amphipolis; Second Region, Thessalonica; Third Region, Pella; Fourth Region, Pelagonia.

5 Wikgren, *op.cit.*, pg. 178.

6 Mason, *GREEK TERMS*, pg. 109.

7 The SC of the *Lex Coloniae* regulated the bases on which the colony was organized, the number of colonists that were to be sent there, the extent of the territory assigned to the city, the land allotment of each colonist and the number of *curatores coloniae deducendae* to be named to preside over the formation of the new city. cf. F. Lenormant, "Colonia", *DAGR*, Tome I, Part 2 (c), pg. 1303–1304; and Kornemann, "Coloniae", *PAULYS-WISSOWA-RE.*, Vol. IV, col. 560. A.N. Sherwin-White notes the influence the citizen colony had on the development and extension of the Roman citizenship in *THE ROMAN CITIZENSHIP*, Oxford, 1939, pg. 75.

occupy a conquered city and its territory or else to establish a new city on land that was part of the *ager publicus*[8]. The word also designated the precise place at which the colonists settled. There were several types of colonies each with a distinct judicial identity and constitutional form which successively appeared throughout the long course of Roman history. Philippi due to its settlement by veterans and its military vocation, can be classified primarily as a military colony[9].

Military colonies could be organized under the terms of a *Senatus Consultum* or instituted by a general or dictator in accordance with a decree arising and proceeding from his *imperium*[10]. Colonies were not founded solely to reward veterans for their service by granting them land therein, but for overriding political and strategic reasons[11]. Colonies were an instrument of Roman policy, used to extend and consolidate Roman domination by the establishment of a loyal city or group of cities, peopled by citizens, in areas needing defence or in danger of revolt[12].

Following the victory of Antony and Octavian over Brutus and Cassius at the Battle of Philippi (42 B.C.), Philippi was made a Roman colony and a certain number of veterans were settled there. After Octavian defeated Antony and Cleopatra at Actium (31 B.C.), more colonists, some erstwhile supporters of the defeated Antony[13], others drawn from Augustus' Praetorian Cohort[14], were settled there and the city received its designation of *Colonia Iulia Augusta Philippensis*[15].

Architecturally and artistically, Philippi resembled other Greek cities with the usual Greek municipal buildings and decoration. There were also strong Greek cultural influences present. Nevertheless the Latin *ethos* was

---

[8] Appian, *Bell.Civ.* I,7; II,140. Dionysius Halicarnassensis VII,13.1–5.

[9] cf. Kornemann, *op.cit.*, col. 549. Military colonies need to be numbered amongst the *coloniae civium Romanorum* as they were settled by soldiers who were Roman citizens. The *coloniae civium Romanorum* constituted one of the integral elements of the state (cf. *Diz. Epigr.* Vol. II, part I, pg. 417). Cicero denounced the establishment of colonies if it were not in the interest of the Republic. (*de Lege Agr.* II,73).

[10] cf. F. Lenormant, *op.cit.*, pg. 1311. J. Bleicken notes that imperium was the "quintessence of Roman might and of the Roman will to rule". (*DER VERFASSUNG DER ROMISCHEN REPUBLIK*, Paderborn, 2e Auflage, 1978, pg. 83). The Emperors gained the *imperium proconsulare maius* by Senate vote at their accession (cf. ILS. 229.10.).

[11] Philippi lay on the great *via Egnatia* which linked the port of Neapolis on the Aegean to Dyrrachium on the Adriatic.

[12] cf. Livy, LVI,3. cf. H.J. Cadbury, *THE BOOK OF ACTS IN HISTORY*, London, 1955, pg. 74–75.

[13] cf. Dio Cassius LI,4.6.

[14] cf. T.H. Watkins, *A STUDY OF THE ORIGIN AND HISTORICAL DEVELOPMENT OF IUS ITALICUM*, Chapel Hill, 1973, pg. 277.

[15] P. Collart points out that Philippi received this name only after January 27 B.C. the date Octavian received the title Augustus from the Senate. P. Collart, *PHILIPPES, VILLE DE MACEDOINE*, Geneva, 1937, pg. 241.

very much in evidence[16]. The Latin language was widely spoken and the coins of the colony bore Latin inscriptions. The colony's political and juridical institutions were designed on the Roman model, Roman law was in usage and the *coloni* enjoyed, both individually and collectively, the rights and privileges afforded their fellow Roman citizens living in Italy itself. This included the possession of *libertas* and of the *ius Italicum*[17]. *Libertas* gave the city the right to autonomous government and was a basic right of all Roman colonies. On the individual level, *libertas* was "first of all the guarantee of a just application of the law to all; and on the collective level of use against dominant oligarchies"[18]. The *ius Italicum* transformed the provincial *solum* into Italian *solum* by the legal extension of Italic rights to the provincial city benefiting from the grant[19].

> "*Ius Italicum* was the pinnacle of colonial status and denoted the closest possible ties with Rome. It was reserved for the relatively few colonies which were the direct historical descendants of the *coloniae maritimae* of the early and middle Republic. Only these colonies were thought worthy of being regarded as part of Italy through a legal fiction"[20].

Thus a Roman colony differed from a *municipium* and from a *civitas libera* in having a Roman form of administration and in the use of Roman law and judicial procedure[21]. It behooves us therefore to recall when examining the sequence of events at Philippi that the apostle Paul was in a com-

---

16 cf. W. Neil, THE ACTS OF THE APOSTLES, London, 1973, pg. 181. Collart writes that nowhere else was the expansion of Latin more complete. (*op.cit.*, pg. 316).
17 Haenchen, pg. 494, note 2.
18 C. Nicolet, LE METIER DE CITOYEN DANS LA ROME REPUBLICAINE, Paris, 1976, pg. 429. Nicolet considers the term *libertas* to be the key word of the Roman civic and political vocabulary.
19 cf. A. von Premerstein, "Ius Italicum". *PAULY-WISSOWA-RE*, Vol. X, 19er Halbband, Cols. 1242–1248 and C. Jullian, "Jus Italicum", *DAGR*, Tome III, Part I (H-K), pg. 746–747. The *ius Italicum* is mentioned by Pliny the Elder, *Nat. Hist.* III,25; 139. Philippi is cited in the *Digest* L,15.6 as being one of the cities possessing the *ius Italicum*.
20 Watkins, *op.cit.*, pg. 434. E. Ferenczy notes the distinctive role the *ius Italicum* played in the imperial régime's policy on citizenship in "Rechtshistorische Bemerkungen zur Ausdehnung des römischen Bürgerrechts und zum ius Italicum unter der Prinzipat", *ANRW* II,14; 1982, pg. 1053 ff.
21 Aulus Gellius made the following comparison between a *municipium* and a *colonia*: "*Municipes*, then, are Roman citizens from free towns (*cives Romani ex municipiis*), using their own laws and enjoying their own rights, merely sharing with the Roman people an honorary *munus*, or "privilege" (from the enjoyment of which privilege they appear to derive their name), and bound by no other compulsion and no other law of the Roman people, except such as their own citizens have officially ratified. (...) But the relationship of the 'colonies' is a different one; for they do not come into citizenship from without, nor grow from roots of their own, but they are as it were transplanted from the State and have all the laws and institutions of the Roman people, not those of their own choice. This condition, although it is more exposed to control and less free, is nevertheless thought preferable and superior because of the greatness and majesty of the Roman people (*propter amplitudinem maiestatemque populi Romani*), of which those colonies seem to be miniatures, as it were, and in a way copies; ...". (*Noct. Att.* XVI,13.6–9; E.T.=J.C. Rolfe, *Loeb*, 1961.)

pletely Roman ambience and as a Roman citizen enjoyed all the rights and protection inherent in his *civitas*.

II. Paul is accused before the *Duoviri*

After a description of Paul's missionary activity in Philippi and the conversion of Lydia of Thyatira (Acts XVI,12b—15), Luke related the event which led to Paul's arrest, that is the driving of a spirit of divination out of a poor slave girl (XVI,16—18). This girl, who could speak in oracles, "brought her owners much gain (ἐργασίαν πολλήν), by soothsaying". (XVI,16b). "But when her owners saw that their hope of gain was gone, they seized Paul and Silas and dragged them into the market place (ἐπιλαβόμενοι τὸν Παῦλον καὶ τὸν Σιλᾶν εἵλκυσαν εἰς τὴν ἀγοράν) before the rulers; (ἐπὶ τοὺς ἄρχοντας); and when they had brought them to the magistrates (τοῖς στρατηγοῖς) they said: 'These men are Jews (Ἰουδαῖοι ὑπάρχοντες) and they are disturbing our city. (οὗτοι οἱ ἄνθρωποι ἐκταράσσουσιν ἡμῶν τὴν πόλιν). They advocate customs which it is not lawful for us Romans to accept or practice! (καὶ καταγγέλουσσιν ἔθη ἃ οὐκ ἔξεστιν ἡμῖν παραδέχεσθαι οὐδὲ ποιεῖν Ῥωμαίοις οὖσιν) (XVI,19—21).

A) ἐργαρσίαν πολλὴν

Luke establishes the mercenary motives of the apostles' accusers (revenge and greed) straight away (XVI, 19a), as he will later do when reporting Demetrius' speech at Ephesus (XIX, 24—27). Thus Luke lets his reader know in an unambiguous way that the real motive for the accusations is disappointment at the loss of profit and not any crime on the apostles' part[22].

B) ἐπιλαβόμενοι/εἵλκυσαν

1) ἐπιλαμβάνω — to "lay hold of", "seize", "attack"; the legal sense is to "make a seizure of", "arrest", to "lay hands on in assertion of a claim"[23].

2) ἕλκω/ἑλκύω — basically to drag by force: here to drag by force before the duly constituted authorities[24].

---

22 cf. C.M. Martini, *ATTI DEGLI APOSTOLI*, Rome, 6th Edition, 1982, pg. 236.
23 *LS*[9], pg. 642. cf. Acts XVII,19; XVIII,17; XXI,30,33. cf. Aristophanes, *Nubes*, 1218.
24 cf. Acts XXI,30.

Luke vividly depicts the violent nature of Paul's accusers and the public disturbance which their charges caused (XVI,19). It was the rowdiness in the streets and the intensity of the tumult which induced the magistrates to deem it quite superfluous to conduct a proper investigation of the two accused apostles' activities. Rather than acting in accordance with normal judicial practice, the magistrates opted to extirpate the alleged evil by summary and expeditious action.

C) εἰς τὴν ἀγοράν (*in Forum*)

The Forum was the centre of public life. Business was transacted there and its porticoes served as a place for intellectual discussion and philosophical and religious discourse[25]. Justice was also administered in the Forum and indeed the term Ἀγορά can be used in the sense of "a judicial assembly"[26].

1. The Officials: *Principes, Duoviri* and *Lictores*

A) ἐπὶ τοὺς ἄρχοντας

In Acts XVI,19, the authorities are referred to as ἄρχοντες (rulers). Five other times in the text the word στρατηγοί (magistrates) is used (XVI,20, 22,35,36,38). We also learn from XVI,35 that the στρατηγοί were attended by ῥαβδοῦχοι (lictors).

The term ἄρχων could be used to describe a number of administrative positions. In Greece, for example, it was used to designate the authorities or magistrates in general and sometimes the chief magistrate[27]. It could also be used to refer to a Roman provincial governor[28]. Polybius uses it in reference to the Roman consuls[29]. In many official documents such as a *Senatus Consultum* or an imperial decree, the word ἄρχων is used as the technical equivalent of magistrate; that is an independent magistrate who could act under his own auspices[30]. In the NT, ἄρχων denotes Jewish and Gentile official of all kinds, normally without naming the particular of-

---

25 cf. Acts XVII,17.
26 *MM.*, pg. 6. cf. *LS*9, pg. 13.
27 This was especially the case at Athens.
28 cf. *OGIS.* 441.59: "*Praeses* (ἡγεμών) *provinciae hic* ἄρχων *appellatur, id quod minus frequens quidem est, sed facilem explicationem habet, quandoquidem de praefectis quos Athenienses olim miserant in oppida regionesque sibi subditas, hoc nomen solenne erat.*"
29 Polybius I,38.6; I,39.1.
30 Mason, *GREEK TERMS*, pg. 111. cf. *ThWb*, Vol. I, pg. 488 (E.T.) which notes that the ἄρχων "has a high position in which he exercises authority; he is thus in the first instance a 'high official'".

fice[31]. In the text at hand, the term ἄρχοντες is used to denote the leading men who, taken together, are the real and effective governing power within the colony of Philippi.

B) τοῖς στρατηγοῖς

The original meaning of στρατηγός was military leader, commander or general. The word appears 10 times in the NT all of them in Luke-Acts.

There were quite a number of civil and military usages for this term in the various official vocabularies of the Ancient East. In Jerusalem, for example, the στρατηγός τοῦ ἱεροῦ designated the commander of the levitical guard who had custody of the Jerusalem temple[32]. It was also the title of the chief magistrates of the cities of Asia Minor[33]. Indeed in official Hellenistic terminology, στραηγός became one of the main ways of designating municipal or provincial officials[34]. In Polybius one finds the terms στρατηγός ὕπατος for Consul[35] and ἑξαπέλεκυς στραρηγός for Praetor[36]. This latter usage is interesting in that one sees how the term στρατηγός had in fact become technically equated with the term Praetor[37] to designate the magistrate responsible for the administration of justice[38]. By assimilation, the title was also used to designate the ruling *Duoviri iure dicundo* of a Roman colony because they too held powers of jurisdiction.

The *Duoviri* were responsible for the overall administration of the colony[39]. One of their duties was to preside at meetings of the Senate and popular Assembly and to carry out measures passed by either of these bodies. The *Duoviri* were invested with judicial authority and their jurisdiction extended to both civil and criminal processes[40]. Their judicial author-

---

31 cf. Acts IV,5: "On the morrow their rulers and elders and scribes were gathered together in Jerusalem". In Acts XIV,5, the word refers to both the leaders of the Jewish community as well as to the Gentile rulers of Iconium.
32 Acts IV,1; V,24 (Captain of the Temple); in Lk. XXII,52 the plural is used.
33 *OGIS*. 329.42 (Aegina, 2nd. Century B.C.). cf. Herodotus V,38.
34 *ThWb*, Vol. VII, pg. 704 (E.T.).
35 Polybius I,52.5 (cf. Polybius I,7.12 where στρατηγός alone means Consul).
36 Polybius III, 106.6; XXXIII,1.5.
37 cf. Mason, *GREEK TERMS*, pg. 157 ff. where the author discusses the special use of στρατηγός for Praetor. cf. A. Giovannini, *CONSULARE IMPERIUM*, Basle 1983, pg. 62.
38 cf. Cicero, who finds the pretention of the magistrates of Capua to the title Praetor rather abusive: "*cum ceteris in coloniis duumviri appellentur hi se praetores appellari volebant*" (*de Lege Agr.* II,34).
39 The conditions of eligibility to the Duumvirate are given in considerable detail in the *Lex Iulia Municipalis* of 45 B.C. The text of this law is given in *CIL*.I,206 and also in Abbott & Johnson, No. 24; Bruns *FIRA*, No. 18; Riccobono, *FIRA*, I,13; Girard, *Textes*4, No. 15. The law, a normative type of constitution, also provides details as to the political and judicial prerogatives of the *Duoviri*. cf. G. Rotondi, *LEGES PUBLICAE POPULI ROMANI*, Hildesheim, 1966, pg. 423–425.
40 *Lex Iulia Municipalis*, line 116.

ity was rather great for although it did not carry with it the same powers which the Praetor had because of the *imperium* with which he had been invested by the people, nonetheless their jurisdiction approached praetorian jurisdiction in that it was not delegated, but like the latter, exercised directly[41].

The *Duoviri* were responsible for keeping the peace and maintaining public order. They had the power to hear cases and to condemn defendants in both civil and criminal proceedings[42]. They held magisterial *coercitio*, the right to inflict summary punishment in order to secure obedience to the magisterial will[43]. A.N. Sherwin-White has pointed out that as far as magisterial *coercitio* was concerned "it is extremely unlikely that the municipal court, even of a Roman colony, which was a privileged organization, had the power to inflict severe punishments"[44]. The *Duoviri* could not order the execution or beating of a Roman citizen[45]. Finally, the *Duoviri* had the power to expel people from the colony, a power akin to the governor's power of relegation from a province.

C) ῥαβδοῦχοι (Vg = *lictores*)

ῥαβδοῦχος or ῥαβδονόμος is the word the Greek writers generally used for the Latin term lictor[46]. The word ῥαβδοῦχος occurs only in this passage in the New Testament.

Like the chief magistrates at Rome, the Philippian *Duoviri* were attended by lictors who preceded them bearing *fasces*. These men were at the disposition of the principal Roman magistrates and their task was to carry out magisterial orders. Their presence was a symbol of the obedience due to the magistrates they accompanied; indeed their duty was to see to it that the latter were rendered all the honours corresponding to their rank[47]. As symbols of law, order and justice they were representatives of the sov-

---

41 J. Marquardt, *ROMISCHE STAATSVERWALTUNG*. Leipzig, 1881, Vol. I, pg. 69.
42 *Lex Iulia Municipalis*, line 119.
43 *Lex Iulia Municipalis*, lines 115–116.
44 Sherwin-White, pg. 75.
45 cf. the *Lex Rubria de Gallia Cisalpina* (49–42 B.C.). The general objective of this law was to establish standard procedure for the municipal courts of Gallia Cisalpina and specific norms to govern relations between them and Rome. Certain limitations were imposed on the local magistrate's judicial competence because of the superior power of the Praetor's jurisdiction. Thus important cases were sent to the Praetor at Rome for judgment as they could not be heard at the municipal instance. The text of this law is given in *CIL*. I,205 and is also reproduced in Abbott & Johnson, No. 27; Bruns, *FIRA*, No. 16; Riccobono, *FIRA*, No. 19 and Girard, *Textes*[4], No. 13.
46 The transliteration λείκτωρ occurs in some inscriptions, cf. *CIL*. III, 6078.
47 cf. Dionysius Halicarnassensis, X,31.

ereign power of the Roman people itself[48]. They bore the *fasces* which were their principal *insignia*. These were *virgae* (rods) tied together around an axe by a red band[49]. The axe (*securis*) was used for carrying out military capital punishment. The rods were also used for capital punishment as well as for the infliction of corporal punishment. The use of the axe is interesting. In Rome (i.e. in the *domi*) only a magistrate not bound by the appeal process (*provocatio ad populum*) could have the use of the axe. After the promulgation of the *Lex Valeria de provocatione*, all other magistrates in Rome had the axe removed from their bundle of rods and had to inflict capital punishment by means of beating with the rods[50]. In the territory outside Rome (i.e. in the *militiae*) the axe was included in the *fasces* and prisoners convicted of a capital crime were executed by that instrument. As Philippi was a Roman colony and thereby an extension of Rome's legal situation, the *fasces* were rods without any axe[51]. The Lictor could summon people into court (*vocatio*), had the power of arrest (*prensio*) and could use the rods for beating. In short, he was the instrument of magisterial *coercitio* in cases of insubordination of any sort.

2. The Accusations

The charges against Paul and Silas made here can be broken down as follows:

A) οὗτοι οἱ ἄνθρωποι ἐκταράσσουσιν ἡμῶν τὴν πόλιν (Vg. = *hii homines conturbant civitatem nostram*)

ἐκταράσσω – to perturb, to agitate, to trouble exceedingly, to throw into confusion[52]. This is the only use of this word in the New Testament. The accusation of disturbing the peace will be made again at Caesarea, where Luke uses the expression κινοῦντα στάσεις (XXIV,5). The slavegirl's

---

48 cf. Kübler, "Lictor", *PAULY-WISSOWA-RE.*, Vol. XIII, 25er Halbband, Stuttgart, 1926, col. 508.
49 E. Samter notes that the *fasces* were a Roman symbol of sovereign authority said to have been borrowed from the Etruscans. (E.Samter, "Fasces" PAULY-WISSOWA-RE., Vol. VI, 12er Halbband, col. 2002.). Th. Mommsen writes that the *Lictor* and the *fasces* "were so intimately linked from the legal point of view that there was neither *fasces* without *Lictor* not *Lictor* without *fasces*." (Mommsen, *STAATSRECHT*, Vol. I, pg. 374.).
50 cf. Suetonius, *Nero*, XLIX,2. Cicero clearly states that the removal of the axe was related to the right of appeal: "Thus Publicola, as soon as that law of his in regard to the right of appeal was passed, ordered the axes to be removed from the bundle of rods." (*de Re Pub.*, II,31.55–E.T. C.W. Keyes, *Loeb*, 1961).
51 Cicero calls *fasces* without axes *bacili* (*de Lege agr.* II,34.).
52 cf. Plutarch, *Coriolanus* XIX,2: "To throw the people into tumult and disorder".

owners did not charge Paul with his *actual deed* — driving out the spirit of divination — as exorcism was not illegal.

B) Ἰουδαῖοι ὑπάρχοντες

Practicing the Jewish religion was not a crime[53]. Judaism was a legally recognized religion which enjoyed official protection throughout the Empire. This exclamation was rather an emotional appeal to the persistant anti-Jewish prejudices of the time[54]. There was a strong mutual dislike between Greeks and Jews and this was especially manifest in the main cities in the Eastern part of the Roman Empire where there were important Jewish communities to be found[55]. The origins of this disaffection were manifold: economic rivalries, the Jewish sense of exclusiveness, political quarrelling over civil rights and rights to citizenship and above all tremendous religious differences. A short, but powerful sentence from the *Histories* of Tacitus reflect the deep and unbridgeable chasm between Jew and Gentile: *"Profana illic omnia quae apud nos sacra, rursum concessa apud illos quae nobis incesta"*[56].

C) καὶ καταγγέλλουσιν ἔθη ἃ οὐκ ἔξεστιν ἡμῖν παραδέχεσθαι οὐδὲ ποιεῖν Ῥωμαίοις οὖσιν (Vg. = *"et adnuntiant morem quem non licet nobis suscipere neque facere cum simus Romani"*)

παραδέχομαι — To admit (as an antonym of reject), to accept, to receive, to take up or recognize as correct.

The slave-girl's owners were not only making an emotional appeal to the anti-Jewish feelings of the city's population, but were calling attention to the proselytizing activities being carried out in a Roman colony, amongst Roman citizens, by two Jewish missionaries[57]. In reality the apostles were being accused of attempting to convert Roman citizens to an alien religion. Their preaching of Jesus Christ was unsettling the local religious scene as it was drawing men away from the worship of the colony's gods especially Roma and Augustus[58].

---

53 W.C. van Unnik writes: "The question as to whether Judaism was a *religio licita* had ... nothing to do with the accusation" ("Die Anklage gegen die Apostel in Philippi", *SPARSA COLLECTA*, Leiden, 1973, pg. 377.).
54 cf. Acts XIX, 33–34.
55 cf. L.C. Ruggini, "Pregiudizi razziali, Ostilità politica e culturale, Intolleranza religiosa nell 'Impero romano", *ATHENAEUM*, Pavia, N.S. 46; 1968, pg. 146. For an overview of anti-Semitism in the Roman world, cf. A.N. Sherwin-White, *RACIAL PREJUDICE IN IMPERIAL ROME*, Cambridge, 1967; pg. 86ff.
56 Tacitus, *Hist.* V,4. In the next verse Tacitus says that the Jews show compassion to each other but *"adversus omnis alios hostile odium"* (V,5). cf. Juvenal, *Satires* XIV,96.
57 cf. C.S.C. Williams, *A COMMENTARY ON THE ACTS OF THE APOSTLES*, London, 1964, pg. 195.
58 cf. van Unnik "Die Anklage gegen die Apostel in Philippi", *op.cit.*, pg. 376.

"It was not lawful for a Roman citizen to accept foreign divinities or new religious practices which had not been publicly ratified by the State. In practice the Roman administration was rather tolerant on this point unless these practices were responsible for public disorder which was precisely what the slave-girl's owners were pretending in this case"[59] .

Roman law did not explicitly interdict the practice of proselytism at this period. Nonetheless proselytism was an act fraught with peril not only for the proselytist, but for the proselyte who could stand liable to the charge of atheism. General Roman policy thus tended toward curtailing the practice for mainly political reasons[60]. Therefore aiming the charges at Paul's missionary work within the Roman colony was an astute move for it was certain to assure a favourable response from the court. The plaintiffs knew perfectly well that the magistrates were sensitive to the problem of maintaining public order and would suppress any religious activity tending to create a breach of peace.

III. Excursus 1: The juridical Situation of Judaism during the Early Principate

As we have seen from the preceding section, practicing the Jewish religion was not a crime as Judaism was authorized by the Roman authorities: "The general Roman policy was to respect local rights insofar as law, cult and administration were concerned"[61]. The overall Roman attitude towards the Jews was one of tolerance and liberal protection which resulted in the safeguarding of religious liberty and autonomy. This tolerant attitude, however, was coupled with a policy of political vassalization[62].

Julius Caesar's rule was characterized by marked favour towards the Jews, a point strongly made in the latter part of Book 14 of the *Antiquities*, where Josephus gives a detailed listing of a number of texts, decrees and speeches emanating from the Caesarian period (49–44 B.C.)[63]. These

---

59 Martini, *op.cit.*, pg. 237.
60 cf. J.L. Daniel, "Anti-Semitism in the Hellenistic-Roman Period", *JBL*, Vol. 98, No. 1; March 1979, pg. 62–64.
61 S. Applebaum, "The Legal Status of the Jewish Communities in the Diaspora", *THE JEWISH PEOPLE IN THE FIRST CENTURY*, Assen, 1974, pg. 420.
62 cf. C. Saulnier, "Rome et la Bible", *SUPPLEMENT AU DICTIONNAIRE DE LA BIBLE*, Paris, 1984, col. 875. Also L.C. Ruggini, *op.cit.*, pg. 146.
63 cf. *Ant*. XIV,10.7 (211–212) for Josephus' account of Caesar's speech to the Senate in which he lauded the loyalty of the Jews. Josephus' understanding of the documents is influenced by his apologetic aims. T. Rajak suggests that Josephus was more concerned with their use in political argument than with their exact legal content. (T. Rajak, "Was there a Roman Charter for the Jews?", *JRS*, Vol. 74, 1984; pg. 121.).

Excursus 1: The juridical Situation of Judaism during the Early Principate

had the cumulative effect of regulating the rights and advantages of the Jews in Judaea, of giving a true charter to the Hasmonaean vassal-state, of confirming or ameliorating rights, privileges and concessions enjoyed by the Jews in Judaea and in the Diaspora, and of formally recognizing the link between the Diaspora communities and the High Priest at Jerusalem, whose hereditary dignities and prerogatives were therein confirmed. These measures created, as it were, a sort of *official Judaism*, "an incorporated body, with an authorized cult, throughout the Empire"[64]. The Jews were able to form legally-recognized religious corporations around their synagogues, enjoy freedom of worship and assembly for the synagogal communities and create special tribunals to settle their differences[65].

The Jews in the West — unlike their coreligionists in the Eastern part of the Empire who were grouped into *politeumata* — were constituted into synagogal communities. The synagogues, as a judicial entity, bore a certain legal resemblance to the *collegia* in that they held meetings open to members only and had a common fund[66]. They differed, however, quite significantly in other ways from the *collegia*. Their functions were much broader than those of the *collegia*, "since they were responsible for the organization and administration of all aspects of the life of the community and not for a single aspect, religious worship alone ..."[67].

Augustus renewed and confirmed the considerable and indeed exceptionable privileges historically enjoyed by the Jews throughout the Empire[68]. Josephus takes great care to stress this point in the *Antiquities*. The Jews could meet freely together and were allowed to construct synagogues in the Diaspora[69]. They were also allowed to levy a tax (the *Didrachma*) each year among male Jews aged 20 or more and send the proceeds to Jerusalem for the upkeep of the Temple. The payment of this tax was a concrete sign that one belonged to the official Jewish community and

---

64 E.M. Smallwood, *THE JEWS UNDER ROMAN RULE*, Leiden, 1976, pg. 135–136. cf. Tertullian, *Apol.* XXI,1 where Judaism is termed an *"insignissima religio, certe licita"*. The expression *religio licita* is a non-juridical one, not belonging to the vocabulary of Roman law.
65 H. Lietzmann, *L'HISTOIRE DE L'EGLISE ANCIENNE*, Paris, 1936, Tome I. pg. 79 (F.T.). cf. E. Lohse, *LE MILIEU DU NOUVEAU TESTAMENT*, Paris, 1973, pg. 40 (F.T.).
66 C. Saulnier, "Rome et la Bible", *op.cit.*, col. 1003.
67 E.M. Smallwood, *op.cit.*, pg. 133. cf. *Digest* XLVII,22.1–4, which is entitled *"de collegiis et corporibus"*. cf. G. La Piana, "Foreign Groups in Rome during the first Centuries of the Empire", *HTR*, Vol XX, No 4, October 1927, pg. 348–350 for an adequate description of the institutional differences between the synagogue and the *collegia*.
68 A.M. Rabello, "The Legal Condition of the Jews in the Roman Empire", *ANRW*. II,13, 1980, pg. 695. cf. M. Goguel, *LA NAISSANCE DU CHRISTIANISME*, Paris, 1946, pg. 507ff ;C. Saulnier, "Lois Romaines sur les Juifs selon Flavius Josèphe", *RB*. Tome 88, 1981, pg. 161–195 for a detailed analysis of the Roman administrative texts concerning the Jews.
69 *Ant.* XIV,10.23–24 (256–261).

submitted to its prescriptions; the tax was also a very important source of revenue for the Temple treasury[70].

The Jews had the right to administer their own local community; its leaders had disciplinary power over its members. This right is reflected in a passage from the *Antiquities* where Flavius Josephus talks of the difficulties the Jews of Sardis were having with the Greek citizens of that city:

> "Jewish citizens of ours have come to me [i.e. the Proquaester] and pointed out that from the earliest times they have had an association of their own in accordance with their native laws and a place of their own, in which they decide their affairs and controversies with one another;..."[71].

It should be noted that the community's disciplinary power even extended to Jewish members who had Roman citizenship.

The Jews were largely exempted from regular military service[72] and could take oaths without invoking the gods[73]. The refusal to worship the local civic gods had its drawbacks for the Jews in their quest to gain local citizenship. In the Greek view, the Jews could not aspire to, or attain, local citizenship unless they unreservedly worshipped the local gods and undertook all the normal prescribed liturgies.

The Jews also had the right to use special forms of service insofar as Emperor-worship was concerned. They did not offer sacrifices to the Emperor himself: rather they offered prayers and sacrifices to God (*Deo aeterno*) for the sovereign's welfare (*pro salute Augusti*). Augustus was well aware of the Jews' resolute monotheism and the repugnance they would feel toward sacrificing to another deity. Augustus, writes Philo, firmly maintained the ethnic and religious customs of each particular nation in the Empire: he "never wished anyone to address him as a god but was annoyed if anyone used the word, and also by his approval of the Jews, who he knew full well regarded all such things with horror"[74].

---

70 cf. Exodus XXX,13–14; Mt. XVII,24–27; *Ant*. XVI,6.1 (163). The levying of this tax and the exporting to Jerusalem of the sums collected caused much bitterness among the local Gentile authorities of the Eastern cities of the Empire. Cicero himself bitterly denounces this privilege in *pro Flacco* XXVIII,66–69.
71 *Ant*. XIV,10.17 (235). The expression Ἰουδαῖοι πολῖται ἡμέτεροι most likely refers to membership in the Jewish *politeuma* of Sardis or possibly to those Jews who were Roman citizens. It should not be taken to mean that the Jewish community residing in Sardis as a whole possessed Sardian citizenship.
72 *Ant*. XIV,10.6 (204); XIV,10.11–14 (223–232).
73 *Ant*. XII,3.2 (125–128); XVI,2.3–5 (27–65).
74 Philo, *Legat. ad Gaium*, XXIII,153–154. A few lines farther Philo writes: "Indeed so religiously did he respect our interests that supported by wellnigh his whole household he adorned our temple through the costliness of his dedications, and ordered that for all time continuous sacrifices of whole burnt offerings should be carried out every day at his own expense as a tribute to the most high God" (XXIII,157b) (E.T. = F.H. Colson, *Loeb*, 1962). This panegyric of Augustus, purposely apologetic, nevertheless reflects the good relations between the Jews and Rome during the first Princeps' long reign.

Excursus 1: The juridical Situation of Judaism during the Early Principate 17

The Jews did acquiesce in substitute forms of emperor-worship in order to manifest their political integration into the Empire and to show their loyalty to the Princeps' person in particular:

"Outside of Palestine they prayed for him in their synagogues, and, if they could not erect temples and statues to him, yet they dedicated their synagogues in his honour, and placed therein tablets, wreaths, shields, and standards, and had recourse to various other symbols, to express their devotion to him"[75].

Tiberius largely continued Augustus' policy of tolerance towards official Judaism. Nonetheless his Principate saw the beginnings of disciplinary measures against the Roman Jews taken mostly for security reasons[75a]. In 19 A.D., Tiberius banished the Jews from Rome largely as a result of their proselytism among the Romans themselves[76]. "As the Jews had flocked to Rome in great numbers," writes Dio Cassius, "and were converting many of the natives to their ways, he banished most of them"[77]. Suetonius relates that the expulsion order not only concerned the Jews, but the Egyptian rites as well:

"[Tiberius] abolished foreign cults, especially the Egyptian and Jewish rites, compelling all who were addicted to such superstitions to burn their religious vestments and all their paraphernalia. Those of the Jews who were of military age he assigned to provinces of less healthy climate, ostensibly to serve in the army; the others of that same race or of similar beliefs he banished from the city, on the pain of slavery for life if they did not obey"[78].

The measures taken by Tiberius against the Jewish and Egyptian rites had a basic political motivation. Stringent limits were placed on religious practices if they were thought to be affecting general state security. The Princeps' overall aim was to remove from Rome those imported rites and cults which had gained too large a following among the governing class, the loyalty of which was so essential to the maintenance of the ruling family's authority[79]. If however the expulsee chose to renounce the religious rites in question he could obtain a rescinding of the order and remain in Italy[80].

---

75 V.M. Scramuzza, "The Policy of the early Roman Emperors towards Judaism", *BC.* Vol. V, pg. 283. cf. Josephus, *contra Apionem* II,73–77.
75a H. Solin, "Juden und Syrer im westlichen Teil der römischen Welt", *ANRW* II, 29.2; 1983, pg. 686.
76 cf. Philo, *Legat. ad Gaium*, XXIV, 159–161.
77 Dio Cassius, LVII, 18,5a – E.T. = E. Cary, *Loeb,* 1961. The immediate cause of the banishment of the Jews was a scandalous outrage: A Jew and three accomplices persuaded a proselyte from the Roman nobility, one Fulvia, to send expensive gifts to the Jerusalem temple, which the four men in question proceeded to embezzle. "Saturninus, the husband of Fulvia, at the instigation of his wife, duly reported this to Tiberius, whose friend he was, whereupon the latter ordered the whole Jewish community to leave Rome." (Josephus, *Ant.,* XVIII,3.5 (81–84). – E.T. = L.H. Feldman, *Loeb,* 1965).
78 Suetonius, *Tib.* XXXVI – E.T. = J.C. Rolfe, *Loeb,* 1960.
79 cf. A. Garzetti, *L'IMPERO DA TIBERIO AGLI ANTONINI,* Bologna, 1960, pg. 37.
80 Tacitus, *Ann.* II,85.

Under Gaius (37–41 A.D.), relations between the Roman state and the Jews deteriorated considerably. A passage from Philo, again not the most objective of sources, reflects the general Jewish disillusionment with the Emperor:

> "When Gaius succeeded to the sovereignty, we were the first of all the inhabitants of Syria to show our joy ... Was our temple the first to accept sacrifices in behalf of Gaius's reign only that it should be the first or even the only one to be robbed of its ancestral tradition of worship"[81] ?

A very dangerous situation developed when Gaius ordered his statue to be placed in the Temple of Jerusalem[82]; only the assassination of the mad Emperor prevented an explosion. "Our own nation", writes Flavius Josephus, "was brought to the very verge of ruin and would have been destroyed but for his sudden death ..."[83].

Communal warfare did develop in Alexandria between the Jews and Greeks of that city[84] over a number of contentious points; one of which was the Jewish quest for full Alexandrian citizenship[85], something which was stoutly resisted by the Greek citizens of the great port city:

> "The Greeks, however, not unreasonably, felt that any such advance should be balanced by an increase in civic responsibilities, resisted the Jews' claim to have the best of both worlds, full citizen rights together with exemption from such civic duties as conflicted with their religion, and gave vent to their annoyance at Jewish aspirations by attacks on their religious privileges or ... on their existing civic position"[86].

Moreover the Greeks considered the Jews as protegés of the Roman Emperors to whose rule the Alexandrians were to a great extent hostile. Alexandrian anti-Semitism was in the main a product of political frustration closely bound up with a strong antipathy to Roman rule[87].

Claudius' reign (41–54 A.D.) was marked by two salient events insofar as relations with the Jews were concerned: the settling of the Alexandrian affair and the expulsion of the Jews from Rome. As we shall examine the latter affair in Chapter 3, we shall limit ourselves here to a brief overview of the Alexandrian affair with particular regard to the question of multiple citizenship.

---

81 Philo, *Legat. ad Gaium*, XXXII, 231–232; E.T. = F.H. Colson, *Loeb*, 1962. cf. Eusebius, *Hist. Eccl.* II,6.1–2.
82 cf. Eusebius, *Hist. Eccl.* II,5.1–7.
83 *Ant.* XIX,1.2 (15); E.T. = L.H. Feldman, *Loeb*, 1965.
84 *Ant.* XIX,5.2 (278).
85 H.I. Bell, *JEWS AND CHRISTIANS IN EGYPT*, London, 1924, pg. 11.
86 E.M. Smallwood, *op.cit.*, pg. 141.
87 E. Badian, "Ancient Alexandria", *STUDIES IN GREEK AND ROMAN HISTORY*, Oxford, 1968, pg. 189. cf. W. Seston, "L'Empereur Claude et les Chrétiens, *RHPR*, Tome 11, 1931, pg. 276. T. Rajak notes that in the Eastern cities the Jews were constantly dependent on Roman support in their struggles against local Greek authorities, provoking even more hostility in the Greek community. (Rajak, *op.cit.*, pg. 118).

Excursus 1: The juridical Situation of Judaism during the Early Principate 19

Flavius Josephus' account of Claudius' διάταγμα/διάγραμμα to Alexandria and Syria (*Ant.* XIX,5.2 ss280–285) as well as the text of the Emperor's ἐπιστολή (*P. Lond.* VI,1912) have given rise to an enormous body of scholarly literature[88]. Both sources shed precious light on the question of the type of civic status which the Jews in the Hellenistic cities enjoyed. The edict and letter were written in Claudius' first regnal year, 41 A.D.

The Jews of Alexandria, as in other Hellenistic cities with large Jewish populations, were constituted as a πολίτευμα, that is as "a corporation of aliens with the right of residence in the city"[89]. This quasi-autonomous body had juridical and administrative authority over its members. It was separate from and independent of the Greek body of citizens and of the local city government, living by its ancestral laws and having independent institutions of leadership[90]. The members of the πολίτευμα thus enjoyed a legally-recognized identity in the Hellenistic city: that of metics having the right of domicile[91].

Many Hellenized Jews of Alexandria, as opposed to the Orthodox faithful for whom pagan civic duties were insupportable, strove to obtain Alexandrian citizenship for a variety of reasons: to escape an inferior civic status, to free themselves from the heavy burden of the poll-tax (λαογραφία) from which the Greek citizenry was exempt, for the social recognition local citizenship would imply, and finally, for some, as a necessary prerequisite for the obtainment of Roman citizenship.

In his account of the edict, Flavius Josephus says "that the Jews in Alexandria called Alexandrians (ἐν Ἀλεξανδρείᾳ Ἰουδαίους Ἀλεξανδρεῖς λεγομένους) were fellow colonizers from the earliest times jointly with the Alexandrians and received equal civil right from the kings (καὶ ἴσης πολιτείας παρὰ τῶν βασιλέων τετευχότας) ..."[92]. Two things should be noted here. By terming themselves *Alexandrians*, the Jews were pressing their claim to Alexandrian citizenship; but although the Jews had lived in

---

88 cf. *inter alia* the comprehensive studies by V. Tcherikover, *HELLENISTIC CIVILIZATION AND THE JEWS*, New York, 4th Printing, 1977; E.M. Smallwood, *op.cit.*; and more recently A. Kasher, *THE JEWS IN HELLENISTIC AND ROMAN EGYPT*, Tübingen, Revised English Edition, 1985. (henceforth abbr. Kasher *op.cit.*). For a detailed chronological review of the events leading to the promulgation of the edict and to the writing of the letter, cf. A. Kasher, "Les Circonstances de la Promulgation de l'Edit de l'Empereur Claude et de sa Lettre aux Alexandrins" *SEMITICA*, Vol. 26, 1976, pg. 99–108.
89 Smallwood, *op.cit.*, pg. 139.
90 Kasher, *op.cit.*, pg. 294.
91 Smallwood, *op.cit.*, pg. 230.
92 *Ant.* XIX,5.2 (281–282) – E.T. = L.H. Feldman, Loeb, 1965. There is similar language in *Contra Apionem* II,38–39 where Josephus says that the Jews residing (κατοικοῦντες) in Antioch are called Antiochenes having been granted rights of citizenship (πολιτείαν) by the founder Seleucus.

Alexandria for a long time (in Josephus' words τοῖς πρώτοις εὐθὺ καιροῖς) and had been granted numerous privileges, they had never been granted Alexandrian citizenship as a bloc. Strictly speaking, the term *Alexandrian* was a legal misnomer for the Jews of that city, its use could only be as an informal and popular turn of phrase. The Jews remained *Jews from Alexandria*, which was something else entirely: "a humble and civically insignificant title"[93] to use Tcherikover's tart phrase. Secondly the use of the expression ἴση πολιτεία = equality of civic rights, was as broad as it was ambiguous. There was no other πολιτεία in the port city save that of the πόλις, the hallmark of which was worship of the local Alexandrian deities. In general Josephus uses the term πολιταί in a rather imprecise way to indicate both citizens of the πόλις as well as members of the Jewish πολίτευμα. The Jews, however, did not have πολιτεία like the Greeks, they were not πολιταί of the πόλις, but metics constituted as a πολίτευμα[94].

Two passages elsewhere in the Josephus-account reflect the underlying situation more accurately. The Emperor, according to Flavius Josephus, desired that none of the rights be lost to τῷ Ἰουδαίων ἔθνει. Here then the meaning would be a national group organized as a separate and distinct political and social body. In the same verse, the Emperor expresses the wish that "their former privileges (δικαιώματα) also be preserved to them, while they abide by their own customs"[95]. This passage is much closer to the real situation: the Jews had greatly benefited from the granting of privileges; but it is incorrect to speak of ἰσηπολιτεία here in the strict legal sense of that word.

Claudius' letter (*P. Lond.* VI,1912) provides a counterbalance to Josephus' version of events. In that letter the Emperor exhorted the Greek citizens of Alexandria not to hinder any of the traditional religious or social practices which had been allowed the Jews by Augustus. For their part, the Jews of Alexandria were exhorted to send no more embassies to Rome to accuse the Greeks, to leave off mixing in the Alexandrian games and festivals and to refrain from seeking to increase the Jewish population of the port city by encouraging the immigration of Jews from Syria or Egypt in order that the ethnic composition of the city not be altered. One has to conclude from a reading of the London papyrus that although some individual Jews doubtless had obtained Alexandrian citizenship, this was exceptional and that the Jews of Alexandria as a whole had not. Indeed Claudius' decision had the effect of ending Jewish hopes of obtaining Alexandrian

---

93 Tcherikover, *op.cit.*, pg. 312.
94 cf. *Ant.* XIV,7.2 (110–118). It is clear from this passage that the Jews were not citizens of the Greek cities; but had their own specific communal organization within them.
95 *Ant.* XIX,5.2 (285). – E.T. = L.H. Feldman, *Loeb*, 1965.

citizenship. The Jews would have to continue to inhabit a 'city not their own' (ἐν ἀλλοτρίᾳ πόλει).

Lastly, Flavius Josephus gives an account of the edict which Claudius addressed to the rest of the world. The Emperor enjoined his subjects to permit "the same privileges to be maintained for the Jews throughout the empire under the Romans as those in Alexandria enjoy"[96]. The edict nonetheless contained a clear warning to the Jews that they would not be allowed to abuse the privileges so graciously granted:

> "It is right, therefore, that the Jews throughout the whole world under our sway should also observe the customs of their fathers without let or hindrance. I enjoin upon them also by these presents to avail themselves of this kindness in a more reasonable spirit, and not to set at nought the beliefs about the gods held by other peoples, but to keep their own laws"[97].

It is interesting to note that Claudius' edict was in answer to a petition addressed him by Kings Agrippa and Herod, whom the Emperor qualifies as "my dearest friends". The confirmation of traditional privileges and rights was a favour granted the Jews on account of their loyalty and friendship to the Romans (διὰ τὴν πρὸς Ῥωμαίους πίστιν καὶ φιλίαν)[98].

Claudius' measures had the effect, then, of restoring to the Jews traditional privileges and rights they had enjoyed and which Gaius had attempted to restrain. It was clear, however, that no further privileges would be granted and that excessive Jewish missionary activity, aimed at winning men over to the one true God would be roundly countered[99].

IV. Excursus 2: Foreign Cults and the Question of Proselytism

The general policy of the Roman State towards foreign cults in the Julio-Claudian period was one of toleration as long as the cult in question remained politically and socially innocuous. This meant that it had to conform to the prevailing sensibility of the time, which expected that religious activity not work against the peace and unity of the Roman body politic. Strictly speaking, a Roman citizen could not practise a foreign cult unless

---

96 *Ant.* XIX,5.3 (288). – E.T. = L.H. Feldman, *Loeb*, 1965.
97 *Ant.* XIX,5.3 (290–291). E.T. = L.H. Feldman, *Loeb*, 1965.
98 *Ant.* XIX,5.3 (289).
99 Tcherikover, *op.cit.*, pg. 511, n.57.cf. G. Lüdemann, *PAULUS DER HEIDENAPOSTEL*, Göttingen, Band I, 1980, pg. 191, who writes that "Claudius' attitude towards the Jews, right from the outset of his reign, could scarcely be characterized as sympathetical; it was on the contrary politically motivated".

it had been duly authorized by the State. Cicero says quite clearly: "No one shall have gods to himself, whether new gods or alien gods, unless recognized by the State" (*nisi publice adscitos*)[100]. In reality, a Roman could practise a foreign cult so long as its usages did not violate Roman law or constitute a threat to the Roman political or social structure. Thus quite a number of foreign cults existed openly and in all quietude[101]. Conversely others were banned because of the immoral, subversive and criminal practices associated with them.

A good example of the concept that alien religions were a permanent menace to the state and to the ancient Roman religion which underpinned it is given in Livy's account of the suppression of the Bacchanalian rites (186 B.C.). The Consul's speech to the Roman populace, which figures in Livy's narration, is dominated by the idea that adherents of an alien religion form a state within a state and that not only do their depraved practices sap the morality and vitality of the population, but that this process goes hand and hand with conscious political conspiracy aimed at undermining the state[102]. Fundamentally their transgression was political: they were a radical seditious group whose aim was to attack state security. Another example is furnished by Valerius Maximus who writes that the *Praetor peregrinus*, C. Cornelius Hispallus, expelled the Chaldaean astrologers and other charlatans from Rome "as they were attempting to corrupt the morals of the Romans"[103]. Druidism had been forbidden to Roman citizens by Augustus and completely prohibited by Claudius even to the Gauls because of its barbaric nature and horrid practices (*Druidarum religionem apud Gallos dirae immanitatis et tantum civibus sub Augusto interdictam penitus abolevit*)[104]. Here too the real reason for Druidism's final prohibition was its nationalistic and anti-Roman content.

The Romans also tended to identify religion ethnocentrically. Thus Judaism was considered the national religion of a particular people — a people which, prior to its incorporation into the Empire, had been a *socius et amicus Populi Romani*[105].

Even though Judaism was the religion of a specific people, there existed strong missionary tendencies in it; a veritable consciousness of the mission

---

100 Cicero, *de Leg.* II,8.19. – E.T. = C.W. Keyes, *Loeb*, 1961.
101 cf. J. Scheid, *LE DELIT RELIGIEUX DANS LA ROME TARDO-REPUBLICAINE*, Rome, 1981, pg. 157.
102 Livy XXXIX,15.1–16.3. cf. Valerius Maximus I,3.1–3.
103 Valerius Maximus I,3.1–3.
104 Suetonius, *Claud.* XXV,5. Technically the criminal rites were known as *flagitia*, i.e. shameful behaviour, dishonour, debauchery, prostitution, horrid practices. Pliny uses this term in the context of the practice of the Christian religion. (*Ep.* X,96).
105 cf. I Macc. VIII,23–30.

Excursus 2: Foreign Cults and the Question of Proselytism

of Israel. This led many Jews to actively work for the conversion of the Gentiles[106].

These missionary tendencies ran counter to the Roman policy of attempting to control the propagation of alien religions. We have to note here that there was no specific crime of *apostasy to Judaism*. "The sole crime", writes A.M. Rabello, "was atheism which meant the failure to perform certain ceremonies, refusal to worship the gods and so forth"[107]. Nevertheless Jewish proselytism was viewed as a pernicious activity and the proselytes themselves considered as renegades. Juvenal, for example, sees in Jewish proselytism an anti-Roman superstition and considers the proselytes to be disdaining the laws of Rome. For the Latin satirist, Jewish proselytism, if left unchecked, would eventually cause the old Roman religion to disappear[108]. For Tacitus, the proselytes were the worst rascals imaginable; people who had renounced their ancestral religion[109].

The Emperors made strenuous efforts to discourage excessive Jewish proselytism especially at Rome itself, while maintaining the grants of privilege the Jews traditionally enjoyed:

> "The Roman government recognized the Jews' moral right to practise their religion without hindrance; but its duties included the maintenance of law and order and public morality, and if the Jews in any individual locality traded on their privileges to contravene Roman law or to act in any way thought to endanger public order or morality, they came under the penalties of the law on equal terms with Gentile offenders[110].

In conclusion we should note two points. First Paul and his followers were very active missionaries. Judaism, in spite of the efforts it made to convert others and the goodly number of proselytes and sympathizers which it attracted, retained its essential ethnic base, remaining the national religion of one specific ethnic group. The Christian missionaries, on the other hand, were men who were striving to convert others to Jesus Christ whatever their beliefs, social class or nationality might have been. Indeed an essential point in Luke's theological programme in Acts is to show how Christianity, in general, became increasingly distant from its Jewish origins and more universalist in its character and composition and how the Pauline mission, in particular, more and more ignored the bonds of ethnic boundaries and legalistic formulae which so hemmed in Judaism. The early

---

106 cf. Horace, *Satires* I, 4.140. G.F. Moore notes that the belief that the true religion must in the end be the universal religion made Judaism a missionary religion: "The forms in which the religion of the golden age to come were imagined were naturally those of the national religion internationalized". (*JUDAISM IN THE FIRST CENTURIES OF THE CHRISTIAN ERA*, Cambridge, 1932, Vol. I, pg. 229–230).
107 A.M. Rabello, *op.cit.*, pg. 697.
108 Juvenal, *Satires* XIV, 96.
109 Tacitus, *Hist.* V,5.
110 E.M. Smallwood, *op.cit.*, pg. 210.

Christian missionaries had the strong inner conviction that theirs was truly a universal religion and that their sacred mission was to bring the message of salvation to all of suffering humanity.

Second it is clear from the text of Acts that Paul and Silas were considered by the Roman authorities to be *Jews* and not members of a new, unknown or unauthorized religion. Christian evangelization was not as yet perceived by the Roman authorities as something distinct from Jewish proselytism. Nonetheless the accusations lodged against the two apostles were of a grave nature. They were aimed at convincing the authorities at Philippi that the apostles' religious activities were illicit and that Paul and Silas were, in Ramsay's terms, "enemies to civilized man and to the customs and laws which regulated society and people bent on relaxing the bonds which held society together"[111]. The violent tumult that the slave girl's owners were so easily able to provoke showed that the crowd understood that these two Jewish missionaries were advocating and promoting customs which were distinctly un-Roman in character. The severe reaction of the *Duoviri* showed that they felt the apostles' missionary work to be "a civic and national rebellion, a sign of open hostility which called for punishment"[112].

V. Paul proclaims his Roman Citizenship

Luke continues the narrative by describing in dramatic terms the violent reaction of the Philippian magistrates to the intensely provocative charges lodged against the apostles: "The crowd joined in attacking them; and the magistrates tore the garments off them (καὶ οἱ στρατηγοὶ περιρήξαντες αὐτῶν τὰ ἱμάτια) and gave orders to beat them with rods (ἐκέλευον ῥαβδίζειν). And when they had inflicted many blows upon them, they threw them into prison (ἔβαλον εἰς φυλακήν), charging the jailor to keep them safely. Having received this charge, he put them into the inner prison (εἰς τὴν ἐσωτέραν φυλακὴν) and fastened their feet in the stocks." (καὶ τοὺς πόδας ἠσφαλίσατο αὐτῶν εἰς τὸ ξύλον) (Acts XVI,22–24).

---

[111] W.M. Ramsay, *THE CHURCH IN THE ROMAN EMPIRE BEFORE 170 A.D.*, London, 1895, pg. 236.
[112] P. Prigent, "Pourquoi les Persécutions?" *RHPR*. Tome LV, 1975, pg. 355.

A) καὶ οἱ στρατηγοὶ περιρήξαντες αὐτῶν τὰ ἱμάτια

Before being beaten, the two apostles were stripped of their garments. Normally beatings were administered on the bared body[113]. It is not likely that the *Duoviri* themselves tore off the apostles' clothing. This was a function of the Lictors.

B) ἐκέλευον ῥαβδίζειν – (Vg. = *iusserunt virgis caedi*)

ῥαβδίζω – to beat with rods, to strike with a stick or a cudgel. Here ῥαβδίζω translates *virgis caedere* for the Roman punishment of *verberatio* and *fustuarium*[114].

According to the narrative the *Duoviri* did not even remotely begin a judicial investigation of the case to see if the accusations were well-founded or not. Rather they immediately used their power of *coercitio* in giving their Lictors orders to beat Paul and Silas[115].

Luke makes no mention of Paul's proclaiming his Roman citizenship at this point. Such a proclamation would have had a suspensive effect on the magistrates' decision to have the apostles beaten; it would have protected them from this exercise of magisterial arbitrariness. Luke, however, is interested in centering the narrative, not on Paul's legal situation, but on the sufferings of the two apostles and on how, in the face of that suffering, they were still able to continue their apostolic ministry. The arrest and jailing of Paul and Silas are the events which lead to the climax of the Philippian pericope which is the miraculous conversion of the jailer. Luke,

---

113 cf. Aulus Gellius, *Noct. Att.* X,3.1–13. In line 11, Aulus Gellius describes the beating given one of Verres' victims who happened to be a Roman citizen: "*Palus ... in foro destitutus est, vestimenta detracta sunt, virgis caesus est*". Cicero talks of illegal action perpetrated by Verres and how the cry "*civis Romanus sum*" was of no succour to the victim as Verres ordered him to be severely beaten (*vehementissime verberari*) notwithstanding. (Cicero, *Verr.* II,v.62.161–162). Cicero concludes by an eloquent condemnation of Verres' action: "Does freedom, that precious thing, mean nothing? nor the proud privileges of a citizen of Rome? nor the law of Porcius, the laws of Sempronius? nor the tribunes' power ...? Have all these things come in the end to mean so little that in a Roman province, in a town whose people have special privileges, a Roman citizen could be bound and flogged in the marketplace (*deligatus in foro virgis caederetur*) by a man who owed his rods and axes to the favour of the Roman people?" (*Verr.* II,v.63.163 – E.T. = L.H.G. Greenwood, *Loeb*, 1960).

114 *ThWb.* Vol. VI, pg. 970 (E.T.). *Verberatio* was the action of beating, thrashing or flogging as a punishment. *Fustuarium* was the military punishment of beating to death. cf. Livy VIII,32.11; Valerius Maximus II,7.8. ῥαβδίζω is not used by the Evangelists in their description of Jesus' beating. Mt XXVII,26 and Mk XV,15 both use the Greek verb φραγελλόω = *flagellatio*, i.e. scourging as a punishment preceding the crucifixion. In Lk XXIII,16, the verb παιδεύω = *fustigatio* is used to indicate a chastisement preceding release. Jn XIX,1 uses the word μαστιγόω i.e. torture by use of the μάστιξ (scourge). The only other use of the verb ῥαβδίζω occurs in 2 Cor XI,25, where Paul has the occasion to mention the beatings which he endured in the course of his apostolic ministry.

115 cf. W.C. van Unnik, "Die Anklage gegen die Apostel in Philippi, *op.cit.*, pg. 374.

in any case, is unambiguous in his depiction of the *Duoviri* as unjust and inequitous magistrates — a rather atypical portrayal of Roman officials in the Lucan narrative. Luke's pro-Roman stance gives way here to a grimly realistic fact: the apostles were indeed victims of magisterial brutality which the author makes no effort to conceal in his account.

C) ἔβαλον εἰς φυλακὴν/εἰς τὴν ἐσωτέραν φυλακὴν

The treatment inflicted on Paul and Silas was that normally meted out to vagrants or the worst elements of society. Their feet were put into stocks and they were flung into prison under military guard. The apostles are considered as itinerant Jews and treated as *humiliores*.

D) εἰς τὸ ξύλον

ξύλον — This was a device used for inflicting punishment: a beam with holes into which the feet, hands and neck of a prisoner were inserted and secured by straps (cf. Latin *nervus*). The text mentions only the feet as being fastened. The stocks were used to confine and torture (by forcing the legs apart)[116].

The story of Paul's legal *démêlés* with the Philippian authorities is now interrupted by the account of the jailer's conversion and resumes only in verse 35: "But when it was day, the magistrates sent the police saying, 'Let those men go' ". Releasing prisoners was one of the rights that the *Duoviri* enjoyed in the exercise of their magisterial *coercitio*.

The narration in the B-Text causes difficulty as it contains no connexion between the story of the release of the apostles and the earthquake. This could very well reflect the fact that originally the two stories were indeed unconnected. The Western Text, however, has the following lesson: "the magistrates met in one and the same place in the Agora and they were filled with fear when they remembered the earthquake which had taken place, and they sent the Lictors saying 'Let those men go' "[117]. Thus we see that the Western version smooths over the awkwardness of the two unconnected tales by providing the necessary link[118].

Paul however gave an unexpected answer to the Lictors: "They have beaten us publicly, uncondemned, men who are Roman citizens, (ἀκατα-

---

116 cf. Job XXXIII,11; Eusebius, *Hist. Eccl.* V,1.27. cf. the *Lex de Astynomis Pergamenorum* (*OGIS*, 483.181).
117 D d sy^hmg (Ephr.). The words "Let those men go ... of whom you received charge yesterday" occur in D 614 sy^h (Ephr.).
118 cf. R.P.C. Hanson, "The Provenance of the Interpolator in the 'Western' Text of Acts and of Acts Itself", *NTS*, Vol. 12, No. 3; April 1966, pg. 214. M. Dibelius notes: "Once more the D-text covers up a seam, in this case a seam between two narrative units". (*STUDIES IN THE ACTS OF THE APOSTLES* (E.T.), London, 1956, pg. 86).

κρίτους, ἀνθρώπους 'Ρωμαίους ὑπάρχοντας) and have thrown us into prison; and do they now cast us out secretly? (λάθρα ἡμᾶς ἐκβάλλουσιν) No! Let them come themselves and take us out (ἐξαγαγέτωσαν)". (XVI,37).

A) ἀκατακρίτους — (indemnatos)

ἀκατάκριτος — 'uncondemned', The context here would indicate 'punished without having been publicly tried'. This word is not a common one in the New Testament, occurring only here and in a parallel circumstance in Acts XXII,25. The Western Text adds the word ἀναιτίους 'guiltless', 'not guilty' along with ἀκατακρίτους[119]. The legal sense of the wording is that the apostle is protesting a magisterial act that is both unjust and illegal.

At both occasions on which Paul proclaimed his Roman citizenship, he states that he is ἀκατάκριτος: Acts XVI,37 reads Δείραντες ἡμᾶς δημοσίᾳ ἀκατακρίτους, ἀνθρώπους 'Ρωμαίους ὑπάρχοντας and Acts XXII,25 εἰ ἄνθρωπον 'Ρωμαῖον καὶ ἀκατάκριτον ἔξεστιν ὑμῖν μαστίζειν. Both verses seem to imply that the bad treatment meted out to Paul was unlawful, not only because he was a Roman citizen, but because he was ἀκατάκριτος as well. In reality a Roman citizen could not be beaten or bound by magisterial order *adversus provocationem*. Roman citizenship was a personal status; inherent in that status was judicial protection against magisterial abuse:

> "The narrative of Acts agrees with the *Lex Iulia* except that it adds the qualification 'uncondemned'. This implies that the provincial authority might administer a flogging after sentence, presumably in a case in which a Roman citizen had not exercised his right of appeal, or alternatively in a special category of cases at present unknown in which the *Lex Iulia* did not apply"[120].

We have to remember that the laws were not always rigourously applied in the provinces. The provincial and municipal magistrates often exceeded their powers even to the point of violating the rights of Roman citizens. In the *Defence of Rabirius*, Cicero bitterly denounces the tribune Titus Labienus for provoking the condemnation of a Roman citizen without his case being heard:

> "The law of Porcius forbade the rod to be used on the person of any Roman citizen: (*Porcia lex virgas ab omnium civium Romanorum corpore amovit*): this merciful man reintroduced the scourge. The law of Porcius wrested the liberty of the citizens from the Lictor: Labienus, the friend of the people, has handed it over to the executioner. Gaius Gracchus carried a law forbidding sentence to be passed on the life of a Roman citizen without your consent [i.e. the Roman people] : this friend of the people has illegally secured without your consent, not indeed that the Duumvirs should put a Roman citizen on trial, but actually that they should condemn him

---

119 D d. cf. Mt XII,5 & 7 for the only N.T. uses of ἀναίτιος.
120 Sherwin-White, pg. 71–72. cf. Dionysius Halicarnassensis V,70.2. cf. W.M. Ramsay who theorizes that Paul, being a Roman citizen, claimed his rights in the Latin language and used the expression *re incognita* = 'without a proper trial', 'an untried' or 'uninvestigated case'. (*SPT.* pg. 224–225).

to death without his case being heard (*sed indicta causa civem Romanum capitis condemnari coegit*)"[121].

B) ἀνθρώπους 'Ρωμαίους ὑπάρχοντας

The use of the plural would indicate that Silas too was a Roman citizen. No better answer could have been given to the plaintiffs' shouts of 'Ιουδαῖοι ὑπάρχοντες than this. Paul's proclamation of his Roman citizenship completely reversed the situation[122]. When he pronounced the formula *civis Romanus sum*, Paul valorized his right as a citizen to protection by invoking a whole legal disposition, the Valerian and Porcian laws and their sequels, which had been enacted precisely to protect a Roman citizen from magisterial abuse. The apostle was in fact declaring that the *Duoviri* had exceeded their legal authority by ordering the beating of a Roman citizen when this action was forbidden by the above legislation. The proclamation *civis Romanus sum* was essentially an appellatory formula: Paul was stressing his right to appeal to a higher judicial authority for protection against the illegal action of the *Duoviri*.

C) ἐκβάλλουσιν/ἐξαγαγέτωσαν

1) ἐκβάλλο – to cast out, drive out, banish.
2) ἐξάγω – to bring out of prison, to release from prison.

Paul insists on an official escort, not so much for protection, but as a visible reprobation of the magistrates' illegal conduct. The two apostles wanted this signal gesture of deference so that the rumour would not go about the city that they had escaped from prison and so that the foes of the Christian mission would not be able to say that the new doctrine was being preached by criminals.

The magistrates' reaction to all this was one of fear and of acquiescence[123]: "The police reported these words to the magistrates, and they were afraid when they heard that they were Roman citizens; so they came and apologized to them. And they took them out and asked them to leave the city." (XVI,38–39). The Western Text adds the following details to

---

121 Cicero, *pro Rab.* IV,12 (E.T. = H.G. Hodge, *Loeb*, 1959). cf. *Verr.* II,ii.17.43; II,v.8.18–20; II,v.42.109; II,v.66.170. Livy, writing about the trial of Caeso, says: "Titus Quinctius cried out that a man who had been charged with a capital crime and whose day of trial was at hand ought not to suffer violence, uncondemned and unheard. (*T. Quinctius clamitat cui rei capitalis dies dicta sit et de quo futurum propediem iudicium eum indemnatum indicta causa non debere violari*). The tribune answered that he did not propose to punish him uncondemned, but that he should keep him in prison notwithstanding, till the day of trial, that the Roman People might have it in their power to punish a homicide." (Livy III, 13.4b–5); E.T. = B.D. Foster, *Loeb*, 1960.
122 cf. Cicero, *Verr.* II,v.57.147. How one proved Roman citizenship to the authorities will be discussed in Chapter 4.
123 cf. Acts XXII,29.

this account: "and having arrived at the prison with many friends, they beseeched them to leave, saying: 'We did not know anything about you, that you are righteous men' (δίκαιοι). And after having led them outside, they beseeched them saying: 'leave this city, lest those who shouted at you, gather together once again'[124]." In underlining the apostles' *righteousness* the Western Text also indicates their *innocence*: those who are righteous cannot be anything but innocent. Nonetheless if no further action is taken against Paul and Silas, it is not because of their δικαιοσύνη but because they enjoyed legal protection as Roman citizens.

Thus the story of Paul's first major encounter with the Roman authorities ends with his being expelled from the colony: "So they went out of prison, and visited Lydia; and when they had seen the brethren, they exhorted them and departed" (XVI,40). It was in Philippi that Paul received the harshest treatment meted out to him in any of the encounters he had with Roman officialdom as described in the Book of Acts[125]. The *Duoviri* had employed heavy-handed methods without first investigating the case to see who these men were and what rights they might have had. As it turned out they had violated Roman legislation protecting citizens from violent magisterial *coercitio* in ordering the apostles to be beaten. The *Duoviri* left themselves open to severe punishment for they could be deprived of office and disqualified from any further government service for having violated the rights of Roman citizens in a Roman colony[126]. It is no wonder then that the magistrates were afraid and wanted to hurry the apostles out of Philippi. Finally we have to note that Paul and Silas were neither condemned nor acquitted of the accusations brought against them. They were simply expelled from the colony. No sentence was handed down at all. Paul's first formal encounter with Roman judges had ended indecisively.

---

124 D d (614 pc sy^h Ephr.).
125 Paul gives his own reaction to his experience in Philippi in the Epistle to the Thessalonians: "But though we had already suffered and been shamefully treated at Philippi, as you know, we had courage in our God to declare to you the Gospel of God in the face of great opposition." (I Thess. II,2).
126 cf. Dio Cassius LX, 24.4.

Chapter II
Thessalonica: Paul, Jason and the Politarchs

I. The Free City of Thessalonica

We have seen how the missionary work of Paul and Silas was brought to an abrupt end at Philippi by their imprisonment and expulsion. Undaunted by this misadventure, the two apostles continued their journey across the province of Macedonia. Luke tells us that after having passed through Amphipolis[1] and Apollonia[2], they came to Thessalonica "where there was a synagogue of the Jews". (Acts XVII,1). Thessalonica was the capital of the second district of Macedonia and the capital of the province, being the seat of the Proconsul. It was also a Free City[3]. In the first Civil War, Thessalonica had been a base of operations for Pompey and the Senate, but it chose the victorious side in the second Civil War having espoused the cause of Antony and Octavian[4]. As a recompense for its fidelity to the Triumvirs, Thessalonica was granted the status of *civitas libera* in the year 42 B.C.[5].

Free cities recognized the sovereignty of Rome and were always bound by her foreign policy. They retained, however, considerable independence in their internal administration[6]. Thessalonica, for example, had its own popular assembly, city council and its own native magistrates, the Politarchs.

The type of privileges and rights enjoyed by a Free City may best be seen from the provisions of the *Lex Antonia de Termessibus*[7]. By this law,

---

[1] Amphipolis, capital of the first district of Macedonia, was also a Free City and had five Politarchs. cf. C. Schuler, "The Macedonian Politarchs", *CP*, Vol. 55, 1960, pgs. 90,96 and 98, n. 6. cf. Fritz Gschnitzer, "Politarches", *PAULYS-WISSOWA-RE*, Supplementband XII, 1973, col. 485.
[2] cf. Pliny the Elder, *Hist. Nat.* IV,38. The apostles were following the *Via Egnatia*.
[3] cf. Pliny the Elder, *Hist. Nat.* IV,36. (*Thessalonica liberae condicionis*).
[4] Plutarch, *Brut.* XLVI,1. cf. Appian, *Bell.Civ.* IV,118.
[5] The granting of the status of *civitas libera* was very often the result of services rendered to Rome in its foreign wars or by the initiative of a victorious general in one of the civil wars. cf. Tacitus, *Ann.* XII,61 ;Appian, *Bell.Civ.* V.7.
[6] Sherwin-White, pg. 96.
[7] The extant text of this law is given in *CIL*. I,204 ; Bruns, *FIRA*, No. 14; Riccobono, *FIRA*, No. 11; Abbott & Johnson, No. 19; Girard, *Textes*[4], No. 11.

dated c. 71 B.C., the city of Termessus in Pisidia became a *civitas sine foedere immunis et libera*, most likely as a reward for loyalty to Rome during the Mithridatic Wars. The first privilege mentioned in the law is the right *uti suis legibus*[8]. Termessus was given the right to govern under its own laws, to change or abrogate them and to create new legislation bound only by the prescription *quod advorsus hanc legem non fiat*[9]. The law implied that justice was to be administered by the local courts; the Free City being thought of as independent to a great extent of gubernatorial control, that is juridically *extra provinciam*.

The jurisdiction of the magistrates of a Free City theoretically extended over all individuals within the territory irregardless of their personal status. The local courts could thus take cognizance even of cases involving Roman citizens. Nonetheless restrictions were likely to have been put on the exercise of the local magistrate's authority in this type of case[10]. Indeed it is quite possible that as a consequence of the pre-eminence of Rome, criminal jurisdiction over Roman citizens was quite circumscribed if not completely removed[11].

II. Paul is accused of acting „*contra decreta Caesaris*"

Luke relates that Paul went to the synagogue "as was his custom" (XVII,2) to proclaim the message of Jesus Christ, first of all to his coreligionists, "explaining and proving that it was necessary for the Christ to suffer and rise from the dead, and saying, 'This Jesus, whom I proclaim to you, is the Christ'" (XVII,3). The narrative notes that Paul argued with the Jews at the synagogue for a period of three Sabbaths (ἐπὶ σάββατα τρία) (XVII, 2). Paul's sojourn in the Macedonian capital, however, may very well have been longer than this mention of a period of three Sabbaths. In I Thess. II,9, we learn that the apostle had had the time to work at a trade while he was conducting his mission in Thessalonica. In Phil. IV,16, Paul writes that the Philippians had aided him "once and again" (with money for his needs) while he was at Thessalonica. Finally Paul relates how successful

---

8 *Lex Antonia de Termessibus*, Col. I, lines 8–9.
9 *Lex Antonia de Termessibus*, Col. I, lines 10–11.
10 Abbott & Johnson, pg. 43–44.
11 Th. Mommsen, *STAATSRECHT*, Vol. III, pg. 702. cf. the article "civitas libera" in *Diz.Epi.* Vol. II, pg. 256–258, especially Section IIc entitled "Giurisdizione e Amministrazione in genere".

his mission had been especially with the Gentiles, those who "turned to God from idols" (I Thess. 1,9). A successful mission would certainly have necessitated a consistent amount of time. The success of Paul's mission to Thessalonica is also stressted by the Acts-narrative: "And some of them were persuaded, and joined Paul and Silas; as did a great many of the devout Greeks and not a few of the leading women." (XVII,4). Jason, the man who received Paul into his house, was most likely one of these converts.

The success of this proclamation provoked a very violent reaction among members of the Jewish community at Thessalonica: "but the Jews were jealous (ζηλώσαντες δὲ οἱ Ἰουδαῖοι) and taking some wicked fellows of the rabble (τῶν ἀγοραίων ἄνδρας τινὰς πονηρούς) they gathered a crowd (ὀχλοποιήσαντες), set the city in an uproar (ἐθορύβουν τὴν πόλιν), and attacked the house of Jason seeking to bring them out to the people (αὐτοὺς προαγαγεῖν εἰς τὸν δῆμον)" (XVII,5).

A) ζηλώσαντες δὲ οἱ Ἰουδαῖοι

Converts to the newly-founded Thessalonian Church were mainly drawn from three categories of people: Jews by birth, devout Greeks, and leading women of the city[12]. The Jewish leadership considered these reverent Greeks as half-Jews already, so that in evangelizing them the apostle was taking prospective converts away from the synagogue. Moreover the content of Paul's Gospel — the proclamation of Jesus as Messiah as well as his preaching salvation to the Gentiles — could not but irritate the Jewish authorities[13]. Jealousy at the success of the Pauline mission moved the Jewish authorities to retaliate against the apostle by making grave accusations against him and by stirring up a crowd in the centre of the Macedonian capital.

B) τῶν ἀγοραίων

The primary sense of the word ἀγοραῖος is someone frequenting the Agora[14]. Very early on, however, the term was used in reference to common or low fellows, worthless idlers or coarse and petty criminals, who abounded in the agora[15]. These people were apparently summoned to

---

12 The Western text notes four categories of converts: Jews, leading women, God-fearers *and* Greeks (A Dpc d g vg bo p m add this καί).
13 cf. Acts XIII,14ff. In the Codex Bezae the Jews are described as ἀπειθοῦντες rather than ζηλώσαντες.
14 In Panegyric IV,10.12, St. John Chrysostom calls Paul the tentmaker and artisan an ἀγοραῖος.
15 cf. Aristophanes, *Ranae* 1015 ("idle loafers"); Theophrastus, *Characteres*, IV,2 ("Ne'er-do-well").

make the attack on the brethren seem like a popular movement[16]. The Jews themselves tried to maintain a low profile:

> "The position of Jews in a predominantly Gentile city was not so strong that they could act as persecutors. Under such circumstances, an excited crowd might turn on the Jews themselves. Instead the Jews made these disturbances appear as uneasiness among the local inhabitants, whom some strangers had provoked to justified anger by acting against the Emperor's decrees and by stating that another, the hitherto unknown Jesus, ought to replace the Emperor"[17].

C) ὀχλοποιήσαντες / ἐθορύβουν τὴν πόλιν (Vg. = *concitaverunt civitatem*)

ὀχλοποιέω — to collect a mob with a view to causing a tumult. This is a very uncommon verb. This is its sole occurrence in the New Testament and it is omitted altogether in the Codex Bezae.

θορυβέω — to make a noise, to be turbulent, to set crowds or assemblies off into an uproar, to exite the multitude. Luke's choice of such a powerful vocabulary highlights the dramatic setting. The plaintiffs do not make the accusations calmly before the δῆμος or the Politarchs according to a regular procedure. Luke clearly sets their legal action in the midst of clamour, riot and tumult[18].

D) αὐτοὺς προαγαγεῖν εἰς τὸν δῆμον

Jason's house is now attacked. Not finding those whom they sought, the crowd dragged Jason and some brethren out where they were without protection from the violence of the mob.

The basic meaning of δῆμος is 'commons' or 'common people', (cf. Latin *plebs:* those who were not chiefs)[19]. There was also a political nuance to the word as it could refer to (a) the 'sovereign people', 'free citizens'; (b) a 'popular government', 'democracy', this being in contrast to oligarchy or tyranny; and finally (c) the people organized into a body politic, the 'popular assembly'[20]. The popular assembly had an important role in the civic life of Thessalonica since it enjoyed a certain number of legislative and juridical prerogatives. Under the Republic the people seemed to have exercised their power to legislate on many matters, but with the introduction of the Principate the main function of the popular assembly was the election of magistrates or priests with real and effective power passing more and more to the magistrates and notables in the local Senate. This

---

16 Haenchen, pg. 507.
17 J. Munck, *THE ACTS OF THE APOSTLES*, New York, 1978, pg. 165. cf. Acts XIV,2.
18 cf. Plutarch, *Aem. Paul.* XXXVIII,3 where the scene depicts Scipio rushing into the Forum "attended by men who were of low birth and had lately been slaves, but who were frequenters of the forum (ἀγοραίους) and able to gather a mob and force all issues by means of solicitations and shouting ..." (E.T. = B. Perrin, *Loeb*, 1961).
19 LS^9, pg. 386–387. cf. Acts XII,22.
20 cf. Plato, *Resp.* 565-B; In *P.Oxy.* I,41.19 δῆμος = the assembly of Oxyrhynchus.

transfer of political and judicial powers was quite in accordance with imperial Rome's policy of preferring to deal with the aristocratic or oligarchic components in a local town's body politic rather than with the democratic element. At this very early period in the Principate, the popular assembly was on the decline as an institution although it still retained a certain number of powers, rights and duties.

The result of the mob's attack on Jason's house was rather disappointing. Paul and Silas were not there. Had they been hidden by the brethren and strongly advised not to confront the mob as later at Ephesus[21]? In any case the brunt of the mob's fury was borne by Jason: "and when they could not find them, they dragged Jason and some of the brethren before the city authorities (ἐπὶ τοὺς πολιτάρχας) (XVII,6a).

A) ἐπὶ τοὺς πολιτάρχας

Thessalonica was governed by a college of five (later six) Politarchs, which was headed by a presiding Politarch[22]. The term Politarch was principally, although not exclusively, used to designate the non-Roman chief civil magistrates of various Macedonian cities[23]. The title is known not only from its mention here in Acts, but from numerous inscriptions as well[24]. The institution seems to have predated the conquest of Macedonia by Aemilius Paulus, although perhaps not in the definitive form it had taken on by Paul's time[25]. The Politarchate was an annual magistracy, but was iterative. It could also be held simultaneously with other offices. The Politarchs were recruited from the wealthier classes and functioned as the magistracy to which the task of administration and police duties fell[26]. Thus the Politarchs were responsible for the maintenance of order in the city and for the surveillance, control and eventual prosecution of troublemakers[27].

The accusations were now made before the Politarchs: "These men who have turned the world upside down (τὴν οἰκουμένην ἀναστατώσαντες) have come here also, and Jason has received them; and they are all acting against the decrees of Caesar, saying that there is another king, Jesus." (καὶ οὗτοι

---

21 cf. Acts XIX,30–31.
22 There was a variability in the number of Politarchs, although their normal number was five.
23 Gschnitzer, op.cit., col. 483.
24 cf. P.Oxy. IV,745.4. In this letter (Egypt, 1st Century A.D.) a Politarch by the name of Theophilus is mentioned. The title however is essentially Macedonian and not Egyptian. cf. CIG. 1967.1. Schuler, op.cit., pg. 96–98, lists some 31 inscriptions referring in some manner to the Politarchs of Macedonia.
25 cf. C. Koukouli-Chrysanthaki, "Politarchs in a new Inscription from Amphipolis", ANCIENT MACEDONIAN STUDIES, 1981, pg. 238.
26 Haenchen, pg. 506.
27 Gschnitzer, col. 491.

πάντες ἀπέναντι τῶν δογμάτων καίσαρος πράσσουσιν, βασιλέα ἕτερον λέγοντες εἶναι Ἰησοῦν). (XVII,6b—7).

The importance of the accusations made in Thessalonica against Paul lay in the fact that they inextricably linked his theological quarrel with the Jewish leadership about the Messiah, the kingship of Jesus and the Gentile mission to the gravest political accusations imaginable. Paul's adversaries were trying to demonstrate that his mission was not only a challenge to the officially-recognized and established Jewish communities, but also sedition against Caesar; a conscious attack on existing imperial decrees.

A) ἀναστατώσαντες (concitant)

ἀναστατόω — here this verb means to disturb by throwing into commotion, to unsettle, to stir up a tumult, to be responsible for sedition[28]. The Jewish leadership is charging Paul with causing disarray and commotion in their communities all over the world[29].

B) τὴν οἰκουμένην

This was the inhabitable world[30]. But the term οἰκουμένη did not only have a geographical sense, but a cultural and political one as well. For the Greeks it was often used to describe that portion of the earth inhabited b ʹ Greeks where religion, philosophy and politics had come together to form a cohesive and ordered human society. The term came later to refer to the Roman Empire (cf. the Latin *orbis terrarum*). Under the Principate, "the philosophic concept of the Hellenistic οἰκουμένη fused with the political and legal structure of the Roman Empire"[31], but the idea that the Empire embraced the οἰκουμένη was of Greek conception.

C) καὶ οὗτοι πάντες ἀπέναντι τῶν δογμάτων καίσαρος πράσσουσιν (*et hii omnes contra decreta Caesaris faciunt*)

ἀπέναντι — should be taken in an emphatic sense: in (total) opposition to.
δόγμα — public decrees, ordinances, used especially of the Roman senate (*senatus consultum*). The Vg. translates the δόγμα of Luke II,1 as *Edictum* (proclamation) and here as *Decretum* (a judicial decision having mandatory force).

---

28 cf. Acts XXI,38. In Gal. V,12, the verb is used in the sense of unsettling someone, disturbing the mind of one's hearers by sowing doubt.
29 cf. Acts XXIV,5.
30 cf. *Ant.* XIV,7.2 (110).
31 *ThWb.* Vol. V, pg. 157. cf. Lk. II,1. cf. *OGIS.* 666.4 ;668.5. Both inscriptions are Neronian.

D) βασιλέα ἕτερον

βασιλεύς was the title used to designate the old Hellenistic monarchs. It entered but slowly into the official language of Rome as a designation for the Emperor: βασιλεύς was applied to the Emperor in verse as early as the time of Augustus, but in prose, βασιλεύς was not generally employed before the second century[32]. Αὐτοκράτωρ was the common designation for the Emperor both in formal imperial titulature as well as in general usage.

In both his Gospel and in Acts, Luke presents Jesus quite clearly as a king, as the One having kingly sovereignty. This can be seen for example in the Annunciation scene where Luke uses such words as *throne, reign,* and *kingdom*[33]. In the Lucan account of Jesus' trial, the Sanhedrin presents Jesus' Messianic kingship to Pilate in a political sense, as an attack on Roman sovereignty: "we found this man perverting our nation, and forbidding us to give tribute to Caesar, saying that he himself is Christ a king". (Lk. XXIII,2). Jesus does not deny the charge. The same politicizing of the charge is recorded in the Gospel of John. There even though Jesus is recognized as innocent by the governor, His adversaries succeed in placing the whole indictment on the political level, thereby forcing Pilate to condemn the Lord. The political dimension given Jesus' Messianic kingship is explicit: "every one who makes himself a king sets himself against Caesar" (Jn. XIX,12b).

There is a parallel set of dynamics at Thessalonica. The accusation against the two apostles is one of sedition by reason of their proclamation of another king, Jesus. The charge of sedition was designed to kindle a terrible fury against the apostles and their followers in the Thessalonian community. For a Roman citizen to proclaim a *regem alium* over against the sovereign head of the Empire would exact the most rigorous punishment. Indeed the text of Acts clearly shows that the crowd present in the Forum and the magistrates were shocked and angered when they heard the accusations (XVII,8).

III. Excursus: The Emperor: His Authority, Majesty, Cult

In 27 B.C., the Senate granted Octavian the title of *Augustus*. With the founding of the principate, Octavian gradually gathered all the reins of

---

32 Mason, *GREEK TERMS*, pg. 120. For NT uses of βασιλεύς meaning the Emperor, cf. I Peter II, 13; II,17. cf. *BJ*. III,8.3 (351) where we see the expression Ῥωμαίων βασιλεῖς.
33 cf. P.W. Walaskay, *AND SO WE CAME TO ROME*, Cambridge, 1983, pg. 17–18 for further discussion.

state authority in his hands. He and his successors came to be vested with the sovereignty formerly held by the *populus Romanus*. The ruler was the *Princeps*, the first of the Romans. He was *Pontifex maximus*, the chief religious leader of the state. He was the *Imperator*, the victorious general. He held the proconsular *imperium*, full military and civil powers. Inherent in this *imperium* was the right to settle matters by edict. This was a comprehensive grant unencumbered by any geographical limitation[34]. His *imperium* was *maius*; he thus exercised wide powers of overriding control on all other magistrates[35]. In 23 B.C. he was also invested with full tribunician power (*tribunicia potestas*)[36]. His person was *sacrosanctus*. He held legislative power and was the highest level of appellate jurisdiction. Proconsular *imperium* and tribunician power together formed the essential juridical base for the imperial power: the fact that they were held by one and the same man transformed the state into an imperial autocracy[37].

The change in regime also affected the concept of *maiestas*[38], a term which could be applied to such criminal offenses as treason, sedition or desertion. Cicero defined lese majesty as a diminishing of the dignity, high estate or authority of the Roman people or to those to whom they had given authority (*Maiestatem minuere est de dignitate aut amplitudine aut potestate populi aut eorum quibus populus potestatem dedit aliquid derogare*)[39]. The crime of *maiestas* was committed against the Roman people (*adversus populum Romanum*) or their safety. Already from the introduction of the *Lex Cornelia Maiestatis* by Sulla, the scope of *maiestas* had been widened enough to include "insults of any kind to persons of importance in the state"[40]. With the founding of the Principate, outrages perpetrated in word or deed against the *Princeps* became assimilated with crimes against the State[41]:

---

34 cf. J.G.C. Anderson, "Augustan Edicts from Cyrene", *JRS*, Vol. 17: 1927, pg. 42–43.
35 Dio Cassius LIII,32,5.
36 Dio Cassius LIII,32,6. cf. *ILS*. 96 for Augustus' titles.
37 cf. J. Gaudemet, *INSTITUTIONS DE L'ANTIQUITE*, 1967, pg. 455 ff. P.A. Brunt, "Lex de Imperio Vespasiani", *JRS*, 67; 1977, pg. 95–97.
38 R.A. Bauman notes that *maiestas* was a peculiarly Roman concept. Greek authors, says Bauman, "in default of an adequate equivalent for the word *maiestas* resorted to approximations". (*CRIMEN MAIESTATIS IN THE ROMAN REPUBLIC AND THE AUGUSTAN PRINCIPATE*, Johannesburg, 1967, pg. 1.).
39 Cicero, *de Inventione* II,17.53. Here of course, magisterial *maiestas* was an extension of the *maiestas populi Romani* and subordinate to it: "A magistrate, possessing no absolute attribute of *maiestas*, could not maintain his *maiestas* against the Roman people. The latter was the *maior* in relation to its delegate, the magistrate, and he in turn was the *maior* in relation to individual citizens" (Bauman, *CRIMEN MAIESTATIS, op.cit.*, pg. 13).
40 J.E. Allison and J.D. Cloud, "The Lex Iulia Maiestatis", *LATOMUS*, Vol. 21 ;1962, pg. 719.
41 cf. *Digest* XLVIII,4.6: "*Qui statuas aut imagines imperatoris iam consecratas conflaverint aliudue quid simile admiserint lege Iulia maiestatis tenentur*".

"The actual enlargement of the scope of *maiestas* was left to Augustus, and the *Lex Iulia* referred to by later jurists is almost certainly his. The actual terms of this law, too, are unknown, but events show that the *crimen minutae maiestatis* was extended to include, as well as the abuse of the divinity of Julius, verbal abuse and slander of the *Princeps* and sometimes even slander of members of his family. It was this extension of the meaning of *maiestas* by Augustus — showing as it did the shift in the balance of power in the State — that was so significant ..."[42].

The enlargement of the concept of *maiestas* and the assimilation of outrages to the dignity of the Emperor or his family with crimes against the State can be clearly seen from Tacitus' account of the revival of the treason laws under Tiberius:

"Tiberius rejected the title *Father of his country* though it had been repeatedly pressed upon him by the people: and, disregarding a vote of the Senate, refused to allow the taking of an oath to obey his enactments. (...) Yet even so he failed to inspire the belief that his sentiments were not monarchical. For he had resuscitated the *Lex Maiestatis*, a statute which in the old jurisprudence had carried the same name but covered a different type of offence — betrayal of an army; seditious incitement of the populace; an act, in short, of official maladministration dimishing the *majesty of the Roman nation*"[43].

A defendant found guilty of a *crimen maiestatis* (cf. the Greek τὸ ἔγκλημα τῆς ἀσεβείας) was a *condemnatus maiestatis*. The type of punishment inflicted varied according to the legal and social status of the guilty party. Crucifixion was common, especially for non-Roman citizens. Being sent to the wild beasts in the arena was another punishment as was deportation to a remote place[44].

"From the establishment of the Principate the trend of Roman criminal law, especially in the law of treason, is towards greater arbitrariness, wider discrimination as between one defendant and another, and crueller and crueller punishments. The beginning of this process can be seen under Tiberius and even under Augustus. The full development is amply clear in the jurists"[45].

A major feature of the growth and spread of the imperial idea was the process of increasing veneration for the Emperor. The idea of divine honours being bestowed on a ruler had its roots in the ancient Greek ideal

---

42 C.W. Chilton, "The Roman Law of Treason under the Early Principate", *JRS*, Vol. 45 ,1955, pg. 75. cf. Dio Cassius, LVII,9.2–3 ; LIX,11.6. cf. Bauman, *CRIMEN MAIESTATIS, op.cit.,* pg. 266–292 for a comprehensive study of the *Lex Iulia Maiestatis*.
43 Tacitus, *Ann.* I,72 (E.T. = J. Jackson, *Loeb*, 1962). cf. Suetonius, *Tib.* LVIII: "It was at about this time that a praetor asked him whether he should have the courts convened to consider cases of lese majesty; to which he replied that the laws must be enforced, and he did enforce them most rigorously". (E.T. = J.C. Rolfe, *Loeb*, 1960). R.A. Bauman writes: "The association of insults to the emperor with treason was productive of many anomalies and inconsistencies. Other legal systems know the crime of lèse-majesté, of injury to the dignity of the sovereign, alongside what is usually known as High Treason, but as a rule the distinction between the two is clear. It was not so in Rome". (R.A. Bauman, *IMPIETAS IN PRINCIPEM*, 1974, pg. 2).
44 cf *Digest* XLVIII,19.38.2: "*Auctores seditionis et tumultus populo concitato pro qualitate dignitatis aut in furcam tolluntur, aut bestiis obiciuntur, aut in insulam deportantur*".
45 C.W. Chilton, *op.cit.*, pg. 81. Allison and Clark note that the Emperors did not need "to take the legally prescribed penalties as more than a guiding line" when handing down a sentence. (Allison and Clark, *op.cit.*, pg. 726).

of kingship and in the later Hellenistic conception of the god-like king, who was a benefactor to and protector of all men[46]. Roman policy strove to establish, promote and institutionalize veneration for the Emperor so as to encourage a sense of unity and patriotism in the vast Empire:

> "Patriotism in ancient times was inseparable from religious feeling, and Roman policy fostered a new imperial religion in which all its subjects should unite, viz., the worship of the divine majesty of Rome incarnate in human form in the series of the emperors and especially in the reigning emperor"[47].

During the latter part of the First Century B.C. and the first half of the following century, the practice of Emperor worship gradually developed and spread throughout the Roman world:

> "The public cult of an emperor was regulated by Augustus. At least before Nero the imperial authorization was necessary for a city, or a province, to establish the cult of an emperor or a member of the imperial house. But each community was free to organize the worship at its own convenience"[48].

In Paul's time, one cannot really speak of the existence of a standard imperial cult with strictly uniform rules and rites throughout the Empire. Rather there was a collective faith in the Emperor as the great benefactor of mankind, manifested by multiple and diverse — yet related — cultic forms expressing this shared faith and common religious phenomenon. Indeed all the different aspects of the imperial cult "were derived from a similar concept, and were inspired by a similar sentiment, which was essentially a religious devotion to the master of the Roman Empire"[49].

The spread of this cult came slowly. After Julius Caesar's assassination in 44 B.C. and the subsequent triumph of the forces of the Second Triumvirate, the slain leader was proclaimed *divus Iulius* by decision of the Senate and enrolled in due form among the deities of the city of Rome: "He died in the fifty-sixth year of his age", writes Suetonius, "and was numbered among the gods, not only by a formal decree, but also in the

---

46 D. Cuss notes: "By the end of the fourth century B.C., few Greeks would have regarded deification or even the rendering of divine honours as an impious act worthy of blame". (D. Cuss *IMPERIAL CULT AND HONORARY TERMS IN THE NEW TESTAMENT*, Fribourg, 1974, pg. 24. D. Cuss goes on to say that the worship of Alexander the Great "was the cornerstone of the developing ruler-cult and formed the basis for the imperial cult which was to play such an important role in the political and religious life of the Empire". (Cuss, *op.cit.*, pg. 25).
47 Ramsay, *SPT*, pg. 134.
48 E. Bickerman, "Consecratio", *LE CULTE DES SOUVERAINS DANS L'EMPIRE ROMAIN*, Vandoeuvres-Genève, 1973, pg. 8–9. cf. F. Millar who writes: "If we look first at the pagan population of the provinces, there is ever-increasing evidence that the Emperor-cult had an important place in public religious life; and that this place was established very early [i.e. from Augustus]". (F. Millar, "The Imperial Cult and the Persecutions", *LE CULTE DES SOUVERAINS DANS L'EMPIRE ROMAIN*, Vandoeuvres-Genève, 1973, pg. 146.
49 D. Cuss, *op.cit.*, pg. 31.

conviction of the common people"[50]. By his adoption, Augustus became the son of the divine Julius and took the name *Augustus divi filius*. Augustus went as close to deification in his lifetime as he could. Tacitus notes rather acidly about Augustus: "He had left small room for the worship of heaven, when he claimed to be himself adored in temples and in the image of godhead by flamens and by priests!"[51]. Augustus was careful however to decline many honours, refusing formal offers to have temples erected to him in the provinces unless the name *Roma* were associated with his own (i.e. *Templum Romae et Augusti*). In Rome itself, he obstinately refused this honour[52]. Augustus was declared a god a short while after his death in 14 A.D.[53].

Tiberius explicitly rejected many of the divine honours that Augustus had enjoyed: "He forbade the voting of temples, *flamens,* and priests in his honour, and even the setting up of statues and busts without his permission; and this he gave only with the understanding that they were not to be placed among the likenesses of the gods, but among the adornments of the temples", writes Suetonius[54]. One does come across the mention *flamen Tiberii*, a tell-tale sign of the sacerdotal, however[55]. Moreover Tiberius strongly encouraged the development of the cult of the divine Augustus[56]. He also agreed to have a temple erected to him (and his mother and the Senate) by the cities of Asia, accepting this honour as a visible sign of their gratitude after he had defended the province of Asia against the nefarious deeds of two venal functionaries, Silanus and Capito[57].

---

50 Suetonius, *Iul.* LXXXVIII, cf. *CIL.* IX, 2628: *"genio deivi iuli parentis patriae quem senatus populusque Romanus in deorum numerum retullit".*
51 Tacitus, *Ann.* I,10. F. Millar notes that although the Emperors are rarely attested as attributing the word *deus* to themselves "the fact of the Imperial cult in its very varied forms was accepted by all the Emperors". (Millar, *op.cit.*, pg. 157). The cult of the Emperor's divinized qualities, e.g. *Victoria, Fortuna redix, Pax Augusta*, etc., was an integral part of the imperial mystique. (cf. L. Cerfaux and J. Tondriau, *LE CULTE DES SOUVERAINS*, Tornai, 1957, pg. 331.).
52 Suetonius, *Aug.* LII.
53 Tacitus, *Ann.* I,11; Dio Cassius LVI, 46.1–5. Following the principle laid down by Augustus, the provincials could worship a living Emperor, but for the Romans the Emperor became a deity only after his death (so E. Bickerman, *op.cit.*, pg. 9–10). cf. the language used in a bilingual inscription on a stele found in Burdur (yr. 18–19 A.D.), where the dead Augustus is *alter deorum* ($\theta\epsilon\tilde{\omega}\nu$) and the reigning Tiberius *alter principum* ($\alpha\dot{\upsilon}\tau o\kappa\rho\alpha\tau\acute{o}\rho\omega\nu$), in G.H.R. Horsley, *NEW DOCUMENTS ILLUSTRATING EARLY CHRISTIANITY*, 1981, Inscription 9 entitled "The regional *Kanon* for requisitioned transport", pg. 36–45. Farther on in this inscription the legate Sotidius threatens infractors of the law by categorically stating that the law would be enforced not only through his own powers (*potestate*) as legate, but by the majesty (*maiestate* /$\theta\epsilon\iota\acute{o}\tau\eta\tau\alpha$) of the most excellent Princeps.
54 Suetonius, *Tib.* XXVI; (E.T. = J.C. Rolfe, *Loeb*, 1960).
55 *CIL* IX,652.
56 Tacitus, *Ann.* I,78; Dio Cassius LVII, 10.2.
57 Tacitus, *Ann.* IV,15.

Tiberius did not refuse a request by the province of Hispania Ulterior to be allowed to erect a temple in his honour, citing as a precedent Augustus' acceptance of a temple at Pergamum dedicated to himself and Rome[58]. Tiberius, writes D.L. Jones, "regarded as absurd claims of divinity for humans, and in his lifetime, conscientiously resisted all honours which did not have their roots in Augustus"[59].

Flavius Josephus notes that there were statues of Emperor Gaius in all the subject cities of the Empire: "... and all the subject nations ... had erected in each of their cities statues of Caesar, along with those of their other gods"[60]. When Gaius' sister Drusilla died in 38 A.D., she was deified. Indeed she was reported to have visibly ascended into heaven[61].

Thus the imperial cult gradually penetrated all social classes and all parts of the Empire. To the Empire's downtrodden classes, especially in the provinces, the Emperor appeared as the victor, the *restitutor pacis*, the providential being who would deliver them from the iniquities of senatorial government and from the heavy burdens laid on them by wicked provincial officials. The Emperor was the great benefactor and the hope of the world[62].

Emperor-worship became an expression of genuine gratitude on the part of much of the Empire's population for the public order, social well-being and peace which had followed the establishment of the Principate[63]. The bonding of the divine and the secular in the Emperor's person gave a certain unity to the vast Roman Empire by providing a focal point around which its far-flung and disparate parts might rally[64]. This political-religious

---

58 Tacitus, *Ann.* IV,37–38.
59 D.L. Jones, "Christianity and the Roman Imperial Cult", *ANRW*, II,23.2; 1980; pg. 1024–25.
60 *BJ.* II,10.3 (194). E.T. = H.St. J. Thackeray, *Loeb*, 1961.
61 Dio Cassius LIX,11.4.
62 cf. *P.Oxy.* VII, 1021.5–13. The type of language used in this notification of the accession of Nero to the throne in 54 A.D. demonstrates the widespread concept of the Emperor = hope of the world: "and the expectation and hope of the world has been declared Emperor, the good genius of the world and the source of all good things, Nero, has been declared Caesar." ὁ δὲ τῆς οἰκουμένης καὶ προσδοκηθεὶς καὶ ἐλπισθεὶς Αὐτοκράτωρ ἀποδέδεικται ἀγαθὸς δαίμων δὲ τῆς οἰκουμένης [αρ]χῇ ὤν [μεγισ]τε πάντων ἀγαθῶν Νέρων Καῖσαρ ἀποδέδεικται. H.I. Bell notes that the letter of Claudius to the Alexandrians (*P. Lond.* VI,1912) shows "very clearly what steady pressure was maintained from the side of the provinces upon the Emperors to sanction extensions of the cult" (H.I. Bell, *op.cit.*, pg. 7.). In the preamble to the letter, the prefect of Egypt states that he had displayed the Emperor's letter publicly so that the Alexandrian population "may admire the majesty of our God Caesar" (μεγαλειότητα τοῦ θεοῦ ἡμῶν καίσαρος θαυμάσητε). In his letter Claudius agreed to have statues erected to himself and his family, but refused a golden statue of the *Pax Augusta Claudiana*, which he ordered to be dedicated instead to *Roma*.
63 cf. Cerfaux & Tondriau, *op.cit.*, pg. 327.
64 C. Munier writes: "The regime used the imperial cult to stimulate a sense of loyalty in those provinces it wished to romanize". (*L'EGLISE DANS L'EMPIRE ROMAIN*, Paris, 1979, pg. 197.)

conception of the person and role of the Emperor constituted one of the secular foundations of the imperial regime[65]. Although at this very early period in the history of the Principate, the imperial cult was not formally obligatory — in fact it was characterized by many and varied forms of expression[66] — refusing to participate in the sacrifices offered to the deified Emperors was considered as anti-Roman and anti-social. Only the dregs of society, the most disloyal of subjects, acted thusly:

> "In the eyes of the Romans, the only religion with a universal vocation was the imperial cult, the seal of unity and the consacration of the established order. Any desire to compete with that cult was tantamount to rejecting the Roman model: For the citizen, this was an act of high treason, for the peregrine an act of rebellion"[67].

Thus one can readily see at what the Jewish plaintiffs were aiming in their accusation. By his missionary endeavours and his proclamation of the Lordship of Jesus, he, Paul, a Roman citizen, was betraying the Emperor by proclaiming another king and by discouraging participation in Emperor-worship. In the view of the Thessalonian Jews, it was necessary and imperative that this enemy, common to both the Jewish and Roman authorities, be duly condemned for sedition. For was it not incumbent on the tribunal to repress any seditious acts, any insubordination and any affront to the dignity, power or majesty of the Princeps?

Paul and other early Church writers were aware of the fact that their enemies were assimilating their proclamation of Jesus' Kingship with sedition against the reigning Emperor. Thus they often exhorted their fellow Christians to pray for the civil authorities and especially for the Emperor so as to demonstrate that Christianity was not a movement inveterately hostile to the imperial system, nor bent on seeking its violent overthrow[68].

Finally, the Jews, as we have seen, were exempt from the usual forms of Emperor-worship. As long as the followers of Jesus were considered by the Roman authorities to be a part of official Judaism, then they too were, of course, exempt. The problem of the irreconcilability of the worship of God and His only-begotten Son on the one hand and of the worship of the Emperor on the other would not become politically or juridically acute until Christianity could no longer officially shelter under the Jewish name.

---

65 cf. L. Homo, *LES EMPEREURS ROMAINS ET LE CHRISTIANISME*, Paris, 1931, pg. 28.
66 cf. F. Millar, *op.cit.*, pg. 164.
67 Scheid, *op.cit.*, pg. 164–165.
68 cf. Rom. XIII,1–7; Titus III,1; I Peter II,13–17, also Clement of Rome LXI,1–2; Tertullian, *Apol.* XXXII,1–3.

IV. Jason gives Security

In the absence of Paul and Silas, legal action was taken against Jason, who as a property-holding resident of Thessalonica, could act as surety for Paul: "And when they had taken security (λαβόντες τό ίκανόν) from Jason and the rest, they let them go." (XVII,9).

A) λαβόντες τό ίκανόν

The basic meaning of the adjective ίκανός when used quantitatively is sufficient, enough, adequate. The expression used here τό ίκανόν λαμβάνειν is a Latinism (*satis accipere*) and means to take security or bail[69]. There is a related legal term τό ίκανόν ποιείν[70] = to be satisfactory to, to give security or bail. The word ίκανοδοτέω[71] is the Latin *satisdare*. The one who gives security or bail (in this case it is Jason who is the guarantor or surety) is the ίκανοδότης.

Jason himself was not accused of sedition. The charge against him was that he received and lodged seditious persons in his house. By exacting the payment of security, the Politarchs made Jason legally responsible for Paul and Silas. The bond would be forfeited and Jason hauled into court anew in the event of any recurring trouble involving the two apostles. To prevent that, as well as to assure the apostles' continued safety, Jason and the brethren organized their hasty and secret departure from Thessalonica: "The brethren immediately sent Paul and Silas away by night to Beroea" (XVII,10a)[72]. Not only did Jason hurry the apostles to Beroea, where the jurisdiction of the Thessalonian Politarchs was not valid, but he also had to see to it that they did not come back to the Macedonian capital. The Politarchs' main concern was to maintain public order and to calm the powerful passions aroused among the population. This was accomplished by Paul's *banishment* which had the effect of putting an impassable chasm between the apostle and the newly-founded church at Thessalonica[73].

The striking fact about Luke's reconstruction of the judicial events which took place at Thessalonica is the remarkable indifference on the

---

69 This expression is also attested in *OGIS* 629.100 (Palmyra, 2nd. Century A.D.). cf. Moulton, *PROLEGOMENA*, pg. 20 for further use.
70 cf. Polybius XXXII,3.13; Justinian, *Novellae* 86.4. Mk. XV,15a also contains this expression.
71 cf. *P.Oxy.* II,259.29 (year 23 A.D.).
72 Beroea was also governed by five Politarchs. cf. Schuler, *op.cit.*, pg. 90,97 and 98, note 6.
73 Not being allowed back into Thessalonica for some time to come saddened Paul; "but since we were bereft of you, brethren, for a short time in person not in heart, we endeavored the more eagerly and with great desire to see you face to face; because we wanted to come to you – I, Paul, again and again – but Satan hindered us." (I Thess. II, 17–18).

part of the Politarchs to charges involving sedition and rebellion against the reigning Emperor. The narrative clearly implies that no effort was made to apprehend the apostles even though they were still in Thessalonica when Jason was dragged before the magistrates and made to act as surety. Thus there seems to be a fundamental contradiction in the Lucan account between the gravity of the charges on the one hand and the behaviour of the Politarchs on the other.

The apostles' departure from the city and Jason's dismissal from the court with a bond to pay did not end the newly-founded church's woes in that city. It continued to be a victim of persecution and vexations due to the dangerous sentiments aroused among the people and their rulers by the circumstances which had so abruptly ended Paul's mission. Indeed a reading of I Thess. II,14–16 shows that the riot in Thessalonica was considerably *more serious than the language used in the Acts-narrative would suggest.*

Paul's second encounter with the authorities in Macedonia had ended in his ignominious banishment from Thessalonica and in lasting difficulties for the community he had founded there.

Chapter III
Corinth: Paul and Gallio

I. The Senatorial Province of Achaia

After his stay in Beroea (Acts XVII,10–15) and Athens (XVII,16–34), Paul went to Corinth. The great commercial city with its two ports of Lechaeum on the Gulf of Corinth and Cenchreae on the Saronic Gulf[1] was the capital of the senatorial province of Achaia[2] and the centre of its political life.

L. Mummius had destroyed Corinth in 146 B.C. at the time of the Roman conquest[3]. In 46 B.C., Julius Caesar refounded Corinth as a Roman colony (*Colonia Laus Iulia Corinthiensis*) and settled some of his soldiers there[4]. Strabo notes that Corinth had been restored because of its favourable position and settled to a great extent by people belonging to the freedmen class[5]. Jews and Syrians also came to settle there; thus the refounded city had a distinctive multi-ethnic flavour[6]. Here too the Latin language was very much in evidence and served as the colony's official tongue during Paul's time[7]. There is thus a strong possibility that the court proceedings involving Paul, a Roman citizen, transpired in Latin both at Philippi and Corinth.

Achaia had been a senatorial province from 27 B.C. to 15 A.D. at which time Tiberius merged both Achaia and Macedonia with the imperial province of Moesia[8]. In 44 A.D., Achaia once again became a senatorial prov-

---

1. Pliny the Elder, *Nat. Hist.* IV,4.cf. Romans XVI,1, where Phoebe, a servant of the church at Cenchreae, is commended to the Roman church.
2. Apuleius Madaurensis, *Metamorphoseon* X,18.
3. Pliny the Elder, *Nat. Hist.* XXXIV,6; Velleius Paterculus, *Hist. Rom.* I,13. Livy gives a succinct but very beautiful description of the city before its destruction (XLV,28). For a pertinent inscription, cf. *CIL.* I,541.
4. Plutarch, *Caesar* LVII,5. cf. Pausanias II,1.
5. Strabo, *Geo.* VIII,6.23. Strabo again mentions the colonization of Corinth in *Geo.* XVII,3.15.
6. cf. J. Wiseman, "Corinth and Rome I: 228 B.C.–A.D. 267", *ANRW* II,7.1; 1979, pg. 497.
7. J. Murphy-O'Connor, *CORINTHE AU TEMPS DE SAINT PAUL* (F.T.) Paris, 1986, pg. 28.
8. Tacitus, *Ann.* I,80.

ince[9] and as such was ruled by a Proconsul. The Greek equivalent for this title was ἀνθύπατος[10], a term which first occurs in the 2nd Century B.C.[11]. This title is used five times in the New Testament, all of them in the Book of Acts. Three of the references are to Sergius Paulus, proconsul of Cyprus (XIII,7,8,12), one is to Gallio (XVIII,12) and one, in the plural, to the proconsuls of Asia (XIX,38).

The Proconsul held the *imperium proconsulare*, which meant that he was the supreme administrative and judicial authority in the province: "*et ideo maius imperium in ea provincia habet omnibus post principem*", writes the jurist Ulpianus[12]. Here again we note that the basic power of criminal jurisdiction, designated by the terms *coercere* and *animadvertere*, stemmed from the *imperium*[13]. Proconsuls could delegate to their legates the examination (*cognitio*) of prisoners, but the legate would have to remit cases to the Proconsul after a preliminary hearing of the prisoners. But the Proconsul could not transfer his own grant of the *ius gladii* (power of the sword) or his power of *coercitio* to another[14].

The Proconsul was not without constraints in the workings of his jurisdiction. Certain statutory laws did provide limits on the Proconsul's use of his *imperium*, among these was the law of *maiestas*. Moreover the Emperor held the *imperium maius* in senatorial provinces as well as in imperial provinces. He could intervene in the province at will, giving instructions to the Proconsuls and regulating any special affairs as he saw fit. As time went on, the Proconsuls tended to consult the Emperor more frequently about any thorny problem which they might encounter. Any formal advice the Emperor gave to the Proconsuls (especially in the form of a Rescript) had the force of law. So even though the Proconsul was competent in the whole realm of civil and criminal jurisdiction, including the hearing of capital cases, he was always subject to the Emperor's overriding *imperium*.

---

9 Suetonius, *Claud*. XXV.
10 cf. Polybius, XXVIII,5.6; *SIG*[4], 684.3.
11 Mason, *GREEK TERMS*, pg. 106. Mason writes further that the title ἀνθύπατος like Proconsul "came to be applied to governors who were not necessarily of consular rank". (pg. 106). W. Neil (*op.cit.*, pg. 197) notes that "It is a mark of Luke's historical accuracy that he knows that Achaia was at this time a 'senatorial' province of the Empire, and therefore governed by a Proconsul – as opposed to an imperial province, which was governed by a legate."
12 *Digest*, I,16.8.
13 Sherwin-White, pg. 4. The term *animadvertere* means to deal with actions punitively, to procede against, to inflict (capital) punishment on persons.
14 *Digest* I,16.6.: "*nec enim potest quis gladii potestatem sibi datam vel cuius alterius coercitionis ad alium transferre*".

II. Paul breaks with the Corinthian Synagogue

According to Acts, Paul arrived in Corinth directly after leaving Athens (XVIII,1) and stayed there for a period of a year and six months (XVIII, 11). It was here that Paul found Aquila "lately come from Italy with his wife Priscilla, because Claudius had commanded all the Jews to leave Rome" (XVIII,2). Paul went to see this couple "and because he was of the same trade he stayed with them, and they worked, for by trade they were tentmakers ($\sigma\kappa\eta\nu\sigma\pi\sigma\iota\sigma\iota$)" (XVIII,3).

A) A year and six months

Luke indicates that Paul's ministry in Corinth was considerable: a year and six months in length. Moreover, the narrative seems to imply that this was one continuous stay. In fact Paul made a number of trips to Corinth in the course of his ministry. We cannot exclude the possibility that Luke has in fact brought together two or more trips into a single narrative sequence. Thus Paul's appearance before Gallio might very well have taken place during another, later, visit to Corinth and not during his first stay in the Achaian capital[15].

B) Aquila and Priscilla

Once again Luke mentions Paul's hosts by name (cf. Lydia at Philippi, Jason at Thessalonica and later Titius Justus at Corinth). By mentioning the reason for their settlement in Corinth, Luke links them to the Chrestus-controversy in Rome. This couple was surely not the only Jewish refugee family to establish itself in Corinth. The expulsion of Jews from Rome had the effect of increasing the size and importance of a number of Jewish communities outside the capital city, in this instance Corinth.

Aquila and Priscilla are mentioned thrice in the Epistles. In I Cor. XVI, 19 Paul transmits their greetings to the Church at Corinth "together with the Church in their house". In 2 Tim. IV,19, Timothy is asked to greet the couple. In Romans XVI,3–5a, Paul writes: "Greet Prisca and Aquila, my fellow workers in Christ Jesus, who risked their necks for my life, to

---

[15] cf. G. Lüdemann who thinks that the text of Acts 18 reflects diverse visits by Paul and not one continuous stay; he motivates this hypothesis "... aus literarkritischen Gründen und der redaktionellen Tendenz des Lukas in der Art der Kompositon der Lokaltraditionen", (Lüdemann, *op.cit.,* pg. 181). For Lüdemann, Paul's appearance before Gallio took place either during his intermediate or final visits to Corinth (pg. 197). J. Knox thinks that Paul's appearance before Gallio took place during the apostle's final stay in Corinth (*CHAPTERS IN A LIFE OF PAUL,* London, 1954, pg. 83.).

whom not only I but also all the churches of the Gentiles give thanks; greet also the church in their house". Thus not only did the couple collaborate with Paul during his Corinthian and Ephesian ministries, but also, according to the Epistle to the Romans, preceded him to Rome where they hosted a church. This friendship and the couple's return to Rome, probably at the end of Claudius' reign or the beginning of Nero's, had important consequences for Paul's ministry. Aquila and Priscilla, writes Ramsay were

> "well-suited to suggest to St. Paul the central importance of Rome in the development of the Church, and form a medium of communication with the great city. We may fairly associate with this friendship the maturing of St. Paul's plan for evangelizing Rome and the West, which we find already fully arranged a little later — Acts XIX,21/Rom. XV,24"[16].

C) σκηνοποιοί

Only Acts mentions that Paul's trade was tentmaking. That the apostle plied a trade is clear from I Cor. IV,12; I Thess. II,9 and 2 Thess. III,8. Curiously enough the phrase ἦσαν γὰρ σκηνοποιοί is missing from the Codex Bezae (and d, g).

In this context it is interesting to compare certain episodes from the life of Dio Chrysostom, who, exiled from Rome by Domitian, also turned to labouring to support himself. In Discourse XIII,10–13 the account given by the great philosopher of his call to service by the god Apollo, his missionary zeal and his efforts at self-support affords a certain similitude to Paul's own story:

> "The case of Dio is especially significant, for his exile meant years of wandering from city to city and from province to province, during the course of which he adopted the role of Cynic missionary; his combining missionary activity and self-support is thus a close parallel to the case of Paul. And so our picture of Paul, of one from the socially privileged classes, who, when faced with finding support turned to a trade, is historically credible"[17].

Paul's primary task lay, of course, in proclaiming the Word of the Lord. As was his wont, he went to the Jewish synagogue "every Sabbath" (XVIII, 4); where he "persuaded" both "Jews and Greeks" (XVIII,4). It was a very busy mission for when "Silas and Timothy arrived from Macedonia, Paul was occupied with preaching, testifying to the Jews that the Christ was Jesus." (XVIII,5). This witness to the Messiahship of the Lord Jesus proved once again to be the major stumbling-block in his relations with the Jews for the latter "opposed and reviled him" (ἀντιτασσομένων καὶ

---

16 Ramsay, "Corinth", *HDB*, Edinburgh, 1898, Vol. I, pg. 479.
17 R.F. Hock, "Paul's Tentmaking and the Problem of his social Class", *JBL*, Vol. 97, No.4; December 1978, pg. 563. Hock concludes (a bit severely perhaps) that Paul's attitude toward work was not that of a typical artisan or rabbi loving labour, but "rather the snobbish and scornful attitude so typical of upper-class Greeks and Romans". (Hock, *op.cit.*, pg. 562).

βλασφημούντων) (XVIII,6a). This in turn led Paul to break off publicly with the Jewish community as he had already done in Pisidian Antioch (XIII,46) and would later do at Rome (XXVIII,28): "he shook out his garments and said to them, 'Your blood be upon your heads! I am innocent." (XVIII,6a). As at Pisidian Antioch and Rome, Paul turned to the Gentiles: "From now on I will go to the Gentiles" (ἀπὸ τοῦ νῦν εἰς τὰ ἔθνη πορεύσομαι) (XVIII,6b).

A) The synogogue

Paul's missionary activity is centered in the synagogue which he leaves only when he is forced out. Luke stresses the centrality of the synagogue to Paul's mission throughout his account of the apostle's travels[18]. The synagogue setting is crucial to Luke's presentation of Christianity as the accomplishment of Old Testament expectations and not a new and illicit religion outside Judaism.

B) ἀντιτασσομένων καὶ βλασφημούντων

Once again Luke chooses very powerful verbs to reveal the depth, extent and quasi-unanimity of the Jewish opposition to Paul's proclamation.
ἀντιτάσσω denotes the act of opposing oneself to something, i.e. absolute resistance.
βλασφημέω means to calumniate, to speak reproachfully or ill of someone, to speak to the prejudice of another person, to rail at. The same verb is used by Luke in his account of Paul's break with the Jews of Pisidian Antioch (XIII,45). For Luke, the Christian writer, the word βλασφημέω signifies speaking irreverently not only of God the Father, but also of the Sonship of Jesus. Thus in this instance, Jewish derision of Paul's proclamation of the Messiahship of the crucified Jesus is perforce blasphemy.

C) ἀπὸ τοῦ νῦν εἰς τὰ ἔθνη πορεύσομαι

Having brought the narrative to a high point of dramatic tension (opposition and reviling by the Jews; shaking out of garments and a malediction by Paul), Luke now introduces the climatic moment of the Corinthian pericope: Paul turns to the Gentiles.

---

[18] Cyprus (XIII,5), Pisidian Antioch (XIII,14), Iconium (XIV,1), Thessalonica (XVII,2), Beroea (XVII,10), Athens (XVII,17), Corinth (XVIII,4), Ephesus (XVIII,19; XIX,8). M. Hengel writes: "In fact we can hardly doubt that the milieu of the synagogue had been an important place for missionary teaching and discussion, both for earliest Christianity and for Jesus himself. It was an area which will have been abandoned reluctantly and only under external compulsion". *(ACTS AND THE HISTORY OF EARLIEST CHRISTIANITY*, London, 1979, pg. 64.).

The apostle is quite clear in his concluding remarks. The Jews themselves are responsible for their rejection of the Gospel of Salvation. Paul is quite free from any blame in that regard having first of all proclaimed the saving message to the Jews. As his own nation was now rejecting Jesus, he would bring the message of salvation to the Gentiles. Luke's use of the prepositions ἀπὸ → εἰς is a literary device to clearly indicate the movement away from one and toward the other[19].

The break with the Corinthian synagogue did not then signify the end of Paul's ministry in Corinth, Paul moves "to the house of a man named Titius Justus, a worshiper of God; his house was next door to the synagogue." (XVIII,7). Moreover at this juncture, a most rewarding event is recorded by Luke: "Crispus, the ruler of the synagogue (ἀρχισυνάγωγος), believed in the Lord, together with all his household;" (XVIII,8a).

A) Titius Justus

Paul will henceforth use the house of Titius Justus, a σεβόμενος τὸν Θεόν, as his base of operations. Paul's host bore the Latin *nomen* and *cognomen* of Titius Justus. This would indicate that he was a colonist and a Roman citizen, and possibly a man of the upper social class of Corinth. Titius Justus' legal and social status would therefore facilitate Paul's access to Corinthian Gentile circles. The text of Acts specifies that the house was contiguous (συνομοροῦσα) to the synagogue, a most dangerous location! Paul's presence and continuing missionary work, especially among the devout Greeks in a building neighbouring the synagogue could only be a constant and visible provocation to the synagogal authorities[20].

B) Crispus

The ἀρχισυνάγωγος was the ruler of the synagogue. This term appears thrice in the Acts-narrative: here in reference to Crispus, slightly later in reference to Sosthenes (XVIII,17) and in XIII,15 where the plural is used. The ruler's duties included the organization of the worship service and the designation of the person who was to lead the assembly in prayer. He also had the right to invite other people to speak about Holy Scripture: in Acts XIII,15, Paul and Barnabas were invited by the rulers of the synagogue of Pisidian Antioch to speak a λόγος παρακλήσεως to the people once the reading of the law and prophets was terminated. The importance of

---

19 The immediacy of the move from the Jews to the Gentiles is made more manifest in the Codex Bezae which uses the present tense πορεύομαι instead of the future πορεύσομαι.
20 cf. Acts XIX,8–9 where Paul withdrew from the synagogue at Ephesus and continued his missionary labours in the Hall of Tyrannus.
21 Crispus was one of the few converts whom Paul himself baptized at Corinth (I Cor. I,14).

the conversion of the ruler of the synagogue, a highly respected person, was that it left a deep and lasting impression on the God-fearers and led to yet more conversions[21].

The success of Paul's mission to Corinth, however, lay almost entirely with the Gentile population and not with the Jews: "and many of the Corinthians hearing Paul believed and were baptized." (XVIII,8b). One could reasonably assume that there was a great deal of tension, if not out and out violence, accompanying this ministry in the wake of the break in relations with the Corinthian Jews, the conversion of Crispus and the evangelization of the God-fearers.

III. Paul before the Proconsul Gallio

The tension between Paul and the Jewish community in Corinth finally culminated in an attack on Paul: "But when Gallio was Proconsul of Achaia, the Jews made a united attack upon Paul (κατεπέστησαν ὁμοθυμαδὸν οἱ Ἰουδαῖοι τῷ Παύλῳ) and brought him before the tribunal (καὶ ἤγαγον αὐτὸν ἐπὶ τὸ βῆμα), saying, 'This man is persuading men to worship God contrary to the law!'" (παρὰ τὸν νόμον ἀναπείθει οὗτος τοὺς ἀνθρώπους σέβεσθαι τὸν Θεόν) (XVIII,12–13).

A) Gallio

For the first time one of Paul's judges steps out of anonymity. Lucius Iunius Gallio (born Marcus Annaeus Novatus) was a well-known historical figure. He was the son of Seneca the Elder, the brother of Seneca, the Philosopher and tutor of the future Emperor Nero[22], and the uncle of the poet Lucan. At this point in his career, he was Proconsul of Achaia. Pliny the Elder says that he also had a Consulship, but does not specify the date[23]. Paul's appearance before the Proconsul Gallio was an important step in the apostle's judicial history for he was appearing before a man intimately linked to the Imperial court and the governing class at Rome[24].

The pericope contains two chronological indications which, taken together, allow an approximate dating of Paul's appearance in the proconsular court in Corinth. Luke mentions: (a) Claudius' expulsion of the Jews from Rome, and (b) Gallio's term as Proconsul of Achaia.

---

22 Cf. Tacitus, *Ann.* XV,73; Dio Cassius LX,35.2; LXII,25.3; Seneca, *Ep. Mor.* CIV,1; *Quaest. Nat.* IVa, praef;IV,9–13; V,11.1.
23 Pliny the Elder, *Nat. Hist.* XXXI,62.
24 Dio Cassius LXI,20.1.

A-1) Claudius' action against the Jews of Rome

In Acts XVIII,2, Luke mentions that Paul stayed with Aquila "lately (προσφάτως) come from Italy with his wife Priscilla, because Claudius had commanded all the Jews (πάντας τοὺς Ἰουδαίους) to leave Rome". Suetonius records that the Emperor expelled the Jews from Rome because of trouble surrounding Chrestus: "Since the Jews constantly made disturbances at the instigation of Chrestus, he expelled them from Rome" (*Iudaeos impulsore Chresto assidue tumultuantis Roma expulit*)[25]. Unfortunately Suetonius gives no date for the enactment of the expulsion order. Dio Cassius, writing about the events of Claudius' first regnal year (41 A.D.), says: "As for the Jews, who had again increased so greatly that by reason of their multitude it would have been hard without raising a tumult to bar them from the city, he did not drive them out, but ordered them, while continuing their traditional mode of life, not to hold meetings"[26]. Orosius, a much later source (beginning 5th Century A.D.), dated the measures taken against the Jews as occurring in 49 A.D.: "In the ninth year of the same reign, Josephus relates that the Jews were expelled from the City by order of Claudius; but what strikes me more is the way in which Suetonius expresses himself: '*Claudius Iudaeos impulsore Christo adsidue tumultuantis Roma expulit*'. Here it cannot at all be discerned whether he ordered the restraining and repression of the Jews who were acting tumultuarily against Christ or if he also wanted to expel the Christians with them as men of kindred religion"[27]. Although he is referred to by Orosius, Josephus is silent on this point. Tacitus' *Annals* for the year 49 A.D. contain no reference to this event; the *Annals* for the year 41 are lost.

Both the date and form of Claudius' measures are the subject of debate among modern scholars. J.B. Frey accepts the date 49 A.D. and writes: "It is most probable that not all the Jews left the city and that many of those who did, did not go very far [to Ariccia, for example] and that they came back at the first opportunity"[28]. C. Saulnier also supports the date 49 A.D.: "It is unlikely that this measure affected the entire community given its numerical importance. It is much better to conceive of the community as having been torn apart by quarrels, probably between Jews and Christians and of the imperial decision as having affected those reputed to be the troublemakers[29]. R. Jewett sees two distinct measures. Dio Cassius' notation concerned events which occurred in 41 A.D.: "The implication

---

25 Suetonius, *Claud.* XXV (E.T. = J.C. Rolfe, *Loeb*, 1959).
26 Dio Cassius LX,6.6. (E.T. = E. Cary, *Loeb*, 1961).
27 Orosius, *Historiarum adversus Paganos*, VII,6.15–16.
28 J.B. Frey, "Les Communautés Juives à Rome", *RSR*, Tome 20,1930, pg. 278.
29 C. Saulnier, "Rome et la Bible", *op.cit.*, Col. 963–964.

is that some public disorder or infraction of Roman regulations raised the question of whether all the Jews should not be expelled and that this impractical idea was dropped"[30]. There is no evidence that this disturbance was Chrestus-related. For Jewett the expulsion noted by Suetonius was caused by strife within the Roman Jewish community in the late 40s and this time was about Chrestus. Contrary to this, R. Penna leans to the earlier date and stresses that both ancient authors are referring to one and not two measures. In his view, the expulsion order concerned only the agitators themselves and other members of the *one* synagogue in which the quarrel over Chrestus took place[31]. Lüdemann writes that an analysis of the existing sources can only lead *mit grosser Wahrscheinlichkeit* to the conclusion that 41 A.D. is incontestably the date of the edict's issuance[32]. Finally M. Stern thinks that Claudius' original intention was to expel all the Jews from Rome and that he had issued an edict to that effect, but that he "shortly afterwards replaced this with an order banning Jewish meetings. Quite a number of Jews undoubtedly left Rome before the original edict was amended including some who moved to Ariccia or, for instance, to Corinth, like Aquila"[33].

In summary it would seem more plausible to discern two separate actions on Claudius' part. The reference in Dio Cassius would indicate that upon accession in 41 A.D., Claudius confirmed the rights of the Roman Jews to live in their traditional mode of life. At the same time he warned them not to agitate or to engage in a massive campaign of proselytism. This would be in the same spirit as his edict which put an end to the Alexandrian controversy. Claudius' accession to the throne in fact was marked by a certain number of measures in favour of the Jews: release of Alexander Lysimachus, Alabarch of the Alexandrian Jews, the establishment of a Palestinian kingdom under Agrippa I and general confirmation of traditional Jewish rights throughout the Empire. It is unlikely that the same year would have witnessed an expulsion of Jews from the capital[34]. The reference in Suetonius, Luke and Orosius would be to a more severe measure taken against certain Roman Jews in 49 A.D. as a result of the turbulence about Chrestus. The reference in Luke to the expulsion order implies

---

30 R. Jewett, *A CHRONOLOGY OF PAUL'S LIFE*, Philadelphia, 1979, pg. 37. Jewett notes that although a late source, Orosius does specifically mention the ninth regnal year; his notation could well reflect a reliable ancient source. (pg. 38). H. Solin (*op.cit.*, pg. 689) also sees two distinct events.
31 R. Penna, "Les Juifs à Rome au Temps de l'Apôtre Paul", *NTS*, Vol. 28; 1982, pg. 331.
32 G. Lüdemann, *op.cit.*, pg. 195.
33 M. Stern, "The Jewish Diaspora", *THE JEWISH PEOPLE IN THE FIRST CENTURY*, Assen, 1974, pg. 182.
34 S. Benko, "The Edict of Claudius of 49 A.D. and the Instigator Chrestus", *TZ*, No. 25, Heft 6, Nov.–Dec. 1969, pg. 407–408. cf. H. Solin, *op.cit.*, pg. 689–690.

that *all* the Jews were expelled from Rome. In view of the importance of the Roman Jewish community, it is unlikely that all were in fact expelled. Claudius' measure would have aimed at restoring order by expelling supporters of Chrestus as well as his adversaries, probably not from more than one synagogue. The expulsion would have been a clear warning on the Emperor's part to the other synagogues in Rome not to get involved in any further agitation springing from the Chrestus-controversy. In a larger sense this restrictive measure, along with others such as the proscription of the Druidic cult and the Romanization of the Eleusynian mysteries, can be considered as a defence of the official religion[35], as well as a purely security measure.

Suetonius and Orosius both categorically state that the action taken against the Roman Jews was caused by quarrelling about *Chrestus*. Already at this early date, the Christian message seems to have reached Rome and to have impacted the Roman Jewish community. For their part the pagan authorities considered the affair to be an internal Jewish controversy and not a Christian-Jewish struggle. The followers of Christ were still considered by the pagan environment to be members of a distinct Jewish party, perhaps, but certainly not as members of an independent religious movement totally outside organized Judaism[36].

A-2) Gallio's Proconsulship in Achaia:

Acts states that Paul was brought before the proconsular court at Corinth during Gallio's term of office. Gallio's proconsulship in Achaia can be dated rather precisely thanks to the *Epistula Claudii ad Delphos*, the famous Delphian inscription which mentions him[37]. The inscription reproduces a

---

35 cf. L. Herrmann, *CHRESTOS*, Brussels, 1970, pg. 165.
36 G. Lüdemann evokes the political context of Claudius' measure: the unrest among the Roman Jews was about a Messianic figure. Whether this figure were Christian or Jewish was of no matter to the Roman authorities. The unrest, notes Lüdemann, "weckte den Verdacht auf beabsichtigte revolutionäre Umtriebe und musste das Eingreifen der Staatsmacht geradezu herausfordern". (Lüdemann, *op.cit.*, pg. 186). L. Herrmann believes that the Chrestus controversy obviously refers to a messianic agitation "which led to the expulsion of people such as Aquila and Priscilla, who were Christians ..." (Herrmann, *op.cit.*, pg. 165). For his part, S. Benko rejects any identification of Chrestus with Christ. He hypothesizes that Chrestus was an extremist (zealot) leader of the Jewish community active in Rome in the year 49 A.D. In Benko's view, the troubles at Rome were not a Jewish-Christian dispute, but part of a larger Jewish-Gentile *Kulturkampf* born of messianic agitation. (Benko, *op.cit.*, pg. 417 ff).
37 The Greek text of the Delphian inscription containing the nine fragments put together by A. Plassart in 1967 is reproduced in Murphy-O'Connor (*op.cit.*, pg. 263). For the older version (i.e. the four fragments published in 1905 by E. Bourguet) cf. *SIG*^{4}, 801.d. The older title given the inscription, the *Epistula ad Gallionem* is a misnomer. The *epistula* was not addressed to Gallio, whose name appears in the Nominative case, but most likely to his successor as Proconsul.

letter composed by Claudius between 25 January and 1 August 52 A.D.[38]. The office of Proconsul was normally held for only one year; the term was sometimes extended, but owing to Gallio's bad health this was unlikely to be the case in this instance. André Plassart dates Gallio's proconsulship from the beginning of May 51 to May 52. This is most probably the case[39]. Both Plassart and J. Wisemann[40] put Paul's appearance before Gallio in the spring or early summer of 51, that is at the beginning of the Proconsul's term of office. J. Murphy-O'Connor suggests the period July-October 51 and hypothesizes that Gallio did not finish his term of office due to ill-health[41]. Nothing in the text of Acts indicates, however, that Paul's appearance was at the very beginning of Gallio's term of office. On the contrary Gallio's response to the Jewish petitioners — at least in the form it has in the Acts-narrative — would seem to indicate a certain experience in dealing with Graeco-Jewish rivalries in an Eastern city and not the inexperience that a newly-arrived governor might have had (cf. Luke's account of Festus' hesitations in Acts 25). We would suggest that Paul's appearance in the proconsular court occurred at the end of Gallio's term of office in Spring 52 A.D.

B) κατεπέστησαν ὁμοθυμαδὸν οἱ Ἰουδαῖοι τῷ Παύλῳ

Once again the Lucan narrative stresses the violence of Paul's Jewish opponents and the unanimity of the Jewish community against the apostle and his mission. Luke's use of the word ὁμοθυμαδὸν shows how complete the alienation was between Paul and the Corinthian Jews.

κατεφίστημι is to come upon suddenly, to rush upon, to assault, to rise up against.

ὁμοθυμαδὸν indicates of one mind and of one accord, together, unanimously.

The Western Text has the following lesson after the word ὁμοθυμαδὸν: "The Jews, after talking among themselves, made a concerted attack against Paul, and laid hands on him and took him before the Bench, yelling and saying ..."[42]. The Western reading stresses even more than the B-Text, the violence of Paul's adversaries.

---

38 A. Brassac, "Une Inscription de Delphes et la Chronologie de St. Paul", RB, Tome 10 ; 1913, pg. 38–45.
39 A. Plassart, "L'Inscription de Delphes mentionnant le Proconsul Gallion". REG, Tome 80 ; 1967, pg. 378. According to E. Fascher, Gallio took office on 1 July 51. (Fascher, "Paulus Apostel", PAULYS-WISSOWA RE., Supplementband 8, 1956, col. 452.
40 J. Wisemann, op.cit., pg. 504, note 255.
41 Murphy-O'Connor, op.cit., pg. 229.
42 D d syh.

C) καὶ ἤγαγον αὐτὸν ἐπὶ τὸ βῆμα (et adduxerunt eum ad tribunal)

βῆμα — step, platform; it is the raised place or tribune from which one speaks at a public assembly. It is the official seat of a magistrate, the place where he sat to hear cases or have proclamations read[43].

D) παρὰ τὸν νόμον ἀναπείθει οὗτος τοὺς ἀνθρώπους σέβεσθαι τὸν Θεόν

ἀναπείθω — to persuade, to convince, to seduce, to mislead.

παρὰ τὸν νόμον: The Corinthian Jews were accusing the apostle of inducing people to worship God *contra legem*. But to which law were they referring? Jewish religious law? Roman law? There was a deliberate and conscious ambiguity in the accusation which demonstrates a certain cunning, but also the weakness of the plaintiffs' case against Paul.

The Jewish authorities at Corinth looked upon the newly-founded Corinthian church, composed as it was of Jews, proselytes, God-fearers and other Greeks of pagan rite, as a hybrid group having nothing to do with official Judaism. The underlying idea implicit in the complaint against Paul is that a church born of the Pauline mission is a new religious group totally distinct from Judaism, indeed a community inveterately hostile to official Judaism's fundamental law, the law of Moses. But this law was the very cornerstone of the organized Jewish community. It was recognized and protected by Rome, being the official statute and the normative rule of an officially-recognized religious group. In the view of his Jewish adversaries, Paul was combatting that law, thereby putting himself and his followers outside the *religio licita*.

IV. *Vos ipsi videritis*

Gallio's reaction was to treat the whole affair with contempt and disdain: "But when Paul was about to open his mouth, (μέλλοντος δὲ τοῦ Παύλου ἀνοίγειν τὸ στόμα), Gallio said to the Jews, 'If it were a matter of wrongdoing or vicious crime, (ἀδίκημά τι ἢ ῥᾳδιούργημα πονηρόν), I should have reason to bear with you, O Jews: (κατὰ λόγον ἂν ἀνεσχόμην ὑμῶν); but since it is a matter of questions about words and names and your own law, (εἰ δὲ ζητήματά ἐστιν περὶ λόγου καὶ ὀνομάτων καὶ νόμου τοῦ καθ' ὑμᾶς), see to it yourselves; (ὄψεσθε αὐτοί); I refuse to be a judge of these things.'" (κριτὴς ἐγὼ τούτων οὐ βούλομαι εἶναι) (XVIII,14–15).

---

43 cf. *BJ.* II,9.3 (172); II,14.8 (301); III,10.10 (532). *P. Tebt.* II,434. For the expression 'to sit on the judgment seat, cf. *infra*, pg. 138.

A) μέλλοντος δέ τοῦ Παύλου ἀνοίγειν τό στόμα

Gallio had spoken so rapidly that Paul did not have time (nor did he need) to make his defence (*apologia*) before the Proconsul even though the *apologia* was an integral and necessary part of Roman procedure[44].

B) ἀδίκημά τι ἤ ῥαδιούργημα πονηρόν (Vg. = *Iniquum aliquid aut facinus pessimum*)

ἀδίκημα — intentional wrong-doing, a wrongful act, or an offence. The word appears later in Acts, when Paul makes his *apologia* before Felix (XXIV,20).
ῥαδιούργημα — a misdeed, wicked act or wicked behaviour. The term has the connotation of fraud, artifice and knavery. It occurs only here in the New Testament.

C) κατά λόγον ἄν ἀνεσχόμην ὑμῶν

κατά λόγον — make him duty bound to deal with the accusation.
ἀνέχομαι — to receive, to take up, to bear with patience, to endure. Here the verb takes on a juridical meaning: to accept a complaint or accusation for further consideration[45].

D) εἰ δέ ζητήματά ἐστιν περί λόγου καί ὀνομάτων καί νόμον τοῦ καθ' ὑμᾶς

ζήτημα — is an 'inquiry' or 'question' of a philosophic nature. It can also mean an 'official' or 'judicial' inquiry[46]. In the plural, the word can mean 'subjects of dispute'.

The accusation against Paul was a disconcerting mixture of theological and political charges, formulated in an ambiguous way. The Proconsul, however, was not duped by all that. For him the accusation was exclusively about the manner of observing Jewish religious law. It was clear to Gallio that Paul had committed no infraction of Roman law. As the Proconsul believed that the *law,* which the accusers alleged was being violated, was in fact Jewish religious law, he declined to hear the case and referred it to the authorities of the Corinthian synagogue for examination and disposal:

> "The narrative in fact agrees very well with the workings of *cognitio extra ordinem*. It is within the competence of the judge to decide whether to accept a novel charge or not"[47].

---

44 cf. *infra*, pg. 156.
45 *ThWb.* Vol. I, pg. 359.
46 *LS*[9], pg. 756. cf. *P. Oxy.* I,97.14 (A.D. 115–116), which is the case of a lawsuit sent by the Strategus of the Nome to the Prefect's court.
47 Sherwin-White, pg. 99–100.

E) ὄψεσθε αὐτοί κριτής ἐγὼ τούτων οὐ βούλομαι εἶναι (Vg. = *vos ipsi videritis: iudex ego horum nolo esse*)

The use of the expression ὄψεσθε αὐτοί is a pertinent reminder to the synagogal authorities that they had the judicial competence to deal with the matter. Gallio is, in fact, referring the case to the Corinthian synagogue, thereby renouncing any further legal role in Paul's affair[48]. The local synagogue had the power to hear cases in which Jews were accused of breaching religious law[49], even if the accused were Roman citizens. Nevertheless the jurisdiction of the self-administering Jewish communities was subject to the competent Roman authorities. Only the latter could inflict capital or other severe punishment on a defendant.

The hearing ended on a rather violent note. After having refused to be a judge in Paul's case, the Proconsul "drove them from the tribunal (καὶ ἀπήλασεν αὐτοὺς ἀπὸ τοῦ βήματος). And they all(πάντες) seized Sosthenes, the ruler of the synagogue (τὸν ἀρχισυνάγωγον), and beat him in front of the tribunal. But Gallio paid no attention to this. (καὶ οὐδὲν τούτων τῷ Γαλλίωνι ἔμελεν)" (XVIII,16—17).

A) καὶ ἀπήλασεν αὐτοὺς ἀπὸ τοῦ βήματος

ἀπελαύνω — to drive out, remove or expel from a place. The petitioners were most likely expelled by the Lictors[50].

B) πάντες

The B-Text is vague as to the identity of Sosthenes' attackers, limiting itself to the word πάντες. The Western version adds the precision οἱ Ἕλληνες after πάντες[51]. If it were indeed the Greeks who had attacked Sosthenes, it would have been a direct expression of their intense dislike and scorn of the Jews. The Jews, too, were unhappy: Sosthenes might very well have been beaten by his dissatisfied coreligionists either because he had mismanaged the case against Paul or because he had personally proven to be too favourable to the apostle's teachings[52].

---

48 J. Gaudemet notes that a magistrate could refuse an *actio* if, *inter alia*, he felt himself juridically incompetent or if the plaintiff's demand was manifestly unfounded. (J. Gaudemet, *op.cit.*, pg. 634–635).
49 *Ant.* XIV,10.17 (235). cf. Mt. X,17: "Beware of men, for they will deliver you up to the councils (εἰς συνέδρια) and flog (μαστιγώσουσιν) you in their synagogues". Mk. XIII,9 reads will be beaten (δαρήσεσθε) instead of flog.
50 cf. A. Wikenhauser, *DIE APOSTELGESCHICHTE*, Regensburg, 1961, 4th Edition, pg. 215.
51 D (pl), E (pl), g.
52 If the Sosthenes mentioned here is the same man as in I Cor I,1, then he too became a Christian.

C) καὶ οὐδὲν τούτων τῷ Γαλλίωνι ἔμελεν

The text depicts Gallio as totally unconcerned about the furious sequel to the petitioners' dismissal from his court. This could imply that Sosthenes' attackers were Jews, for the Proconsul would have acted with alacrity had the violence mentioned by Luke been of an inter-communal stripe between Greeks and Jews[53]. The Proconsul was probably annoyed that Jewish accusers had made a formal complaint against someone on a matter affecting their own law and cognizable by the synagogal authorities. The Proconsul remained a disinterested party in this matter which he clearly considered to be an intra-Jewish religious dispute.

The narrative concludes with the departure of Paul for Syria: "After this Paul stayed many days longer, and then took leave of the brethren and sailed for Syria, and with him Priscilla and Aquila". (XVIII,18a). Unlike his departures from Philippi and Thessalonica, Paul's exit from Corinth was orderly and unhurried. He does not seem to have been banished from the Roman colony for Luke speaks of his staying "many days" (ἡμέρας ἱκανάς) after his appearance before Gallio[54].

The events in Corinth have a considerable importance in Paul's legal history.

A) The narrative stresses the widespread opposition of the Jewish community to Paul's mission. Consequently the apostle had little other choice than to break with the synagogue. Although the newly-founded Church at Corinth had some distinguished Jewish members, its composition was largely Gentile from the very beginning.

B) In the opinion of the Jewish authorities, Paul's preaching, the whole of his missionary work, the indiscriminate mixing of Jew and Gentile in the newly-founded church communities without a strict observance of Mosaic law, meant that these Pauline churches were outside the structure of official Judaism and formed a new and alien religion.

C) Thus if the Proconsul had undertaken a full and comprehensive examination of the case, Paul might very well have found himself in a difficult legal situation. The disavowal of the synagogue, confirmed by Paul's break with it and his founding of a rival, mainly Gentile community in which Jewish laws were not observed, would have made it quite difficult

---

53 E. Delebecque writes: "Gallion n'a pas à connaître d'une affaire qui intéresse, non pas deux communautés différentes, mais des Juifs entre eux". (*LES DEUX ACTES DES APOTRES*, Paris, 1986, pg. 112).

54 F.F. Bruce notes that the apostle "was not likely to hurry away immediately after Gallio's favourable verdict". (Bruce, pg. 348). Maurice Goguel for his part is quite sceptical that Paul's appearance in Gallio's court ended so favourably for the apostle: "For the narrator the affair ended completely to the advantage of the apostle. However it was only a few days after having appeared before the Proconsul that Paul left Corinth." (M. Goguel, "La Vision de Paul à Corinthe", *RHPR*, No.4–5, 1932; pg. 322.)

for him to make a plausible case to Gallio that it was the new community and not the familiar, established synagogue which represented true Judaism.

D) Gallio, however, refused to take cognizance of the case. He took no legal action against Paul despite the gravity of the charges. His dismissal of the case in effect declared the apostle innocent of any infraction of Roman law. The Proconsul doubtlessly realized from the vehemence of the Jews that they deemed Paul a threat to the stability of their community. This did not necessarily mean, however, that Paul was practicing an illicit religion or was otherwise engaged in seditious actions. Gallio's attitude was typical of the Roman officials who appear in the Acts story. The Proconsul judged the affair to be a purely theological dispute between Jewish sectaries, judicially irrelevant in a Roman court of law.

E) The Roman judiciary's opinion as to whether the Christian community was part of official Judaism or not was a key element in Paul's legal history. If the State were led to believe that the Christians had lost the quality and status of Jews, the situation of newly-born Christianity would rapidly become much more precarious: "For confessing the Lord Jesus and refusing to honour the divine Emperor would lay the faithful open to the charge of lese-majesty. They would thus be pursued as atheists and enemies of the State"[55].

F) Finally the rather favourable results which Paul obtained in the proconsular court at Corinth had the effect of directing his attention to the protection which a Roman court could give him against his Jewish adversaries.

---

55 P. Menoud, "L'Eglise naissante et le Judaisme", *JESUS-CHRIST ET LA FOI*, Neuchâtel, 1975, pg. 309.

Chapter IV
Jerusalem (Part 1): Paul and Lysias

I. Paul's last Journey to Jerusalem

The last seven chapters of Acts deal extensively with the apostle's legal history. As Acts approaches its climax, Luke relates Paul's case in much greater detail, refining the terms of the indictment and outlining the apostle's legal defence. It is essentially in the latter chapters of Acts, and especially in Paul's speeches, that the theological and apologetic programme of Acts is brought to its culminating point. The story of Paul's legal history is intimately bound up with that programme. It forms the framework against which the overall narrative unfolds and it is used as the point of departure for the great apologetic speeches. Luke consistently presents Paul both as a Pharisee and as a Roman. The author sees no contradiction in this at all. As a Pharisee, Paul stands well within the mainstream of Judaism, he is therefore not the ringleader of a heretical, illegal or subversive sect. Paul's Roman citizenship plays a key role in his case. It allows him to make his appeal to Caesar which transforms the nature of his case and which enables him to come to Rome, the goal of Acts and the goal of Paul.

Luke tells us that the apostle, following his long stay in Ephesus and his visit to Greece and the lands adjacent to the Aegean Sea, "was hastening to be at Jerusalem, if possible, on the day of Pentecost." (Acts XX,16b). There were two basic reasons motivating this trip to the Holy City:

A) The Acts-narrative stresses Paul's *religious* motive in hurrying to Jerusalem. He wished to participate in the Pentecost feast in order to demonstrate to the Judeo-Christian community there his loyalty to Jewish tradition and practice.

B) There was also a more *practical* reason as is clear from the Epistles and from Acts XXIV,17. Paul wished to take the alms and offerings collected in the Gentile churches he had founded to the mother church at Jerusalem to help relieve the latter's great necessity. By this concrete gesture, the apostle was endeavouring to promote a greater sense of solidarity and unity between Christians of Jewish and Gentile origin[1]. The

---

1 cf. Romans XV,25–27.

apostle meant his stay in Jerusalem to be a brief one for he intended to go thence to Rome and later to Spain[2].

Luke stresses how dangerous the projected trip to Jerusalem was by creating in the narrative an appropriately ominous ambience. Already the Jews had fomented a plot against Paul which had obliged him to modify his planned route. Instead of sailing to Syria from Greece, he took a more circuitous route overland by Macedonia (XX,3). At Tyre, Paul and his party stayed with the local disciples for seven days. The latter warned the apostle not to go on to Jerusalem (XXI,4), because of the difficulties and perils which they knew awaited him in the Holy City. At Caesarea, Agabus the prophet came down to the apostle and "took Paul's girdle and bound his own feet and hands, and said, 'Thus says the Holy Spirit, so shall the Jews at Jerusalem bind the man who owns this girdle and deliver him into the hands of the Gentiles' " (XXI,11). Agabus' prophecy points to the very dangerous situation the apostle had to expect to encounter in Jerusalem.

Paul, however, as was his wont, would not be deterred. He responded to his friends who begged him not to go up to Jerusalem by saying: "I am ready not only to be imprisoned but even to die at Jerusalem for the name of the Lord Jesus." (XXI,13). The apostle was quite conscious of the dangers he was courting by going to the Holy City[3].

When he finally reached Jerusalem, Paul was well received by the brethren (XXI,17) and went the day after his arrival to see James and the elders (XXI,18), to whom he related the things "God had done among the Gentiles through his ministry" (XXI,19). This joyful story of a successful mission caused James and the elders to glorify God (XXI,20a). All however was not well because James and the elders told Paul of the bad impression his mission to the Gentiles had made on the Jewish Christians: "You see, brother, how many thousands there are among the Jews of those who have believed; they are all zealous for the law." (XXI,20b): These Jewish Christians were unhappy with Paul's activities as "they have been told about you that you teach all the Jews who are among the Gentiles to forsake Moses, telling them not to circumcize their children or observe the customs." (XXI,21). This obviously was the core of Paul's problem with the Jewish community, a central problem which had caused much hostility to his missionary labours on the part of the Jewish leadership. Paul was being accused of encouraging Jewish believers to abandon their ancestral customs and of refusing to impose Mosaic observances on Gentile converts[4].

---

[2] cf. Acts XIX,21; Romans XV,24; XV,28.
[3] cf. Romans XV,30–31.
[4] Paul's view is that faith in Jesus Christ is the only ground for salvation for both Jews and Gen-

To counter this, James and the elders suggested Paul make a gesture to show the brethren in Jerusalem that he himself still honoured Jewish ancestral customs. Four men were under a vow. Paul was to take the four and purify himself along with them, paying their expenses, so that they could shave their heads (XXI,23–24a): "Thus all will know that there is nothing in what they have been told about you, but that you yourself live in observance of the law." (XXI,24b). Luke stresses Paul's agreement to do exactly what James and the elders suggested in order to demonstrate that the apostle was not in fact teaching Jews to renounce their religious customs or established ritual[5].

Paul, however, was too well-known and had too many enemies among the Jews for his presence in the temple to go unnoticed at festival time: "When the seven days were almost completed, the Jews from Asia, who had seen him in the temple, stirred up all the crowd, (συνέχεον πάντα τὸν ὄχλον), and laid hands on him, (καὶ ἐπέβαλαν ἐπ' αὐτὸν τὰς χεῖρας), crying out, 'Men of Israel, help! This is the man who is teaching men everywhere against the people and the law and this place; (οὗτός ἐστιν ὁ ἄνθρωπος ὁ κατὰ τοῦ λαοῦ καὶ τοῦ νόμου καὶ τοῦ τόπου τούτου πάντας πανταχῇ διδάσκων) moreover he also brought Greeks into the temple, and he has defiled this holy place!." (ἔτι τε καὶ Ἕλληνας εἰσήγαγεν εἰς τὸ ἱερὸν καὶ κεκοίνωκεν τὸν ἅγιον τόπον τοῦτον (XXI,27–28).

A) συνέχεον πάντα τὸν ὄχλον (Vg. *concitaverunt omnen populum*)

συγχέω – to stir up a crowd, to cause a riot. In Acts XXI,31 = to be in confusion. The only NT uses of this verb are in Acts.

Luke places the blame for the tumult in the Temple precincts squarely on the Asian Jews, underlining once again Jewish hostility to the apostle, this time in the setting of Judaism's holiest place. Luke's description of the tumult is entirely plausible. Disturbances were not uncommon in the Temple precincts which is why they were under continuous military supervision. This was especially the case at festival time as riots could more easily be provoked with many pilgrims filling the Temple grounds.

---

tiles. cf. Romans III,29–31; IV,14; IV,16. cf. E.P. Sanders, "Jesus, Paul and Judaism", *ANRW* II, 25.1; 1982; pg. 431–432.

5 cf. I Cor. IX,20: "To the Jews I became as a Jew, in order to win Jews; to those under the law I became as one under the law – though not being myself under the law – that I might win those under the law." J. Jervell notes: "The vow story in Acts 21 emphasizes that Paul is a Jewish Christian, and as such is a venerator of the Mosiac Torah". (J. Jervell, *THE UNKNOWN PAUL: ESSAYS ON LUKE-ACTS AND EARLY CHRISTIAN HISTORY*, Minneapolis, 1984, pg. 71.

B) καὶ ἐπέβαλαν ἐπ'αὐτὸν τὰς χεῖρας (*et iniecerunt ei manus*)

Luke uses this expression twice before in Acts both times in a precise legal context. In Acts IV,3, the priests, captain of the temple and the Sadducees came upon Peter and John teaching the people and proclaiming in Jesus the resurrection from the dead. As they were greatly vexed by this, they arrested the apostles and placed them in custody, their case to be heard on the following day. In Acts V.18 the High Priest and the Sadducees again arrested the two apostles and put them in the common prison to await a hearing before the council. On both occasions the expression 'lay hands on' refers to a formal arrest per order of the competent Jewish authorities with a view to a subsequent trial[5a]. Here that type of legal context is absent. It was the Asian Jews who made the accusations against Paul with the purpose of stirring up the crowd. Paul was *seized* by the rioters not so that he could be bound over to the Sanhedrin for trial, but so he could be dragged out of the temple precincts and slain forthwith. Paul's formal arrest will be made by the Roman tribune Lysias and not by the Jews.

C) οὗτός ἐστιν ὁ ἄνθρωπος ὁ κατὰ τοῦ λαοῦ καὶ τοῦ νόμου καὶ τοῦ τόπου τούτου πάντας πανταχῇ διδάσκων Vg. = *hic est homo qui adversus populum et legem et locum hunc omnes ubique docens*

These charges in themselves would have sufficed to ostracize Paul from the official Jewish community[6]. Yet it would have been difficult to obtain official ratification for a sentence handed down for simply *teaching* against the people, law or temple. Therefore a new and more serious charge was now preferred.

D) ἔτι τε καὶ Ἕλληνας εἰσήγαγεν εἰς τὸ ἱερὸν καὶ κεκοίνωκεν τὸν ἅγιον τόπον τοῦτον Vg. = *insuper et gentiles induxit in templum et violavit sanctum locum istum*

κοινόω — In Classical Greek this verb basically means to make common. Here Paul's adversaries are using the term in the sense of defiling, rendering *ritually* unclean[7]. The use of the Perfect Tense indicates that the profana-

---

[5a] The Latin expression *manum inicere alicui* means to seize or hold a person against whom one has certain types of claims.

[6] cf. The charge against Stephen (Acts VI,13–14): "This man never ceases to speak words against this holy place and the law; for we have heard him say that this Jesus of Nazareth will destroy this place, and will change the customs which Moses delivers to us."

[7] The Vg. translates by *violare*: to disturb the sanctity of a sacred place, to profane that which is sacred, to pollute by an unholy deed.

tion of the Temple subsists[8]. The word ἱερόν refers here to the Inner courtyard and raised terrace in front. Non-Jews were permitted to enter the Outer courtyard (the Court of the Gentiles)[9], but could not penetrate any farther. Josephus describes the notices debarring the Temple's Inner court to foreigners:

> "Proceeding across this [open, outer court] towards the second court of the temple, one found it surrounded by a stone balustrade, three cubits high and of exquisite workmanship; in this at regular intervals stood slabs giving warning, some in Greek, others in Latin characters, of the law of purification, to wit that no foreigner was permitted to enter the holy place, for so the second enclosure of the temple was called"[10].

For an ἀλλογενῆς[11] to proceed any farther, i.e. beyond this balustrade (δρύφακτος) was unlawful: it constituted a desecration of the holy place. This was a capital crime, for any profanation of the Temple had to be immediately punished lest the whole community be polluted[12]. "Still more abounding and peculiar is the zeal of them all for the temple", Philo writes, "and the strongest proof of this is that death without appeal (θάνατος ἀπαραίτητος) is the sentence against those of other races who penetrate into its inner confines"[13]. The notices on the slabs referred to above clearly state this. One of the them was discovered in Jerusalem in 1871 by C.S. Clermont-Ganneau and is now in Istanbul. Its inscription reads: μηθένα ἀλλογενῆ εἰσπορεύεσθαι/ἐντὸς τοῦ περὶ τὸ ἱερὸν τρυφάκτου/καὶ περιβόλου ὃς δ᾽ ἂν ληφθῇ/ἑαυτῷ αἴτιος ἔσται διὰ τὸ/ἐξακολουθεῖν θάνατον[14] = "Let no one of another nation penetrate beyond the balustrade and into the inner precinct around the sanctuary. Whoever is caught will himself be to blame for what ensues: death".

A second inscription on a slab half a meter high and a third of a meter thick was discovered in December 1935 near St. Stephen's Gate. The text, although in a less skillful style of lettering, is virtually the same as the text

---

8 cf. *Bl. Debr.* sect. 342.4: The Greek's entrance *in the past* "produced defilement as a *lasting effect*".
9 Josephus, *Contra Apionem*, II, 103: "*In exteriorem itaque ingredi licebat omnibus etiam alienigenis*".
10 *BJ.* V,5.2 (193–194). E.T. = H. St. J. Thackeray *Loeb*, 1961. cf. *Ant.* XV,11.5 (417).
11 i.e. "*qui non sit Iudaeus*" (cf. *OGIS.* 598, note 1).
12 cf. *Ant.* XII,3.4 (145) for the decree of Antiochus III concerning the Temple: "It is unlawful for any foreigner to enter the enclosure of the temple which is forbidden to the Jews, except to those of them who are accustomed to enter after purifying themselves in accordance with the law of the country", (E.T. = R. Marcus, *Loeb*, 1961).
13 Philo, *Legat. ad Gaium* XXXI,212. (E.T. = F.H. Colson, *Loeb*, 1962). cf. E. Bickerman, "The Warning Inscriptions of Herod's Temple", *JQR*, Vol. 37, No. 4; April 1947; pg. 389.
14 *OGIS.* 598. The Greek text and a photo of the inscription is to be found in *CII*, II,1400. Bickerman notes that the Temple was not unique in barring the alien or impure from its inner sanctum: "In all ancient religions there were *sancta* inaccessible to the profane crowd and separated by a rail of wood or stone". (Bickerman, "Warning Inscriptions", *op.cit.*, pg. 389.

figuring on the Clermont-Ganneau stone (only the word ἑαυτῷ has been contracted into αὐτῳ)[15].

Luke explains the origin of this accusation in the next verse: "For they previously had seen Trophimus the Ephesian with him in the city and they supposed (ἐνόμιζον) that Paul had brought him into the temple." (XXI,29).

A) *Trophimus*

We first hear of Trophimus in Acts XX,4, where he and Tychicus are called Asians[16]. These two men, along with Sopater, Aristarchus, Secundus, Gaius of Derbe and Timothy, were mentioned as having preceded Paul to Troas[17].

B) ἐνόμιζον

νομίζω — to deem, to think, to hold, to suppose (that). Strictly speaking it was Trophimus who would have been guilty of profaning the Temple. The apostle would have been guilty of introducing a Gentile into the inner precincts and thereby of sanctioning the presence of a foreigner in the part of the Temple exclusively reserved for Jews.

II. The Tribune Lysias arrests Paul

Luke's description of the population's reaction to the accusations forms a very dramatic episode, one of the most compelling in the narrative: "Then all the city was aroused, and the people ran together; they seized Paul and dragged him out of the temple and at once the gates were shut. (ἐπιλαβόμενοι τοῦ Παύλου εἷλκον αὐτὸν ἔξω τοῦ ἱεροῦ καὶ εὐθέως ἐκλείσθησαν αἱ θύραι). And as they were trying to kill him, word came to the tribune of the cohort (τῷ χιλιάρχῳ τῆς σπείρης) that all Jerusalem was in confusion. He at once took soldiers and centurions, and ran down to them; when they saw the tribune and the soldiers, they stopped beating Paul. Then the tribune came up and arrested (ἐπελάβετο) him, and ordered him to be bound with two chains." (δεθῆναι ἁλύσεσι δυσί) (XXI,30—33a).

---

15 cf. J.H. Iliffe, "The *Thanatos* Inscription from Herod's Temple: Fragment of a Second Copy", *QDAP*, Vol. VI; 1938; pg. 1—3. The article contains illustrations of both stones.
16 They are called *Ephesians* in D δ sy[hmg] sa. Another reference to Trophimus occurs in 2 Tim. IV,20.
17 Acts XX,4—5.

A) εἷλκον αὐτὸν ἔξω τοῦ ἱεροῦ καὶ εὐθέως ἐκλείσθησαν αἱ θύραι

The verb εἷλκον is in the Imperfect as it is used to portray the manner of action: The description lies in the indication of the direction[18] i.e. ἔξω τοῦ ἱεροῦ. The use of the Imperfect points to the completion of the first action: 'they dragged him out' and then to the following sequence of events: 'at once the gates were shut': 'they were trying to kill him'. Paul was dragged out of the Temple so that it would not be defiled by an act of blood. The shutting of the Temple gates and the expulsion of Paul from Judaism's holiest site is a powerful symbol of the rejection of God's message of salvation by the Jews.

B) χιλίαρχος – *tribunus cohortis*

The Tribune was the chief Roman authority in Jerusalem. His hierarchical superior was the Governor of Judaea who resided at Caesarea. The legionary tribunes were six in number and combined military and administrative duties. They were normally young men doing military service at the start of their official careers[19]. Lysias intervened in the fray as it was his duty to quell any disorders in the city and to do all he could to maintain public order.

C) σπεῖρα – *cohors (auxiliaris)*

During the late Republic and early Principate, the armies fell into three components: the legions, the professional *auxilia* and additional troops provided by client kings, local tribes or other sources[20]. Regular Roman legions were stationed in Syria to defend the Eastern frontier against enemy powers the foremost of which was Parthia[21]. The Governor of Judaea had auxiliary troops under his command. In general, the auxiliary units were composed of peregrines. Very often the auxiliaries received Roman citizenship at the end of their service. The auxiliary force was composed of infantrymen (*cohors peditata*) and calvarymen, grouped into *alae*. Some infantry forces had horsemen attached to them (*cohors equitata*)[22].

The Jerusalem garrison was a *Cohors milaria equitata*, i.e. it was composed of 760 infantrymen and 240 cavalrymen. The cohort was garrisoned in the Fortress Antonia, which overlooked the temple[23]. The tribune thus

---

18 *Bl. Debr.* sect. 327.
19 T.R.S. Broughton, "The Roman Army", *B.C.*, London, 1933, Vol. V, pg. 428.
20 D.B. Saddington, "The Development of the Roman Auxiliary Forces from Augustus to Trajan", *ANRW*. II,3; 1975, pg. 183.
21 The legion numbered about 6000 men divided into 10 cohorts.
22 R.W. Davies, "Cohortes Equitatae", *HISTORIA*, vol. 20; 1971, pg. 75.
23 Josephus gives us a description of the Roman garrison stationed at the Antonia and its police

commanded considerable military forces that he could use for police purposes. At least 200 of his men were called out to rescue Paul.

D) ἐπελάβετο[24] (*adprehendit*)

The apostle's arrest by the Roman tribune had two important consequences:
1. Paul's life had been saved by Lysias' timely action;
2. Paul was arrested by the Roman authorities and not by the temple police. Thus from the very outset of the legal process at hand, the apostle was in Roman custody. Had the temple police arrested the apostle instead of the Roman soldiers, he would have been tried and sentenced forthwith by the Sanhedrin. Now the supreme Jewish body would have to obtain his extradition in order to try him. Paul had no intention of leaving Roman jurisdiction; he would fight any attempt by the Sanhedrin to have him extradited.

E) δεθῆναι ἁλύσεσι δυσί

ἅλυσις – is a hand-chain, the chain for feet (fetters) being πέδαι[25]. Paul was chained to two attending soldiers one on each side[26]. It can be seen from the text that Lysias had arrested Paul without knowing beforehand that he was a Roman citizen (contrary to what he later wrote to the Governor Felix). It was of course impossible in the midst of the tumult to learn for certain the victim's identity. Thus Paul was immediately secured with two chains – normal police procedure when placing non-Roman citizens under arrest[27].

III. The Preliminary Investigation begins

Lysias' action can be divided into three distinct phases. First of all he had intervened in the riot because he felt compelled to act: as tribune his

---

role (*BJ.* V, 5.8 (243–245): "At the point where it [the Antonia] impinged upon the porticoes of the temple, there were stairs leading down to both of them, by which the guards descended; for a Roman cohort was permanently quartered there, and at the festivals took up positions in arms around the porticoes to watch the people and repress any insurrectionary movement. For if the temple lay as a fortress over the city, Antonia dominated the temple, and the occupants of that post were the guards of all three; ...". (E.T. = H.St.J. Thackeray, *Loeb*, 1961).

24 cf. *supra*, pg. 8.
25 cf. Mk. V.4; Lk. VIII,29.
26 cf. Acts XII,6 where Peter was also bound with two chains. In Eph. VI,20, Paul calls himself "an ambassador in chains". cf. 2 Tim. I,16. Ignatius (*Rom.* V.1) talks of being chained to "ten leopards", i.e. a detachment of soldiers. cf. Seneca, *Ep.Mor.* V.7.

primary responsibility was the maintenance of Roman order in the city and especially in the temple area adjacent to the Antonia. Secondly, he had arrested Paul, who was on the point of being killed by the enraged mob. Lysias took Paul into custody on the basis of *the oral denunciation* of the rioters:

> "This part of the proceedings shows a considerable analogy to legal proceedings as described in the papyri. Denunciation is the normal way by which police proceedings are instituted. Denunciation is usually in writing; oral denunciation being the exception"[28].

Finally Lysias instituted the police inquiry itself. He had to ascertain the prisoner's identity and learn the exact nature of the charges against him (XXI,33b). He queried the denouncers — but to his surprise the rioters could tell him nothing. Luke writes: "some in the crowd shouted one thing, some another" (XXI,34a). As Lysias could not learn the facts, he ordered Paul to be brought into the barracks ($\pi\alpha\rho\epsilon\mu\beta o\lambda\dot{\eta}\nu$) (XXI,34b) to be examined by torture. Getting the prisoner into the barracks, however, was not an easy task for the mob was inflamed against Paul and determined to kill him. Luke graphically portrays the scene: "And when he came to the steps, he was actually carried by the soldiers because of the violence of the crowd: for the mob of the people followed, crying, 'Away with him!'" (XXI,35–36).

Luke does not inform his readers of how badly Paul was injured as a result of the mistreatment he sustained. The narrative indicates only that Paul was able to dialogue with the tribune and to address the rioters *immediately* after the beating. What is important to Luke is the coming apologetic speech for which the preceding actions lay the groundwork. From the strictly juridical point of view, the narrative is realistic. Lysias' duty as police officer was to ascertain Paul's identity which the apostle discloses in part before and in part after his speech. "As Paul was about to be brought into the barracks, he said to the tribune, 'May I say something to you?' And he said, 'Do you know Greek? Are you not the Egyptian, ($o\dot{v}\kappa$ $\ddot{\alpha}\rho\alpha$ $o\dot{v}$ $\epsilon\dot{\iota}$ $\dot{o}$ $A\dot{\iota}\gamma\dot{v}\pi\tau\iota o\varsigma$), who recently stirred up a revolt and led four thousand men of the Assassins ($\ddot{\alpha}\nu\delta\rho\alpha\varsigma$ $\tau\tilde{\omega}\nu$ $\sigma\iota\kappa\alpha\rho\dot{\iota}\omega\nu$) out of the wilderness?'"(XXI,37–38).

A) $\pi\alpha\rho\epsilon\mu\beta o\lambda\dot{\eta}\nu$

This is the Fortress Antonia, about which Josephus writes:

> "At an angle on the north side [i.e. of the temple precinct] there had been built a citadel, well fortified and of unusual strength. It was the kings and high priests of the Hasmonaean

---

27 cf. *P. Lond*, II,422 (A.D. 350).
28 R. Taubenschlag, "Le Procès de l'Apôtre Paul en lumière des Papyri", *OPERA MINORA*, Warsaw, 1959, Vol. II, pg. 722.

family before Herod who built it and called it *baris*. Here they had deposited the priestly robe which the High Priest put on only when he had to offer sacrifice. (...) Herod, the King of the Jews, made this *baris* stronger for the safety and protection of the temple, and to gratify Antony, who was his friend and at the same time ruler of the Romans, he called it Antonia"[29].

B) οὐκ ἄρα σὺ εἶ ὁ Αἰγύπτιος

One of the reasons for Lysias' quick police action was his mistaken belief that Paul was this Egyptian[30]. Josephus mentions the Egyptian's seditious activites in *BJ*:

"A still worse blow was dealt at the Jews by the Egyptian false prophet. A charlatan, who gained for himself the reputation of a prophet, this man appeared in the country, collected a following of about thirty thousand dupes[31], and led them by a circuitous route from the desert to the mount called the Mount of Olives. From there he proposed to force an entrance into Jerusalem and, after overpowering the Roman garrison, to set himself up as tyrant of the people, employing those who poured in with him as his bodyguard. His attack was anticipated by Felix, who went to meet him with the Roman heavy infantry, the whole population joining him in the defence. The outcome of the ensuing engagement was that the Egyptian escaped with a few of his followers; most of his force were killed or taken prisoners[32]; the remainder dispersed and stealthily escaped to their several homes[33].

C) ἄνδρας τῶν σικαρίων

This is the only passage in the NT in which the word *sicarius* appears. As a technical term in Roman law, *sicarius* denotes not only the murderer, but any malefactor armed with the *sica* (dagger) who *intends* to commit a murder[34].

The Jewish *sicarii* or Assassins were extreme nationalist elements which sprang up in Jerusalem and its environs during Felix's Governorship and flourished during the time of his successor Festus[35]. Josephus portrays them in the blackest of terms. The *sicarii*, he writes,

" ... committed murders in broad daylight in the heart of the city. The festivals were their special seasons, when they would mingle with the crowd, carrying short daggers concealed under their clothing, with which they stabbed their enemies. Then, when they fell, the murderers joined in the cries of indignation and, through this plausible behaviour, were never discovered. The first to be assassinated by them was Jonathan the high-priest[36]; after his death there were

---

29 *Ant.* XV,11.4 (403–409); E.T. = R. Marcus, *Loeb*, 1963. cf. *Ant.* XVIII, 4.3 (92); *BJ.* V,5.8 (238–242).
30 Lysias' question to Paul beginning with οὐκ ἄρα denotes astonishment. cf. *Bl. Debr.* 440.3.
31 4000 according to Acts XXI,38.
32 According to *Ant.* XX,8.6 (171), there were 400 killed and 200 taken prisoner.
33 *BJ.* II,13.5 (261–263). – E.T. = H.St.J. Thackeray, *Loeb*, 1961.
34 cf. Tacitus, *Ann.* XIII,44. cf. the *Lex Cornelia de Sicariis,* which was promulgated by Sulla in 81 B.C. (*Digest* XLVIII,8). For an example of court being held under the provisions of the *Lex Cornelia de Sicariis* to try a case of assassination, cf. Seneca, *Apoc.* XIV,1. cf. M. Hengel, *DIE ZELOTEN*, Leiden/Köln, 1961, pg. 47.
35 cf. Morton Smith, "Zealots and Sicarii", *HTR*, Vol. 64, No. 1; Jan. 1971, pg. 18. Smith's article is a critical overview of scholarly literature (through 1970) on this subject.
36 High Priest from 36 to 37 A.D. Josephus implicates Felix in his murder in *Ant.* XX,8.5 (161–163).

The Preliminary Investigation begins 71

numerous daily murders. The panic created was more alarming than the calamity itself; every one, as on the battlefield, hourly expecting death"[37].

The tribune's question to Paul reflected the worsening political situation in Palestine and the ever-increasing violence there[38]. The Roman authorities were continually fighting revolutionary movements born of political Messianism. Was Paul a part of this? So the tribune must have wondered:

> "That the tribune voices this suspicion and then lets it drop constitutes the first acquittal of Christendom: the suspicion that Paul belongs in this company is immediately abandoned. (...) Christianity had nothing to do with political Messianism, and is also immediately recognized in this its non-political character"[39].

Paul then replies to the tribune's question about his identity: "I am a Jew from Tarsus in Cilicia, a citizen of no mean city ;(ἐγὼ ἄνθρωπος μέν εἰμι Ἰουδαῖος Ταρσεύς τῆς Κιλικίας οὐκ ἀσήμου πόλεως πολίτης); I beg you let me speak to the people. And when he had given him leave, Paul, standing on the steps, motioned with his hand to the people; and when there was a great hush, he spoke to them in the Hebrew language, (τῇ Ἑβραΐδι διαλέκτῳ)", (XXI,39–40).

A) ἐγὼ ἄνθρωπος μέν εἰμι Ἰουδαῖος Ταρσεύς τῆς Κιλικίας οὐκ ἀσήμου πόλεως πολίτης.

We shall examine the question of Paul's Tarsian πολίτης in the excursus. It is interesting to note that the apostle did not mention his Roman citizenship in his reply. He spoke of his being a Tarsian πολίτης which sufficed to prove that he was not the seditious Egyptian. This self-identification also seemed sufficient to persuade the tribune to allow him to address the crowd.

The Acts-narrative has now arrived at the first of the great apologetic speeches related within the framework of Paul's legal history. Three things should be noted here. First the text of Acts stands well within the tradition of Greek historical writing since speeches appear at key places and times in the narrative. Second the speeches are not word for word renditions of what was actually said by the speaker at a given time; they are suited to the speaker, to the audience and to the occasion by the author[40]. Third

---

37 *BJ*. II,13.3 (254–256) E.T. = H.St.J. Thackeray, *Loeb*, 1961.
38 cf. *Ant*. XX,8.5 (160). S. Applebaum notes that the influence of the *Sicarii* was not confined to the strict limits of Palestine: "The *Sicarii* were also the one group that is recorded to have exercised some influence on Jewish communities in the Diaspora". (Shimon Applebaum, "Judaea as a Roman Province. The Countryside as a Political and Economic Factor", *ANRW*. II,8, 1977, pg. 381.). cf. *BJ*. VII, 10.1 (407–419) for a gripping account of the fate of the *Sicarii* who took refuge in Egypt after the fall of Jerusalem.
39 Haenchen, pg. 622.
40 cf. F.F. Bruce, "The Acts of the Apostles: Historical Record or Theological Reconstruction", *ANRW*. II,25.3; 1985, pg. 2582. F. Veltman compares the defence speeches that Paul makes in

Luke pays much attention to the formalities of judicial procedure and presents his readers with a legally realistic reconstruction of the main events in Paul's judicial history. Luke has consciously intertwined the legal and theological (kerygmatic) dimensions in carrying out his apologetic strategy in this last part of Acts.

B) τῇ Ἑβραΐδι διαλέκτῳ

Aramaic was the principal language spoken by the Jews in Palestine during this period. Many people in Jerusalem doubtlessly learned and spoke some Greek, but Greek was a foreign language to them, while Aramaic was their own[41]. By using Aramaic in his speech, Paul was identifying himself linguistically with his listeners and thereby creating a bond of fellowship with them. Luke notes the effect on the crowd: "When they heard that he addressed them in the Hebrew language, they were more quiet." (XXII,2).

Two of Luke's apologetic aims are quite obvious in his account of the apostle's speech to the Jerusalemites. First he emphasizes Paul's Jewishness throughout the speech. Paul addresses the rioters who had very nearly killed him as "brethren" and "fathers" (XXII,1). The apostle identifies himself as a "Jew, born in Tarsus in Cilicia", (XXII,3), and goes on to describe his orthodox education: "but brought up in this city at the feet of Gamaliel, educated according to the strict manner of the law of our fathers, being zealous for God as you all are this day" (XXII,3). The above is a very good example indeed of how Luke's reconstruction of the Pauline discourse in Acts aims constantly at showing Paul's faithfulness to Judaism[42]. Secondly Luke is careful to provide justification for the Gentile mission. Paul had earlier persecuted the Church (XXII,4–5; 19–20), but the Christophany on the road to Damascus, described at length in XXII, 6–11, had altered his life forever. Ananias, "a devout man according to the Law" (XXII,12) was the one who informed him of his divinely appointed mission to "be a witness for him to all men" (XXII,14–15), he is baptized (XXII,16), and while at prayer in the temple of Jerusalem itself,

---

Acts with the defence speech in ancient literature (Greek, Roman and Jewish historiography, martyrdom and romance literature) and concludes that "the defense speeches of Paul in Acts exhibit the same form, the same arrangement, and the same general elements which are characteristic of defense speeches in other narrative literature from ancient times". (F. Veltman, "The Defense Speeches of Paul in Acts", in *PERSPECTIVE ON LUKE-ACTS*, Danville, Virginia/Edinburgh, 1978, pg. 256).

41 W.C. van Unnik, "Tarsus or Jerusalem" in *SPARSA COLLECTA*, Leiden, 1973, pg. 304.
42 cf. A. George, "Israel dans l'Oeuvre de Luc", *RB*, Vol. 75, No. 4, October 1968, pg. 517–518. Paul himself writes in Gal. I,14: "I advanced in Judaism beyond many of my own age among my people, so extremely zealous was I for the traditions of my fathers."

he falls into a trance (XXII,17) and then receives the Lord's command: "Depart;for I send you far away to the Gentiles" (XXII,21).

The justification of the Gentile mission was the most sensitive point of all and it is significant that upon hearing this, and not before, that the Jews renewed the tumult: "they lifted up their voices and said, 'Away with such a fellow from the earth! For he ought not to live'. And they cried out and waved their garments and threw dust into the air" (XXII,22b–23). Paul's opponents could never accept that he was preaching the message of Salvation to the nations without requiring converts to observe the precepts of the law. They were essentially demanding the death penalty against the apostle.

The apologetic speech was now at an end ; Luke once again turns his attention to Paul's legal situation. Paul's speech had not helped Lysias in his investigation of the case so he commanded Paul "to be brought into the barracks and ordered him to be examined by scourging, (εἴπας μάστιξιν ἀνετάζεσθαι αὐτόν) to find out why they were shouting against him." (XXII,24).

A) μάστιξιν

Here μάστιξ refers to the instrument of torture known as the *flagrum* (Roman scourge). This terrible whip tore the flesh and broke the bones causing grievous wounds to the victim. One version of the *flagrum,* the *plumbata,* was made up of three parts: a handle of twisted iron metal, small iron chains and then terminated by heavy metal balls which dangled at the end of the small chain. A variant form was made up of a leather strap, interwoven bones and small pieces of metal[43].

B) εἴπας μάστιξιν ἀνετάζεσθαι αὐτόν

ἀνετάζω – to inquire of, to examine judicially, to investigate. Here it means to examine by torture. The Vg. translates ἀνετάζω by *torqueo* – to torture in order to extract evidence.

Examining by torture was a dreadful affair. The victim was stripped of his clothing and tied to a column or pillar. He was then beaten with the μάστιξ until his body was torn to shreds. This type of treatment, which Paul was about to undergo, was quite a bit severer than that which had been meted out to him in Philippi. There the Lictors had beaten him with their rods, whereas at Jerusalem, the apostle faced a scourging, which was used as a method of examination in the preliminary investigation of

---

43 G. Fougères, "Flagellum, *DAGR*, Paris, 1896. Tome II, Part 2, pg. 1154–1155. The article has three illustrations of the different varieties of the *flagrum.* cf. Hebrews XI,36; Apuleius, *Met.* VIII,28; VIII,30; *Codex Theodosianus,* IX, 35.1–2.

cases involving the vilest malefactors, slaves or others of comparable low rank[44]. It will be remembered that scourging was not only an inquisitorial means of coercion. It was also employed as a punitive measure for convicted criminals and indeed even inflicted on innocent victims of magisterial tyranny[45].

When Paul saw that his speech to the Jews was unsuccessful and that he was now being tied with thongs to be scourged, he proclaimed his Roman citizenship, saying to the Centurion who was standing by: "Is it lawful for you to scourge a man who is a Roman citizen and uncondemned?" (εἰ ἄνθρωπον Ῥωμαῖον καὶ ἀκατάκριτον ἔξεστιν ὑμῖν μαστίζειν) (XXII,25). This was basically a repetition of his question to the authorities at Philippi (XVI,37)[46]. On both occasions the apostle reminded the officials that

A) he was a Roman citizen and that beating and binding a Roman citizen was forbidden;

B) and that he was uncondemned and that his affair was still a *re incognita*. Not only had the apostle not been sentenced by any court; but a thorough investigation of the affair had not yet even taken place.

The proclamation of Roman citizenship had an immediate suspensive effect on the punishment about to be meted out. Once again one sees how advantageous it was to hold Roman citizenship and how Paul's *civitas* was the key factor in the case. Luke reports the subsequent sequence of events in direct literary style: "When the centurion heard that, he went to the tribune and said to him, 'What are you about to do? For this man is a Roman citizen'." (XXII,26)[47]. Having received this information the tribune went to Paul and said, "Tell me, are you a Roman citizen?". And he said "Yes". (XXII,27)[48]. The tribune of course was also a Roman citizen; but Lysias had not been born a citizen as had the apostle: "The tribune an-

---

44 cf. *P.Lille*, I,29. col.I, lines 19—26. We see from this fragment of a code (Egypt, 3rd Century B.C.) that torture was applied to slaves if the evidence they had given in a case was of such an ambiguous nature that the magistrates were unable to give a verdict. In the Roman provinces it was the Roman soldiers who administered the whipping, cf. Jn. XIX,1: "Then Pilate took Jesus and scourged (ἐμαστίγωσεν) him". Jewish law also allowed whipping as a punitive measure. Unlike Roman law, which set no maximum number of blows, Jewish law limited the blows to a maximum of forty. cf. Deuteronomy XXV,3, where the reason given for the imposition of a maximum number of blows is to prevent an offender from being degraded in the sight of all.
45 cf. *BJ*. II,13.7 (269); II,21.5 (612); Philo, *Flaccus* X,75; Suetonius, *Caligula*, XXVI,3.
46 cf. *supra*, pg. 27 ff.
47 The Western text has the centurion adding a cautious note to his remarks as reported in the B-Text: "Take care (ὅρα) what you are about to do" (D al, g,p,sa,). The direct question of the B-Text is transformed into a warning. The centurion sees that his hierarchical superior is about to commit a serious infraction of the law and is urging another type of response.
48 The Western text reads: "Tell me, are you a Roman citizen?" And he said, "I am" (εἶπεν εἰμί) (D g). This is a more formal and solemn proclamation which such a critical moment would require.

swered, 'I bought this citizenship for a large sum' (πολλοῦ κεφαλαίου). Paul said, 'But I was born a citizen' (ἐγὼ δὲ καὶ γεγέννημαι) (XXII,28).

A) πολλοῦ κεφαλαίου

It was during the reign of Emperor Claudius (41–54 A.D.) that the traffic in citizenship took on enormous proportions. Dio Cassius has a caustic comment to make on this practice:

> "For inasmuch as Romans had the advantage over foreigners in practically all respects, many sought the franchise by personal application to the emperor, and many bought it from Messalina and the imperial freedmen. For this reason, though the privilege was at first sold only for large sums, it became so cheapened by the facility with which it could be obtained that it came to be a common saying, that a man could become a citizen by giving the right person some bits of broken glass"[49].

The tribune's *nomen*, Claudius, would indicate that he had bought his citizenship during Claudius' principate as it was the custom of new citizens to take the family name of the reigning Emperor.

B) ἐγὼ δὲ καὶ γεγέννημαι

The Greek phrase can be technically equated with the Latin *ingenuus*, meaning the native-born citizen.

The effects of this declaration of Roman citizenship were immediately felt: "So those who were about to examine him withdrew from him instantly; and the tribune also was afraid, (ἐφοβήθη), for he realized (ἐπιγνοὺς) that Paul was a Roman citizen and that he had bound him." (XXII, 29).

A) ἐφοβήθη

We saw in Chapter I that the Philippian magistrates were also afraid when they learned that they had mistreated a Roman citizen (ἐφοβήθησαν δὲ ἀκούσαντες ὅτι Ῥωμαῖοί εἰσιν) (Acts XVI,38). Officials might very well be discharged from their office for having violated the diverse laws protecting a Roman citizen from arbitrary punishment and abuse. The use of the verb φοβέω is hardly an exaggeration; on the contrary it provides a striking demonstration of the extent to which the Tribune, ever mindful of the law, respected Paul's status as a Roman citizen.

B) ἐπιγνοὺς

ἐπιγινώσκω – to know, recognize, ascertain, find out, acknowledge. One

---

[49] Dio Cassius LX,17.5–6. E.T. = E. Cary, *Loeb*, 1961. cf. Dio Chrysostom XXIV,23, where the writer expresses his strong contempt for trafficking in Roman citizenship.

would assume that Paul provided adequate proof of his citizenship to satisfy the tribune [50].

The dialogue between the apostle and the tribune is a good example of the Lucan understanding of Paul's attitude towards his citizenship. Lysias had purchased his citizenship to enjoy its privileges and to advance his career. Paul, on the other hand, never had to seek Roman citizenship. Acts is prompt to show that except in very perilous circumstances the apostle neither invokes its protection nor avails himself of his rights. Paul accepts his citizenship as a consequence of his birth, but he never boasts of his status to his various interlocutors. The apostle attaches no undue importance to his status. In his mind, his primary identity is religious and not legal, i.e. he is first and foremost a Christian apostle fulfilling his ministry[50a].

IV. Excursus: Paul's triple Identity

1. *The Concept of Multiple Citizenship*

It was not at all uncommon for a man coming from a higher social class to enjoy dual citizenship especially in the Eastern part of the Empire. A good example of this is the case of Harpocras, Pliny the Younger's physician, who was an Egyptian. Pliny petitioned Emperor Trajan to accord Harpocras Roman citizenship ; he subsequently realized that Harpocras ought to have obtained Alexandrian citizenship beforehand, as the holding of Alexandrian citizenship was a prerequisite for an Egyptian asking for a grant of Roman citizenship[51]. It is interesting to note that in his reply Trajan is more reticent about granting Alexandrian citizenship to Harpocras than he was in granting Roman *civitas* to the physician: *"Civitatem Alexandrinam secundum institutionem principum non temere dare proposui. Sed, cum Harpocrati, iatraliptae tuo, iam civitatem Romanam impetraveris, huic quoque petitioni tuae negare non sustineo"*[52]. Citizenship in the *polis* was a highly valued and sought after legal status whose obtention depended generally on hereditary possession or special grant[53].

---

50 cf. *infra*, pg. 83 ff.
50a R.J. Cassidy, *SOCIETY AND POLITICS IN THE ACTS OF THE APOSTLES*, Orbis Books, Maryknoll, Maryland, 1987; pg. 100–103.
51 Pliny, *Ep.* X,6.
52 Pliny, *Ep.* X,7.
53 S. Applebaum, "The Legal Status of the Jewish Communities in the Diaspora", *op.cit.*, pg. 434.

Excursus: Paul's triple Identity

Despite the great value, social and otherwise, of citizenship in a Greek *polis*, the holding of Roman citizenship, with all its inherent rights, guarantees and privileges[54], superseded all other status in the law and in the opinion of society. In response to the question "Have you two fatherlands (*duas patrias*)?" Cicero writes:

> "Cato, for example, though born in Tusculum, received citizenship in Rome, and so, he was a Tusculan by birth and a Roman by citizenship, had one fatherland which was the place of his birth, and another by law; ... so we consider both the place where we were born our fatherland, and also the city into which we have been adopted. But that fatherland must stand first in our affection in which the name of republic signifies the common citizenship of all of us. (...) But the fatherland which was our parent is not much less dear to us than the one which adopted us. Thus I shall never deny that my fatherland is here, though my other fatherland is greater and includes this one within it; [and in the same way every native of an Italian town, in my opinion], has [two] citizenships but thinks of them as one citizenship"[55].

The apostle Paul might call himself a πολίτης of Tarsus and a Pharisaic Jew, but he was above all a Roman citizen.

The problem of the status of the Jews in the cities of the eastern Roman Empire is a complex one. Jews who became Roman citizens and who elected to continue the practice of their ancestral religion were permitted to keep the traditional privileges which they had enjoyed as peregrines. There was no incompatibility in a practising Jew's accepting a grant of Roman citizenship as Jewish Roman citizens were exempt from those state duties which might conflict with their monotheistic faith.

In the Hellenistic cities of the east, the Jews traditionally enjoyed many specific rights akin to those of local citizens, but the members of the *politeuma* remained alien residents and not citizens of the Greek *polis*[56]. Moreover there was no reciprocity of citizenship between the Jewish *politeuma* and the Greek *polis*. Isopolity was a strictly reciprocal agreement amongst Greek city-states; no such arrangement is known to have existed between a Greek city and a Jewish *politeuma*[57]. Individual Jews and their families may have received citizenship in the Greek *polis* as a grant of favour from the old Hellenistic monarchs or from the Roman rulers or

---

54 Nicolet, *op.cit.*, pg. 34–35.
55 Cicero, *de Leg.* II,2.5. (E.T. = C.W. Keyes, *Loeb*, 1961). cf. A.N. Sherwin-White, "The Roman Citizenship. A Survey of its Development into a world Franchise", *ANRW*. I,2; 1972, pg. 36 ff.
56 W.A. Meeks, *THE FIRST URBAN CHRISTIANS*, New Haven, 1983, pg. 36.
57 cf. S. Applebaum, "The Legal Status of the Jewish Communities in the Diaspora", *op.cit.*, pg. 436–438. A. Kasher, *op.cit.*, pg. 280. V. Tcherikover notes: "The meaning of the term *isopoliteia* ... was the granting of the citizenship of one city to all the citizens of another ... Such instances were very rare, and I know of no single instance of the granting of *isopoliteia* or *sympoliteia* by a Greek city to a *politeuma* of non-Greeks" (Tcherikover, *op.cit.*, pg. 515, note 86). For a discussion of the development of double citizenship in the Hellenistic world, cf. M. Hammond, *THE CITY IN THE ANCIENT WORLD*, 1972; pg. 273. The same author analyzes the Greek concept and practice of double citizenship and its influence on Rome in "Germana Patria", *HSCP*, Vol. 60; 1951; pg. 148–154.

indeed individual Jews might leave the *politeuma* and become (pagan) local citizens; but it is clear that the Jews did not enjoy local citizenship as a *bloc* in either Alexandria, the best documented example, or elsewhere in the Greek East[58].

2. Paul, a πολίτης of Tarsus

According to Acts XXII,3, Paul was born in Tarsus in Cilicia (γεγεννημένος ἐν Ταρσῷ τῆς Κιλικίας); in Acts XXI,39, Paul says that he is from Tarsus in Cilicia, a citizen of no mean city (ἐγὼ ἄνθρωπος μέν εἰμι Ἰουδαῖος Ταρσεύς τῆς Κιλικίας οὐκ ἀσήμου πόλεως πολίτης). The Vg. reads here: *Ego homo sum quidem a Tarso Ciliciae non ignotae civitatis municeps*[59]. The Codex Bezae has the following lesson: ἐγὼ ἄνθρωπος μέν εἰμι Ἰουδαῖος ἐν Ταρσῷ δὲ τῆς Κιλικίας γεγεννημένος), thus omitting the key words οὐκ ἀσήμου πόλεως πολίτης)[60]. In Acts IX,11, Paul is termed "a man of Tarsus" (Σαῦλον ὀνόματι Ταρσέα). Acts states that Paul lived in Tarsus after his conversion. In IX,30 we learn that Paul was sent away to that city by the Jerusalem brethren; it was there that Barnabas went to bring him to Antioch (XI,25). The epistles contain only the scantest reference to Paul's Tarsian connexion. In Gal. I,21, the apostle limits himself to saying that following his first visit to Jerusalem he went to the region of Syria and Cilicia (εἰς τὰ κλίματα τῆς Συρίας καὶ τῆς Κιλικίας). Finally Jerome says in *de Viris Illustribus V*:

> "Paulus apostolus, qui ante Saulus (Act. VII,57), extra numerum duodecim apostolorum, de tribu Benjamin et oppido Iudaeae Giscalis fuit, quo a Romanis capto, cum parentibus suis Tarsum Ciliciae commigravit (Acts. XXII,3), a quibus ob studia legis missus Hierosolymam, a Gamaliele viro doctissimo, cuius Lucas meminit, eruditus est". (*PL*, Vol. 23)

The problem of determining whether Paul was a citizen of the πόλις or merely a resident officially domiciled in the Jewish community of Tarsus is complicated by a lack of sources. Paul is silent on his Tarsian connexion in his Epistles, although it is safe to conclude on the basis of Galatians and

---

58 cf. S. Applebaum, "The Legal Status of the Jewish Communities in the Diaspora, *op.cit.*, pg. 445–449 for a look at evidence that Cyrene appears to have admitted a small group of wealthy Hellenized Jewish families to Cyrenaic citizenship. The author stresses, however, that the great majority of Cyrenaic Jews remained unenfranchised.

59 The Vg. reading is interesting as it translates the word πολίτης by the Latin *municeps*, rather than the *civis* of the Old Version. This preference is all the odder as the notion of *municipium* was in fact inapplicable to Tarsus, which was a *civitas libera*. The choice of the word *municeps* may very well be due to Jerome's belief that Paul was a resident, but not a native of Tarsus. cf. J Schwartz, "A propos du Statut personnel de l'Apôtre Paul", *RHPR*. No. 1; 1957, pg. 92–93.

60 The *pars latina* (d) however brings them back: *ego homo quidem sum iudaeus tarse[n]sis ex ciliciae non ignotae civitatis cuius (civis?) rogo obsegro autem mihi loqui ad populum*.

Acts that he spent time there after his conversion and that that city was most likely his official home. Acts also stresses the fact that Tarsus was Paul's birthplace, not only in the B-text, but also and especially in the D-text which replaces πολίτης by γεγεννημένος. Thus the only reference to Paul's possible Tarsian citizenship occurs in the B-text of Acts XXI,39, where Luke has Paul say that he is a πολίτης of no mean city. Strictly speaking the word πολίτης refers to a citizen of a town or state, a member of the πόλις as a political entity, someone who participates actively in the city's civic and religious life and who shares in the privileges, but also the duties, of the πόλις in its political quality. Finally the πολίτης is completely distinct on the juridical plane from a resident alien or slave.

In Scripture and in the Hellenistic writers, however, the word oftentimes loses its strict political and juridical connotation, taking on a much wider meaning. In the *LXX*, the word πολίτης is used 17 times most often in the sense of a co-religionist, neighbour or compatriot, reflecting the Hebrew stress on the ethical and religious rather than the Greek idea of citizen, whose nuance would be more political and legal. In Genesis XXIII,11, for example, the word means "my people"; in Proverbs XI,9, it means "neighbour". It is only in 2 Maccabees IX,19 and 3 Maccabees I,22 that the term denotes a "citizen" in the stricter meaning. Both Josephus and Philo tend to use the word in a wider sense, taking it out of its legal context and using it in a distinctively philosophical, if not spiritualizing transposition. In Josephus' writings the word πολίτης occurs very nearly 100 times; it most often denotes "fellow-countrymen", "co-religionists"[61], or members of the same people[62]. Josephus also uses the word in reference to the legitimate inhabitants of a city, free persons, Jews as citizens of the cities of Israel and subject to the king. He also uses it to refer to Jews who are Roman citizens[63]. In the NT, the word occurs only four times: in Hebr. VIII,11, it denotes neighbours or kinsmen dwelling together in a New Covenant; in Lk XV,15, its use is also non-political (the prodigal son's employer is socially an independent land-owner); in Lk XIX,19, also a parable, the citizens are independent inhabitants freely dwelling in that place and contrasted with the king's δοῦλοι. The sense of these two uses from Luke's Gospel is social and economic rather than legal or political. The NT usage of the term πολίτης is therefore generic and has no strict juridical implication[64].

---

61 cf. *Ant.* XII,2.5 (46); *Ant.* XIV,10.12 (226).
62 cf. *Contra Apionem* II, (170).
63 cf. *Ant.* XIV,10.13 (228); XIV,10.14 (232); XIV,10.16 (234); XIV,10.18 (237); XIV,10.19 (240).
64 cf. Eph. II,12, where the expression πολιτεία τοῦ Ἰσραηλ does not, of course, refer to a political citizenship, but to a spiritual citizenship without any specific political implication. Believers share with each other a sympoity of the ἅγιοι.

Another element militating against Paul's holding Tarsian citizenship is the fact that the obtaining of citizenship in an Eastern Greek city was the heartfelt wish of only a strict minority of highly Hellenized Diaspora Jews whose aim was total integration into the surrounding Greek ambience. This would be in complete disaccord with Paul's Orthodox Pharisaic heritage and education. Moreover, a young Jewish man, who was a citizen of the Greek city, would most likely have attended a gymnasium, a most sought-after institution of education. Paul's upbringing was clearly rabbinical. Local citizenship would have required participation in all aspects of civic life, including worship of local or tutelary gods. It is hard to imagine a strict monotheist such as Paul worshipping the local pagan deities. As in Alexandria and other Hellenistic cities in the East, it is unlikely that the Jewish community of Tarsus possessed Tarsian citizenship *en bloc*; only a few Hellenized Jews enjoyed that status. The Jews of Tarsus might form a legally-recognized body with specific rights and privileges, but the great majority of the Jewish residents of Tarsus nonetheless remained ἔξωθεν τῆς πολιτείας[65]:

> "The very fact that the internal organization of the Jewish community resembled the organization of the *polis* whose privileges were so great, proves, indeed, that it stood side by side with the *polis* as an independent political organization requiring no citizen-rights within it. Only isolated Jews could aspire to equality of franchise with the Greeks, but not complete communities"[66].

We would like to conclude by saying that Paul's Tarsian citizenship cannot be proved on the basis of Acts XXI,39. The use of the word πολίτης in that passage was in a non-juridical sense and most likely refers to Paul's membership in the resident Jewish community at Tarsus rather than to any citizenship in the Greek πόλις. His mention of Tarsus in this verse is a statement of domicile and not a proclamation of citizenship. His identification as a resident of Tarsus was enough to dispel any suspicion on the tribune's part that he was the seditious Egyptian. But as Acts makes clear, it had no suspensive effect on the actions or decisions of the Roman official and thus could not save the apostle from the threat of scourging. Paul's statement that he was a πολίτης of Tarsus did not — and could not — have the same legal effect on the supreme Roman authority in Jerusalem as did his subsequent proclamation of Roman citizenship.

---

65 For the status of the Jews in the Hellenistic cities of Asia and Syria, cf. S. Applebaum, "The Legal Status of the Jewish Communities in the Diaspora" *op.cit.*, pg. 440–444. Michael Grant writes: "Paul was not one of the small body of Jews who became, in their individual capacity, citizens of Greek cities, though he may have been the potential beneficiary of an arrangement (going back to Seleucid times) by which he could become a citizen on demand, if he worshipped the city's gods: a right which he did not choose to exercise" (Grant, *THE JEWS IN THE ROMAN WORLD*, New York, 1973; pg. 118.

66 V. Tcherikover, *op.cit.*, pg. 515, note 861.

3. Paul, the Pharisaic Jew

In Acts XXII,3, Paul emphasizes not only his belonging to the Jewish nation, but also his Pharisaic background and upbringing: "I am a Jew, born at Tarsus in Cilicia, but brought up in this city at the feet of Gamaliel, educated according to the strict manner of the law of our fathers, being zealous for God as you all are this day". The apostle's Jewish identity is stressed elsewhere in the Acts narrative: in Acts XXIII, 6a, Paul tells the Sanhedrin that he is "a Pharisee, a son of Pharisees"; in XXIV,14b, he tells Felix "I worship the God of our fathers, believing everything laid down by the law or written in the prophets"; in XXVI,5b, the apostle tells King Agrippa " ... that according to the strictest party of our religion I have lived as a Pharisee". In his narrative Luke presents Paul as a Pharisee "who remains a Pharisee after his conversion and never becomes an ex-Pharisee"[67]. Thus Luke recalls that although Paul was born in the Diaspora, he was educated in strictly Pharisaic circles. He did not belong to a liberal Hellenistic Judaism strongly influenced by the surrounding Greek ambience, but to Palestinian orthodoxy[68].

Paul himself explicitly asserts his Jewish identity in the Epistles. In Romans XI,1b, he says "I myself am an Israelite, a descendant of Abraham, a member of the tribe of Benjamin". In 2 Cor. XI,22, he writes "Are they Hebrews? So am I. Are they Israelites? So am I. Are they descendants of Abraham? So am I". In Gal. I,14, he notes that he showed much zeal for the tradition of his fathers. Finally in Phil. III,5, the apostle identifies himself as being "of the people of Israel, of the tribe of Benjamin, a Hebrew born of Hebrews; as to the law a Pharisee".

> "It is perfectly plain, however, both from the letters and from Acts, that Paul the Christian was still Paul the Pharisee and that, like many other Christian Jews, he saw no contradiction in this (cf. 15:5). Christianity was for him the fulfillment of the law and of prophecy, and his hope as a Jew loyal to the traditions of his people was that all Jews might come to recognize this as he himself had done"[69].

4. Paul, the Roman Citizen

a) *Aspects of Roman Citizenship*

In Acts XXII,24, Paul, who was on the point of being scourged with the dreaded *flagrum*, proclaimed his Roman citizenship. The cry *civis Romanus sum* had a suspensive effect on the proceedings; this proclamation freed

---

67 J. Jervell, *op.cit.*, pg. 71.
68 cf. J. Daniélou, "Paul dans les Actes des Apôtres" *AXES*, Paris, Tome V, May 1969; pg. 6.
69 Neil, *op.cit.*, pg. 228.

him from the torture about to be inflicted. Acts states that Paul was born a Roman citizen, but not how his father or forebears received the grant of *civitas*[70].

In fact there was more than one way to obtain it. Slave manumission or citizenship by emancipation was one possibility. Another was by service in the Roman armed forces. Except for officers, the soldiers in the auxiliary forces were not Roman citizens, but at the end of their service they were given the grant of Roman citizenship. The Roman colony was another form of citizen extension. The existing native population as well as the non-Romans who settled in the colonies acquired Roman citizenship in due time[71]. Finally there was the old and rather extensive practice of granting citizenship to individual free *peregrini*, to whole *collegia*, or indeed to entire communities which had distinguished themselves by their exemplary service to Rome:

1) As early as 89 B.C., Gnaeus.Pompeius Strabo, father of Pompey the Great, had granted citizenship to some Spanish cavalrymen[72]. Pompey himself had been authorized by provisions of the *Lex Gellia Cornelia de Civitate* (72 B.C.) to grant Roman citizenship as a reward to individual peregrines[73].

2) Julius Caesar had granted citizenship to political leaders and diverse nobles in various parts of the Empire as a reward for their support and loyalty[74].

3) Mark Antony had sold Roman citizenship for money[75].

4) There was a large traffic in citizenship during Claudius' reign, in which Messalina and the Emperor's freedmen sold citizenship for large sums of money[76].

---

70 Ramsay writes: "In the first century, when citizenship was still jealously guarded, the *civitas* may be taken as proof that his [Paul's] family was one of distinction and at least moderate wealth. It also implies that there was in the surroundings amid which he grew up, a certain attitude of friendliness to the Imperial government ..." (*SPT*, pg. 30–31).
71 Suetonius (*Iul*. XXVIII) gives an example of the power to grant citizenship that a military commander enjoyed in a Roman colony and how this power was still contested even in the late Republic: "Not content with depriving Caesar of his provinces and his privilege, Marcellus also moved that the colonists whom Caesar had settled in Novum Comum ... should lose their citizenship, on the ground that it had been given from political motives and was not authorized by the law." (E.T. = J.C. Rolfe, *Loeb*, 1960).
72 *ILS*. 8888.
73 Cicero, *pro Balbo*, VIII,19. E. Badian gives a comprehensive list of peregrine individuals who were granted Roman citizenship during the last half century of the Republic. The list includes the name of the new citizen, his native city, the enfranchiser, evidence and notes. (E. Badian, *FOREIGN CLIENTELAE*, Oxford, 1958, pg. 302–308.
74 Strabo, *Geo*. V,1.6.
75 cf. Cicero, *Philippicae* II,92; V,11–12 for an account of Mark Antony's trafficking.
76 cf. *supra*, pg. 75.

One can conjecture that Paul's forebears, having emigrated to Tarsus either under the Seleucid rulers or more likely in the resettlement carried out under Pompey the Great, had served in the mercenary forces and were consequently awarded Roman citizenship. This is most likely to have occurred during one of the Civil Wars as a recompense for some signal service to the Roman state or to a particular victorious commander.

In the NT, the apostle uses or is referred to by his *cognomen*, Paul, (except for earlier in Acts as Saul). As a citizen, Paul would have had a regular Roman triple name consisting of a *praenomen, nomen* and *cognomen*. It is a pity of course that only one of Paul's three names is known to us. As enfranchised persons normally took the *praenomen* and *nomen* of their benefactor (retaining their own original single name as the *cognomen*), Paul's gentilic middle name might have suggested with a good deal of probability the moment and possibly the circumstances under which his family had come onto the list of Roman citizens.

We have seen how twice Paul proclaimed his Roman citizenship and what effects his declaration had on the Roman magistrates. An interesting question to be raised in this context is in what manner Roman citizenship was proved. Peregrine auxiliary soldiers received Roman citizenship when their term of service with the army was over. The certificate of citizenship was recorded on a document known as a *diploma civitatis Romanae*, which was portable and could be used for purposes of identification. These *diplomata* were folded in two to form a diptych: "They were written on bronze and refer to official lists of veterans discharged and enfranchised, kept at the Capitol in Rome. The earliest of them are dated contemporary with the events in Acts"[77]. Such documents could also be used in grants of citizenship to civilians. One famous example is recorded by Suetonius: "He [Nero] also exhibited ... Pyrrhic dances by some Greek youths, handing each of them certificates of Roman citizenship (*diplomata civitatis Romanae*) at the close of his performance"[78].

As time went on, it became customary for the Emperor to send to the beneficiary of a grant of citizenship or other privilege a *libellus* which recorded the measure in his favour. The *libellus* was recorded not only in the tribal lists at Rome, but most probably in the municipal registers of the beneficiary's hometown as well[79].

---

77 Cadbury, *THE BOOK OF ACTS IN HISTORY, op.cit.*, pg. 83, n. 18.
78 Suetonius, *Nero* XII. E.T. = J.C. Rolfe, *Loeb*, 1960.
79 cf. Ehrenberg & Jones, No. 301 and Riccobono, *FIRA*, No. 55 which give the text of letters by Augustus granting citizenship and other privileges to one Seleucus of Rhosos (41 B.C.) and ordering the text of the decree already inscribed on a column at Rome to be copied in the public records of Tarsus and Antioch.

The lists of Roman citizens were reviewed every five years in the municipal census taken in the local communities which possessed Roman citizenship. The local census was taken at the same time as the census was being taken in Rome. The *Lex Iulia Municipalis* gives interesting particulars on census-taking:

1) The highest magistrates in all *municipia, coloniae* or *praefecturae* shall take a census of all those persons who are Roman citizens belonging to those respective entities.

2) The magistrate shall receive their gentilic names, *praenomina* and *cognomina*, their fathers or patrons, their tribes, their age and a statement of their property.

3) These details shall be entered into the public records of the respective communities,

4) and then dispatched to the officials taking the census at Rome who shall see that they are entered into the public records.

5) The aforesaid public records are to be kept in the same place with other census records[80].

The Roman citizen could thus turn to a corpus of properly-kept census archives and communal lists to prove his citizenship. If for some reason or other the census archives were not consulted, then a native-born Roman citizen "could produce a copy of the original *professio* or registration of his birth recording his Roman status and made before a magistrate"[81]. In the provinces this *professio* was most likely made at the *tabularium publicum* of the *praeses provinciae*:

> "Only children in possession of the Roman citizenship could be registered. (...) If one or the other of the parents did not possess the Roman citizenship, the child was a *peregrinus* (or *peregrina*) according to the *Lex Mincia*, and it might be taken for granted even without any further proof that *peregrini* could not be enrolled in the purely Roman register. Moreover apparently in all our documents concerning legitimate children, the father asserted in his *professio* that his child was a Roman citizen"[82].

---

80 *CIL*. I,206: the *Lex Iulia Municipalis*, lines 142–156.
81 Sherwin-White, pg. 148.
82 F. Schulz, "Roman Registers of Births and Birth Certificates" (Part I), *JRS*, Vol. 32; 1942; pg. 80. cf. Apuleius, *Apol.* LXXXIX,2–3: "Pudentilla's father, at the birth of his daughter, declared her as was customary. The record of this was kept both in the public archives and at home ("*Pater eius natam sibi filiam more ceterorum professus est. Tabulae eius partim tabulario publico partim domo adseruantur*") and it can be put before your very eyes." cf. *Scriptores Historiae Augustae* – Marcus Antoninus IX,7–8: "[he ordered] ... that every citizen should bestow names upon his free-born children within thirty days after birth and declare them to the prefects of the treasury of Saturn. In the provinces, too, he established the use of public records, in which entries concerning births were to be made in the same manner as at Rome in the office of the prefects of the treasury, the purpose being if that any one born in the provinces should plead a case to prove freedom, he might submit evidence from these records." (E.T. = D. Magie, *Loeb*, 1960.)

The portable certificates which were held by the citizen himself were certified copies made from the registers and their authenticity could be tested by referring back to the public records. They most likely indicated his name, age, heirship to his father's estate and his Roman citizenship.

The partially preserved text of Michigan Papyrus 2737 is an example of the regular form of the birth certificate. The fragment in question, published by H.A. Sanders in 1931, is the lower half of the second tablet of a diptych. The certificate is on the waxed part of the tablet and four of the seven customary signatures of witnesses figure on the surrounding wooden parts. The extant text reads as follows:

> [. Cornel] i[u] s M. filius Iustus HS xx
> [fil.nat.] M. Cornelium Iustum ex
> [. . . . . .] a M. f(ilia) Herade IV Idus Septemb.
> q p.f.c.r.e. ad K

Sanders reconstructs the text:

> "I Marcus Cornelius Iustus, the son of Marcus, possessed of property worth twenty thousand sesterces, have published in the Kalendarium that on the fourth day before the Ides of September just past a son, Marcus Cornelius Iustus, a Roman citizen, was born from the mother ... a Heras, the daughter of Marcus"[83].

Forgery of the certificate or registration was a very serious offense. Roman citizenship had an almost sacred quality to it, reflecting the many privileges associated with it. Falsifying one's status called for the severest punishment[84].

Did Roman citizens carry the certificates around with them as modern man carries his identity card?

> "They were convenient in shape and size, being small wooden diptychs. But it is more likely that they were normally kept in the family archives. The itinerant is the exception in the ancient world. The general mass of the population stayed in one place from one generation to another, except for merchants and soldiers; hence the latter were given metal certificates of citizenship, ..."[85].

It is quite likely then that Paul produced a copy of his birth registration in order to corroborate his claim to Roman citizenship[86].

---

83 H.A. Sanders, "Two Fragmentary Birth Certificates from the Michigan Collection" *MEMOIRS OF THE AMERICAN ACADEMY IN ROME*, Vol. IX, 1931, pg. 62. Sanders dates the fragment as 103 A.D. He reconstructs the letters q.p.f. as *"quae proximae fuerunt"* and c.r.e. ad K. as *"c(ivem) R(omanum) e(scripsi) ad K (alendarium)."*
84 cf. Epictetus, *Arrian Discourses*, III,24.41: "those who falsely claim Roman citizenship are severely punished" (E.T. = W.A. Oldfather, *Loeb*, 1959). Suetonius writes: "Those who usurped the privileges of Roman citizenship he [Claudius] executed in the Esquiline field". (*Claud.* XXV; E.T. = J.C. Rolfe, *Loeb*, 1959.).
85 Sherwin-White, pg. 149.
86 cf. F. Schulz, "Roman Registers of Births and Birth Certificates" (Part 2), *JRS*, Vol. 33; 1943, pg. 63.

One last thing to be noted is that the Roman citizen was expected to be fluent in Latin. Dio Cassius relates an interesting episode in this regard:

> "During the investigation of this affair [i.e. the slaying of a Roman by some Lycians] which was conducted in the Senate, he [Claudius] puts a question in Latin to one of the envoys who had originally been a Lycian, but had been made a Roman citizen; and when the man failed to understand what was said, he took away his citizenship, saying that it was not proper for a man to be a Roman who had no knowledge of the Romans' language"[87].

One might reasonably infer that Paul was conversant with the Latin language. He was a learned man, and his being a Roman citizen could very well have provided further impetus to acquire Latin. Acts depicts Paul as being quite knowledgeable of Roman court procedure — he never consults a rhetor and always seems to know what legal steps to take. The narrative also stresses his trust in the fairness of the Roman judicial system. All this would indicate that Roman civilisation was not foreign to the apostle and that it was made accessible by the vehicle of the language. Finally Latin would have been most useful to the apostle in his many encounters with Roman officials, especially at Rome itself.

b) *Was the Apostle Paul Indeed a Roman Citizen?*

The key to Paul's legal history lies in his possession of the Roman citizenship. Paul's *civitas* put him into a precise juridical relationship with the Roman authorities with whom he came into contact and signified that on the purely legal level at least, Paul's trial was fundamentally different than those of Jesus and Stephen, neither of whom were Roman citizens.

Yet Luke's account in Acts is the only New Testament witness to Paul's Roman citizenship. The Pauline Epistles make no reference to the apostle's citizenship status. Although Tradition and the vast majority of scholars have accepted Paul's possession of Roman citizenship as a historical fact, the Lucan identification of Paul as a Roman citizen has not gone unquestioned or unchallenged.

Two recent publications in German scholarly literature on Acts provide a clear illustration as to the divergence of opinion on this subject. Gerd Lüdemann has devoted a short but comprehensive Excursus ("Zum römischen Bürgerrecht des Paulus") to this question in his commentary, *Das frühe Christentum nach den Traditionen der Apostelgeschichte,* (Vandenhoeck & Ruprecht, Göttingen), which appeared in 1987. Lüdemann, whose work is in general characterized by a great scepticism as to the historical trustworthiness of Acts, nonetheless accepts as positively founded that Paul did indeed possess Roman citizenship.

---

87 Dio Cassius, LX,17.4 (year 43 A.D.) E.T. = E. Cary, *Loeb*, 1961.

Lüdemann begins his Excursus by examining the arguments militating against the apostle's having Roman citizenship: (1) Paul does not mention his Roman citizenship in his Epistles, (2) Paul was thrice beaten with rods, (3) Paul's manual activity reflected his lower middle class origins and thus contradicted any possession on his part of the Roman citizenship, which was normally granted only to leading upper class provincials. Lüdemann provides brief but pertinent answers to counter the above arguments: (1) Paul did not mention his Roman citizenship in his Epistles because he attached no particular importance to his legal status in them, (2) The *Lex Iulia* did indeed protect a Roman citizen from the rods, but its provisions were sometimes contravened by abusive magistrates. Moreover, for one reason or other Paul might not have had the opportunity to proclaim his Roman citizenship before being beaten with rods, (3) Paul's manual labour was most likely motivated by his rabbinical education and training and does not conclusively indicate his social class provenance. Lüdemann also places great importance on the fact that the apostle had a Roman name, *Paulus*. He also notes that surprisingly many of Paul's real or intended missionary stations were either Roman colonies (e.g. Philippi, Corinth) or areas which had been subject to an extensive and on-going policy of Romanization (e.g. Spain).

Despite his great scepticism as to the basic historical reliability of Acts, Lüdemann was not able in his Excursus to eschew the testimony found in Luke's second volume: Paul's transferral to Rome is best explained by the exercise of his right of appeal to the Roman Emperor to hear his case; the aforesaid right of appeal being a fundamental prerogative of the Roman citizenship. For the above reasons, Lüdemann rightly concludes the historicity of Paul's Roman citizenship.

The second publication is a thirty page article by Wolfgang Stegemann entitled "Was der Apostel Paulus ein römischer Bürger?", which appeared in *ZNW*, Band 78; 1987. The author is extremely critical (to say the least!) of the Lucan account of Paul's legal history. In Stegemann's view, it was highly improbable that Paul possessed the Roman citizenship and this for three basic reasons: (1) Paul's low social class and Jewish background would preclude a grant of Roman citizenship to his family, (2) Paul is silent in his Epistles on his Roman citizenship whence Stegemann concludes that he did not possess it, (3) the reports in Acts are Luke's own composition, written purely for his own apologetic purposes and therefore quite unreliable.

The points raised in Stegemann's article are familiar ones and many of them are answered elsewhere in this book so we shall restrict ourselves here to responding to some of the more dubious conclusions he draws regarding Paul's citizenship. As stated above, Paul's tentmaking activity cannot be used as conclusive evidence to prove a low social class background. Lüdemann has pointed out in his Excursus the influence on Paul of rabbinical training and education in this matter of self-support. Moreover Paul himself is rather loathe to take mony for preaching the Gospel and ministering to the communities and only does so exceptionally, not wishing to be a burden on the churches he founded (cf. 2 Cor. XI,7—9). Appeals and appearances in the imperial court were expensive affairs more indicative of personal wealth than of inferior social status. Stegemenn also depicts Paul's Jewishness as being completely antithetical to his holding Roman citizenship. Yet it is surely incorrect to portray the relationship between Jews and Romans as one of inveterate hostility. In Chapter I we noted the relatively favourable position held by the Jews in the early Principate. Anti-Semitic reflexes did exist, stimulated to some extent by the Jewish sense of exclusiveness, but this should not obscure the fact that there was a certain integration of the Jewish communities both in Palestine and in the Diaspora into the overall political, economic, social and legal framework of the Roman Empire. Jewish communities did not exist in a vacuum of time or space totally cut off from their environment. There was interaction at many levels between Jews and Romans as the writings of Josephus and Philo amongst others show. Jews were granted Roman citizenship no less than were other provincials and being a Jew did not in itself disqualify a man from the grant of Roman citizenship.

Stegemann attaches great importance to the fact that the Pauline Epistles say nothing of the apostle's citizenship and concludes from their silence that he was not in fact a citizen. We have already mentioned that Paul attached no particular importance to his Roman citizenship in the Epistles. Luke's portrayal of Paul in Acts is consistent with this attitude. The apostle, after all, proclaims his citizenship only in the direst circumstances (magisterial abuse at Philippi, threat of scourging at Jerusalem, threat of transferral to the Sanhedrin's jurisdiction at Caesarea). Legally speaking Paul's status was that of a Roman citizen, resident in Tarsus and of Jewish origin, but to the apostle himself his premier identity was that of a Christian, a citizen of the Kingdom, a man who cared little for human courts or their judgments (cf. 1 Cor. IV,3ff).

The fact that Paul did not sign the Epistles with his Roman *tria nomina*, but with the simple *cognomen* of Paul cannot be used as evidence to disprove Paul's possession of the Roman citizenship. Paul was writing as a Christian apostle and brother to fellow Christians with precise doctrinal or ecclesiological aims in mind; he was not writing a decree, judicial brief or epitaph which would require the use of his full official Roman name.

Stegemann's main point however is that as Acts was Luke's own composition, its indication that Paul possessed Roman citizenship is unhistorical along with the rest of the narrative. Still in his reconstruction, Stegemann conjectures (from the Acts narrative?) that Paul was indeed transferred from the governor's court at Caesarea to the imperial court at Rome. Luke then is said to have taken this historical fact and extrapolated that Paul was a Roman citizen. It is at this point that the author's whole argument concerning the historical inaccuracy of Paul's Roman citizenship collapses. Stegemann does not adequately explain on what *legal basis* Paul was able to appeal to the Emperor's court at Rome for protection against the decision of a governor *sedens pro tribunali* if he were the inconsequential Jewish manual labourer and peregrine that Stegemann says he was. Over against this viewpoint, we maintain that the only plausible way to explain Paul's transferral to the highest court is that he was in fact a Roman citizen, who had exercised his right of appeal — a basic prerogative of Roman citizenship — a right to justice, equitable treatment and protection from magisterial abuse absolutely inherent in the *civitas*.

Luke of course has his apologetic aims and theological concerns and he sometimes limits his material and omits things which do not fit in with his overall theological purpose. Yet his work contains a real historical programme. Luke's account of Paul's trial is of historical value indicating as it does the essential characteristics of that event and providing a historical understanding of Paul's relationship to the Roman judicial system.

Chapter V
Jerusalem (Part 2): Paul and the Sanhedrin

I. *Paulus ante Synedrium*

1. *The Convening of the Sanhedrin*

Lysias had learned very little from the preliminary investigation conducted up till then. He now decided on a new way of investigating this mystifying case: "But on the morrow, desiring to know the real reason why the Jews accused him, (βουλόμενος γνῶναι τὸ ἀσφαλές τὸ τί κατηγορεῖται ὑπὸ τῶν Ἰουδαίων), he unbound him, (ἔλυσεν αὐτόν), and commanded the chief priests and all the council to meet, (καὶ ἐκέλευσεν συνελθεῖν τοὺς ἀρχιερεῖς καὶ πᾶν τὸ συνέδριον) and he brought Paul down before them." (καὶ καταγαγὼν τὸν Παῦλον ἔστησεν εἰς αὐτούς) (XXII,30).

A) βουλόμενος γνῶναι τὸ ἀσφαλές

Paul was led from the Fortress Antonia to the Council Chamber. His appearance before the Sanhedrin was not a formal trial, but a part of the preliminary investigation into the case after which Lysias would have to decide if Paul should be released or remanded to the governor's jurisdiction for trial at Caesarea. At this stage of the proceedings, the Sanhedrin is not meeting to formulate charges against the apostle nor to prepare a regular case against him. The Sanhedrin is not as yet the plaintiff as it will later be when the case is heard by the governors. Lysias is trying to clarify his thoughts so as to know what to do with his prisoner; the meeting of the Sanhedrin was convened according to Luke to help him. At the beginning of the passage, the judicial role of the Sanhedrin is more advisory than anything else.

B) τὸ τί κατηγορεῖται ὑπὸ τῶν Ἰουδαίων

κατηγορέω — to accuse, to make accusations before a judge; to accuse formally and before a tribunal. In the passive = to be brought as an accusation against. Luke uses the word here in its exact judicial sense: the putting forth before a magistrate of a formal request for the punishment of an accused person[1].

C) ἔλυσεν αὐτόν

The verse presents a certain number of difficulties due to its syntax and the exact sense of the words ἔλυσεν αὐτόν. The tribune is *afraid*, yet the text indicates that Paul was unbound only *on the morrow*!

1) It is clear that the apostle was still in custody. He is referred to as a prisoner (δέσμιος) in XXIII,18 and was left a prisoner (δεδέμενον) in XXIV,27.

2) Paul had already been released from the whipping post or bench to which he had been bound by thongs to keep him immobile for the scourging. His cry *civis Romanus sum* had suspended the action of the Roman officials and provoked his *immediate* release from the instruments of torture[2].

3) The unbounding *on the morrow* (ἐπαύριον) refers to the apostle's release from the rigours of *custodia militaris*, i.e. he was no longer bound to two soldiers[2a].

D) καὶ ἐκέλευσεν συνελθεῖν τοὺς ἀρχιερεῖς καὶ πᾶν τὸ συνέδριον

The Acts-narrative seems to infer that the Tribune of Jerusalem had the power to convene the Sanhedrin. R. Taubenschlag finds an analogy to this situation in the papyri:

> "Another question which the procedure against St. Paul suggests is to see if we possess an analogy in our papyrological sources wherein an administrative official ... convenes a meeting of a judicial body to serve as a council. We do not possess similar cases in sources from the Roman period; but we do find some in the papyri of the Ptolemaic period ..."[3].

E) καὶ καταγαγὼν τὸν Παῦλον ἔστησεν εἰς αὐτούς

κατάξω — The verb indicates descent: to bring down to a place, to lead down. Paul was led from the Antonia *down* to a lower place when he appeared in the Council Chamber. The place where the Sanhedrin heard Paul cannot be determined with certitude. Lysias had accompanied Paul to the Council Chamber and later sent Roman soldiers to fetch the apostle when the session threatened to break up violently. Thus the Inner Court of

---

[1] As he does in Lk.XXIII,10;14; Acts XXIV,2;8b;13;19; XXV,5;11; XXVIII,19.
[2] The immediacy is stressed in the lesson in 614, syh and sa. which add the words καὶ παραχρῆμα ἔλυσεν αὐτόν to vs. 29.
[2a] H L and P add ἀπὸ τῶν δεσμῶν for more precision.
[3] R. Taubenschlag, "Le Procès de l'Apôtre Paul en Lumière des Papyri", *op.cit.*, pg. 723. cf. *P. Amh.* II,33.6–9. Lüdemann for his part, believes that the convening of the Sanhedrin by a Roman officer as well as his presence at the ensuing session is probably unhistorical. (Lüdemann, *DAS FRUHE CHRISTENTUM...*, *op.cit.*, pg. 251.).

the Temple has to be excluded from consideration as non-Jews were forbidden to enter it. The inquiry most likely took place in the βουλή which Josephus mentions as being the Sanhedrin's usual meeting place[4].

2. In the Council Chanber

In accordance with the customary judicial procedure used by the Sanhedrin, the defence stated its case first followed in turn by the prosecution[5]. The text of Acts nowhere indicates the existence of any defence witnesses nor or any defence counsel. It was the defendant who spoke on his own behalf: "And Paul, looking intently (ἀτενίσας) at the council, said 'Brethren, (ἄνδρες ἀδελφοί), I have lived before God in all good conscience up to this day'. (ἐγὼ πάσῃ συνειδήσει ἀγαθῇ πεπολίτευμαι τῷ Θεῷ ἄχρι ταύτης τῆς ἡμέρας). And the high priest Ananias commanded those who stood by him to strike him on the mouth". (XXIII,1–2).

A) ἀτενίσας

ἀτενίζω – to fix one's eyes upon, to look intently, to gaze earnestly at. Almost all the NT uses of this verb occur in Luke-Acts, especially at moments of high and expectant drama: e.g. Acts I,10, the Ascension narrative; III,4 the miracle at the Beautiful Gate; VI,15; VII,55, the Stephen pericope; X,4, Cornelius and the angel; XI,6, vision of Peter; XIII,9, Paul vs. Elymas; XIV,9, the miracle at Lystra. Here Luke uses the intensive ἀτενίζω as a literary device: not only does it draw the attention of the reader to the significant statement to come, – Paul's declaration of his Pharisaic status and belief in the hope and resurrection – but also to the whole conflictual situation between the apostle and the Sanhedrin.

B) ἄνδρες ἀδελφοί

By his use of the word *brethren* instead of *fathers*, Paul, from the outset of his speech, showed that he did not consider the members of the Sanhedrin as his judges or his superiors, but simply as equals.

C) ἐγὼ πάσῃ συνειδήσει ἀγαθῇ πεπολίτευμαι τῷ Θεῷ ἄχρι ταύτης τῆς ἡμέρας

πολιτεύω – Here the meaning of the verb is more spiritual than legal: to

---

[4] *BJ.* V,4.2 (144). This was the chamber in or near the southern part of the temple precincts in which the Sanhedrin was wont to meet. cf. *m.Sanh.* XI,2.
[5] cf. *m.Sanh.* IV,1.

order or govern one's life and conduct according to religious and ethical norms, standards and principles[6].

συνείδησις — conscience, consciousness of what is morally right or wrong, commending the former and renouncing the latter. The term signifies the inward moral impression and ethical evaluation of one's principles and actions. The apostle judges that he has a good conscience because his conduct is governed by a devout and godly sincerity. He is thus innocent before God, the sole judge who matters[7].

In his statement, Paul declares that he is serving God according to the divine directives given him. Having acted in good conscience and in a right way, he cannot accept being judged by a body such as the Sanhedrin. It is clear from his gestures and opening remarks what Paul thought of human courts in general and of this one in particular[8]. This type of attitude on a defendant's part was highly unusual[9]. Most often defendants were as obsequious as possible when their case was before the Sanhedrin so as to stir up feelings of mercy and compassion in their judges[10]. By speaking before being questioned or asked to speak, Paul showed that he did not consider himself a defendant and certainly not a transgressor. Moreover he was implying that the conduct of the Sanhedrin and of his immediate accusers, the Asian Jews, was most unethical. In contrast to their violence and inequity, he had a clear conscience and could truly maintain his innocence even though a prisoner. Thus the authority of the Sanhedrin was rejected from the very start on moral and ethical grounds.

Once again in vivid and unambiguous terms, Luke highlights one of the key points of the Acts-narrative. Paul is a loyal Pharisaic Jew. Nonetheless he is forced by the stubbornness of his unpersuaded adversaries to renounce the authority of the supreme Jewish Council whose unrighteousness and disbelief are dramatically symbolized by the gesture of the slap in the face given Paul at the beginning of the hearing.

D) *Ananias*

Ananias, son of Nebedaeus, was appointed High Priest by Herod of Chalcis in 47 A.D.[11]. In 52 A.D. he was sent to Rome by Quadratus, Legate of Syria, as he had been implicated in insurrectional activity in Judaea[12]. He was found innocent of the charges and returned to the High Priesthood

---

6 cf. Phil. I,27; Clement, *Ep.Cor.* XXI,1.
7 cf. Acts XXIV,16; 2 Cor. I,12; I Tim III,9; 2 Tim I,3.
8 cf. I Cor. IV,3.
9 cf. Jn. XVIII, 19–24 for the attitude of the Lord before the Sanhedrin.
10 *Ant.* XIV,9.4 (172).
11 *Ant.* XX,5.2 (103).
12 *Ant.* XX,6.2 (131).

which he left in 58 A.D., when Ishmael, son of Phabi, was appointed in his stead by Herod Agrippa II[13].

Paul responded to being struck by saying to the High Priest, "God shall strike you, you whitewashed wall[14]! Are you sitting to judge me according to the law, (καὶ σὺ κάθῃ κρείνων με κατὰ τὸν νόμον), and yet contrary to the law (παρανομῶν) you order me to be struck?" (XXIII,3).

A) καὶ σὺ κάθῃ κρείνων με κατὰ τὸν νόμον

Jewish law considered a defendant innocent until he had been proved guilty. The High Priest ought to have been impartial in this affair. Instead he had violated Jewish law by ordering the prisoner struck before he had been found guilty on any charge. A certain evolution in the account has to be noted here. Lysias' original intention in bringing Paul before the Sanhedrin was to learn the facts of the accusations brought by the Jews (XXII, 30). The Sanhedrin was brought together to give advice in the case. Here, however, Paul's question, with its two verbs, *sit* and *judge* implies that the Sanhedrin is now functioning as a veritable tribunal hearing the case in a formal way. The account is very abbreviated here. Luke's main interest is Paul's declaration and the Sanhedrin's reaction and not the legal details or procedural aspects of the case.

B) παρανομῶν

The apostle could not allow such an offensive and illegal action to pass without protest:

> "He would have appeared as a dreg in the eyes of the tribune had he accepted being treated like a slave without protesting. Indeed the tribune might well have been more easily induced to extradite him to the Jews. What would the tribune have thought hearing this order given to strike a Roman citizen[15]?"

After this stormy start, Paul concentrated his remarks on the question of the resurrection[16]: "But when Paul perceived that one part were Sadducees and the other Pharisees, (γνοὺς δὲ ὁ Παῦλος ὅτι τὸ ἓν μέρος ἐστὶν Σαδδουκαίων τὸ δὲ ἕτερον Φαρισαίων), he cried out in the council, 'Brethren, I am a Pharisee, a son of Pharisees; with respect to the hope and the resurrection of the dead I am on trial'." (ἐγὼ Φαρισαῖός εἰμι υἱὸς Φαρισαίων· περὶ ἐλπίδος καὶ ἀναστάσεως νεκρῶν κρίνομαι) (XXIII,6).

---

13 *Ant.* XX,8.8 (179).
14 Ananias was assassinated in September 66 because of his pro-Roman policy. cf. *BJ.* II,17.9 (441).
15 Jacquier, *LES ACTES DES APOTRES*, Paris, 1926, pg. 658.
16 cf. Paul's other apologetic speeches in the latter part of Acts (XXIV,15; XXIV,21; XXVI,6–8; XXVI,22–23; XXVIII,20) and his remarks in I Cor. XV,12 ff.

A) γνοὺς δὲ ὁ Παῦλος ὅτι τὸ ἓν μέρος ἐστὶν Σαδδουκαίων τὸ δὲ ἕτερον Φαρισαίων

It was during the reign of Queen Alexandra (76–67 B.C.) that the Pharisaic scribes, who had formerly been opposed to the Hasmonaeans, began to sit in the *Gerousia* in increasing numbers and with increasing influence. The Sadducees still made up the majority of the council, but they were obliged to take into account the opinions of the Pharisees[17]. This they did quite unwillingly as Josephus informs us:

> "For whenever they [the Sadducees] assume some office, though they submit unwillingly and perforce, yet submit they do to the formulas of the Pharisees, since otherwise the masses would not tolerate them"[18].

B) ἐγὼ Φαρισαῖός εἰμι υἱὸς Φαρισαίος

Luke strongly emphasizes (ἐγὼ εἰμι) Paul's identity as a Jew and Pharisee. By re-affirming that he was a Pharisee (and still is), Paul was appealing to the Pharisaic party in the Council as one of their fellows. The appeal to the Pharisees served to remind them that he shared in common with them a certain number of fundamental doctrines opposed to the more naturalistic beliefs of the Sadducees. By stating that he was the son of Pharisees, Paul was underlining the fact that his attachment to the Pharisaic party was not merely a personal affair, but an ancient family tradition as well. Finally the appeal to the Pharisees is a spiritual parallel to his later – political – appeal to Caesar in that both appeals sprung from the need the apostle felt for protection against his violent foes.

C) περὶ ἐλπίδος καὶ ἀναστάσεως νεκρῶν κρίνομαι

This declaration was quite pertinent for it created a diversion which worked in Paul's favour. The apostle knew that the Sanhedrin was divided along party lines[19], so he brought the discussion around to the question of the

---

17 Lohse, *op.cit.*, pg. 91.
18 *Ant.* XVIII,1.4 (17). E.T. = L.H. Feldman, *Loeb*, 1965.
19 cf. *Ant.* XIII, 10.6 (297–298): " ... the Pharisees had passed on to the people certain regulations handed down by former generations and not recorded in the Laws of Moses, for which reason they are rejected by the Sadducaean group, who hold that only those regulations should be considered valid which were written down in Scripture, and that those which had been handed down by former generations need not be observed. And concerning these matters the two parties came to have controversies and serious differences, the Sadducees having the confidence of the wealthy alone but no following among the populace, while the Pharisees have the support of the masses."
E.T. = R. Marcus, *Loeb*, 1961. Josephus is rather unflattering to the Sadducees in *BJ*. II,8.14 (166) when he says: "The Pharisees are affectionate to each other and cultivate harmonious relations with the community. The Sadducees, on the contrary, are, even among themselves, rather boorish in their behaviour, and in their intercourse with their peers are as rude as to aliens,"
E.T. = H.St.J. Thackeray, *Loeb*, 1961. cf. *Ant* XX,9.1 (200).

resurrection which was one of the central doctrinal points dividing the two parties: "for the Sadducees say that there is no resurrection, nor angel nor spirit; but the Pharisees acknowledge them all." (XXIII,8).

> "The hope of Israel, as Paul saw it was bound up with the resurrection of Christ, and thus with the general principle (held by the Pharisees) of the resurrection of the dead, ... Therefore Paul's message could be fitted into the Pharisaic framework, but not onto the Sadducaean[20]."

From the strictly legal point of view, Paul's centering his remarks on the resurrection was no response to the charges lodged against him[21]. Once again a legal confrontation had been transformed into a theological dispute.

Paul's speech succeeded in dividing the Sanhedrin along party lines: "And when he had said this, a dissension arose between the Pharsisees and the Sadducees; and the assembly was divided" (τοῦτο δὲ αὐτοῦ λαλοῦντος ἐγένετο στάσις τῶν Φαρισαίων καὶ Σαδδουκαίων καὶ ἐσχίσθη τὸ πλῆθος) (XXIII,7). The Council Chamber thus became the scene of quarreling over this point. This renewal of party antagonisms was beneficial to Paul: "and some of the scribes of the Pharisees' party stood up and contended, 'We find nothing wrong in this man. (οὐδὲν κακὸν εὑρίσκομεν ἐν τῷ ἀνθρώπῳ τούτῳ) What if a spirit or an angel spoke to him'?" (XXIII,9).

A) ἐγένετο στάσις

ἡ στάσις – here the word is used in the sense of discord, dissension or division.

The Pharisees displayed great solidarity with each other. Paul no doubt was counting on this clannish reflex when he identified himself squarely as a Pharisee and as a believer in the doctrine of the resurrection.

B) οὐδὲν κακὸν εὑρίσκομεν ἐν τῷ ἀνθρώπῳ τούτῳ

The text clearly shows that the Sanhedrin was very divided in its evaluation of the apostle's activities[22]. Some of the scribes belonging to the Pharisaic party could find nothing wrong in the apostle as his teaching on the question of the resurrection seemed to lie within the framework of traditional Pharisaic thought on this doctrinal point[23].

---

20 Bruce, pg. 411. cf. Mt. XXII,23; Mk, XII,18; Lk. XX,27. cf. *BJ* II,8.14 (162–166).
21 K. Lake, "Paul's Controversies", *BC.* Vol. V, 1933, pg. 214.
22 This is in contrast to Jesus' appearance before the Sanhedrin, where the Saviour was confronted by the total hostility of both major parties. cf. Mk. XIV,53; XIV,64; XV,1. Lk. XXII,66; XXIII, 1.
23 cf. B. Lifshitz, who writes: ".The Pharisees saw the Nazarenes as a Jewish sect just like all the others. Only the Sadducees were opposed to the Judeo-Christian community. This was certainly the reason for the sect's rather rapid expansion." (B. Lifshitz, "Jérusalem sous la Domination romaine", *ANRW.* II,8, 1977, pg. 462).

No proper investigation of Paul's case could take place in such a highly-charged atmosphere. The increasingly violent nature of the discussion and the growing danger to Paul caused Lysias to remove the apostle: "And when the dissension became violent, the tribune, afraid that Paul would be torn in pieces by them, commanded the soldiers to go down (καταβάν) and take him by force from among them and bring him into the barracks" (XXIII,10).

At the beginning of the pericope both Paul and Lysias were in the *Antonia*; then Lysias brought Paul down to the Council Chamber (κατάγω). Here Luke states that the tribune ordered his soldiers to go down (καταβαίνω) to rescue Paul. The account seems to imply — by its use of a verb indicating downward motion — that Lysias was still (or was once again) in the fortress and not with Paul in the Council Chamber. Whether the tribune did actually stay with Paul throughout his appearance in the Council Chamber is unclear from the narrative. Once again, Luke's main interest is not to describe at length the sequence of events during Paul's appearance before the Sanhedrin, but to make a precise theological point. In doing so, Luke has certainly omitted facts concerning the exact judicial nature of Paul's appearance.

Despite the legal *lacunae*, the episode plays an important role in Paul's legal history. It marked a deepening involvement of the Sanhedrin in his case. In the beginning, according to the narrative, the Sanhedrin was consulted by the tribune to give advice. Then its role seemed to change into that of a proper court. Finally a bit later, the Sanhedrin will appear as the the plaintiff formally introducing the case against Paul and demanding his extradition to its jurisdiction. Thus the episode here marks the point in Paul's legal history at which the Sanhedrin finally evolved into the formal accuser in the case. Luke uses the episode to demonstrate that the apostle's dispute with the Sadducaean party in the Sanhedrin was nothing other than doctrinal. It is here in fact that Luke transforms Paul's case from a legal issue into a mainly theological one and then goes on to develop the theological points in the subsequent apologetic speeches[24]. Luke is careful to stress that Paul's theological stand had much in common with the Pharisaic view and was therefore to be considered as a mainstream position within official Judaism. It is thus deeply significant that the Pharisaic party in the Sanhedrin found Paul guiltless of any transgression of the law and allowed the possibility that his religious activities might be due to divine directives.

---

24 P. Schubert, "The Final Cycle of Speeches in the Book of Acts", *JBL*, Vol. 87, No.1; March 1968, pg. 11.

II. Excursus: The Judicial Prerogatives of the Sanhedrin

The Sanhedrin played a significant role in the three big trials related at length in Luke-Acts: those of Jesus, Stephen and Paul. Of the three, Paul's case was by far the most complicated juridically speaking:

A) He was the only one of the three who was a Roman citizen. This gave him the benefit of a whole range of civil rights not available to Jesus or Stephen.

B) Paul was arrested by Roman officials. He thus had to be removed from Roman custody before any trial could take place before the Sanhedrin. Extraditing Paul from Roman to Jewish custody would be a long process. Just at the moment when the extradition was about to be achieved, the apostle appealed to Caesar (Acts XXV,1–11). He thus thwarted the Sanhedrin's designs by definitively removing any threat of extradition.

The Sanhedrin was a venerable institution. The Chronicler traces the constitution of the supreme tribunal at Jerusalem to King Jehoshaphat[25]. Before the Maccabaean uprising the powers of the aristocratic council of elders (*Gerousia*) were rather extensive as it was the practice of the Hellenistic kings to leave considerable freedom to the subject cities to regulate their internal affairs[26]. In the period following the Maccabaean revolt, the *Gerousia* still existed although its power had waned with the assumption of the royal title by the Hasmonaeans[27].

Josephus tells us that young Herod was summoned before the συνέδριον[28] to answer for his actions in Galilee in putting down brigands who were largely extreme nationalists[29]. This would indicate that the political and judicial power of the Sanhedrin had again increased. However when Herod had firmly established his kingdom, the Sadducees were persecuted and the Sanhedrin practically done away with[30]. The wily monarch did not rely on the various Jewish parties, but on Rome for support. He surrounded himself with Hellenistic advisers and was protected by a body of mercenary troops who were mostly Gentile.

---

25 cf. II Chronicles XIX,8.
26 E. Schürer, *THE HISTORY OF THE JEWISH PEOPLE IN THE AGE OF JESUS-CHRIST*, Edinburgh, Vol. II, 1979, pg. 203. (revised edition)
27 II Macc. I,10; IV,44; XI,27.
28 cf. *Ant.* XIV,5.4 (91); *BJ.* I,8.6 (170). Schürer notes that the term συνέδριον is used repeatedly to denote the Jerusalem council: "Since it is not usually applied to Greek city councils, the usage is somewhat peculiar, but is probably to be explained by the fact that the Jerusalem council was primarily regarded as a court of law. Indeed, this is the sense given to συνέδριον in later Greek usage". (Schürer, *op. cit.*, pg. 205).
29 *Ant.* XIV,9.4 (168–169).
30 *Ant.* XIV,9.4 (175).

Excursus: The Judicial Prerogatives of the Sanhedrin

After the deposition of Archelaus (6 A.D.) and the establishment of a provincial régime under a governor of equestrian rank whose seat was in Caesarea, the authority of the Sanhedrin again increased. This does not mean that the Sanhedrin had unlimited political or judicial power in the period after 6 A.D. The Roman governors always remained the ultimate authority in the province because they alone had the *imperium*. The Romans also reserved for themselves the right to supervise the Temple's finances and they frequently deposed the High Priests and named others to succeed them[31]. Nonetheless with the abolition of the monarchy, the Sanhedrin not only continued to direct the religious life of the population, but it also regained a measure of control in the administration of civil and criminal justice[32] even though it was still accountable to the Romans in many instances[33].

The Sanhedrin had 71 members (70 plus the president)[34]. It was presided over by the reigning High Priest[35]. The Sanhedrin was composed of three categories of persons: the High Priests, the elders and the scribes[36]. The high priestly group took in the reigning High Priest, his predecessors and the other chief priests exercising a sacerdotal or administrative role in the Temple. The elders sprang from the lay nobility of Jerusalem. Both groups were Sadducaean. The scribes were mostly Pharisees and were the theologians as it were, of the Sanhedrin. They played an important role when the Sanhedrin was called on to render justice[37].

---

31 *Ant.* XX,10.5 (249–251).
32 One of the problems in trying to determine the precise nature of the judicial competence enjoyed by the Sanhedrin is the often conflictory data furnished by the different Rabbinical and Hellenistic sources. H. Mantel notes: "While in the Hellenistic sources, in Josephus and the Gospels, it appears as a political and judicial council headed by the ruler, the Tannaitic sources depict it chiefly as a legislative body dealing with religious matters, and in rare cases, acting as a court — for instance, to try a false prophet or high Priest". (H. Mantel, "Sanhedrin", *ENCYCLOPAEDIA JUDAICA*, Jerusalem, 1971, Vol. 14, pg. 836).
33 Jn. XI,47–48.
34 *M. Sanh*. I,6. cf. Numbers XI,16; XI,24–25.
35 cf. I Macc. XIV,44; Acts V,17; VII,1; IX,1–2; XXII,5; XXIV,1. cf. *Ant.* XX,10.5 (251).
36 cf. Mk. XIV,53; Lk. XXII,66.
37 Josef Blinzler in his comprehensive book, *LE PROCES DE JESUS*, Paris, 1962 (F.T.) is cautious about the influence of the Pharisaic party in cases heard by the Sanhedrin prior to the Jewish Wars. He points out that until that event "the Sanhedrin stuck to the Sadducaean penal code of the Old Testament" (pg. 233). He notes that "the Sadducaean element in the Sanhedrin in Jesus' time still set the tone at least in certain formalities; what demonstrates this fact is that the presidents of this tribunal, the High Priests, were Sadducaean ..." (pg. 236). Comparing the Sanhedrin of before 70 A.D. with the *Beth-Din* of Jamnia, Blinzler says: "While in the old Jerusalem Sanhedrin the Pharisees asserted their influence with the Sadducees, who had their own penal code, the court of justice of Jamnia was a college of scribes whose judicial conceptions were purely Pharisaic; the Sadducaean doctrine having collapsed at the same time as the Temple". (pg. 203).

We have a certain number of indications as to the judicial procedure used when a case was heard before the supreme Jewish body. The members of the Sanhedrin were seated on raised chairs placed in a semi-circle. Two bailiffs were standing to note all the arguments for and against the defendant. The latter was in the middle of the semi-circle as were the witnesses. The defence stated its case first, followed by the plaintiffs. The accusers had to produce a minimum of two or three witnesses[38] whose testimony tallied. If the testimonies of the witnesses for the prosecution were discordant, then the case could not be sustained and the defendant was dismissed[39].

As we have seen the Sanhedrin constituted the supreme native court which the Romans allowed to continue to function even though its judicial competence was limited by the governor's *imperium*:

> "It was therefore the forum for every judicial decision and every administrative measure which could either not be dealt with by the lesser local courts or was reserved to the Roman governor himself"[40].

The Sanhedrin also exercised moral authority over the Jews in the Diaspora. Its decrees were recognized by all Jews and not only by those living in Palestine.

The Sanhedrin had the right to judge non-capital cases involving Jews and to inflict punishment in them[41]. This type of power in civil and criminal justice would point to the existence of an indigenous Jewish police force and the exercise of police power by that force where non-Roman citizens were involved[42]. The Sanhedrin could hear capital cases involving Jews and it seems likely that it could still hand down a guilty verdict in them[43]. But

---

38 cf. Deuteronomy XVII,6; XIX,15. The early Church borrowed this judicial practice from Judaism. cf. Mt. XVIII,16; 2 Cor. XIII.1; 1 Tim. V,19.

39 In Jesus' trial, the false witnesses proved to be an obstacle to the High Priest's successful prosecution of the case. cf. Mk. XIV,55–56 where the testimonies of the false witnesses neither tallied with each other nor with reality. They were thus useless to the prosecution. cf. *Bab. Talmud*, Yoma I, 19b which states that whosoever throws suspicion on an innocent party must himself bear the consequences of his act.

40 Schürer, *op.cit.*, pg. 218. H.J. Cadbury notes that "it was the general policy of Rome to leave local matters of many sorts to be settled in native courts by native law". (Cadbury, "Roman Law ...", pg. 301.). C. Saulnier sees the reason for Rome's allowing native princes and courts a certain amount of power as being due to a penury of competent Roman officials to administer the vast Empire: "In fact it seems that Rome was quite lacking when it came to administering regions which did not have a tradition of urban life in the Greek manner. In such cases Rome preferred to delegate the management of such places to princes who were more familiarized with local customs". C. Saulnier, *op.cit.*, col. 880.

41 cf. the corporal punishment meted out to Jesus (Mt. XXVI,67; Mk. XIV,65; Lk. XXII,63) and to Peter and John (Acts V,40). cf. the case of the doomsayer Jesus ben Ananias as related in *BJ*. VI,5.3 (300–309).

42 cf. Acts IV,3; V,18. Roman participation in the arrest of a non-Roman citizen was not necessary.

43 cf. Mk. XIV,64: "You have heard his blasphemy. What is your decision? And they all condemned him as deserving death." cf. Mt. XXVI, 66; XXVII,1.

the Sanhedrin could not lawfully execute a sentence of death in its own right. The martyrdom of Stephen (Acts VII,54–VIII,2) was more of an act of mob violence than anything else. The account in Acts clearly states that Stephen was dragged out of the Council Chamber before the Sanhedrin could formally pronounce sentence[44]. Carrying out the death penalty was a sign of sovereignty and sovereignty in Judaea belonged exclusively to Rome. Therefore the Sanhedrin could not carry out the death penalty without the ratification of the Roman governor[45]. This was a crucial limitation on its judicial competence. Supreme judicial power in an Imperial province remained in the governor's hands at all times as he alone was vested with the *imperium*. The governor was under no judicial constraint to carry out a death penalty decided by the Sanhedrin as his *imperium* was free-working[46]:

> "Sundry facts that we have from elsewhere in the Empire converge in this matter with testimonies relative to the situation in Judaea. They allow us to conclude that it was quite probable that the Governor of Judaea; vested with the *imperium*, alone had the power to ratify the execution of a capital sentence. Thus a Jewish trial, which finished in the handing down of a capital sentence, was relevant only to the extent that the governor accepted the condemnation and allowed the execution"[47].

An interesting example of the Sanhedrin's judicial incompetence in capital cases is given by Josephus in his account of the death of the apostle James, the brother of the Lord, in the year 62 A.D. It is clear from Josephus' account that Ananus profited from a gubernatorial interregnum to have St. James done away with:

> "Upon learning of the death of Festus, Caesar sent Albinus to Judaea as Procurator. The King removed Joseph from the High Priesthood, and bestowed the succession to this office upon the son of Ananus, who was likewise called Ananus. (...) Ananus thought that he had a favourable opportunity because Festus was dead and Albinus was still on the way. And so he convened

---

44 B. Lifshitz notes: "Stephanos' harangue irritated the multitude gathered round the Sanhedrin and some zealots judged him to be liable to death. The stoning of Stephanos, the first Christian martyr (between 31 and 36), was therefore a lynching, as the verdict of the Sanhedrin had not been handed down ...". (B. Lifshitz, "Jerusalem sous la Domination romaine", *op.cit.*, pg. 461.) So Dibelius: "In Stephen's case, it is a question of mob-law, and the event therefore does not take place as the Mishna prescribes". (Dibelius, *op.cit.*, pg. 208, note 3).
45 cf. Jn. XVIII,31: "Pilate said to them, 'Take him yourselves and judge him by your own law.' The Jews said to him, 'It is not lawful for us to put any man to death'." (ἡμῖν οὐκ ἔξεστιν ἀποκτεῖναι οὐδένα). Blinzler writes: "During the time of the Procurators, the Sanhedrin had the right to hear criminal cases and to pronounce death sentences, but the execution of the sentence was reserved for the governor, as, it seems, was the case in all Roman provinces." (J. Blinzler, *op.cit.*, pg. 239). Lemonon demonstrates rather convincingly the Sanhedrin's loss of the right to carry out the death penalty in his excellent analysis of key texts from the rabbinical tradition (e.g. the *Megillat Taanit*, the *Mekhiltas* of Rabbi Ishmael and Simeon ben Yohai etc.), J.P. Lemonon, *PILATE ET LE GOUVERNEMENT DE LA JUDEE*, Paris, 1981, pg. 81–90.
46 cf. Jn. XIX,10.
47 Lemonon, *op.cit.*, pg. 92.

the judges of the Sanhedrin and brought before them a man named James, the brother of Jesus who was called the Christ, and certain others. He accused them of having transgressed the law and delivered them up to be stoned. Those of the inhabitants of the city who were considered the most fair-minded and who were strict in the observance of the law were offended at this. They therefore secretly sent to King Agrippa urging him, for Ananus had not even been correct in his first step, to order him to desist from any further such actions. Certain of them even went to meet Albinus, who was on his way from Alexandria, and informed him that Ananus had no authority to convene the Sanhedrin without his consent. Convinced by these words, Albinus angrily wrote to Ananus threatening to take vengeance upon him. King Agrippa, because of Ananus' action, deposed him from the High Priesthood which he had held for three months and replaced him with Jesus the son of Damnaeus"[48].

The Sanhedrin was, of course, judicially incompetent in capital cases involving Roman citizens charged with political offences against Rome, such as treason. In these type of cases only the Roman authorities were legally competent[49]. So even though the Sanhedrin enjoyed a tolerably extensive jurisdiction, it was always limited by the fact that the Roman authorities could intervene in an affair and proceed independently which is exactly what they did in Paul's case[50].

As we have indicated earlier on[51], there was one sole instance in which the Sanhedrin had the right to punish a transgressor by death even if he were a Roman citizen. This was in cases where non-Jews entered the inner precincts of the Temple and thus profaned its holiness[52].

The right to execute non-Jews even if these latter were Roman citizens represented a concession of exceptional dimension accorded the Jews by Rome. Normally Roman citizens appeared before Roman judges for trial and sentencing in capital cases. So even though Paul was a Roman citizen, he could have lawfully been judged by the Sanhedrin on the charge of profanation, had the Roman authorities chosen to remand him to their custody. Moreover if the Sanhedrin had found Paul guilty of violating the inner precincts of the Temple, sentencing him to death as a result, the

---

48 *Ant.* XX,9.1 (197–203) – E.T. = L.H. Feldman, *Loeb*, 1965. Eusebius explains James' arrest as being one of the consequences of Paul's appeal to Caesar: "When Paul appealed to Caesar and was sent over to Rome by Festus the Jews were disappointed of the hope in which they had laid their plot against him and turned against James ..." (*Hist. Ecc.* II,23.1; E.T. = K. Lake, *Loeb*, 1959).
49 J. Juster, *LES JUIFS DANS L'EMPIRE ROMAIN*, Paris, 1914, Vol. II, pg. 109.
50 Schürer, *op.cit.*, Vol. II, pg. 223.
51 cf. *supra*, pg. 65 ff.
52 cf. *BJ.* VI, 2.4 (124–126). Here Josephus mentions this right in his account of Titus' speech to the besieged Jews of Jerusalem during the Jewish Wars: "Titus, yet more deeply distressed, again upbraided John and his friends. 'Was it not you,' he said, 'most abominable wretches, who placed this balustrade before your sanctuary? Was it not you that ranged along it those slabs, engraved in Greek characters and in your own, proclaiming that none may pass the barrier? And did we not permit you to put to death any who passed it, even were he Roman?" E.T. = H.St.J. Thackeray, *Loeb*, 1961. According to Philo, *Legat. ad Gaium* XXXIX, 307, a Jew, who profaned the Holy of Holies, was also liable to execution without appeal.

governor would very likely have found himself bound to ratify the sentence as Rome took cognizance of the Sanhedrin's judicial competence in matters affecting the sanctity of the Temple's holiest sections[53]. Nonetheless one should not conclude that in granting this special privilege Rome gave the Jewish court general license to impose and execute capital sentences. Jurisdiction in the case of the profanation of the Temple remained an isolated and indeed unique exception[54].

As a final note we have to remember that the Herodian rulers often played an important judicial role. This too somewhat circumscribed the Sanhedrin's jurisdiction and authority. During his long reign, Herod the Great dispensed justice and exercised capital jurisdiction[55]. Even after the establishment of gubernatorial rule in Palestine in 6 A.D., the Herodian rulers continued to pronounce the death penalty[56].

III. Paul is transferred to Caesarea

1. *The Plot to Assassinate Paul*

The preliminary investigation into Paul's case had terminated with his withdrawal from the Sanhedrin. The tribune now decided to send his prisoner to the Governor Felix at Caesarea so that the latter might be able to fully and comprehensively examine the case and hand down a decision. Lysias had conducted the police inquiry and had gathered enough information to enable him to send letters of report to Felix, but he lacked the necessary *imperium* to deal any further with the case of a Roman citizen

---

53 cf. Bruce, pg. 408; Scramuzza, *op.cit.*, pg. 282.
54 T.A. Burkill has argued that the Sanhedrin had the power to inflict capital punishment in general and was not restricted to just cases of profanation: "For if in certain circumstances the Jewish authorities could put a Roman citizen to death, a right which was not even enjoyed by the procurator himself, surely they would be formally empowered to pass and execute a capital sentence on any ordinary Jewish citizen who was found guilty of a religious offence for which the law of Moses required the infliction of the death penalty". (T.A. Burkill, "The Competence of the Sanhedrin", *VC*, Vol. 10, 1956, pg. 96). Burkill errs by not taking sufficiently into account the exclusivity of the governor's sovereign power nor the truly exceptional nature of the concession Rome granted the Jews insofar as dealing with crimes of violating the sanctity of the Temple were concerned.
55 cf. *Ant.* XV,6.2 (173).
56 Herod Antipas, the Tetrarch of Galilee, had John the Baptist killed without referring the case to the Sanhedrin (Mk. VI, 17–29; *Ant.* XVIII,5.2 (116–119). King Herod Agrippa I had James the son of Zebedee executed (Acts XII,2).

against whom serious charges had been preferred[57]. Lysias did not have the authority either to send the prisoner directly to the Emperor thereby bypassing the governor or to hand him over to a native court on a capital charge. From a judicial point of view, Lysias could do nothing else but transfer the apostle to the custody of the gubernatorial court once he had completed the preliminary examination. The Lucan account is in harmony with this standard judicial procedure.

Luke however heightens the drama and tension surrounding the first period of Paul's imprisonment by emphasizing the plot against Paul as the event precipitating the apostle's transference to Caesarea. This plot was instigated by more than forty Jews (XXIII,13), who "bound themselves by an oath neither to eat nor to drink till they had killed Paul" (XXIII, 12). These conspirators went to the chief priests and elders to inform them of their intended action and to procure their help (XXIII,14). The scribes are not mentioned in this verse; this silence would imply that the plotters approached the Sadducaean section of the Sanhedrin alone to ask their help: "You, therefore, along with the council, give notice now to the tribune (ἐμφανίσατε τῷ χιλιάρχῳ) to bring him down to you, as though you were going to determine his case more exactly. (ὡς μέλλοντας διαγινώκειν ἀκριβέστερον τὰ περὶ αὐτοῦ). And we are ready to kill him before he comes near." (XXIII,15).

A) ἐμφανίσατε τῷ χιλιάρχῳ

ἐμφανίζω – the basic meaning of the verb is to manifest, show forth or exhibit. In the legal sense it can mean to inform, to lay an information against someone or to declare something against someone[58]. The phrase "give notice now to the tribune" should not be understood as implying that the Sanhedrin could give orders to the tribune, but rather that the Sanhedrin was laying information before the Roman official in order to bring about Paul's re-appearance before them. The overall sense of the verse is that the priests and the elders are being asked to aid and abet the conspirators in their dastardly deed.

B) ὡς μέλλοντας διαγινώσκειν ἀκριβέστρον τα περὶ αὐτοῦ (Vg. = *tamquam aliquid certius cognituri de eo*)

διαγινώσκω – to 'distinguish', 'discern exactly', to 'determine'. As a law

---

[57] Sherwin-White, pg. 54.
[58] cf; Acts XXIV,1 = 'to lay their case against'; XXV,2 = to 'inform against'; XXV,15 = to 'give information about'. R. Taubenschlag notes two further legal terms related to the verb ἐμφανίζειν (the introduction of the denunciation): ἐμφανιστής, the technical term for designating the denouncer, and ἐμφανισμός, the denunciation itself. R. Taubenschlag, "Il Delatore e la sua Responsibilità nel Diritto dei Papiri", *OPERA MINORA*, Warsaw, 1959, Vol. II, 729.

term the verb means to examine or inquire into something judicially; to 'determine' or 'decide' a suit ; to 'take cognizance of an action'. cf. the expressions ὁ βασιλεὺς διαγνώσεται, the king shall take cognizance[59], and διαγινώσκω περί τινος, to give judgment[60]. The term not only denotes an investigation or inquiry, but also a determination or a decision in a case. The verb διαγινώσκω appears only twice in the NT, both times in Acts. Here it means 'making further inquiry into the case'; in XXIV,22 it means to decide a case[61].

The plot, however, was destined to be foiled: "Now the son of Paul's sister (ὁ υἱὸς τῆς ἀδελφῆς Παύλου) heard of their intended ambush; so he went and entered the barracks and told Paul. And Paul called one of the centurions (προσκαλεσάμενος δὲ ὁ Παῦλος ἕνα τῶν ἑκατονταρχῶν) and said, 'Bring this young man to the tribune; for he has something to tell him'." (XXIII,16–17). The centurion complied with Paul's wishes and Paul's nephew related the story of the plot to Lysias.

A) ὁ υἱὸς τῆς ἀδελφῆς Παύλου

This is the only mention in the Book of Acts of a member of Paul's family. The exact state of his relations with them is unknown. How the nephew learned of the plot is not stated in the text.

B) προσκαλεσάμενος δὲ ὁ Παῦλος ἕνα τῶν ἑκατονταρχῶν

Paul's imprisonment is that of a distinguished prisoner. He can receive visitors and can ask the centurion to do his bidding.

In view of this dangerous plot, Claudius Lysias decided that Paul's continued safety depended on his being removed straightaway to Caesarea. He commanded two of the centurions as follows: "At the third hour of the night get ready two hundred spearmen to go as far as Caesarea. Also provide mounts for Paul to ride and bring him safely to Felix the Governor." (XXIII,23–24)[62]. This was a change in the place of custody, not an extradition. Paul still remained a Roman prisoner.

---

59 *LS*[9], pg. 391. cf. *P. Petr.* III,43: recto, col.I, 27; III,7; IV,43–44; verso, col. III, 14; V, 13. (year 245 B.C.). cf. *P. Amh.* II, 29.18 (c. 250 B.C.). *MM*, pg. 147, notes that the expression ὁ βασιλεὺς διαγνώσεται "is to be classified with other instances of the technical legal use of διαγινώσκειν, which appears in Acts 24.22".
60 cf. Lysias VII,22.
61 cf. Acts XXV,21 for the usage of the noun διάγνωσις in the expression 'for the decision of the Emperor'.
62 cf. R.W. Davies, *op.cit.*, pg. 758–760 for evidence suggesting that the *cohortes equitatae* were often employed in police duties, in maintaining communications and in escort duty. Certain later witnesses give a vividly clear explanation of the reason for which Lysias transferred Paul to Felix: "For he (Lysias) was afraid lest the Jews snatch him away and kill him and that subsequently he himself be accused of having taken money". (sy[h], p[48] (614,2147) c g p vg[s, cl]).

2) Lysias' 'Dimissoriae Litterae'

Luke mentions letters of report (*dimissoriae litterae*) on two occasions in his account of Paul's legal history, once again manifesting that careful attention to the formalities of legal procedure which characterizes his narrative. In Acts XXV,26–27, Festus asks Agrippa to hear Paul's case because he is perplexed as to what to write to the Emperor in the letters of report which were to accompany Paul to Rome. At that moment Paul was an appellant. This situation required the judge to send the letters of report to the higher court at Rome[63]. In XXIII,25, the legal situation is different. It is the tribune who is remitting Paul to gubernatorial jurisdiction without any sort of prior appeal having been made by the prisoner. In both cases, however, the letters of report would contain the results of both the inquiry into the case and the interrogation of the prisoner as well as the reasons motivating the remission to a higher jurisdiction.

Here Luke not only mentions the letters of report, but also proceeds to represent that letter, dividing it into five distinct parts: (a) the greeting, (b) the description of the arrest, (c) the summary of the police inquiry, (d) the tribune's own opinion in the case, (e) the reasons motivating the decision to remit the prisoner.

A) *The Greeting*

"Claudius Lysias to his Excellency the Governor Felix (τῷ κρατίστῳ ἡγεμόνι Φήλικι) greeting." (XXIII,26).

κράτιστος — The Vg. translates by *optimus*. The noun κρατιστεία denotes the title of excellency. The adjective was used in addressing members of the *equester ordo* from which the procurators were often drawn[64].

ἡγεμών — The Vg. renders this term by the Latin *praesis*. The word ἡγούμενοι was used as a general designation for the Roman authorities in their diversity. The term ἡγεμών was a more precise designation for the governor[65]. The word occurs six times in Acts always in reference to the Governor of Judaea.

B) *The Resumé of Paul's Arrest*

"This man was seized by the Jews, and was about to be killed by them,

---

[63] cf. *Digest*, XLIX,6.1: "*Post appellationem interpositam litterae dandae sunt ab eo, a quo appellatum est, ad eum, qui de appellatione cogniturus est, sive principem sive quem alium, quas litteras dimissorias sive apostolos appellant*".
[64] cf. Lk. I,3: (κράτιστε Θεόφιλε). cf. *P.Fay.*, pg. 33 for the expression ὁ κράτιστος ἡγεμών which appears on an inscription from the 1st Century A.D.
[65] cf. L. Robert, "Recherches Epigraphiques", *REA*, Tome 62; 1960, pg. 329.

when I came upon them with the soldiers and rescued him, having learned that he was a Roman citizen." (XXIII,27).

This of course was not the exact sequence of events for Lysias had originally thought that Paul might have been the trouble-making Egyptian. Far from intervening to save the life of the man because he was a Roman citizen, Lysias had had him bound and had ordered his scourging. The tribune rather craftily re-arranged the facts so that he might not be discredited for his actions at a later date. He was no doubt happy to take the occasion to stress his role as a protector of a Roman citizen's life and well-being. It is nonetheless undeniable that his timely action had certainly saved Paul's life.

C) *The Summary of the Preliminary Investigation*

"And desiring to know the charge on which they accused him, (τὴν αἰτίαν δι' ἣν ἐνεκάλουν αὐτῷ), I brought him down to their council." (XXIII,28).

1) τὴν αἰτίαν

ἡ αἰτία – a cause deserving punishment (cf. Latin *causa*); hence accusation or charge of crime. Fundamentally ἡ αἰτία implies the imputation of guilt in a crime. It is the ground of accusation, the crime involved in the charge.

2) δι' ἣν ἐνεκάλουν αὐτῷ Vg. = *quam obiciebant illi*)

ἐγκαλέω – The word occurs seven times in the NT, six of them in Acts. It means to 'bring a charge' or 'accusation' against someone, to 'accuse'. As a law term, it means to 'prosecute', 'take proceedings against'[66]. The verb ἐγκαλέω is akin to κατηγορέω in meaning. κατηγορέω signifies the formal and public accusation of a defendant by plaintiffs before a court. ἐγκαλέω also denotes the bringing forth publicly of an accusation, but not necessarily in a formal procedure before the court. Κατηγορέω stresses the formal judicial procedure involved; ἐγκαλέω the open averment.

D) *His Opinion of Paul's Case*

"I found that he was accused about questions of their law, but charged with nothing deserving death or imprisonment." (ὃν εὗρον ἐγκαλούμενον περὶ ζητημάτων τοῦ νομου αὐτῶν μηδὲν δὲ ἄξιον θανάτου ἢ δεσμῶν ἔχοντα ἔγκλημα) (XXIII,29).

---

[66] *LS*^{9}, pg. 469–470.

1) ἔχοντα ἔγκλημα

τὸ ἔγκλημα – the accusation, crime with which one is charged. (cf. Latin *crimen*). The word appears only twice in the NT, here and at XXV,16. J. Dupont defines the ἔγκλημα as "the criminal act of which the defendant is accused and by which his foe would like to have him condemned"[67].

Luke once again stresses a very important point in his relation of Paul's legal history: a Roman official judges the dispute between Paul and the Sanhedrin to be essentially theological involving no infraction of Roman law. Lysias' opinion parallels that of Gallio and is part of a conscious pattern on Luke's part aimed at demonstrating to his Roman audience that Paul was really innocent of all political charges.

E) *Paul's Transfer*

"And when it was disclosed to me that there would be a plot against the man, I sent him to you at once ordering his accusers (παραγγείλας καὶ τοῖς κατηγόροις) also to state before you what they have against him." (λέγειν πρὸς αὐτὸν ἐπὶ σοῦ). (XXIII,30).

1) παραγγείλας καὶ τοῖς κατηγόροις λέγειν πρὸς αὐτὸν ἐπὶ σοῦ

Luke introduces a piece of information in his account of Lysias' letter which he had not earlier mentioned in the narrative: the accusers were also ordered to appear before the governor to restate their accusations. Here the tribune was following normal procedure. The law required that during the court proceedings, the accused be confronted face to face with his accuser before the judge. If the accuser failed to appear, he could very well lose the case by default. The judge had to allow the defendant the possibility of refuting the accusations and of defending himself as completely as possible. He always had to have the right to make his *apologia*[68]. Confronting one's accusers in front of the judge was of paramount importance in safeguarding the rights of the defence. If the defendant were not able to answer his accuser directly in front of the judge, "*aequitas* would not be assured"[69].

Thus Paul, accompanied by a heavily-armed escort, was transferred to Caesarea: "So the soldiers according to their instructions, took Paul and brought him by night to Antipatris." (XXIII,31). From there only the horsemen accompanied him to Caesarea (XXIII,32), where upon arrival they delivered Paul and the letters of report to Felix (XXIII,33).

---

67 J. Dupont, "Aequitas Romana", *ETUDES SUR LES ACTES DES APOTRES*, Paris, 1967, pg. 539.
68 *Ant.* XVII,5.6 (127).
69 Dupont, "Aequitas Romana", *op.cit.*, pg. 535.

Chapter VI
Caesarea (Part 1): Paul and Felix

I. The Procuratorship in Judaea: Judicial Competence and Exercise of Criminal Jurisdiction

As we have seen from Acts XXIII,33, Paul's guard delivered Lysias' letter to the Governor Felix in Caesarea and presented Paul before him:

A) *Caesarea*

Originally Strato's Tower, Caesarea Maritima was re-built by Herod the Great and was finished in c. 13 B.C.[1]. It was the capital of the province of Judaea and a port of strategic importance. Although a large number of Jews lived there, the city had no real Jewish character. Greeks and Hellenized Orientals were far more numerous than the Jewish inhabitants[2]. The city is mentioned several times in Acts in addition to the account of Paul's imprisonment there. It was the scene of Philip's ministry (Acts VIII,40; XXI,8), of Cornelius' conversion (X,1 ff) and of Herod's death (XII,19 ff). Acts also mentions the existence of a group of disciples in Caesarea (XXI, 16). The scene of Paul's trial thus moves from a Jewish to a Hellenistic setting.

B) *Felix*

Paul's case was to be heard by Antonius Felix, the Governor of Judaea since 52 A.D.[3]. Like Gallio, Felix was a well-known and well-connected

---

1 cf. *Ant.* XV,9.6 (331–341) and *BJ.* I,21.5 (408–415) for a description of the building of Caesarea.
2 cf. B. Lifshitz, "Cesarée de Palestine, son Histoire et ses Institutions", *ANRW*, II,8; 1977, pg. 514.
3 The Province of Judaea in Felix' time consisted of Archelaus' old ethnarchy (Idumaea, Judaea proper, Samaria) and a portion of Herod Antipas' tetrarchy (part of Galilee and Peraea). Philip's tetrarchy and the other portion of Antipas' tetrarchy were ruled by King Herod Agrippa II.

figure at Rome. He was a freedman of the imperial family[4] and a member of the socially prestigious and politically powerful Equestrian Order[5].

Felix was the brother of Pallas, the favourite of Emperor Claudius. Suetonius notes that Claudius was also fond of Felix "giving him the command of cohorts and of troops of horse, as well as of the province of Judaea"[6]. Tacitus mentions Felix in the *Annals* where he stigmatizes him for his iniquity and misgovernment:

> "The like moderation [of Pallas], however, was not shown by his brother, surnamed Felix; who for a while past had held the governorship of Judaea, and considered that with such influences behind him all malefactions would be venial"[7].

The great Latin historian was even more scathing (but not more objective) in the *Histories*:

> "Claudius made Judaea a province and entrusted it to Roman knights or to freedmen; one of the latter, Antonius Felix, practised every kind of cruelty and lust, wielding the power of a King with all the instincts of a slave"[8].

The governor had had considerable experience in Palestine[9] and was well acquainted with the Jewish nation, the diverse and sundry tendencies present in Judaism and with the vicissitudes of Roman rule in that troubled land. Felix' governorship was marked by a disregard for the Jewish religion and for Jewish customs, provoking in turn an ever-increasing hostility to Roman rule.

There were three terms which were generally used to designate the provincial governors of equestrian rank in Judaea: the official terms *Procurator* ($\grave{\epsilon}\pi\acute{\iota}\tau\rho o\pi o\varsigma$) and *Praefectus* ($\check{\epsilon}\pi\alpha\rho\chi o\varsigma$) and the more general designation of Governor ($\acute{\eta}\gamma\epsilon\mu\acute{\omega}\nu$)[10]. During the later Republic and the reigns of the first two Emperors, the title procurator was a private law term designating a person to whom the charge, responsibility or administration of something

---

4 E. Schürer notes that "the conferring of a Procuratorship with military command on a freedman was unprecedented, and can only be accounted for by the influence exercised by freedmen at the court of Claudius." (Schürer, *op.cit.*, Vol. I, pg. 460–461). J.P. Lemonon *op.cit.*, pg. 55 writes of the growing importance of the freedmen in the imperial administration during the reign of Claudius: "They often directed the imperial services in Rome and Italy. In the provinces they were more often than not assistants to the Knights. Nonetheless freedmen were to be found in the government of the provinces; such was Felix' case in Judaea. Indeed Felix had doubtlessly been assimilated into the Equestrian Order beforehand, because, although freedmen played an important role under Claudius, officially their duties were linked to a domestic function".
5 cf. G. Alföldy, "Die Stellung der Ritter in der Führungsschicht des Imperium Romanum", *CHIRON*, Munich, Band 11; 1981, pg. 182.
6 Suetonius, *Claud.* XXVIII. – E.T. = J.C. Rolfe, *Loeb*, 1959.
7 Tacitus, *Ann.* XII,54. – E.T. = J. Jackson, *Loeb*, 1963.
8 Tacitus, *Hist.* V,9. – C.H. Moore, *Loeb*, 1962.
9 *Ant.* XX,7.1 (137); *BJ.* II,12.8 (247). cf. Tacitus, *Ann.* XII,54.
10 cf. *Digest* I,18.1: "*Praesidis nomen generale est eoque et proconsules et legati Caesaris et omnes provincias regentes ... praesides appellantur;*".

was entrusted. He was a private steward, intendant and financial manager[11]. The procurators of the first two Emperors were their private agents:

> "They fall into two classes, the procurators of the provinces, who handled all the Emperor's financial affairs within each and the lesser procurators who were bailiffs of individual estates which the Emperor owned in a private capacity"[12].

Thus under Augustus and Tiberius, it was the prefect who had real administrative power and who enjoyed civil and criminal jurisdiction in a province of equestrian rank[13]. Starting from Claudius' reign, however, the term procurator evolved into an accepted title designating the governor of imperial provinces of equestrian rank (*procurator Augusti*), the main exception being the prefect of Egypt. The adoption of this title revealed the increasingly significant role the Emperor played in the administration of the Empire as well as the more important place accorded the Equestrian Order[14]:

> "Several times in this year [53 A.D.], the Emperor was heard to remark that judgements given by his procurators ought to have as much validity as if the ruling had come from himself. In order that the opinion should not be taken as a chance indiscretion, provision — more extensive and fuller than previously — was made to that effect by a senatorial decree as well. For an order of the deified Augustus had conferred judicial powers on members of the equestrain order, holding the government of Egypt; their decisions to rank as though they had been formulated by the national magistrates. Later, both in other provinces and in Rome, a large number of cases till then falling under the cognizance of the praetors were similarly transferred; and now Claudius handed over in full the judicial power so often disputed by sedition or by arms"[15].

In the province of Judaea all three designations were used. In the *Jewish Wars*, Josephus names Coponius, the first Governor of Judaea (6–9 A.D.) and Pontius Pilate, the fifth governor (26–36 A.D.) as procurators[16]. Tacitus and Philo also call Pilate a procurator[17]. In the *Jewish Antiquities*, Josephus uses the term ἡγεμών to designate Pilate[18]. This is the less formal

---

11 cf. Lemonon, *op.cit.*, pg. 51 for a description of the private functions of the earlier procurators, and P.A. Brunt, "Princeps and Equites", *JRS*, Vol. 73; 1983, pg. 52–53 for a description of the functions of the patrimonial and fiscal procurators. cf. Tacitus, *Ann.* IV,15 and Dio Cassius LIII,15.1–5.
12 A.H.M. Jones, "Procurators and Prefects in the Early Principate", *ROMAN GOVERNMENT AND LAW*, Oxford, 1968, pg. 123.
13 J.P. Lemonon, *op.cit.*, pg. 52. In the smaller imperial provinces, the same man could hold both these distinct offices. Thus Pontius Pilate was the *Praefectus* of Judaea with all the military, judicial and administrative powers inherent in the governorship. At the same time he took care of the Emperor's private financial affairs in the province (procurator). The term *Procurator et Praefectus* occurs in a number of inscriptions especially under the Flavians. cf. *CIL.* X,8023.4; *ILS.* 5350. The title prefect was probably added to stress the military functions of the officials in question. cf. *CIL.* II,3271; XII,2455.
14 cf. P.A. Brunt, "Procuratorial Jurisdiction", *LATOMUS*, Tome 25, 1966, pg. 463; J.P. Lemonon, *op.cit.*, pg. 56–57.
15 Tacitus, *Ann.* XII,60. — E.T. = J. Jackson, *Loeb*, 1963.
16 *BJ.* II,8.1 (117); II,9.2 (169).
17 Tacitus, *Ann.* XV,44; Philo, *Legat. ad Gaium* XXXVIII,299.
18 *Ant.* XVIII,3.1 (55).

title to which the NT writers, especially Matthew, have recourse when describing Jesus' judge[19]. Josephus calls Valerius Gratus, Pilate's predecessor (15—26 A.D.) a prefect[20]. An inscription in Latin discovered during the third season of excavations at the theater in Caesarea (1961) provides vital epigraphical evidence that Pilate had the title of prefect[21]. The designation of Cuspius Fadus (44—46 A.D.) is more complicated. Josephus refers to him as a prefect[22] and as a procurator[23]. He designates Cumanus (48—52 A.D.) and Felix (52—59 A.D.), as procurators[24] and Felix' successor, Festus (59—62 A.D.) as a prefect[25]. In the final analysis, it would seem more correct to term the Governors of Judaea from the deposition of Archelaus to the reign of Agrippa I (6—41 A.D.) as prefects and the governors from the restoration of the Roman province to the Jewish Wars (44—66 A.D.) as procurators[26].

The governor of an imperial province had wide powers[27]. He had his own *imperium* which he enjoyed as a result of his appointment by the Emperor and which lasted as long as his term of office[28]. This does not mean of course that he was totally free in his jurisdiction. He was bound by his own Edict, which he fixed at the beginning of his term of office, setting out the actions he was prepared to follow (*ius edicendi*). These carefully-framed magisterial edicts had to be, in turn, in conformity with existing *leges* and *senatusconsulta*. The whole body of edicts constituted one of the essential and most original sources of classical law[29]. Moreover, when-

---

19 Mt. XXVII,2,11,14,15,21,27; XXVIII,14; cf. Lk. XX,20.
20 *Ant.* XVIII,2.2 (33).
21 From 1959 to 1964 the Italian Archeological Mission of the Istituto Lombardo (Milan) conducted six series of excavations on the site of ancient Caesarea. In 1961 a stone was found in the theater on which was inscribed the name of Pontius Pilate and his title *Praefectus*. Dr. Frova writes: "The major importance of the inscription lies in the fact that for the first time there is an epigraphical witness to the name of Pontius Pilate, governor of Judaea from 26 to 36 A.D., who is known solely from Graeco-Roman literary sources and almost exclusively in relationship to Christ". (A. Frova, "L'Iscrizione di Ponzio Pilato a Cesarea" *RENDICONTI*, Classe di Lettere e Scienze Morali e Storiche, Istituto Lombardo, Milan, Vol. 95; 1961, pg. 428. cf. J. Vardaman, "A New Inscription which mentions Pilate as *Prefect*", *JBL*, Vol. 81, No. 1, March 1962, pgs. 70—71.
22 *Ant.* XIX,9.2 (363).
23 *Ant.* XX,1.1 (2); *BJ.* II,11.6 (220).
24 *Ant.* XX,6.2 (132); XX,8.5 (162); *BJ.* II,12.8 (247).
25 *Ant.* XX.8.11 (193).
26 H.J. Mason notes that the classical authors "are in fact of little use in solving the question of the change of titulature. (...) It is unlikely therefore that any term used by these authors for the Governor of Judaea reflects his precise title or any change in it". (Mason, *GREEK TERMS*, pg. 142—143).
27 Josephus mentions the governor's administrative and judicial powers in *Ant.* XVIII,1.1 (2); *BJ.* II,8.1 (117).
28 Dio Cassius LIII, 13.6—8.
29 J. Gaudemet, *op.cit.*, pg. 574—580.

ever the interests of the state were at stake, the governor was duty bound to intervene and to punish and repress if necessary. The governor's actions could also be cancelled by the Emperor if he chose to intervene in an affair through his *imperium maius*[30].

The governor had the power to inflict the death penalty in a certain number of circumstances. He held the *ius gladii* over the troops under his command[31]. His right of *coercitio* over the citizen soldiers was unfettered as the troops were not protected by the right of *provocatio* once they were outside Rome[32]. The governor had the power to inflict the death penalty on civilians in military matters[33]. He could also inflict it on non-Roman citizens living in the province without hindrance[34]. The *ius gladii* and other sanctions were possessed by the governors as an integral and inherent part of their office[35]. In the case of Judaea, Josephus notes that when Coponius was sent out by Augustus to be the first governor of that province, he was entrusted by the Princeps with full powers, including the infliction of capital punishment[36].

The governor could also try, condemn and execute a Roman citizen on a capital charge provided that an appeal from the prisoner did not suspend the sentence handed down[37]. The Roman citizen's right to appeal to Rome to have his case heard there put a significant limitation on the workings of the provincial governor's jurisdiction. The legal protection which a Roman citizen enjoyed due to his right to appeal to Rome was real, comprehensive and effective. The *ius provocationis* was a citizen's personal right, inherent in his citizenship and was his no matter where he went in the Empire[38].

We have to note the existence of cases in which Roman citizens were in fact executed by provincial governors. These cases point to exceptions (or loopholes) in the laws protecting Roman citizens from capital punishment at the hands of provincial governors[39].

---

30 *Digest* I,18.4. P. Horovitz writes that the procurator had judicial independence and that his power was "without limit and without restriction on the part of any authority except that of the Emperor himself". ("Essai sur les Pouvoirs des Procurateurs-Gouverneurs", *RBPH*, Tome 17; 1938, pg. 54).
31 Dio Cassius LIII,13.6–8. A.H.M. Jones notes that the *ius gladii* was originally "a power granted to army commanders to execute Roman soldiers, but not civilians, under their jurisdiction". ("I appeal to Caesar", *ROMAN GOVERNMENT AND LAW*, Oxford, 1968, pg. 60.)
32 A. Giovannini, *op.cit.*, pg. 26.
33 Th. Mommsen, *STAATSRECHT*, Vol. II, pg. 270.
34 *BJ*. II,14.1 (271).
35 *Digest* I,18.6.8. cf. P. Garnsey, "The Criminal Jurisdiction of Governors", *JRS*, Vol. 58; 1968, pg. 52.
36 *BJ*. II,8.1 (117).
37 P. Garnsey, *op.cit.*, pg. 54.
38 A. Giovannini, *op.cit.*, pg. 26.
39 Th. Mommsen, *STAATSRECHT*, Vol. II, pg. 269, n.5.

Suetonius gives an account of a trial which illustrates this point. The judge in the legal proceedings was none other than Galba, the future Emperor, but who was at that time governor of Hispania Tarraconensis. According to Suetonius' account, Galba

> "crucified a man for poisoning his ward, whose property he was to inherit in case of his death; and when the man invoked the law and declared that he was a Roman citizen (*implorantique leges et civem Romanum se testificanti*), Galba, pretending to lighten his punishment by some consolation and honour, ordered that a cross much higher than the rest and painted white be set up, and the man transferred to it"[40].

Another example is given by Josephus in his account of an event that occurred during the administration of Florus, Governor of Judaea from 65 to 66 A.D.:

> "For Florus ventured that day to do what none had ever done before, namely, to scourge before his tribunal (μαστιγῶσαί τε πρὸ τοῦ βήματος) and nail to the cross men of equestrian rank, men who, if Jews by birth, were at least invested with that Roman dignity"[41].

The governor's main administrative concern was the *salus publica*. Consequently he tended to leave cases of lesser importance to be heard by municipal or native courts while he himself concentrated on weightier matters affecting public order or well-being:

> "These were largely but not solely the capital crimes of the Roman *ordo*. But since the traditions of provincial government were established long before the *ordo* was completed, provincial jurisdiction was based on the *imperium* and the free exercise of the governor's judgement. He might follow local custom if he liked, and in the period of the Principate he was also free to adopt the rules of the *ordo* where this was appropriate. There was no compulson to do so ..."[42].

Sherwin-White goes on to write that the governor "would probably follow the lead of the *ordo* in the field covered by the statutory criminal laws, *leges publicae*, though more in the formulation of the charges than of penalties"[43].

Not all offenses were covered by the *ordo*. Others came under a type of administrative justice called *cognitio extra ordinem*[44], a term which refers to those proceedings not authorized for the *quaestiones perpetuae*. In *extra ordinem* procedure, the governor could render justice directly in virtue of his personal *cognitio*. Justice was rendered in the name of the Emperor, in the absence of formally constituted juries.

---

40 Suetonius, *Galba* IX – E.T. = J.C. Rolfe, *Loeb*, 1959.
41 *BJ*. II.14.9 (308) – E.T. = H.St.J. Thackeray, *Loeb*, 1961.
42 Sherwin-White, pg. 14–15.
43 *Ibid*, pg. 22–23.
44 I. Buti notes that the birth of *extra ordinem* procedure coincided with the assertion of the authority of the imperial régime and "appeared in its diverse forms as one of the expressions of the tendency of the Princeps to make his own presence increasingly felt with what one might term *creative interventions* in the field of law as in other fields". I. Buti, "La '*Cognitio extra Ordinem*'", *ANRW*. II,14; 1982, pg. 31.

In *extra ordinem* cases, judicial procedure was usually as follows:

A) The case was heard by the governor in person (personal *cognitio*). He was normally seated on the tribunal (*in sede tribunalis*) and was assisted by his *consilium* or council of advisers. A *notarius* was responsible for writing up the minutes of the proceedings. The trial itself (although not the preliminary hearing) was usually open to the public[45].

B) There was a formal act of accusation made in court by private accusers (*delatores*). The method was accusatorial (i.e. use of private accusers) and not inquisitorial, where the prosecutor was the judge on the bench (*inquisitor*).

C) The defendant was called to the courtroom where he confronted his accusers face to face. If the accuser failed to appear, it was assumed that he had dropped his case against the defendant. After the prosecution had rested its case, the defendant was allowed to make his *apologia*. The burden of proof rested on the accuser[46].

D) The magistrate could arbitrarily define the nature and extent of the defendant's alleged misdeeds. J. Dupont has pointed out that in trial procedure, the magistrate had the power to weigh the merits of the charges contained in the indictment and could do so even in the absence of the accusers[47] i.e. on the basis of a simple *delatio* alone[48]. This was however exceptional as normally the accusers had to appear in court. The magistrate could also arbitrarily decide what range of penalties might be applied if the defendant were found guilty[49]. The governor was not obliged to deal with the accusation precisely as it was formulated by the accusers. He had flexibility in both establishing the *crimen* and in determining the punishment.

E) The governors had the power of immediate decision. They could release a prisoner, sentence him themselves, hand the case over to a competent local court, or in more complicated cases, send the prisoner on to Rome. They also had the right to postpone their decision indefinitely (as Felix did in Paul's case). The prisoner, although uncondemned, remained in custody.

Paul's appearances before the Governors Felix and Festus are very good examples of the workings of *extra ordinem* procedure in the provincial court of an imperial province:

---

45 E.J. Urch, "Procedure in the Courts of the Roman Provincial Governors", *CJ.* Vol. 25, No. 2; November 1929, pg. 93.
46 *Ibid*, pg. 98.
47 J. Dupont, "Aequitas Romana", *op.cit.*, pg. 530, note 11a.
48 Munier, *op.cit.*, pg. 228.
49 Jones, "I Appeal unto Caesar", *op.cit.*, pg. 58.

A) The governors heard the case in person, i.e. there was a formal prosecution of the case in court. Luke notes that Festus heard the case seated on the tribunal (Acts XXV,6) and that he later consulted his *consilium* before declaring that Paul's appeal to Caesar had been allowed (XXV,12).

B) The charges were made by private accusers:

1) The denunciation by the Asian Jews in the Temple court had led to the apostle's arrest and the institution of the police proceedings (XXI, 28);

2) The formal charges laid against Paul in the governor's court by the Jewish leading men set the judicial proceedings in motion (XXIV,5–6; XXV,7).

C) Paul was allowed to make his *apologia* (XXIV,10–21; XXV,8).

D) Felix decided to postpone making any decision in Paul's case (XXIV, 22) and kept the apostle imprisoned. Festus allowed Paul's case to go before Caesar (XXV,12).

II. Paul is handed over to Felix: the Question of *Forum Domicilii*

The first thing that Felix did upon reading Lysias' letter was to ask Paul "to what province he belonged (ἐκ ποίας ἐπαρχείας ἐστίν)." (XXIII,34a). Paul's answer to that question was that he was "from Cilicia" (XXIII,34b). Whereupon Felix answered: "I will hear you when your accusers arrive." (διακούσομαί σου ἔφη ὅταν καὶ οἱ κατήγοροί σου παραγένωνται). (XXIII, 35a). In the interim, Paul was "to be guarded in Herod's Praetorium". (ἐν τῷ πραιτωρίῳ τοῦ Ἡρῴδου). (XXIII,35b).

A) ἐκ ποίας ἐπαρχείας ἐστίν / ἀπὸ Κιλικίας

The initial step in the procedure was to ascertain where Paul was officially domiciled. In cases where a crime took place outside the accused's native province, the examining magistrate had the possibility of either sending him back to his native province to be judged there (*forum domicilii*) or of conducting the trial in the province in which the crime took place (*forum delicti*). In the Lucan account of Jesus' trial, the question of *forum domicilii* also comes up: "When Pilate heard this, he asked whether the man was a Galilean. And when he heard that he belonged to Herod's jurisdiction (ὅτι ἐκ τῆς ἐξουσίας Ἡρῴδου ἐστίν), he sent him over to

Herod, who was himself in Jerusalem at that time"⁵⁰. In commenting this passage, F. Bovon notes that *forum domicilii* was never more than an option:

> "It was said that a criminal should have been judged in his home province (*forum domicilii*) and not in the province in which the crime was committed (*forum delicti*). In fact this appears to be a late usage and it appears that it concerned only *ordo* jurisdiction. In the early Principate, cases were handled in the province in which the act had been perpetrated"⁵¹.

The jurist Celsus writes that there is no dobut that a person charged should be judicially examined by the governor of the province in which the action took place whatever the accused's home province might have been. The jurist makes it clear that the practice of remitting a man held in custody to his own province is a practice of some governors, but is by no means either mandatory or universally applied: *"Illud a quibusdam observari solet, ut, cum cognovit et constituit, remittat illum cum elogio ad eum, qui provinciae praeest, unde is homo est, quod ex.causa faciendum est"*⁵².

In Paul's case, Felix' question about his province of origin remained an isolated fact, one of information-gathering more than anything else. The governor did not seem to have drawn any conclusions from the fact that Paul was from Cilicia nor did he seem to have seriously entertained the idea of referring Paul's case back to his native province.

B. διακούσομαι σου ἔφη ὅταν καὶ οἱ κατήγοροί σου παραγένωνται (Vg. = *audiam te inquit cum accusatores tui venerint*)

διακούω — to hear through, fully or to the end. The legal sense here is to hear a case in court (*audire*). When used with the Genitive of persons, the verb means to hear both parties to a dispute⁵³. Felix promises to formally hear the case as soon as the accusers arrive to press charges. This first exchange between the governor and the prisoner was an informal audience. Its purpose was to enable Felix to establish the juridical competence of his court in the case at hand and to determine the *nominis delatio*⁵⁴. The promise of an early audience was a great boon to all parties in the case as delays in court procedure were very often lengthy.

C. ἐν τῷ πραιτωρίῳ τοῦ Ἡρῴδου

The *Praetorium* was originally the place, a tent or a more stable building, which was attributed in the Roman camp to the military commander

---

50 Lk. XXIII,6—7.
51 F. Bovon, *LES DERNIERS JOURS DE JESUS*, Neuchâtel, 1974, pg. 66.
52 *Digest* XLVIII,3.11.
53 cf. Dio Cassius XXXVI,53.2; *SIG*⁴, 599.20; 685.29.
54 C. Munier, *op.cit.*, pg. 229—230.

(*praetor*) and which was his headquarters. In addition to this military usage, the term *Praetorium* was also used in the later Republic to denote the official residence of a Roman governor. Under the Principate the word designated the residence of any provincial governor whether he be a proconsul, a propraetor, a procurator or a prefect[55]. The *Praetorium* referred to here was the palace built by Herod the Great and subsequently taken over and used as headquarters by the Roman governors of Judaea[56].

III. Tertullus the Rhetor presents the Case against Paul

The governor had told Paul that the hearing would take place quite soon and such proved to be the case: "And after five days the High Priest (ὁ ἀρχιερεύς) Ananias came down with some elders (μετὰ πρεσβυτέρων τινῶν) and a spokesman (ῥήτορος), one Tertullus. They laid before the governor their case against Paul" (οἵτινες ἐνεφάνισαν τῷ ἡγεμόνι κατὰ τοῦ Παύλου)(XXIV,1).

A) ἀρχιερεύς /μετὰ πρεσβυτέρων τινῶν

Paul's accusers were no longer some anonymous Jews visiting Jerusalem from Asia, but the High Priest himself and some of the elders — the highest authority of the Jewish nation. Their presence is meant to underline the seriousness of the case and serves as a justification for all the precautions Lysias took in protecting Paul.

B) ῥήτορος

The presence of a Rhetor was not mandatory. Tertullus' presence also underlines the importance and complexity of the case.

The basic meaning of ῥήτωρ is speaker or orator. In Athens especially, οἱ ῥήτορες were the public speakers in the ἐκκλησία. The word came to mean a rhetorician or a teacher of eloquence. In this passage, it denotes a

---

[55] P. Benoit, "Prétoire, Lithostraton et Gabbatha", *RB*, Tome 59; 1952, pg. 533.
[56] It was not infrequent for provincial governors to be installed in former royal palaces. Cicero mentions in *Verr.* II,v.31.80 that King Hiero's palace in Syracuse was now the regular quarters of the governors of Sicily. The term appears in the Gospel accounts of our Lord's Passion: Mt. XXVII,27; Mk. XV,16; Jn. XVIII,28; XVIII,33; XIX,9.
Paul writes in the Philippians that it had become known in the whole *Praetorium* that his imprisonment was for Christ (Phil. I,13).

speaker in court, i.e. an advocate[57]. The rhetor was one who was trained in the art of Greek rhetoric and a man experienced in Roman legal procedure[58]. The Romans were impressed by beautiful rhetoric and responded favourably to it[59].

It cannot be determined from the text if Tertullus were Roman, Greek or Jew, but Acts XXIV,6b (Western Text) implies that he was a Greek-speaking Jew as he spoke of "our" Law[60].

C) οἵτινες ἐνεφάνισαν τῷ ἡγεμόνι κατὰ τοῦ Παύλου (*qui adierunt praesidem adversus Paulum*)

ἐμφανίζω[61] — By formally putting forth the complaint, the plaintiffs set into motion the whole trial procedure. The beginning of a judicial action consisted of a formal declaration on the accuser's part that he wished to pursue such and such person as being guilty of a crime.

It was for the plaintiffs to speak first: "And when he was called, (κληθέντος δὲ αὐτοῦ), Tertullus began to accuse him, saying, 'Since through you we enjoy much peace, (πολλῆς εἰρήνης τυγχάνοντες), and since by your provision, most excellent Felix, reforms are introduced on behalf of this nation, in every way and everywhere we accept this with all gratitude. But, to detain you no further, I beg you in your kindness (ἐπιεικείᾳ) to hear us briefly'." (XXIV,2–4).

A) κληθέντος δὲ αὐτοῦ

The subject of the Genitive Absolute construction is ambiguous[62]. The word αὐτοῦ could either refer to Paul's being called to the courtroom or Tertullus' being called on to present the case for the plaintiffs. The former seems the more likely. Τέρτυλλος is in the nominative and is the subject of the main verb. Classical Greek usage would call for another subject for

---

[57] *P. Oxy.* I, 37, col. I, 3–4 (49 A.D.): "In court, Pesouris vs. Saraeus. Aristocles, advocate (ῥήτωρ) for Pesouris ...". cf. *P. Flor.* I, 61.24 (The papyrus is entitled 'Processo verbale di una udienza del Prefetto').
[58] A Wikenhauser, *op.cit.*, pg. 256.
[59] cf. Pliny, *Ep.* IV,22. Here Pliny writes that Trebonius Rufinus, Duumvir of Vienna in Gallia Narbonensis, "pleaded his own cause so successfully as eloquently; and what particularly recommended his speech was, that he delivered it with the deliberate gravity proper to a true Roman and a good citizen in dealing with a personal matter." E.T. = W.M.L. Hutchinson, *Loeb*, 1961. This text shows that a rhetor's presence was not an indispensable part of legal procedure at least in the imperial court.
[60] The Western Text Ψ (E 69 614)pm c e g p^c dem vg^{scl} sy∫ R^m reads καὶ κατὰ τὸν ἡμέτερον νόμον ἠθελήσαμεν κρῖναι = Vg. *voluimus secundum legem nostram iudicare*.
[61] cf. *supra*, pg. 104.
[62] cf. *P. Oxy.* IX.1204.13. In this papyrus the record of the hearing starts with a Genitive Absolute construction. For the use of the Genitive Absolute in Hellenistic Greek, cf. *Bl. Debr.* 423.6; Zerwick, *GB.*, pg. 19.

the Genitive Absolute construction, although admittedly NT usage might be more flexible on this point. Secondly Luke may have intended κληθέντος to stand for the Latin *vocare*: to summon to court. In that case Paul would be meant and not the rhetor. Indeed the Vg. is quite specific here as to whom is meant when it translates: "*Et citato Paulo, coepit accusare Tertullus, dicens ...*".

B) πολλῆς εἰρήνης τυγχάνοντες

Tertullus' phrase *much peace* rings hollow. It is quite the contrary to the real situation prevailing in Palestine at that time. Tertullus made the statement merely to flatter Felix as Roman governors in general prided themselves on having maintained peace and public order in their provinces.

C) ἐπιείκεια

Luke as always is sensitive to literary norms and considerations. He has the rhetor begin his speech with a *captatio benevolentiae*. Luke gives us a good example of this rhetorical device in his reconstruction of Tertullus' exordium. It contains the standard vocabulary customarily used in such introductions: *great peace, detain/weary you no further, briefly*. The use of the word ἐπιείκεια for example was frequent in just such complimentary expressions when appealing to officials.

The *captatio benevolentiae* had an important role to play in Tertullus' presentation:

1) This laudatory introduction to his main speech was in accordance with the standard form of rhetoric in use in the ancient world:

2) Tertullus was enthusiastic in his praise of Felix. This surely would not damage his clients' standing in the eyes of the governor.

3) Tertullus took care to depict the Jewish nation and authorities as being friendly to Felix, grateful for all the benefits they had enjoyed during his governorship. Felix would certainly not want to shake this friendship to its foundations by rendering a verdict unfavourable to the Jewish leadership. All this was perhaps a subtle reminder to the governor of the difficulties which his predecessors had had with the Jewish leadership and how detrimental those differences could be to their careers.

After this promising exordium, Tertullus went into the main body of his speech, the putting forth of the charges against Paul: "We have found this man a pestilent fellow, (εὑρόντες γὰρ τὸν ἄνδρα τοῦτον λοιμόν), an agitator among all the Jews throughout the world, (καὶ κινοῦντα στάσεις πᾶσιν τοῖς Ἰουδαίοις τοῖς κατὰ τὴν οἰκουμένην), and a ringleader of the sect of the Nazarenes. (πρωτοστάτην τε τῆς τῶν Ναζωραίων αἱρέσεως). He even tried to profane the Temple, but we seized him." (ὃς καὶ τὸ ἱερὸν ἐπείρασεν βεβηλῶσαι ὃν καὶ ἐκρατήσαμεν) (XXIV, 5–6a).

A) εὑρόντες γὰρ τὸν ἄνδρα τοῦτον λοιμὸν

λοιμός – In the LXX, the term denotes a rebel, plotter or conspirator[63]. The only other NT use of the word is in Lk. XXI,11 where it means pestilence, rather than a pestilent fellow as here. λοιμός was a term of abuse[64]. In the first century A.D. it was used to describe those accused of sedition. By qualifying Paul as a λοιμός, Tertullus was explicitly categorizing him amongst those who were fomenting unrest against Roman rule. At the same time the rhetor was stressing the fact that the local Jewish authorities were as much opposed to political agitators as the Roman government. Moreover it has to be noted that the word *pest* had a particular shade of meaning in the context of Roman-Jewish relations. Its use called to mind the decree of the Roman Senate in which the alliance between Rome and Simon Maccabeus was guaranteed. According to the Book of Maccabees this decree enjoined the neighbouring states to hand over to the High Priest *pests* who had fled Judaea in order that the High Priest might judge them *according to the law*. Here the Sanhedrin's spokesman was asking to have the apostle, whom he deemed a *pest*, handed over for trial *according to the law* in conformity with the spirit of that ancient alliance[65].

B) Καὶ κινοῦντα στάσεις πᾶσιν τοῖς Ἰουδαίοις τοῖς κατὰ τὴν οἰκουμένην (Vg. = *et concitantem seditiones omnibus Iudaeis in universo orbe*)

The charge here is parallel to the one lodged against Paul by the Thessalonian Jews (οἱ τὴν οἰκουμένην ἀναστατώσαντες οὗτοι καὶ ἐνθάδε πάρεισιν) (XVII,6). The rhetor was attempting to convince Felix that Paul's preaching was causing public disturbances in the constituted Jewish communities throughout the empire and that the imperial authorities could not remain indifferent to such subversive activity. Tertullus was aware that the governor would be very reticent to convict Paul on purely religious charges. His speech thus highlights the political ramifications of Paul's deeds.

C) πρωτοστάτην τε τῆς τῶν Ναζωραίων αἱρέσεως (Vg. = *et auctorem seditionis sectae Nazarenorum*)

ὁ πρωτοστάτης – was a military term meaning the person who marches in the front rank of the army. By extension, it is the leader or chief of a party. This is the only NT use of this word.

---

63 cf. II Chron. XIII,7; Ps. I,1.
64 The word had already been used by Demosthenes in a very virulent way (Dem. XXV,80).
65 cf. I Macc. XV, 16–21. In verse 21 one reads: "If therefore any traitors (λοίμοι) have escaped from their country to you, hand them over to Simon the High Priest to be punished by him according to the law of the Jews."

ἡ αἵρεσις — is that which is *chosen*. It connotes a chosen course of deed or thought; hence a system of philosophic principles or a school or philosophy. It can mean a party or sect, a group of men who have separated themselves from others in that they follow their own tenets. The word αἵρεσις was used in reference to parties, factions and sects within Judaism. "Jewish philosophy", writes Josephus, "in fact takes three forms. The followers of the first school are called Pharisees, of the second Sadducees, of the third Essenes"[66]. Similarly the Book of Acts calls the Sadducees and the Pharisees a αἵρεσις: cf. Acts V,17 αἵρεσις τῶν Σαδδουκαίων); XV,5 ἀπὸ τῆς αἱρέσεως τῶν Φαρισαίων and again of the Pharisees in XXVI,5. It is thrice used to denote Christians (Acts XXIV,5,14; XXVIII, 22). In these three references, however, the connotation is rather pejorative. Its usage by opponents of the Christians would signify that the former not only thought that the Christians had separated themselves from and were in earnest conflict with orthodox Rabbinic tradition, but that Christianity was in fact a new faith outside Judaism. Consequently, the word is never used by the Christians to refer to their own community in the Acts-narrative. On the contrary Acts stresses that the Christians did not consider themselves to be a αἵρεσις *outside* Judaism, since their proclamation of Jesus as the Messiah was firmly rooted in the Old Testament prophecies on the coming Redeemer, the Hope of Israel.

2) Ναζωραῖος

This designation presupposes a connexion to Jesus' hometown of Nazareth[67]: being derived from the patrial name used by the Jews for Jesus. In this passage, Ναζωραῖος is applied by the Jews to Christ's followers. As the term has a depreciatory sense, it was not used by the Christians to describe their own community.

In his reconstruction of Tertullus' speech, Luke has made one point exceedingly clear: the high priests and elders considered the "sect of the Nazarenes" as a group completely outside the framework of official Judaism. The central Christian belief that Jesus was the long-awaited Messiah could never be accepted by the Jewish leadership. For the Jews, a group accepting the Messiahship of Jesus could no longer belong to the legally

---

66 *BJ*.II,8.2 (119). — E.T. = H.St.J. Thackeray, *Loeb*, 1961.
67 cf. Mt. II,23. Tertullian says: "According to the prophecy, the Creator's Christ was to be called a Nazarene. For that reason, and on his account, the Jews call us by that very name, Nazarenes" (*Adv. Marc.* IV,8.1). cf. *ThWb*, Vol. IV, pg. 874 for a discussion of the terms Ναζαρηνός/Ναζωραῖος: "Luke took Ναζαρηνός from an older tradition but prefers Ναζωραῖος, though the two forms mean the same for him".

constituted and officially recognized nation of Israel. Disowning the "sect of the Nazarenes" thus had a legal consequence of immense importance. It meant that the group of Christ's followers was no longer a part of a legally recognized religion and was thus illicit. Moreover the Jewish authorities were attempting to demonstrate that as the "sect of the Nazarenes" proclaimed Jesus to be "another King" and "Lord", it was professing a dangerous brand of *political* Messianism which was a direct challenge to Roman rule in Palestine. Thus the charge against Paul was particularly grave for it was aimed at connecting him to an anti-Roman Messianic movement.

Luke, of course, attempts to disprove these allegations by placing Paul's apologetic discourse within the mainstream of Pharisaic thought. He thus disconnects Paul from any sort of anti-Roman or anti-Jewish political activity.

D) ὃς καὶ τὸ ἱερὸν ἐπείρασεν βεβηλῶσαι

Βεβηλόω – to profane, to desecrate. The adjective βέβηλος applied to persons signifies those who are very far from God, unreceptive to his Holiness and indeed an enemy of the Deity. In Acts XXI,28 the verb κοινόω, which has the nuance of rendering (levitically) unclean, is used to describe the alleged profanation. Here the more secular word βεβηλόω[68] is used as the setting is that of a Roman court of law. In this passage Paul is accused of trying to profane the Temple. In Acts XXI,28 he was accused of actually defiling it. Whatever the phraseology, the charge of profaning the Temple was a key one in Paul's present indictment because for this crime alone could the Sanhedrin condemn a transgressor to death and entertain a confident hope that the governor would execute the sentence.

E) ὃν καὶ ἐκρατήσαμεν

κρατέω – to take hold of by force, to 'secure'; hence to 'arrest'[69]. The rhetor's account of Paul's arrest differs from Luke's earlier account of what transpired in the temple precincts. Tertullus says nothing of the attempted murder of Paul, but does state that Paul was arrested by the temple police and not by the Roman soldiers under the command of Claudius Lysias. The main thrust of Tertullus' legal argumentation here is that Paul was originally a temple-prisoner snatched away illegally by the tribune. Tertullus' point is made even clearer in the Western text which supplies verses 6b,7 and 8a missing from the B-text:

---

[68] cf. Ezekiel XXIII,38–39; Mt. XII,5. The Vg. translates both verses by *violare*.
[69] *LS*[9], pg. 991. As a term denoting arrest, cf. Mt. XIV,3; Mk. VI,17 (John the Baptist); Mt. XXVI, 4; Mk. XII,12; XIV,1 (Jesus). cf. Polybius VIII,18.8.

6b) "... and we wished to judge him according to our law,
7) but Lysias the tribune came and with great violence he took him out of our hands,
8a) commanding his accusers to come before you ..."[70].

According to Tertullus, Paul's arrest was conducted in an orderly and regular way. The violence that occurred was attributed to the tribune's clumsy handling of a matter which should have normally concerned the Jewish authorities alone. It was vital to the Jewish leadership's case to depict Lysias as having exceeded his powers by taking Paul out of their hands. The implication in the rhetor's speech is that Felix could right a grievous wrong done to the Jewish leadership if, after examining the prisoner, he were to hand him over to the Sanhedrin's jurisdiction. This benevolent deed would be favourably seen by the authorities and would go a long way towards restoring good relations between governor and subjects.

Tertullus now brought his speech to a close; "By examining (ἀνακρίνας) him yourself you will be able to learn from him everything of which we accuse him. The Jews also joined in the charge (συνεπέθεντο) affirming (φάσκοντες) that all this was so." (XXIV,8b—9).

A) ἀνακρίνας (iudicans)

ἀνακρίνω – to interrogate, to examine, to inquire into, to hold an investigation[71]. The verb can be used of a judicial inquiry, especially prior to the trial itself[72].

B) συνεπέθεντο

συνεπιτίθημι – to assail at the same time, to unite in impeaching, to join together in attacking. This is the only NT use of this verb.

C) φάσκοντες

φάσκω – to affirm, to make an assertion. Luke concludes the rhetor's speech by mentioning the supporting testimony offered by the Jewish leaders.

Luke's reconstruction of Tertullus' speech is greatly compressed. The full speech would have certainly been a great deal longer than the account given in Acts and would presumably have developed the case's legal side in greater detail by reference to the specific laws alleged to have been breached.

---

70 The Western lesson: Ψ (E 69 614) pm c e g p^c dem vg^{s,cl} sy$\int$; Rm.
71 cf. Acts IV,9; XII,19; I Cor. IX,3.
72 cf. Demosthenes, *Orat.*, XLVIII,31.

IV. Paul makes his *Apologia* before Felix

At the end of Tertullus' speech, Felix motioned Paul to speak (XXIV,10a); i.e. to make his *apologia*, the judicial counterbalance to the indictment. Luke presents Paul's apologetic speeches before the Governors Felix and Festus and later King Agrippa as occasions for proclaiming the Gospel before the authorities in the midst of danger and opposition. We must not lose sight of the fact, however, that juridically speaking, Paul remained a defendant throughout and that he simultaneously had to defend himself against the charges as well as proclaim the Gospel. One might very well surmise that the authorities were less interested in a religious dissertation or sermon than in elucidating the actual case that had to be judged[73].

Paul's speech before Felix also began with a *captatio benevolentiae* which, though complimentary towards the governor was considerably less servile in tone than the rhetor's: "Realizing that for many years you have been judge over this nation, I cheerfully make my defense" (εὐθύμως τὰ περὶ ἐμαυτοῦ ἀπολογοῦμαι (XXIV,10b).

A) εὐθύμως τὰ περὶ ἐμαυτοῦ ἀπολογοῦμαι

ἀπολογέομαι — to make one's defence, so speak in defence, to defend oneself. It is the juridical antithesis to κατηγορεῖν[74].

The verb occurs ten times in the NT, six times in Acts and twice in Luke. Both occurrences in the Gospel stress the divine inspiration for the *apologia*. In Lk. XII,11–12 Jesus tells his disciples to have no feelings of anxiety before making their defence in front of the synagogal authorities for the "Holy Spirit will teach you in that very hour what you ought to say". The same idea of divine succor occurs in Lk. XXI,14–15: "Settle it therefore in your minds, not to meditate beforehand how to answer; for I will give you a mouth and wisdom which none of your adversaries will be able to withstand or contradict". The divine dimension also underpins the apologetic speeches in Acts. What is of central importance to Luke in his account of Paul's speech here is the proclamation of the divine word, of the doctrine of the resurrection with Jesus Christ as its foundation, and not a systematic legal defence or a categorical refutation of the specific indictment. These are only lateral concerns in the author's apologetic strategy.

---

[73] cf. J.M. Gilchrist, "On what Charge was St. Paul brought to Rome?", *Expository Times*, Vol. 78; Oct. 1966–Sept. 1967; pg. 265.
[74] In Rm. II,15, Paul uses the antithetical pair κατηγορούντων/ἀπολογουμένων in the context of the final judgement. cf. Dionysius Halicarnassensis, *Ant. Rom.* VII,58.1. (τὴν ἀιτίαν ἀπολογησόμενου).

Paul begins his defence by denying the charges, this denial serves as a veritable introduction to his profession of faith: "As you may ascertain, it is not more than twelve days since I went up to worship at Jerusalem; and they did not find me disputing with anyone or stirring up a crowd, whether in the temple or in the synagogues, or in the city. Neither can they prove (παραστῆσαι) to you what they now bring up against me." (XXIV, 11–13).

παρίστημι – (cf. Latin *probare*) is to provide proof, to produce evidence to support the charge. The verb is very often used in just this type of description of judicial proceedings.

Paul emphasizes that he had come to Jerusalem as a pilgrim to worship in the temple. His action was that of an orthodox Jew observing the prescriptions of the law. He challenges Tertullus to produce cogent evidence to support the charges he has made.

Paul's confession of faith made up the next part of the *apologia*. Its proclamation of his belief in the resurrection of both the just and the unjust is the central doctrinal point of the whole apologetic speech before Felix: "But this I admit (ὁμολογῶ) to you, that according to the Way (κατὰ τὴν ὁδόν), which they call a sect, (αἵρεσιν) I worship the God of our fathers (λατρεύω τῷ πατρῴῳ Θεῷ), believing everything laid down by the law or written in the prophets, having a hope in God which these themselves accept, that there will be a resurrection of both the just and the unjust." (XXIV,14–15).

A) ὁμολογῶ – (*confiteor*)

ὁμολογέω – Here the verb has a double nuance. It is used by the apostle to express his *confessio fidei*: to declare openly his profound conviction. It is also used here as a judicial term: to acknowledge, to avow something, to recognize something (in court before a judge)[75].

B) κατὰ τὴν ὁδόν

ἡ ὁδός can be defined as a religious condition, a manner of life and behaviour prescribed and approved by God (ἡ ὁδὸς τοῦ Θεοῦ). Paul uses it here to signify the course or method by which God is known and worshipped: *through Christ, in Christian fellowship*. The contrast which the apostle made between ὁδός and αἵρεσις was important from the juridical point of view. The ὁδός did not represent a forsaking of the ancestral religion, but rather its providential fulfillment. The thrust of Paul's argumentation

---

[75] cf. the legal language in *P. Amh.* II,66.41 (year 124 A.D.): "and not even the witnesses produced by you (ὑπὸ σοῦ παρασ[τ]αθέντες) acknowledged (ὡμολόγησαν) that they knew of the murder".

was that believers following the ὁδός were an integral part of Judaism, they were wholly within the nation of Israel and so part of a duly recognized religion. Paul rejects the word αἱρέσις in the sense in which it had been used by the rhetor for it was of primary importance to his defence to demonstrate that the Christian ὁδός was a legitimate form of Judaism and could dwell under the Jewish name[76]. The idea that the Christian ὁδός was the accomplishment of Judaism and not a new and illicit religion is one of the principal themes of the apologetic discourse in Acts. Leaving aside Luke's purely theological aims, we should note his judicial motive, which was to secure for the Christian Way the continued protection of the State.

C) λατρεύω τῷ πατρῴῳ Θεῷ

In Acts, Paul consistently represents Christianity as being firmly rooted in Judaism in order to counter the charge of his being the ringleader of an illicit religious group whose activities were seditious. Paul stresses here that he has remained faithful to his nation's ancestral God. His use of the word πατρῷος was more than just a rhetorical device. It was an argument of defence, conveying the idea of loyalty and continuity in faith[77]. It is significant that the word πατρῷος occurs only thrice in the NT, all in the Lucan account of Paul's apologetic speeches (here, in Acts XXII,3 and XXVIII,17). Luke's aim is clear. He wishes to stress Paul's continuing Jewish identity and the place of Christianity within Judaism[78].

Paul continued his *apologia* by describing his own mood at the moment: "So I always take pains to have a clear conscience toward God and toward men" (XXIV,16). Paul's conscience was clear for his mission had been divinely ordained and he considered "his teaching as true Judaism, as the fulfillment of the promises and assurances of authentic Judaism"[79]. His conscience was clear for his motives in coming to the Temple had been pure: "Now after some years I came to bring my nation alms and offerings" (XXIV,18). This offering from the Gentile Churches to the Jerusalem Church was the visible sign that the Church was one and that there was

---

76 The Vg. reads here: "*confiteor autem hoc tibi quod secundum sectam quam dicunt heresim sic deservio patrio Deo meo ...*".
77 cf. Romans IX,3b—5a: Here the apostle calls the Jews my "kinsmen by race" and says "They are Israelites, and to them belong the Sonship, the glory, the covenants, the giving of the law, the worship and the promises; to them belong the patriarchs, and of their race according to the flesh is the Christ".
78 cf. A.M. Perry, "Acts and the Roman Trial of Paul", *HTR*, Vol. 17, No. 2; April 1924, pg. 195 for further discussion.
79 J. Klausner, *FROM JESUS TO PAUL*, London, 2nd. Edition, 1946, pg. 325.

no disunity between the Gentile and Jewish Christian congregations[80]. The apostle had come to the Holy City with financial help for his fellow countrymen and not with the aim of causing trouble or dissension.

After describing his motives, Paul evoked his arrest and in so doing emphasized the various weaknesses in the plaintiffs' case: "As I was doing this, they found me purified in the temple, without any crowd or tumult. But some Jews from Asia — they ought to be here before you and to make an accusation (οὓς ἔδει ἐπὶ σοῦ παρεῖναι καὶ κατηγορεῖν), if they have anything against me. Or else let these men themselves say what wrongdoing[81] they found when I stood before the council, except this one thing which I cried out while standing among them, 'With respect to the resurrection of the dead, I am on trial before you this day'." (XXIV,18–21).

A) οὓς ἔδει ἐπὶ σοῦ παρεῖναι καὶ κατηγορεῖν

This question was an extremely embarrassing one for Tertullus and Ananias. Where were the actual eyewitnesses of Paul's alleged profanation of the Temple, the Jews of Asia? Paul's present accusers were not the ones who had supposedly found him sullying the Temple. The Jews of Asia ought to have been in court to reiterate their accusations. Their very absence was already a major point in Paul's favour.

As we have already seen, if a plaintiff failed to formally lodge his accusation in court before a judge, he could lose the case by default. Paul was no doubt alluding to the absence of the Asian Jews for this reason.

The apostle was careful to note in his defence that he was ritually purified at the moment of the tumult. He was observing a prescribed Jewish rite in full accordance with the Law's precepts. Paul rejects the charge of defiling the sanctity of the Temple as totally unfounded.

B) The defence closes by Paul's dramatic cry: "With respect to the resurrection of the dead, I am on trial before you this day". The apostle reiterates this central doctrinal theme — this time as the culminating point of his whole apologetic speech. Once again one sees how pivotal a role the doctrine of the resurrection played in Luke's reconstruction of Paul's defence.

---

80 Paul is doubtlessly referring to the collection mentioned in Rom. XV,25 ff; I Cor. XVI,1–4; 2 Cor. VIII, 1ff.
81 For ἀδίκημα, cf. *supra*, pg. 57.

V. Felix leaves Paul in Prison

1. Paul in Custody

Both parties to the case had now finished their presentations. The moment had come for the governor to decide the case. Felix' decision, however, was to reserve judgement till a later date: "But Felix, having a rather accurate knowledge of the Way, put them off, (ἀναβάλετο δέ αὐτοὺς ὁ Φῆλιξ) saying, 'When Lysias the tribune comes down, I will decide your case'. (διαγνώσομαι τὰ καθ' ὑμᾶς). Then he gave orders to the centurion that he should be kept in custody but should have some liberty, and that none of his friends should be prevented from attending to his needs." (τηρεῖσθαι αὐτὸν ἔχειν τε ἄνεσιν καὶ μηδένα κωλύειν τῶν ἰδίων αὐτοῦ ὑπηρετεῖν αὐτῷ) (XXIV,22–23).

A) ἀνεβάλετο δέ αὐτοὺς ὁ Φῆλιξ

ἀναβάλλω – means to put off, to 'delay'. In the legal sense, to defer hearing and judging a case, to 'adjourn' a trial[82]. Here it is a juridical formula meaning that there is cause for establishing new evidence or hearing new te..nony. cf. the Latin legal expression *pronuntiavit amplius*[83].

B) διαγνώσομαι τὰ καθ' ὑμᾶς

For the verb διαγινώσκω cf. *supra*, pg. 104. According to Luke, Felix' reason for delaying the verdict was to have fuller information from Lysias, who, as author of the letters of report, would normally have to testify at the prisoner's trial[84]. Luke mentions no visit by the tribune to Caesarea. Felix had succeeded in blocking all judicial action in the case, which was now at a stalemate. The apostle was neither handed over to the Jewish authorities, nor judged by Roman law, nor set free.

C) τηρεῖσθαι αὐτὸν ἔχειν τε ἄνεσιν καὶ μηδένα κωλύειν τῶν ἰδίων αὐτοῦ ὑπηρετεῖν αὐτῷ

Luke is careful to inform his readers of how lenient Paul's conditions of imprisonment were in Caesarea. In Rome too, Paul benefited from liberal conditions. In Luke's literary design, this positive attitude is intended to

---

[82] *LS*⁹, pg. 98; Bauer, *Wb*. pg. 50. cf. *P. Tebt*. I,22.9 (yr. 112 B.C.) where ἀναβάλλω is used in the sense of referring a litigation to another official so as to delay it.
[83] cf. Cicero, *Verr*. II,i.29.74: where *amplius pronuntiaretur* means further trial is required. cf. the *Lex Acilia Repetundarum* (especially line 47) in *CIL*. I,198.
[84] cf. Sherwin-White, pg. 55.

show that the Roman authorities thought the apostle innocent and would have released him had it not been for the frenetic pursual of the case against him by the Jewish authorities. Felix' decision to allow Paul privileges meant that he could be helped by his friends for the duration of his imprisonment at Caesarea. In practical terms, this meant that he could communicate with them freely and obtain food[85].

Luke is very vague as to the identity of those succouring Paul ($\tau\tilde{\omega}\nu$ $i\delta\iota\omega\nu$ $\alpha\dot{\upsilon}\tau o\tilde{\upsilon}$). No mention is made of the Christian community at Caesarea or of Philip the Evangelist in whose house Paul had sojourned not so long before (XXI,8–10). This silence may very well indicate that Paul had been abandoned by the Caesarean brethren. On the other hand Luke's silence may be simply due to a literary consideration. In the latter part of Acts, Luke concentrates his attention on Paul and on no other Christian individuals: "only by this strict limitation of his material can he put his heroes in the right perspective"[86].

The adjournment of the case did not mean that contact between the governor and his prisoner was broken off: "After some days Felix came with his wife Drusilla, who was a Jewess; and he sent for Paul and heard him speak upon faith in Christ Jesus." (XXIV,24).

A) Drusilla

Luke introduces yet another historical character into his narrative as he will later do with Bernice[87]. Drusilla was the younger daughter of Herod Agrippa I and the sister of Agrippa II[88], Josephus notes that Agrippa II gave her in marriage to Azizus, King of Emesa, but that shortly afterwards this marriage was dissolved when Felix wooed her away[89]. Suetonius writes that Felix was the husband of three queens, but does not mention their names[90]. Tacitus does mention in the *Historiae* that Felix married a Drusilla, whom the Latin writer says was the granddaughter of Cleopatra and Mark Antony (making Felix their *progener*)[91].

The Harclaean margin states that it was Drusilla who was responsible for Felix' summoning Paul in order to hear him speak of Christ Jesus: "Felix came with his wife Drusilla, who was a Jewess, and she asked to

---

85 cf. Lucian, *de Morte Peregrini* 12, for an interesting account of the favours one Proteus received while in prison.
86 M. Hengel, *op.cit.*, pg. 36.
87 Acts XXV,13.
88 *BJ.* II,11.6 (220). In *Ant.* XIX,9.1 (354), Josephus writes that Drusilla was six years old when Herod Agrippa I died in 44 A.D.
89 *Ant.* XX,7.1 (139–143).
90 Suetonius, *Claud.* XXVIII.
91 Tacitus, *Hist.* V,9.

see Paul and hear the word. Wishing therefore to please her, he summoned Paul"[92].

B) Felix and Drusilla had two motives for conversing with Paul. One reflected, in Ramsay's words, "a curiosity and intelligent interest in the new doctrine"[93]. This interest in the Word did not, however, lead to Felix' or Drusilla's conversion. Luke tells us that after having heard Paul "argue about justice and self-control and future judgement, Felix was alarmed and said, 'Go away for the present; when I have an opportunity I will summon you'." (XXIV,25)[94]. The second motive was far less noble as Luke plainly states: "At the same time he hoped that money would be given him by Paul. So he sent for him often and conversed with him" (XXIV,26).

Under the provisions of the law on extortion, the *Lex Repetundarum,* anyone holding a position of power or administration was forbidden to solicit or accept a bribe either to bind or unbind a man, to give judgement or not or to release a prisoner[95]. This law was frequently violated by the provincial governors, many of whom were infamous for their extortionate depredations. Josephus gives a good example of the official misbehaviour in his description of Albinus, Festus' successor as Governor of Judaea (61–65 A.D.):

> "Not only did he, in his official capacity, steal and plunder private property and burden the whole nation with extraordinary taxes, but he accepted ransoms from their relatives on behalf of those who had been imprisoned for robbery by the local councils or by former procurators; and the only persons left in gaol as malefactors were those who failed to pay the price"[96].

One question this last exchange between the governor and the apostle raises is the question of Paul's personal financial situation. Acts implies that Paul had considerable sums of money at his disposal during the period of his imprisonement both at Caesarea and at Rome. This is clear from the deferential treatment and respect shown him by the Roman authorities in general and by Felix and Festus in particular. Trials and especially appeals were expensive and for that reason usually reserved for the rich who could afford all the costs, such as making a hefty deposit, etc. When the apostle appealed to Rome, he chose a very expensive line of judicial procedure[97].

Luke maintains a curious silence as to the provenance of Paul's money. In his narrative, he never mentions the churches as having provided the

---

92 The expansion in the *Hcl. Mg.* helps explain the mention of Drusilla in the B-Text.
93 W.M. Ramsay, *THE CHURCH IN THE ROMAN EMPIRE BEFORE 170 A.D. op.cit.*, pg. 133.
94 C.M. Martini writes: "By means of faith in the resurrected Jesus, the Christian opens himself to a new life which is manifested by justice and by a moderating of the passions. He is thus able to escape the judgement of condemnation which falls on those who do evil deeds". (Martini *op.cit.,* pg. 301). These moral and ethical considerations were the last things Felix wanted to hear.
95 cf. *Digest* XLVIII,11.3;7. cf. Aulus Gellius, *Noct. Att.* XX,1.7.
96 *BJ.* II,14,1 (273) – E.T. = H.St.J. Thackeray, *Loeb,* 1961.
97 J.H. Oliver, "Greek Applications for Roman Trials", *AJP.*, Vol. 100; 1979, pg. 555–556.

apostle with financial help during his long imprisonment. We can only surmise that money from Paul's personal estate was used to cover his legal expenses.

2. Biennis Captivitas Caesariensis

Despite all this personal benevolence on Felix' part and the deference with which he was treated, Paul remained imprisoned: "But when two years had elapsed, (διετίας δὲ πληρωθείσης), Felix was succeeded by Porcius Festus; and desiring to do the Jews a favour (θέλων τε χάριτα καταθέσθαι τοῖς Ἰουδαίοις) Felix left Paul in prison." (ὁ Φῆλιξ κατέλιπε τὸν Παῦλον δεδεμένον) (XXIV,27).

A) διετίας δὲ πληρωθείσης

ἡ διετία — the space of two years. (cf. the Latin *biennium*).
πληρόω — in the passive = to be fulfilled, to come to an end.
The text indicates that the apostle was imprisoned for a full two years subsequent to his appearance in Felix' court. This is most likely what transpired. There is a body of opinion, however, that takes the *biennium* in question to mean the period of Felix' rule in Palestine and not the length of Paul's imprisonment[98].

B) θέλων τε χάριτα καταθέσθαι τοῖς Ἰουδαίοις (*volens autem gratiam praestare Iudaeis*)

κατατίθημι[99] — in the Middle Voice, the verb can mean to 'deposit for oneself', to 'lay by', to 'lay up in store'. Hence the expression χάριτα/χάριν κατατίθεσθαι + Dative, which means to 'lay up a store of favour', to lay up a claim of gratitude[100]. Here and in Acts XXV,9, it has the

---

98 cf. C. Saumagne, "St. Paul et Félix, Procurateur de Judée", *MELANGES PIGANIOL*, Paris, 1966, Vol. III, 1386. Saumagne proposes the following dates for Paul's legal itinerary:
  52 A.D. — beginning of Felix' procuratorship;
  54 A.D. (Pentecost) — Paul arrives in Jerusalem;
  54 A.D. (November—December) — Paul before the Sanhedrin and before Felix;
  55 A.D. (winter) — Festus takes over the case;
  55 A.D. (spring) — Festus grants Paul's appeal;
  55 A.D. (August) — Paul's leaves for Rome;
  56 A.D. (January—February) — Paul arrives in Rome;
  56—58 A.D. Paul a prisoner in Rome (*biennium*);
  58 A.D. — Paul is executed in Rome.
  Contrary to Saumagne, we do not believe that Paul was executed as early as 58 A.D. (cf. note 103).
99 LS^9, pg. 917.
100 cf. Thucydides I,33.

sense of to curry or court favour with or to ingratiate oneself with. There is a marked nuance of reciprocity, i.e. doing a favour/later receiving thanks for the favour: "The emphasis is on the thanks that the party now benefited in the action will feel or show in the future ..."[101].

Felix felt himself obliged to curry favour with the local Jewish authorities at this point in time. His personal misconduct and his attacks on Jewish guerrillas had alienated a large part of the Jewish population of Palestine. The Caesarea riots completely marred the end of his term of office[102]. In 59 A.D., the Emperor recalled Felix from Palestine[103]. The Emperor's ostensible reason for removing Felix was the latter's unsatisfactory handling of the Caesarea riots and all the complications which arose therefrom. Thus Felix needed to act to curry favour with the Jewish authorities who had sent a delegation to Rome to accuse him before Nero. Moreover Nero had already removed Felix' brother Pallas from office[104]. Pallas nonetheless seems to have retained some of his former influence even after his fall:

> "When Porcius Festus was sent by Nero as successor to Felix, the leaders of the Jewish community of Caesarea went up to Rome to accuse Felix. He undoubtedly would have paid the penalty for his misdeeds against the Jews had not Nero yielded to the urgent entreaty of Felix's brother Pallas, whom at that time he held in the highest honour"[105].

---

101 *BC.*, Vol. IV, pg. 306.
102 The Caesarea riots which occurred at the time Paul was being held a prisoner in Caesarea, arose over disputes between the Jews and Greeks (Syrians) about citizenship rights. Caesarea was a Greek *polis* and the Greeks enjoyed membership in the *polis*; they thus had superior standing to the Jews of Caesarea who were grouped in their *politeuma*. Here as elsewhere, the Jews were contesting the Greek community's identification with the *polis* which left them masters of the city. For Josephus' description of the Caesarea disturbances, cf. *Ant.* XX,8.7 (173–178); *BJ.* II,13.7 (266–270).
103 The proposed date uses a *medium* chronology for later events of Paul's life (as opposed to Saumagne's *short* chronology):
52 A.D. beginning of Felix' governorship;
57 A.D. (Pentecost) – Paul arrives in Jerusalem;
57–59 A.D. – Paul's two-year imprisonment in Caesarea;
59 A.D. (summer) – Festus grants Paul's appeal;
59 A.D. (September) – Paul leaves for Rome;
60 A.D. (February) – Paul arrives in Rome;
60–62 A.D. – Paul a prisoner in Rome;
62 A.D. – end of Paul's detention in Rome.
E. Fascher, "Paulus (Apostel)", *op.cit.*, col. 453, dates everything a year later: Paul would have been sent to Rome in the summer of 60 A.D. and his sojourn there would have lasted from 61 to 63 A.D.
104 cf. Tacitus, *Ann.* XIII,14 (for the year 55 A.D.): "Nero ... removed Pallas from the charge [of *libertus a rationibus*, i.e. Financial Secretary] to which he had been appointed by Claudius, and in which he exercised virtual control over the monarchy". E.T. = J. Jackson, *Loeb*, 1962.
105 *Ant.* XX,8.9 (182). E.T. = L.H. Feldman, *Loeb*, 1965. cf. R. Jewett, *op.cit.*, pg. 43, who writes: "In short up until the year 62, Pallas had the influence of an immensely rich bachelor from whom senators and even the emperor had hoped to receive legacies. There is little doubt that such influence would suffice to thwart a Jewish delegation complaining about the behaviour of his brother".

C) ὁ Φῆλιξ κατέλιπε τὸν Παῦλον δεδεμένον

It was not an uncommon practice for a departing governor to free prisoners whose cases were still pending[106]. Felix may very well have released other prisoners in his custody, but he kept Paul in prison. The text of Acts motivates this refusal to release the apostle by mentioning Felix' desire to curry favour with the Jewish authorities[107].

This whole period in Paul's legal history was marked by a judicial stalemate. On the one hand, it seems clear that Felix never had any intention of handing Paul over to the Sanhedrin in spite of his desire to be as appeasing as possible. Paul's Roman citizenship was the major factor blocking Felix from extraditing him to the Sanhedrin. The governor was aware that if he handed over the apostle, the Sanhedrin would demand a sentence of death on the charge of profanation. Felix then would have had to have shouldered the responsibility for the legal lynching of a Roman citizen. On the other hand, it also seems clear that Felix never intended to free the apostle. By keeping Paul in prison, the governor had effectively put an end to his apostolic ministry, which was so irksome to the Jewish authorities. Paul was powerless to prevent this period of imprisonment as there was no judicial recourse against a *postponement* of a trial. Luke stresses Felix' benevolence toward his prisoner, but the fact of the matter remains that Paul was kept in prison for the rest of the governor's term of office. His case would be heard anew only with the arrival in Judaea of Felix' successor, Porcius Festus.

---

[106] cf. *Ant.* XX,9.5 (215), where the Governor Albinus cleared out the prison when he heard that Florus was coming to succeed him.
[107] The sy^{hmg} (614, 2147) states that Felix left Paul in prison because of Drusilla.

Chapter VII
Caesarea (Part 2): Paul and Festus

I. Festus at Jerusalem

As we have seen, Felix was succeeded by Porcius Festus. Contrary to his predecessor, Festus left few traces among the ancient writers. Neither Tacitus nor Suetonius speaks of him and he is known to the modern reader only through Luke and Josephus[1]. He remained Governor of Judaea for two years, dying in that post in the year 61 A.D. In Acts, Luke portrays the new governor as a more competent and honest administrator not given over to Felix' well known venality.

Festus lost no time in going to Jerusalem to visit the Jewish authorities there: "Now when Festus had come into his province, after three days he went up to Jerusalem from Caesarea." (XXV,1). This was a visit he was compelled to make, not only for reasons of protocol, but for eminently political ones as well: it was absolutely necessary to put his relationship with the Jewish authorities on the best footing possible in the wake of the Caesarea riots, which had been the cause of the break between the Jewish leadership and his predecessor.

Paul's case was among the things discussed: "And the chief priests and the principal men of the Jews informed him against Paul:" (ἐνεφάνισάν τε αὐτῷ οἱ ἀρχιερεῖς καὶ οἱ πρῶτοι τῶν Ἰουδαίων κατὰ τοῦ Παύλου (XXV, 2).

A) οἱ ἀρχιερεῖς

This time the reigning High Priest is not mentioned by name, the plural οἱ ἀρχιερεῖς is used. The plural usage is not surprising. The word designated not only the reigning High Priest, but also those of his predecessors who were still alive as well as the select sacerdotal group from which the high priests were chosen.

---

1 *BJ.* II,14.1 (271): "Festus, who succeeded Felix as Procurator, proceeded to attack the principal plague of the country: he captured large numbers of the brigands and put not a few to death." E.T. = H. St.J. Thackeray, *Loeb,* 1961. cf. *Ant.* XX, 8.10 (185–188).

B) οἱ πρῶτοι τῶν Ἰουδαίων

The word πρῶτοι is used to designate the foremost members of the Sanhedrin.

C) ἐνεφάνισαν

For the verb ἐμφανίζω cf. *supra*, pg. 104.

The text once again demonstrates the continuing hostility of the Jewish authorities to Paul. By informing the new governor against Paul, the Jewish authorities started the same judicial proceedings against the apostle as they had two years earlier. Once more the plaintiffs were exerting pressure on the governor to have Paul remanded to their custody: "And they urged him, asking as a favour[2] to have the man sent (μεταπέμψηται) to Jerusalem, planning an ambush (ἐνέδραν) to kill him on the way." (XXV,3).

A) μεταπέμψηται

μεταπέμπω – to send for, to summon. The noun μεταπέμψις means a summons. The verb occurs eight times in the NT, all of them in Acts.

B) ἐνέδραν

Once again Luke creates a background of tension and violence against which Paul's case unfolds. The ambush planned on the Jerusalem-Caesarea road offers a parallel to that described in Acts XXIII,12ff[3]. The plot serves a double role in the narrative. It enhances the drama of the scene and it serves as an explanation for the actions and decisions of the various Roman officials.

At first Festus held firm against the plaintiffs. Paul was a prisoner at Caesarea, so his hearing would take place there. Let the Jews accuse him in Caesarea if they wished: "Festus replied that Paul was being kept at Caesarea, and that he himself intended to go there shortly. 'So', said he, 'let the men of authority (δυνατοί) among you go down with me, and if there is anything wrong about the man (εἴ τί ἐστιν ἐν τῷ ἀνδρὶ ἄτοπον), let them accuse him'." (XXV,4–5).

---

2 αἰτούμενοι χάριν κατ' αὐτοῦ – cf. *supra*, pg. 132.
3 The expansion in the *Hcl. Mg.* states that the plot was revived by the same men who made the vow to murder the apostle two years earlier: *illi qui votum fecerant quomodo obtinerent ut in manibus suis esset.*

A) οἱ δυνατοί

In this passage Luke designates the men who had the highest rank and who exercised the greatest influence within the Jewish community[4].

Unlike his account in Ch. 24 where he uses specific names to describe the plaintiffs (Ananias, Tertullus, some elders), Luke restricts himself here to more generalized categories: high priests, principal men, men of authority.

B) εἴ τί ἐστιν ἐν τῷ ἀνδρὶ ἄτοπον

ἄτοπος – wicked, wrong, ethically improper, injurious. Luke uses it here and in XXVIII,6 in his account of the trial of Paul and in Lk. XXIII,41 in his account of the trial of Jesus[5].

Initially Festus seemed adamant in his refusal to consider a change of venue in Paul's case:

A) Festus may very well have been shocked by the violent nature of the Jewish authorities' request. He later told King Herod Agrippa II that "the whole Jewish people petitioned me ... shouting that he ought not to live any longer." (XXV,24).

B) The Sanhedrin's conception of a legal proceeding was certainly alien to Festus' own ideas of due process and to Roman legal custom. He later told Agrippa that he had replied to the Jews "that it was not the custom of the Romans to give up any one before the accused met the accusers face to face and had the opportunity to make his defense concerning the charge laid against him." (XXV,16). Festus readily recognized that a judicial lynching was in the works against a Roman citizen presently in his custody.

C) It is possible that the governor had information that some violent act might be perpetrated on Paul's person and so did not want to remove him from the security of Caesarea.

II. Festus in Favour of a Change of Jurisdiction

The next sequence of events is of vital importance to Paul's case. Here the trial begins anew (Acts XXV,6), the Jews accuse Paul (XXV,7), the apostle

---

4 cf. *Ant.* XIV,13.1 (324) where Josephus uses the expression οἱ δυνατοί to describe the Jewish officials who went to Mark Antony to accuse Phasael and Herod. cf. *BJ.* I,12.4 (242).

5 cf. 2 Thess. III,2.

makes his defence (XXV,8), Festus asks Paul to consider returning to Jerusalem to be tried there (XXV,9), Paul categorically refuses (XXV,10), he appeals to Caesar (XXV,11), Festus grants the appeal (XXV,12).

Festus' stay in Jerusalem was not long, "not more than eight or ten days" (XXV,6a). He then returned to Caesarea. The next day "he took his seat on the tribunal (καθίσας ἐπὶ τοῦ βήματος) and ordered Paul to be brought." (XXV,6b).

A) καθίσας ἐπὶ τοῦ βήματος

For τὸ βῆμα cf. *supra*, pg. 56. The Greek phrase here finds its technical equivalent in the Latin legal expression *sedens pro tribunali*. The term also appears in the accounts of our Lord's Passion[6]. The judge's taking his place on the judgement seat was a solemn gesture indicating that his forthcoming decision would have legal effect[7]. The tribunal mentioned in this passage was probably in the auditorium of Herod's palace[8].

The Jews began to make their accusations once the apostle had been brought in: "the Jews who had gone down from Jerusalem stood about him (περιέστησαν αὐτόν), bringing against him many serious charges (πολλὰ καὶ βαρέα αἰτιώματα καταφέροντες) which they could not prove." (ἃ οὐκ ἴσχυον ἀποδεῖξαι) (XXV,7).

A) περιέστησαν αὐτόν

περιίστημι — to stand around, to encircle. The Lucan account stresses the physical confrontation between plaintiffs and defendant: they surround the apostle while making the accusation.

B) πολλὰ καὶ βαρέα αἰτιώματα καταφέροντες

τὸ αἰτίωμα — charge, accusation. This is a rarer form than αἰτία and appears only here in the NT[9], contrary to αἰτία which appears twenty times.

The narrative is very abbreviated here. Luke does not give an account of the specific charges forming the indictment. On the basis of Paul's reply in XXV,8 and the content of past indictments, the "serious charges" can be reconstructed as follows:

---

6 cf. Mt. XXVII,19; Jn. XIX,13. cf. *Ant.* XX,6.2 (130); where Quadratus sat on the judgement seat from which he gave a second thorough hearing to the case of the Samaritans.
7 Bruce, pg. 430; Th. Mommsen, *STRAFRECHT*, pg. 361–362.
8 cf. *BJ.* II,9.3 (172) where Pontius Pilate took his place on the tribunal (καθίσας ἐπὶ βήματος) not in the auditorium of Herod's palace, but in the great stadium of Caesarea. The tribunal was not necessarily in the governor's headquarters.
9 cf. *P. Fay.* CXI,8 (yr. 95–96 A.D.): [Heraclidas], shifted the blame from himself (τῷ αἰτίωμα περιεπύησε).

1) The apostle had violated the sanctity of the Temple;

2) Paul was attempting to dislocate the official Jewish communities by his hostile speeches and actions. He was systematically denigrating basic Mosaic law and practices and was combatting the duly constituted authorities of his people;

3) The apostle's proclamation of Jesus as King was doubtlessly portrayed as a seditious action against the reigning Princeps. His evangelization was thus disturbing the *salus publica*.

C) ἃ οὐκ ἴσχυον ἀποδεῖξαι

ἀποδείκνυμι — to prove by argument, to show, to demonstrate. It was incumbent upon the plaintiffs to produce direct evidence in support of their accusations. Their failure to do so revealed the tremendous weakness of their case.

According to Roman procedure, it was now Paul's turn to speak in order to make his defence. His reply was similar to that in XXIV,2. Once again the apostle denied all the charges against him: "Paul said in his defense[9a], 'Neither against the law of the Jews, nor against the temple, nor against Caesar have I offended at all'." (οὔτε εἰς τὸν νόμον τῶν Ἰουδαίων οὔτε εἰς τὸ ἱερὸν οὔτε εἰς Καίσαρά τι ἥμαρτον (XXV,8).

A) οὔτε εἰς τὸν νόμον τῶν Ἰουδαίων οὔτε εἰς τὸ ἱερὸν οὔτε εἰς Καίσαρά τι ἥμαρτον

ἁμαρτάνω — to err, sin, violate God's law; in a judicial sense to do wrong in a matter, to violate set laws. Luke gives a brief but detailed refutation of the charges lodged against Paul.

Both the plaintiffs and the defendant had now finished presenting their cases, so the moment had come for the governor to give his opinion: "But Festus wishing to do the Jews a favour (θέλων τοῖς Ἰουδαίοις χάριν καταθέσθαι) said to Paul, 'Do you wish (θέλεις) to go up to Jerusalem, and there be tried on these charges before me'?" (ἐκεῖ περὶ τούτων κριθῆναι ἐπ' ἐμοῦ) (XXV,9).

A) ὁ Φῆστος δὲ θέλων τοῖς Ἰουδαίοις χάριν καταθέσθαι[10]

Festus had just arrived in Judaea to begin his governorship and was doubtlessly aware of the turbulence which had marked several of his predecessors' relations with the Jews. Luke presents him as wishing to avoid a ser-

---

9a τοῦ Παύλου ἀπολογουμένου cf. *supra*, pg. 125.
10 cf. *supra*, pg. 132.

ious conflict with the Sanhedrin at the very outset of his term of office by trying to accommodate their demands. He certainly would try to avoid having any complaint lodged against him at Rome all the more so as any complaint would most likely have charged the governor with negligence and laxity in prosecuting a man accused of seditious deeds, a point on which the Emperors were extremely sensitive[11].

> "Felix had left Paul in prison when he departed as he wished to do the Jews a *favour*, thereby showing himself to be accomodating insofar as they were concerned. The High Priests and leading men were asking Festus for a *favour* when they asked him to transfer Paul to Jerusalem. In order to do the Jews the favour they had been asking, Festus requested Paul to go to Jerusalem"[12].

B) θέλεις

The narrative accentuates Festus' change of attitude towards Paul's case. The governor is portrayed as being in favour of Paul's accepting not only a change of venue from Caesarea to Jerusalem, but also a change of jurisdiction from Governor to Sanhedrin. Luke clearly states that Festus' question to Paul is motivated by a desire to accomodate the Jewish authorities. At the same time however, Luke also notes Festus' sense of justice and the respect he shows to Paul's Roman citizenship. He requests — not orders — the apostle to agree to the change. Paul's consent to be brought from Caesarea to Jerusalem was necessary; as a Roman citizen he could not be forced to renounce his right to be judged by a Roman court[13].

C) ἐκεῖ περὶ τούτων κριθῆναι ἐπ' ἐμοῦ (Vg. = *ibi de his iudicari apud me*)

Κρίνω — to judge, give judgement. In the passive voice — to be brought to trial so that one's case may be examined and judgement given.

Festus' suggestion that the trial take place in Jerusalem but before him, reflected the ambiguity of the case. On the one hand the political charges remained unsubstantiated as Festus himself stated later on: "When the accusers stood up they brought no charge in his case of such evils as I supposed." (XXV,18). He himself felt Paul to be innocent of any political misdeed: "I found that he had done nothing deserving death." (XXV,25a). The governor was in fact rejecting as unfounded the political charges in

---

11 cf. Jn. XIX,12b for the thinly-veiled threats addressed by the Jews to Pontius Pilate during Jesus' trial: "If you release this man, you are not Caesar's friend;".
12 J. Dupont, "Aequitas Romana", *op.cit.*, pg. 530.
13 The *Lex Rupilia*, drawn up by P. Rupilius in 131 B.C. and in force in Sicily offers an interesting parallel. One of the provisions of this law stated that if a Roman citizen were sued by a Sicilian, the judge had to be Roman. Cicero notes that a Sicilian was appointed to try cases where a Sicilian was sued by a Roman citizen and a Roman judge was appointed to try cases in which a Roman citizen was sued by a Sicilian (*Verr.* II,ii.13.32).

the case. For Festus, the affair was really a theological dispute between Paul and the Jewish authorities "about their own superstition and about one Jesus, who was dead, but whom Paul asserted to be alive." (XXV,19). Festus understood nothing at all of the theological aspect of the case as he himself admits: "Being at a loss how to investigate these questions ..." (XXV,20a). It would seem logical to him that the trial take place before the Sanhedrin which had judicial competence in cases dealing with Jewish law, beliefs and the sanctity of the Temple. Nonetheless Paul was a Roman citizen who had been indicted on capital charges. It was the governor's responsibility to safeguard his rights to protection over against the pretentions of a native court. Consequently Festus was reluctant to completely disassociate himself from the case.

Festus' request to Paul raises a number of interesting questions:

A) The governor was judicially competent to make a decision in Paul's case. We have already seen that a governor could determine the nature and scope of the indictment and, if the defendant were found guilty, determine his punishment[14]. Paul's case however was a capital case and as A.N. Sherwin-White notes, "Festus could not hand over his capital jurisdiction, either in earlier or in later usage, to a provincial tribunal such as the Sanhedrin, or to any third party"[15]. Basically Festus thought Paul innocent of the charge of sedition. There was thus no question at any point of his handing over his jurisdiction to the Sanhedrin to judge that charge, for the charge of sedition could only be judged by the competent Roman authorities. But by retaining the religious indictment against Paul and especially the charge of profanation — which normally fell within the Sanhedrin's jurisdiction — Festus was in fact extraditing Paul on a capital charge to a body whose decision was a foregone conclusion. Festus then was going against the spirit of the laws protecting a Roman citizen in order to please those asking the favour[16].

B) If the case had finally reached the Sanhedrin, that body would have been both plaintiff and judge in the matter. One wonders how Festus would have reconciled himself to a legal procedure so diametrically opposed to Roman procedure, if he had, in fact, really intended to play an active part in the trial once the change of jurisdiction had been effected.

C) The key word in the text is thus ἐπ' ἐμοῦ. It should not be taken to mean that the Roman governor would be the presiding officer at a formal session of the Sanhedrin. Rather it most likely signifies that Festus intended to be physically present at Paul's trial before the Sanhedrin.

---

14. cf. *supra*, pg. 114.
15 Sherwin-White, pg. 67.
16 Dupont, "Aequitas Romana", *op.cit.*, pg. 532.

This presence would be intended to dissuade the Sanhedrin from perpetrating any injustice on a Roman citizen. This presence — with its intended dissuasive effect — could, however, hardly counterbalance the plain fact that Paul would have been in the complete legal custody of the Jewish authorities. It would be the Sanhedrin alone which would have pronounced final judgement in the apostle's case.

D) Two phrases in the text indicate that Festus was not simply asking Paul to accept a change of venue; but that he intended to give Paul up to the Sanhedrin. First Luke stresses that the governor wanted to do the Jews a favour. A mere change of venue from the Praetorium of Caesarea to the Praetorium of Jerusalem would not satisfy their demands as Paul would have remained under Roman jurisdiction throughout. Second, Paul's strong reply in XXV,10—11 reminding Festus that he was a Roman citizen, that he wished to remain in Roman jurisdiction and finally that he was appealing to Caesar in order to do so would indicate that Festus' request to Paul implied nothing less than a total change of jurisdiction — an extradition to the highest Jewish court on a capital charge.

III. Paul appeals to Caesar

For the apostle, Festus' request that there be a change of jurisdiction was disastrous. Paul's overall strategy consisted of doing all within his power to remain under Roman jurisdiction. To accept the governor's proposal meant embarking on the road to a legal lynching. Paul had no illusions as to Festus' capacity to resist the plaintiff's violence and fury once the case was transferred to Jerusalem. Thus Paul's answer was firmly negative: "I am standing before Caesar's tribunal, where I ought to be tried; (ἑστὼς ἐπὶ τοῦ βήματος καίσαρός εἰμι οὗ με δεῖ κρίνεσθαι); to the Jews I have done no wrong as you know very well[17]! If then I am a wrong-doer[18], and have committed anything for which I deserve to die, I do not seek to escape death; but if there is nothing in their charges against me, (εἰ δὲ οὐδέν ἐστιν ὧν οὗτοι κατηγοροῦσίν μου), no one can give me up to them." (οὐδείς με δύναται αὐτοῖς χαρίσασθαι)(XXV,10—11).

---

17 ἐπιγινώσκεις: cf. supra, pg. 75.
18 εἰ μὲν οὖν ἀδικῶ: cf. supra, pg. 57.

A) ἐστὼς ἐπὶ τοῦ βήματος Καίσαρός εἰμι οὗ με δεῖ κρίνεσθαι (*ad tribunal Caesaris sto ubi me oportet iudicari*)

The apostle was asking that the trial take place before a Roman court. He was a citizen and could therefore demand that his right to be heard in a Roman court be respected. He had absolutely no intention of being forced to leave Roman jurisdiction. Moreover, the Jewish plaintiffs had made grave political accusations in their indictment. Such charges fell outside the judicial competence of the Sanhedrin for only a Roman court could try a Roman citizen on the charge of sedition. Contrary to Festus, Paul retained only the charge of sedition as a motive for further trial and categorically refused to agree to be sent to the Sanhedrin to be tried on religious charges.

B) εἰ δὲ οὐδέν ἐστιν ὧν οὗτοι κατηγοροῦσίν μου (*si vero nihil est eorum quae hii accusant me*)

The accent is on the word οὐδέν. Bruce notes that "even after εἰ, the negative οὐδέν is here preferred to μηδέν, as denoting greater absoluteness, 'nothing at all' "[19].

C) οὐδείς με δύναται αὐτοῖς χαρίσασθαι (*nemo potest me illis donare*)

χαρίζομαι[20] — (+ Dative) to 'say' or 'do something agreeable' to a person; to 'show' him 'favour' or 'kindness', 'oblige', 'gratify', to 'court favour' with. Hence (+ Dative and Accusative) = to 'give up' someone 'as a favour'[21], as a result of a partial verdict, or unjust condemnation. In the abstract, it means to make oneself agreeable to others or to comply (with their wishes).

In his narrative, Luke stresses the point that the governors wanted to do the Jewish authorities a favour in order to gain their benevolence. First Felix had kept Paul in prison to block the apostle's ministry which the Jews found so threatening. Now Festus asks Paul to agree to a change of jurisdiction in order to satisfy the Sanhedrin's pressing demand. The apostle emphatically rejects this request by reminding the governor that as a Roman citizen he is entitled to be heard in a Roman court before a Roman judge.

The apostle is in mortal danger. Only one recourse remains, the appeal to Rome. So Paul cries out at the end of his defence: "I appeal to Caesar!" (XXV,11b).

---

19 Bruce, pg. 432.
20 LS^9, pg. 1978. The judge, says Plato "is not here to grant favours in matters of justice but to give judgement; and his oath binds him not to do favours according to his pleasure, but to judge according to the laws;" (Plato, *Apologia*, 35 C). E.T. = H.N. Fowler, *Loeb*, 1960.
21 cf. Acts III,14–15.

IV. Excursus: The Appeal under the early Emperors

Καίσαρα ἐπικαλοῦμαι – *Caesarem appello*! As soon as a Roman citizen had uttered this solemn cry for protection, all judicial action was broken off in the court at which his trial was taking place and the appellate process set in motion: "The filing of the appeal had a suspensive effect and prevented execution until the appeal had been disposed of"[22].

Paul was not appealing a final verdict handed down by the governor following a formal legal proceeding in his court. Rather the apostle was appealing an interlocutory decision: the request by the governor to Paul to consider a change of jurisdiction. When the apostle answered Festus' question "*Vis Ierosolymam ascendere et ibi de his iudicari apud me?*" by "*ad tribunal Caesaris sto ubi me oportet iudicari ... Caesarem appello*", he was not only designating the Princeps' legal competence for his case by invoking ancient legal provisions which protected the Roman citizen from magisterial abuse[23], but also formally opposing the Sanhedrin's judicial competence to hear and decide his case. Until the affair was taken up by the court at Rome, Paul would remain in Roman custody and could not be sent before the Sanhedrin.

The appeal marked the beginning of the last period of Paul's long legal history. There was no higher court in the Empire than Caesar's court and no higher legal authority than the *Princeps*. No further appeals could be lodged; the case normally would be disposed of one way or another at Rome.

> "In capital cases both the Emperor and the Senate exercised a primary jurisdiction against which there was, it would seem, no *provocatio ad populum*: these jurisdictions are well attested under Tiberius and can be traced back to Augustus' reign"[24].

A) προκαλοῦμαι/*provocare*

A.W. Lintott has pointed out in his article on the *provocatio* that the early usage of the verb *provocare* was "to call citizens out into the street to witness an outrage and to afford assistance"[25]. Afterwards the term was used to refer to an appeal made by a citizen against a decision of a magistrate.

The word *provocare* (cf. the Middle Voice προκαλοῦμαι) basically means to challenge. A.H.J. Greenidge defines *provocatio* in Roman criminal

---

22 R. Taubenschlag, *THE LAW OF GRECO-ROMAN EGYPT IN THE LIGHT OF THE PAPYRI*, Warsaw, 2nd Edition, 1955, pg. 522.
23 J. Bleicken, *SENATSGERICHT UND KAISERGERICHT*, 1963, pg. 181.
24 A.H.M. Jones, "Imperial and Senatorial Jurisdiction in the Early Principate", *ROMAN GOVERNMENT AND LAW*, Oxford, 1968. pg. 69.
25 A.W. Lintott, "Provocatio", *ANRW*. I,2; 1972, pg. 232.

law as "a challenge by an accused to a magistrate to appear before another tribunal on the ground that he is not acting within his own right"[26]. Reduced to its simplest expression, *provocatio* is the denial of a magistrate's judicial competence by the interdiction of the execution of the magisterial *coercitio* inherent in his *imperium*[27]. What an appellant was asking the higher legal authority to do was to set aside the judgment that had been handed down in a lower court and to replace it by a decision of his own.

It is important to note that by Paul's time the right of appeal had been extended to Roman citizens living in the provinces[28]. The right of a Roman citizen living anywhere in the vast Empire to appeal to Rome, thereby suspending the execution of a provincial magistrate's verdict of death or flogging, was of primordial importance in protecting his civil rights from being usurped. The right to appeal was an intrinsic right inherent in the *civitas*:

"The *ius provocationis* is a citizen's right because he is a citizen. Due to this fact, it is independent of the place where the citizen finds himself at the moment he exercises this right"[29].

B) ἐπικαλοῦμαι / *appellare*

Luke has Paul use the Greek formula Καίσαρα ἐπικαλοῦμαι to invoke the Emperor's legal competence in his case[30]. In the Middle Voice, the verb has the sense of calling upon, or invoking someone in one's behalf. The Vg. translates by *Caesarem appello*. In its legal sense the Latin verb means to seek the aid of someone (especially the tribune) or to refer to a higher judicial authority, i.e. to appeal.

H.J. Cadbury defines *appellatio* as "the request made by a citizen to the magistrate's colleague or to the tribune to intervene (*intercessio*) to protect him"[31]. The *intercessio* entailed the "complete invalidity of the act against which it was levelled"[32]. The *appellatio* was a right that could be exercised

---

26 A.H.J. Greenidge, *THE LEGAL PROCEDURE OF CICERO'S TIME*, London, 1901, pg. 306.
27 cf. Dionysius Halicarnassensis, V,70.2.
28 Lintott, *op.cit.*, pg. 251; Jones, "I Appeal to Caesar", *op.cit.*, pg. 53.
29 Giovannini, *op.cit.*, pg. 22–23. cf. Cicero, *de ReP.* II,31.54.
30 cf. Dionysius Halicarnassensis IX,39.1–2, who relates an incident wherein the Consuls ordered their Lictors to beat a man named Valero Publius with their rods. "The young man called upon the tribunes for assistance (τοὺς τε δημάρχους ἐπεκαλεῖτο), and asked, if he were guilty of any crime to stand trial before the plebeians". (E.T. = E. Cary/E. Spelman, *Loeb*, 1963). The case is interesting in that it shows how strong a Roman citizen's rights were. Dionysius notes that the consuls paid no heed to Publius' appeal. This in turn caused a tumult in the Forum, the plebeians forcing the consuls to flee. Then the plebeians asked that the case be heard before the people. cf. Plutarch, *Marcellus*, II,4, who relates the rejection of an an appeal by the tribunes of the people.
31 H.J. Cadbury, "Roman Law ... ", pg. 315.
32 A.H.J. Greenidge, *op.cit.*, pg. 288.

at any point in the course of the legal action, i.e. against either a final or an interlocutory decision[33]:

> "Any and all measures taken by the magistrate could be quashed: the institution of the proceedings, the arrest itself, ... the formulation of the indictment, the verdict handed down by the magistrate"[34].

In lodging an appeal, a defendant was aiming at a judicial reconsideration of a magisterial decision[35]. The appeal effectively suspended the ongoing legal action until such a time as it could be examined. The judge to whom the appeal was addressed would then have to completely re-examine the affair and hand down a new decision. In so doing, he could apply new principles of law or indeed modify any previous evaluation of the facts in the case[36].

Finally A.W. Lintott notes that the two forms of appeal for protection were "superficially different ways of achieving the same end, using the same basic source of power"[37]. Indeed the two words came to have a synonymous usage[38]:

> "This appeal procedure could equally well have been described as a *provocatio*, or *appellatio*. It seems to me [Lintott] that the interchangeability of these expressions ... is a natural consequence of, first the interdependence of *provocatio* and appeal to the tribunes in the Republic and second, the grant to Octavian of powers which enabled him to act like a united college of tribunes without the need to refer matters to the people at all"[39].

This does not mean that there was a significant lessening in the protection afforded by the law to a Roman citizen during the First Century A.D. Indeed the right to appeal was re-affirmed by the promulgation in Augustus' reign of the *Lex Iulia de vi publica et privata*. This law basically forbade an official holding the *imperium* to bind, torture or kill a Roman citizen who had appealed to Rome. The importance of the *Lex Iulia de vi publica et privata* lay in the fact that from the date of its promulgation "the Roman citizen was protected throughout the Roman Empire from the capital jurisdiction and violent *coercitio* of provincial governors"[40]. The general intention of this legislation was that Roman citizens, who

---

33 I. Buti, *op.cit.*, pg. 55.
34 Th. Mommsen, *STAATSRECHT*, Vol. I, pg. 276.
35 I. Buti, *op.cit.*, pg. 54.
36 J. Gaudemet, *op.cit.*, pg. 647.
37 A.W. Lintott, *op.cit.*, pg. 234.
38 cf. J. Bleicken, "Provocatio", *PAULYS - WISSOWA - RE*, 26er Halbband (Nachträge), 1959, col. 2445. In Col. 2456, Bleicken writes: "Der synonyme Gebrauch von *provocatio* und *appellatio* in den Quellen der Kaiserzeit ist wohl auf antiquarische Studien der Juristen zurückführen, die als den Hauptinhalt beider Institutionen die Herbeiführung des höchsten Gerichtes ansprachen und darum miteinander gleichsetzten."
39 A.W. Lintott, *op.cit.*, pg. 264.
40 Sherwin-White, pg. 59.

made an appeal from the provinces, should not in any way be hindered from having their case heard in Rome[41].

C) The *Princeps*: Recipient of the Appeal

With the founding of the Principate, the *Princeps* came to possess the appellate authority once vested solely in the Roman people. Thus appeals, formerly addressed *ad populum*[42], were now addressed to the sovereign *Princeps* who had the authority to hear the appeal (*ex provocatione cognoscere*). He enjoyed the customary right, once held only by the people, to ratify or to reverse (pardon) a death sentence handed down by a lower-ranking magistrate[43]. The *Princeps* also possessed the powers of the tribune (*tribunicia potestas*), that is the power to defend the people's liberty against any abuses of a lower magistrate[44]. Having the *tribunicia potestas* and the tribune's special power of *ius auxilii*, i.e. the power to give aid in response to an appeal, meant that the *Princeps* had the right to hear and judge an appeal (*ex appellatione cognoscere*) and the right of cassation. The *Princeps* was therefore truly the *maior potestas* or *maior collega* vis-à-vis all other Roman magistrates since this one and the same man held both the *proconsulare imperium* and the *tribunicia potestas*[45].

> "He intervened moreover in the appellate process by re-examining decisions taken by another judge either to amend them or replace them. (...) What interested the *Princeps* more than anything else, however, was the *political* affirmation of his authority in this area. This objective was pursued and accomplished by the assumption of judicial competence in the first instance or in appellate jurisdiction and by the promulgation of rescripts which decided controversies or resolved doubtful matters which had been submitted to him"[46].

V. Festus grants Paul's Appeal

We have examined the sequence of events which led to Paul's appeal. The text of Acts now goes on to describe the governor's reaction to the appeal: "Then Festus, when he had conferred with his council (συλλαλήσας μετὰ

---

41 Jones, "I Appeal to Caesar", *op.cit.*, pg. 54.
42 cf. Cicero, *de Leg.* III,4.11; *pro Sestio* XXX,65; *de ReP.* II,36.61.
43 cf. Suetonius, *Nero*, X,2: "When he was asked according to custom to sign the warrant for the execution of a man who had been condemned to death, he said: 'How I wish I had never learned to write!.'". (*Et cum de supplicio cuiusdam capite damnati ut ex more subscriberet admoneretur: 'Quam vellem,' inquit, 'nescire litteras.*) E.T. = J.C. Rolfe, *Loeb*, 1959.
44 For a description of the powers held by the tribune during the Republican period, cf. J. Bleicken, *DIE VERFASSUNG DER ROMISCHEN REPUBLIK, op.cit.*, pg. 86–88.
45 I. Buti, *op.cit.*, pg. 35.
46 *Ibid*, pg. 35.

τοῦ συμβουλίου), answered, 'You have appealed to Caesar; to Caesar you shall go'." (Καίσαρα ἐπικέκλησαι ἐπὶ Καίσαρα πορεύσῃ) (XXV,12).

Festus was doing two things in this verse, both in accordance with established custom in appellate cases: (a) consulting his council, (b) and taking his decision.

A) συλλαλήσας μετὰ τοῦ συμβουλίου (*cum consilio locutus*)

συλλαλέω – to talk with.

The text of Acts does not indicate any time lapse between Paul's making the appeal and Festus' granting it. It is quite possible, however, that Festus did not consult his council on the same day that Paul had made his appeal. Normally the governors were wont to allow a short time to pass before answering an appeal. It was indispensable that the magistrate be left with sufficient time to determine whether the appeal was well-founded or not. Th. Mommsen suggests that this delay was perhaps "limited to three days"[47].

The council of advisers (συμβούλιον = *consilium*)[48] was a deliberative body made up of συνέδροι (*consiliarii*). The council functioned as a jury or board of assessors. It was customary for the magistrate to call upon the council to give an advisory opinion in all important matters under examination[49]. The number of councilors was variable, but normally ranged from eight to twenty depending on the case's complexity and the locality in which the trial was taking place[50].

The council was normally made up of two categories of members:

1) A panel of Roman citizens who resided in the particular locality or district in which the chief magistrate was holding his assizes (*conventus civium Romanorum*)[51].

2) Military men and civilians who were in the governor's entourage and who attended him in one official capacity or another. Later on in the Principate, this category of councilor became a permanent class of auxiliary

---

47 Mommsen, *STAATSRECHT*, Vol. I, 279. Mommsen's hypothesis of a three day maximum delay is based on his reading of a provision in the municipal law of the Latin city of Salpensa in Spain. For the text of this law, cf. CIL. II,1963.27, Riccobono, *FIRA*, No. 23 and Girard, *Textes*[4], pg. 108–122. The *Lex Municipii Salpensani* dates from 82–84 A.D. and is a splendid example of a municipal charter of a Latin city.
48 cf. *SIG*[4], 684.11.
49 cf. J. Bleicken, *DIE VERFASSUNG DER ROMISCHEN REPUBLIK, op.cit.*, pg. 132.
50 cf. Cicero, *Verr.* II,i.29.73. cf. *CIL*. X,7852 which is the *Decretum Proconsulis Sardiniae de Finibus Patulcensium et Galillensium* (69 A.D.). In the decree one reads that the Proconsul L. Helvius Agrippa had a *consilium* of eight members assisting him in determining a case.
51 The *conventus civium Romanorum* was basically the Roman community resident in a non-Roman district and which formed a separate and distinct group. In Cicero, *Verr.* II,ii.13.32, the *conventus* signifies a panel of Roman citizens resident in a district from which a court is nominated. In *Verr.* II,ii,29.70 the word *conventus* means a particular district as a judicial entity.

bureaucrat, the *assessores consiliarii*, who were remunerated by the *praeses provinciae*.

The procedure used in the council's deliberations was relatively uncomplicated.

A) The governor consulted his council on a specific matter;

B) The councilors had to be sufficiently informed of the facts in the case;

C) After debating, each member gave his opinion;

D) The governor would state in his final decision that the council had been consulted. As the council was only an advisory body, the governor was under no constraint to accept its opinion. The final decision lay in his hands alone[52].

B) Καίσαρα ἐπικέκλησαι ἐπὶ Καίσαρα πορεύσῃ

The verse raises an interesting legal question: Was the governor automatically obliged to grant the appeal of a Roman citizen in a capital case? Could he disallow the appeal and try the case himself? If this were so, would he later need to seek ratification of the sentence handed down in his court from Rome? Finally could the governor send a case to Rome even if the defendant had not lodged an appeal?

P. Garnsey, for one, is categorical in denying that the governor was obliged to grant Paul's appeal to Rome:

" ... Festus was under no obligation to grant Paul his request. He could have tried the case and passed sentence. The fact that he conferred with his advisers (v.12) itself suggests that the sending off of Paul was not something automatic, something Festus was compelled to do. Why then did he let him go? Paul was a man of some importance because of his citizen status, and his fame – or notoriety. He was a difficult man to handle, and caused trouble wherever he went. Festus would be glad to be rid of him, especially as he really did not know how to deal with him"[53].

A.H.J. Greenidge states that in the Republican period, the governor enjoyed vast power over those Roman citizens residing in his province: "The power of the governor over Roman citizens in his province was, from a legal point of view, absolute and unlimited, and even extended to the infliction of capital punishment of every type"[54]. Nonetheless the eminent British jurist does go on to point out that in practice there were a certain number of legal restraints on gubernatorial power:

1) It was customary for the governor to consult the *consilium*. Even

---

52 cf. Cicero, *Verr.* II,ii.33.81; II,v.8.18.
53 Peter Garnsey, "The *Lex Iulia* and Appeal under the Empire", *JRS*, Vol. 56, 1966, pg. 184–185.
54 Greenidge, *op.cit.*, pg. 411–412.

though only an advisory body, the council's opinion could influence the governor's final decision in a case[55].

2) When the crime at hand was treasonable or seditious in nature it was more customary for the magistrate to send the ringleaders to be tried at Rome.

3) Customary law and judicial usages at Rome acted to limit the governor's *imperium* to a certain extent by determining the general form of the appropriate legal procedure needed:

> " ... the criminal procedure of the provinces was, in the protection of the citizen as in other respects, closely modelled on that of Rome: and custom seems to have directed that the governor should remit capital cases of Roman citizens to the home government, and that, in the exercise of his jurisdiction, he should inflict on them no degrading punishment"[56].

Cicero's rhetoric reached one of its most compelling and sublime moments when the great orator evoked just this question:

> "To bind a Roman citizen is a crime, to flog him is an abomination, to slay him is almost an act of murder: to crucify him is — what? There is no fitting word that can possibly describe so horrible a deed." (*Facinus est vincire civem Romanum, scelus verberare, prope parricidium necare: quid dicam in crucem tollere? Verbo satis digno tam nefaria res appellari nullo modo potest*)"[57].

Therefore the declaration *civis Romanus sum* should have sufficed to afford the Roman citizen the full protection of Roman law as it had the effect of valorizing his right to the *provocatio*[58].

Th. Mommsen is clearly of the opinion that the governor was bound to send the appellant to Rome once he had lodged his appeal:

> "In view of the shape which the right of *provocatio* had taken in the last century of the Republic, the Governor did not have the right to inflict the death sentence on a Roman citizen. Under the Principate, he was duty-bound to send a citizen threatened by corporal or capital punishment to Rome to be judged there if the said citizen so requested"[59].

As time went on, the referral of cases to Caesar's court became more frequent[60]. Indeed it became customary for the *legati* "to pass on to the Emperor cases involving subversion or danger to the Emperor's person"[61].

---

55 E.J. Urch goes too far when he states categorically that "the customary consultation of *consilia* limited the executive and judicial powers of a provincial governor". (Urch, *op.cit.*, pg. 97).
56 Greenidge, *op.cit.*, pg. 413.
57 Cicero, *Verr.* II,v.66.170. E.T. = L.H.G. Greenwood, *Loeb*, 1960.
58 cf. Cicero, *Ep..ad Fam.* X,32.3 where the cry *civis Romanus sum* was of no help.
59 Th. Mommsen, *STAATSRECHT*, Vol. II. pg. 269. Ulpianus writes that any official holding the *imperium* who orders a Roman citizen put to death or flogged is liable under the *Lex Iulia de vi publica:* "*Lege Iulia de vi publica tenetur, qui, cum imperium potestatemue haberet, civem Romanum adversus provocationem necaverit verberaverit iusseritue quid fieri aut quid in collum iniecerit ut torqueatur*", (*Digest,* XLVIII,6.7). cf. Paulus, *Sententiae*, V,26.1–2.
60 cf. J.H. Oliver, *op.cit.*, pg. 555.
61 F. Millar, "The Emperor, the Senate and the Provinces", *JRS*, Vol. 56, Parts 1 & 2; 1966, pg. 159.

By the Antonine period, governors were regularly sending capital cases involving Roman citizens to the imperial tribunal even if the defendant had made no prior appeal[62].

Finally there were certain types of cases in which the governor could try, condemn and execute Roman citizens for capital offences without acting contrary to the law of *provocatio*[63]. Th. Mommsen himself cites some examples of cases where the governor could reject an appeal: (a) if the appeal had been made solely to prolong the trial; (b) if postponing the execution of a sentence would have posed risks or dangers to public order and the common weal, or (c) if the crime in question involved charges such as counterfeiting, violence or kidnapping, etc., from which cases the appeal was generally excluded[64]. What is quite clear is that had the governors referred all the appeals made by the growing number of Roman citizens living in the provinces to the imperial tribunal, the whole court system would have collapsed from the sheer volume of cases.

Paul's case, however, did not lie within the framework of the exceptions outlined above:

> "The charges against Paul were either *extra ordinem*, as is probably the case, or if they could be subsumed under any statutory crime of the *ordo* it would be one of those, such as the treason law, which were not left to the authority of the provincial governors"[65].

The nature of the indictment against Paul was such that the appeal could not be rejected as invalid by the governor. Paul would thus have to be sent to Rome once he made the appeal. This is what the Lucan account in Acts goes on to relate in its final two chapters.

---

62 cf. Pliny, *Ep.* X.96. In this famous letter to Emperor Trajan, Pliny tells how he dealt with the Christians in the province of Bithynia of which he was governor and of the distinction he made between Christians who were not Roman citizens and those who were: "In the meanwhile, the method I have observed towards those who have been denounced to me as Christians is this: I interrogated them whether they were Christians; if they confessed it I repeated the question twice again, adding the threat of capital punishment; if they still persevered, I ordered them to be executed. (...) There were others also possessed with the same infatuation, being citizens of Rome, I directed them to be carried thither." (*Fuerunt alii similis amentiae; quos, quia cives Romani erant, adnotavi in Urbem remittendos*). Pliny then made no effort to judge their cases or hand down a verdict under his own authority, but rather routinely referred their cases to Trajan. Indeed in the prologue to this letter, Pliny writes: "It is a rule, Sir, which I inviolably observe, to refer myself to you in all my doubts; for who is more capable of guiding my uncertainty or informing my ignorance?" (E.T. = W. Melmoth, *Loeb*, 1963). It seems very likely that there had been *cognitiones de Christianis* before Pliny's consultation with Trajan, cf. Eusebius, *Hist. Eccl.* V,1.44 ff.
63 Sherwin-White, pg. 60–61.
64 Th. Mommsen, *STRAFRECHT*, pg. 470–471. cf. J.H. Oliver, *op.cit.*, pg. 555, who notes: "Even Roman citizens of western-origin could not be allowed to insist on Roman trials in unimportant cases".
65 Sherwin-White, pg. 62.

Chapter VIII
Caesarea (Part 3): Paul and Agrippa

I. Festus summarizes Paul's Case to Agrippa

We have seen how a sequence of dramatic events led to Paul's appeal and to Festus' granting the appeal. The governor now had to write the letters of report which would accompany the apostle to Rome in order to inform the imperial tribunal of the particulars of the case.

According to Acts XXV,26, Festus was at a loss as to what to say in his letters of report. Luke gives this legal necessity as the reason which motivated the governor to consult Agrippa. Festus twice gives an account of Paul's case to the King. The first (XXV,13–22) is presented as a rather informal summary of the case given in the absence of the defendant. The second account (XXV,23–27) takes place in the more formal framework of a hearing held in the presence not only of Paul but of assessors and other dignitaries. Luke's primary authorial aim, however, is not to give a detailed account of the hearing, nor does he supply a reconstruction of Festus' letter. Rather he centers the apostle's apologetic speech in Chapter 26 on the salvation message. The procedural considerations which appear in the latter part of Chapter 25 thus serve as the point of departure for Paul's powerful proclamation of the Messiah and the justification of the Gentile mission, which are the principal themes of the apologetic speech in Chapter 26.

Luke opens the story of this last formal hearing in Acts by the announcement of the arrival of Agrippa and Bernice at Caesarea: "Now when some days had passed, Agrippa the King and Bernice arrived at Caesarea to welcome (ἀσπασάμενοι) Festus. And as they stayed there many days, Festus laid Paul's case before the King," (ὁ Φῆστος τῷ βασιλεῖ ἀνέθετο τὰ κατὰ τὸν Παῦλον) (XXV,13–14a).

A) King Herod Agrippa II

Marcus Iulius Agrippa, the son of Herod Agrippa I, was born in 27 A.D. and educated in Rome. He did not succeed his father upon the latter's death in 44 A.D. as Judaea once again became a Roman Province under a governor [1]. Emperor Claudius gave Agrippa the Kingdom of Chalcis in 50 A.D. following the death of Agrippa's uncle Herod [2]. The Emperor also appointed him "curator of the temple" (ἐπιμελητής τοῦ ἱεροῦ) [3] and gave him the right of appointing the Jewish High Priest. In 53 A.D., Claudius granted to him the tetrarchy of Philip together with Batanaea, as well as Trachonitis and Lysanias' former tetrarchy of Abila; but deprived him of Chalcis [4]. In 54 A.D. Agrippa obtained parts of Galilee and Peraea from Nero [5]. It was at this time that he changed the name of his capital city from Caesarea Philippi to Neronias. His title was βασιλεὺς μέγας φιλόκαισαρ εὐσεβὴς καὶ φιλορώμαιος [6] which says much about his politics. When possible Agrippa tried to promote the cause of Judaism; yet his policy was one of unconditional subordination to Rome. He remained loyal to Rome during the Jewish wars [7] and was subsequently awarded more territory. Paul thus appears before a man well-known in the Roman court [8].

Luke's account of Herod Agrippa's role in Paul's trial is much more detailed and developed than his account of the Herodian role in the trial of Jesus. There are nonetheless interesting parallels between the two accounts. In both Gospel and Acts, Luke introduces the Herodians at a crucial moment in the legal process and for a specific reason: "As in the trial of Jesus, Luke has stylized the Herodian as a half-way figure. Being neither fully Jewish nor fully Roman, Agrippa has been asked to shed some light on the Jewish charges" [9]. The literary pattern is the same. Herod Antipas, intrigued by Jesus reputation, desires to see him (Lk. IX,9; XXIII, 8); similarly Herod Agrippa expresses a desire to hear Paul (Acts XXV, 22). Neither man proves receptive to the Christian message (Luke XXIII, 11; Acts XXVI,28).

B) Bernice

Bernice was the daughter of Agrippa I, sister of Agrippa II and Drusilla and the widow of her uncle, Herod of Chalcis. At the time of Paul's appearance, she was closely associated and reputedly living notoriously with her brother [10].

---

1 *Ant.* XIX,9.2 (360–366); XX,6.3 (134–136).
2 *Ant.* XX,5.2 (104); *BJ.* II,12.1 (223).
3 *Ant.* XX,9.7 (222).
4 *Ant.* XX,7.1 (138). cf. *BJ.* II,12.8 (247).
5 *Ant.* XX,8.4 (159); *BJ.* II,13.2 (252).
6 *OGIS.* 419; 420.
7 cf. *BJ.* II,16.4 (345–401) in which Josephus gives an account of Agrippa's speech to the Jews trying to dissuade them from war with the Romans.
8 For a convenient summary of Agrippa II's life and reign, cf. R.D. Sullivan, "The Dynasty of Judaea in the First Century", *ANRW.* II,8; 1977, pg. 329–345.
9 Walaskay, *op.cit.*, pg. 57.
10 *BJ.* II,11.5 (217); *Ant.* XX,7.3 (145); Juvenal, *Satire* VI,155–160.

C) ἀσπασάμενοι

ἀσπάζομαι – to greet, to pay one's respect to (cf. Latin *salutare*). Here the verb is used in a more technical sense: paying respects officially and formally to the governing authorities[11], paying homage to them by making an official call. King Agrippa was careful to maintain very friendly relations with Festus throughout the latter's term as governor[12].

D) ὁ Φῆστος τῷ βασιλεῖ ἀνέθετο τὰ κατὰ τὸν Παῦλον

ἀνατίθημι – in general to 'refer' a thing to a person, to 'communicate' with a view to consultation; hence the judicial nuance of 'remit' or 'refer' something to an examining body[13]. There is no suggestion in the account that Paul was being remanded into Agrippa's custody, but simply that the King was being officially consulted.

Festus began by summarizing what had already transpired in the case: "There is a man left prisoner by Felix; and when I was at Jerusalem, the chief priests and the leaders of the Jews gave information about him[14] asking for sentence against him." (αἰτούμενοι κατ' αὐτοῦ καταδίκην) (XXV, 14b–15).

A) αἰτούμενοι κατ' αὐτοῦ καταδίκην (Vg. = *postulantes adversus illum damnationem*)

ἡ καταδίκη – 'judgement given against' someone, 'sentence', 'condemnation'[15]. This is the only NT usage of this word. The related verb καταδικάζω means to condemn (in the Active), while the sense in the Middle is for a plaintiff to aim at or to obtain the pronouncing of a damnatory sentence on his opponent. Festus' statement reflects the real essence of the Sanhedrin's demand: they wanted Paul transferred to the Jewish high court, where his condemnation would be a foregone conclusion.

Festus tells Aprippa that he had been firm – at least in the procedure's initial stages – in refusing this demand: "I answered them that it was not the custom of the Romans to give up anyone (οὐκ ἔστιν ἔθος Ῥωμαίοις χαρίζεσθαί τινα ἄνθρωπον) before the accused met the accusers face to face (πρὶν ἢ ὁ κατηγορούμενος κατὰ πρόσωπον ἔχοι τοὺς κατηγόρους)

---

11 cf. *OGIS.* 219.43; *P. Flor.* 296.57. cf. *MM*, pg. 85.
12 cf. *Ant.* XX,8.11 (189–196).
13 *LS⁹*, pg. 123; *MM.* pg. 38. A good example of this usage is in Polybius XXI,45.11: they were in doubt and referred (ἀνέθεντο) the affair to the Senate.
14 For the verb ἐμφανίζω cf. *supra*. pg. 104.
15 *LS⁹*, pg. 889. cf. Wisdom XII,27. For the juridical sense of condemnation, cf. Plutarch, *Coriolanus* XX,4; *BJ.* IV,5.2(317). As a financial penalty, cf. *Ant.* XVII,12.2 (338). Thucydides V,49.1.

and had the opportunity to make his defense concerning the charge laid against him." (τόπον τε ἀπολογίας λάβοι περὶ τοῦ ἐγκλήματος) (XXV,16).

J. Dupont has amply shown the significance of this verse in his magisterial study *"Aequitas Romana"*. He considers Festus' formulation as an "expression of a fundamental principle of Roman law and indeed of all human justice"[16]. Festus' speech reflects the important role of customary law in Roman jurisprudence:

> "No Roman legislative text that has come down to us expresses in precise terms the judicial prescription set forth by Festus, but nonetheless, his declaration quite splendidly conveys what was a constant practice of Roman procedure"[17].

A) οὐκ ἔστιν ἔθος 'Ρωμαίοις χαρίζεσθαί τινα ἄνθρωπον (Vg. = *non est consuetudo Romanis donare aliquem hominem*)

ἔθος – cf. the Latin *consuetudo*. In Scripture the word usually designates custom, habit or use, the customary practice of cultic ordinances and observance of religious prescriptions and rites[18]. In the present passage, it has a more technical, legal meaning: "common practice or use which thereby is law"[19]. Custom as a source of law is expressly acknowledged as far back as the Third Century B.C. It played an important part in all branches of law, private, penal and administrative[20]. When he pronounced the word ἔθος, the governor was not merely mentioning a procedural norm; rather, he was evoking a whole judicial use both ancient and standard. Festus states that he refused to hand over Paul to the Sanhedrin because this would have violated the ἔθος; implying that such action would have flouted all that was lawful, fought all that was right and scorned all that was just. Festus' sense of justice and equity is thus highlighted in the account, forming a stark contrast to the injustice, violence and inequity of the Jewish plaintiffs.

B) πρὶν ἢ ὁ κατηγορούμενος κατὰ πρόσωπον ἔχοι τοὺς κατηγόρους (Vg. = *prius quam is qui accusatur praesentes habeat accusatores*)

The procedure admitted no anonymous denunciations; the two parties had to confront one another in front of the judge[21].

---

16 Dupont, "Aequitas Romana", *op.cit.*, pg. 528.
17 *Ibid.* pg. 542.
18 cf. Lk. I,9; II,42; Acts VI,14; XV,1; XXI,21; XXVIII,17.
19 Dupont, "Aequitas Romana", *op.cit.*, pg. 531.
20 R. Taubenschlag, "Customary Law and Custom in the Papyri", *OPERA MINORA*, Warsaw, 1959, Vol. II, pg. 91–92.
21 cf. Pliny, *Ep.* X,97 in which Trajan clearly states that anonymous denunciations were to be considered as juridically invalid. Here Trajan says: *"Sine auctore vero propositi libelli nullo crimine locum habere debent. Nam et pessimi exempli, nec nostri saeculi est"*. cf. Hadrian's Rescript

The verse contains two Optatives (ἔχοι and λάβοι), a grammatical usage which is rather rare in Acts. Luke fits his rhetoric to the scene. In presenting Paul's case, Festus speaks in a more polished form of Greek.

C) τόπον τε ἀπολογίας λάβοι περὶ τοῦ ἐγκλήματος (Vg. = *locumque defendendi accipiat ad abluenda crimina*)

ὁ τόπος — cf. the Latin *locus*[22]. Here the sense of the word is metaphorical: opportunity, occasion for acting[23].

ἡ ἀπολογία — J. Dupont defines *apologia* as "the plea by which the accused answers the charges which have been made against him and provides explanations which would be likely to justify his case"[24]. Here Festus uses the word in its strict legal sense of a defence against accusations before a judge, the antithesis of ἡ κατηγορία[25]. The same legal usage appears in 2 Tim IV,16a: "At my first defence, no one took my part; all deserted me". Paul himself uses the word twice in the Epistle to the Philippians. In Phil. I,7 he writes, "I hold you in my heart, for you are all partakers with me of grace, both in my imprisonment and in the defence and confirmation of the gospel". In Phil. I,16, Paul explains the reason for his imprisonment: "I am here for the defence of the gospel". In Philippians the word *apologia* is still used in a judicial setting (Paul's imprisonment) but takes on a wider meaning. Paul offers no defence on the specific charges for which he has been imprisoned. Rather than dwelling on the strictly judicial aspects of his case, the apostle uses the occasion for the defence and confirmation of the Gospel. In Luke's account of Paul's apologetic speeches, the word *apologia* also has this wider meaning. It is first and foremost a witnessing to and a defence of the Gospel. The apologetic speeches in Acts also occur in the context of a precise legal setting; yet their main thrust is clearly theological and not juridical.

Finally, the accused could not normally be judged without having had the opportunity to make his *apologia*. Appian writes in the *Bella Civilia*: "Our law, Senators, requires that the accused shall himself hear the charge preferred against him and shall be judged after he has made his own defence"[26].

τὸ ἔγκλημα — cf. Latin *crimen*, the accusation or charge[27]. Vs. 16 is thus a key one in the Lucan account of Paul's trial. This is not only due to the

---

addressed to Minucius Fundanus, Proconsul of Asia (124 A.D.), in Justin, *I Apol.* LXVIII; Eusebius, *Hist. Eccl.* IV,9.
22 Cicero, *de Prov. Cons.* I,2.
23 cf. *Ant.* XVI,8.5 (258).
24 Dupont, "Aequitas Romana", *op.cit.*, pg. 536.
25 cf. *Ant.* XVIII,8.1 (259): οἷος ἦν ἐπ' ἀπολογίᾳ χωρεῖν τῶν κατηγορημένων.
26 Appian, *Bell. Civ.*, III,54.
27 For the word ἔγκλημα, cf. *supra*, pg. 108.

legal vocabulary it contains, but also in that it clearly shows the workings of Roman judicial procedure and how much Paul, the Roman citizen, benefited from the rights and privileges inherent in that citizenship when he appealed for protection against his adversaries.

Festus continues his summary of Paul's case by telling Agrippa that he acted quickly in the matter: "When therefore they came here I made no delay, (ἀναβολὴν μηδεμίαν ποιησάμενος), but on the next day (τῇ ἑξῆς) took my seat on the tribunal and ordered the man to be brought in." (XXV,17). The governor says that he quickly concluded that the apostle had done nothing evil and that the dispute was basically theological: "When the accusers stood up, they brought no charge in his case of such evils as I supposed; but they had certain points of dispute with him about their own superstition (τῆς ἰδίας δεισιδαιμονίας) and about one Jesus, who was dead, but whom Paul asserted to be alive". (XXV,18–19). Festus explained his request for the case to be heard at Jerusalem – not as currying favour with the Jewish authorities – but as a necessity in investigating the case born of his own perplexity: "being at a loss how to investigate these questions, (ἀπορούμενος δὲ ἐγὼ τὴν περὶ τούτων ζήτησιν) I asked whether he wished to go to Jerusalem and be tried there regarding them. But when Paul had appealed to be kept for the decision of the Emperor, (εἰς τὴν τοῦ Σεβαστοῦ διάγνωσιν) "I commanded him to be held until I could send him to Caesar." (ἕως οὗ ἀναπέμψω αὐτὸς Καίσαρα) (XXV, 20–21).

A) ἀναβολὴν μηδεμίαν ποιησάμενος / τῇ ἑξῆς

Once again the promptness of the Roman examining magistrate in dealing with Paul's case is underlined.

B) τῆς ἰδίας δεισιδαιμονίας (sua superstitione)

This is the only NT occurrence of the word δεισιδαιμονία. The precise meaning of this term varied according to the stress put on one of its two component parts: δείδω (to fear) or δαίμων. Thus δεισιδαιμονία could either denote a pious attitude or deportment towards the gods[28] or an excessive fear of them, a fear of provoking their hostility or of upsetting the *pax deorum*[29].

---

28 cf. Acts XVII,22: "Men of Athens, I perceive that in every way you are very religious (δεισιδαιμονεστέρους)." In this passage the sense of δεισιδαίμων is positive: a pious discharge of religious duties.
29 S. Calderone, "Superstitio", *ANRW*, I,2; 1972, pg. 382.

There is a certain ambiguity in the usage of this word in the text at hand. Δεισιδαιμονία in the sense of *religion* or *beliefs*[30] would have a positive connotation. This is the complimentary sense that such a scene would require. Δεισιδαιμονία in the sense of *superstition*, i.e. the fear of evil spirits[31] would, of course, be more negative. Now throughout much of the literature of Republican Rome, the term *superstitio* was pejorative:

> "Apparently metaphorical meanings arose in the literature of the early Empire, and the word itself comes into vogue only in Silver Latin, where it is with few exceptions derisive and abstract"[32].

Finally the term could be used in reference to any legally unrecognized religion or to religious behaviour which was uncultured and unrefined or not in conformity with the spirit of the official religious tradition of the Roman state[33].

C) ἀπορούμενος δὲ ἐγὼ τὴν περὶ τούτων ζήτησιν

ἀπορέω – to be in doubt, not to know which way to turn, not to know how to decide or what to do, to be perplexed or puzzled[34].

ἡ ζήτησις – debate, matter of controversy, judicial inquiry. cf. the Latin *quaestio*.

Festus realized to some degree that the dispute between the apostle and the Sanhedrin was about the resurrection and Messiahship of Jesus. The theological controversy, however, remained incomprehensible to the governor. In his view, a religious dispute between Jews ought to be heard by the Sanhedrin. Festus thus justifies his request to Paul for a transfer of the case on that legal ground.

D) εἰς τὴν τοῦ Σεβαστοῦ διάγνωσιν (Vg. = *ad Augusti cognitionem*)

σεβαστός – reverend, venerable. It is the Greek equivalent of the Latin *augustus*. As an adjective, the word conveyed the meaning of holy or sacred when used in reference to the deities or to sacred places. *Augustus* was also the title of the Roman Emperors first conferred on Octavian by the Senate in 27 B.C.[35]. The use of this title elevated the Emperor above all other Romans. It was in this spirit that Philo wrote:

---

30 cf. *Ant.* XIX,5.3 (290).
31 cf. Theophrastus, *Characters* XVI,1: "Superstitiousness (δεισιδαιμονία), I need hardly say, would seem to be a sort of cowardice with respect to the divine." (πρὸς τὸ δαιμόνιον). (E.T. = J.M. Edmonds, *Loeb*, 1961).
32 R.C. Ross,"Superstitio", *CJ*, Vol. 64; 1968–1969, pg. 356.
33 Calderone, *op.cit.*, pg. 383–385. *Superstitio*, writes the Italian scholar, "puo essere ogni *religio iniusta*, non riconosciuta" (pg. 383).
34 cf. 2 Cor. IV,8; Gal. IV,20.
35 cf. *Res Gestae divi Augusti*, 34. cf. Lucian, *Laps* 18 where σεβαστός means the Emperor. In Lk. II,1, the transliteration Αυγοῦστος is used as a proper name to designate the first Emperor.

"Again, consider him who in all the virtues transcended human nature, who on account of the vastness of his imperial sovereignty as well as nobility of character was the first to bear the name of the August or Venerable (πρῶτος ὀνομασθεὶς Σεβαστός), a title received not through lineal succession as a portion of its heritage but because he himself became the source of the veneration which was received also by those who followed him; who from the moment that he had charge of the common weal took in hand the troubled and chaotic condition of affairs[36].

Thus one has the expression σεβαστοὶ θεοί which was very likely used in reference to the deified Emperors[37]. Apart from Acts XXVII,1, the only NT use of this word occurs in Festus' speech. The term καῖσαρ, which Festus also uses, is the more common NT designation for the Emperor.

ἡ διάγνωσις — distinguishing, discerning, examination, decision. It is the equivalent of the Latin *cognitio*. Thus the expression ἐπὶ διαγνώσεων τοῦ Σεβαστοῦ means *a cognitionibus Augusti*[38]. The use of this expression would signify a full judicial trial during which evidence was received and at whose conclusion a judgement was handed down. This is the only NT use of the noun διάγνωσις although the verb διαγινώσκω appears elsewhere[39].

E) ἕως οὗ ἀναπέμψω αὐτὸν πρὸς καίσαρα

ἀναπέμπω — to send up, to remit someone to another, normally higher, judicial authority[40]. cf. the Latin term *remitto*. Here of course it means Paul's transference to the appellate court at Rome. In his Gospel, Luke uses the verb in its precise legal sense when he describes Jesus' being sent to Herod and then back to Pilate[41]. Four of the five NT uses of this verb occur in Luke-Acts.

II. Festus lays Paul's Case before Agrippa

The case greatly interested the King: "And Agrippa said to Festus, 'I should like to hear the man myself'. (ἐβουλόμην καὶ αὐτὸς τοῦ ἀνθρώπου ἀκοῦσαι)". To which the governor replied: "Tomorrow (αὔριον) you shall hear him" (XXV,22).

---

36 Philo, *Legat. ad Gaium* XXI,143. — E.T. = F.H. Colson, *Loeb*, 1962.
37 cf. *IG*. VII,2233; *SIG*[4], 820.6.
38 *IG*. XIV,1072.
39 For the verb διαγινώσκω, cf. *supra*, pg. 104.
40 *P. Hib.* I,57 (year 247 B.C.); *P. Tebt.* VII,7 (year 114 B.C.).
41 cf. Lk. XXIII,7; 11;15.

A) ἐβουλόμην καὶ αὐτὸς τοῦ ἀνθρώπου ἀκοῦσαι (volebam et ipse hominem audire).

The verb is in the Imperfect expressing wish[42]. The grammatical turn of the verse could signify that King Agrippa had previously heard of Paul and now desired to hear him personally out of curiosity or out of personal interest.

B) αὔριον

Once again a hearing is promptly arranged[43].

We have now come to the last of the hearings recorded in the Book of Acts: Festus lays Paul's case before King Agrippa (XXV,23–27), the apostle makes his defence (XXVI,1–23), there is an exchange between the apostle and the King (XXVI,24–29) and the King gives his opinion in Paul's case (XXVI,30–32).

Luke begins the narrative with a description of the solemn opening of the hearing: "So on the morrow Agrippa and Bernice came with great pomp, and they entered the audience hall (ἀκροατήριον) with the military tribunes (σύν τε χιλιάρχοις) and the prominent men of the city (καὶ ἀνδράσιν τοῖς κατ' ἐξοχὴν τῆς πόλεως). Then by command of Festus Paul was brought in." (XXV,23).

A) ἀκροατήριον (auditorium)

The Auditorium was the room used by the Emperor or a magistrate to hear cases[44]. The ἀκροατήριον mentioned here was most likely in Herod's palace. This is the only use of this word in the NT.

B) σύν τε χιλιάρχοις

According to Josephus, there were five cohorts in Caesarea[45]. These were troops from the Roman Legions in Syria, each commanded by a military tribune. All these officers, like Claudius Lysias, were Roman citizens.

---

[42] M. Zerwick writes: "The Potential Optative for modest assertion has (unlike its counterpart in questions) disappeared from popular speech, and is to be found in Luke alone, who uses it with obvious aiming at literary effect, e.g. where Paul is made to say to Agrippa εὐξαίμην ἄν Acts 26,29, or to Felix εἴ τι ἔχοιεν πρὸς ἐμέ Acts 24,19. In place of this optative we often find the future ... or the imperfect, as Acts 25,22 ἐβουλόμην for βουλοίμην ἄν; ... " (M. Zerwick, GB, pg. 123, No. 356 E.T.).
[43] cf. Acts XXII,30; XXIV,1; XXV,6.
[44] Digest IV,4.18.1 cf. P. Benoit, op.cit., pg. 545.
[45] Ant. XIX,9.2 (365).

C) ἀνδράσιν τοῖς κατ' ἐξοχὴν τῆς πόλεως

The city referred to here is Caesarea and not Jerusalem. The men in Agrippa's train were probably all Gentiles.

As soon as Paul had entered the audience hall, the governor began to lay his case before the King: "King Agrippa and all who are present with us (καὶ πάντες οἱ συνπαρόντες ἡμῖν ἄνδρες), you see this man whom the whole Jewish people petitioned me. (θεωρεῖτε τοῦτον περὶ οὗ ἅπαν τὸ πλῆθος τῶν Ἰουδαίων ἐνέτυχόν μοι), both at Jerusalem and here, shouting that he ought not to live any longer. But I found (ἐγὼ δὲ κατελαβόμην) that he had done nothing deserving death; (μηδὲν ἄξιον αὐτὸν θανάτου πεπραχέναι); and as he himself appealed to the Emperor, I decided to send him. But I have nothing definite to write my Lord about him. (περὶ οὗ ἀσφαλές τι γράψαι τῷ Κυρίῳ οὐκ ἔχω). Therefore I have brought him before you, and especially before you King Agrippa, that, after we have examined him, I may have something to write. (διὸ προήγαγον αὐτὸν ἐφ' ὑμῶν καὶ μάλιστα ἐπὶ σοῦ Βασιλεῦ Ἀγρίππα ὅπως τῆς ἀνακρίσεως γενομένης σκῶ τί γράψω). For it seems to me unreasonable, (ἄλογον), in sending a prisoner, not to indicate the charges against him." (XXV,24–27).

A) καὶ πάντες οἱ συνπαρόντες ἡμῖν ἄνδρες

The purpose of this hearing was to enable the governor to gain a clearer understanding of the case so that he could write a coherent and reasonable dismissory letter to the Princeps. Paul had not been transferred to Agrippa's jurisdiction; he was still in Roman custody. Indeed in this hearing before Agrippa, normal trial procedure was adhered to as strictly as possible. The *men who are present* were basically functioning as the King's council. In this passage they are termed οἱ συνπαρόντες ἡμῖν ἄνδρες. Later in the narrative they will be referred to as οἱ συγκαθήμενοι αὐτοῖς (XXVI, 30). After Paul finishes the *apologia pro sua vita*, these men go out to consult with Festus and Agrippa.

B) θεωρεῖτε τοῦτον περὶ οὗ ἅπαν τὸ πλῆθος τῶν Ἰουδαίων ἐνέτυχόν μοι

ἐντυγχάνω – to petition the authorities.
ἅπας – is the strengthened form for πᾶς; hence, 'quite all'. 'the whole of', 'every one' together[46]. Ἅπας is the preferred form "when something impressive is to be said, especially with implicative meaning"[47]. A signi-

---
46 *LS*[9], pg. 181.
47 *ThWb*. Vol. V, pg. 889.

ficant modification in the identify of the plaintiffs has to be noted here. In Festus' first account to Agrippa, he says that it was the High Priests and elders of the Jews who laid information against the apostle (XXV,15), here he tells the king that the *whole* of the Jewish community petitioned him.

C) ἐγὼ δὲ κατελαβόμμν μηδὲν ἄξιον αὐτὸν θανάτου πεπραχέναι

Luke emphasizes the governor's opinion in Paul's case: he has committed no political crime meriting the death penalty. This is the second time that a Roman official declares the political indictment against Paul to be unsubstantiated. Indeed Festus' viewpoint is expressed in very nearly the same terms as those used by Lysias in XXIII,29.

D) περὶ οὗ ἀσφαλές τι γράψαι τῷ κυρίῳ οὐκ ἔχω

κύριος – a person in supreme authority, the lord or master, cf. Latin *dominus*; cf. the adjective κύριος – vested with legal power. The term was used in reference to Herod the Great and Herod Agrippa I[48]. It was used of the gods, especially in the East[49] and of deified rulers[50]. It was also used of the Roman emperors[51]. The title κύριος became associated with the veneration offered the Emperor[52]. From a political point of view, its use denoted the Princeps' absolute position in the State and implied acceptance of an oriental-style monarchy. Augustus had rejected the title *dominus*[53] as had his successor Tiberius[54] because these two rulers strove to camouflage under a constitutional cover and Republican façade the triumph of a type of absolute monarchy, associated in the Orient with the term *dominus*[55]. Despite this rejection by Augustus and Tiberius, the word slowly established itself in the official political vocabulary of the Principate. The term *dominus* thus became increasingly accepted as a title for the Emperor; by Trajan's time it had become quite normal to call the Emperor *dominus*[56].

---

48 *OGIS*. 415.1; 418.1.
49 cf. *P. Oxy*. CX,2 (Lord Sarapis); *IG*. XIV,1124 (Artemis).
50 cf. *OGIS*. 186.8 (year 62 B.C.) where Ptolemy XIII is described as τοῦ κυρίου βασιλέυς θεοῦ.
51 *P. Oxy*. XXXVII,6 (Claudius); *P. Tebt*. II, 286.2 (Hadrian). *P. Oxy* II,246.37 might very well refer to Nero, but this is not entirely certain.
52 C.S.C. Williams, *op.cit.*, pg. 261.
53 Suetonius, *Aug*. LIII,1: "*Domini appellationem ut maledictum et obprobrium semper exhorruit*".
54 cf. Suetonius, *Tib*. XXVII,1; Tacitus, *Ann*. II,87; Dio Cassius, LVII,8.1–2.
55 *ThWb*. Vol. III, pg. 1056.
56 cf. Pliny, *Ep*. X,96.

E) διὸ προήγαγον αὐτὸν ἐφ' ὑμῶν καὶ μάλιστα ἐπὶ σοῦ Βασιλεῦ Ἀγρίππα ὅπως τῆς ἀνακρίσεως γενομένης σκῶ τί γράψω

Here the words προάγω and ἐφ' ὑμῶν are being used in a legal sense as the scene describes a judicial investigation. Agrippa was being consulted as an authority on Jewish religious problems and not because the governor was legally obliged to do so. As governor, Festus was supreme in Judaea. The purpose of the hearing was for Festus to obtain enough pertinent information to enable him to write a coherent account of the case to the Emperor. This is made perfectly clear in XXV,27 when Festus terms it unreasonable (ἄλογον) to send a dimissory letter to the imperial court without a clear listing of the charges making up the indictment.

III. Paul makes his Defence

Paul's speech before Agrippa is the longest and most detailed of his apologetic speeches in Acts. The speech is a literary masterpiece of great spirituality and profound beauty; a magnificent exposition of the apostle's life and work. It is here that Luke's apologetic programme – summarized in the final verse of the speech – is carried through:
1) Christ must suffer,
2) He is the first to rise from the dead,
3) He proclaims light to both the People and to the Gentiles (καταγγέλλειν τῷ τε λαῷ καὶ τοῖς ἔθνεσιν)

In view of Luke's overriding theological interests, it is not surprising (although perhaps disappointing to us!) that he does not have Paul defend himself at length and in detail against the specific political charges. From the strictly judicial point of view, Paul's *apologia* was irrelevant in a Roman court of law.

After Festus had finished laying the case before Agrippa, Paul was given permission to speak (XXVI,1a)[57]. Luke writes that Paul "stretched out his hand (ἐκτείνας τὴν χεῖρα) and made his defense" (XXVI,1b)[58].

A) ἐκτείνας τὴν χεῖρα

According to the Acts-narrative, Paul made this same gesture before delivering his sermon in the synagogue at Pisidian Antioch (XIII,40) and before

---

[57] The prophecy that Ananias of Damascus heard at the moment of Paul's conversion is now fulfilled: "But the Lord said to him, 'Go, for he is a chosen instrument of mine to carry my name before the Gentiles and kings and the sons of Israel;'" (Acts IX, 15).
[58] ἀπελογεῖτο cf. *supra*, pg. 125.

making his speech at the temple gate in Jerusalem (XXI,40). Such freedom of movement would indicate that the apostle was only very lightly chained to a soldier at the moment he began his speech. The Syriac Harclean Margin adds the beautifully spiritual words *confidens et in spiritu sancto consolationem accipiens* between *Paul* and *stretched out his hand*.

Paul's defence began with the customary *captatio benevolentiae*[59]: "I think myself fortunate (ἥγημαι ἐμαυτὸν μακάριον) that it is before you, King Agrippa, I am to make my defense today against all the accusations of the Jews (περὶ πάντων ὧν ἐγκαλοῦμαι ὑπὸ Ἰουδαίων), because you are especially familiar with all the customs and controversies of the Jews (μάλιστα γνώστην ὄντα σε πάντων τῶν κατὰ Ἰουδαίους ἐθῶν τε καὶ ζητημάτων); therefore I beg you to listen to me patiently." (XXVI,2–3).

A) ἥγημαι ἐμαυτὸν μακάριον

μακάριος can be compared to εὐθύμως in Paul's speech before Felix (XXIV,10). Paul, in a very diplomatic way, is expressing confidence in the man who is hearing the case.

B) περὶ πάντων ὧν ἐγκαλοῦμαι ὑπὸ Ἰουδαίων

The article is also missing in Acts XXV,10; XXVI,4,7,21. It is interesting to note the absence of the article with the name of an opponent in Attic court case speeches[60].

C) μάλιστα γνώστην ὄντα σε πάντων τῶν κατὰ Ἰουδαίους ἐθῶν τε καὶ ζητημάτων

In his introduction, Paul recalls the King's considerable knowledge of Jewish religious problems. From the beginning of his speech the apostle centers his remarks on the doctrinal aspects of the case. Paul's defence consists of a theological presentation of his beliefs and an explanation of his mission. Once again Luke's aim is primarily apologetic and not the presentation of a detailed legal defence.

After having finished the *captatio benevolentiae*, the apostle began the main part of his speech by stressing his belonging to the Jewish nation: "My manner of life from my youth, spent from the beginning among my own nation (ἐν τῷ ἔθνει μου) and at Jerusalem, is known by all the Jews. They have known for a long time, if they are willing to testify, that according to the strictest party of our religion I have lived as a Pharisee" (ὅτι

---

[59] cf. *supra*, pg. 120.
[60] cf. *Bl. Debr.*, section 262.1: "Names for peoples, if they denote the group as a collective whole, do not require the article any more than do personal names".

Paul makes his Defence

κατὰ τὴν ἀκριβεστάτην αἵρεσιν τῆς ἡμετέρας θρησκείας ἔζησα Φαρισαῖος) (XXVI,4–5).

A) ἐν τῷ ἔθνει μου

In gente mea probably refers to Paul's life in the Jewish community in Tarsus, as it is clearly distinguished from his subsequent life in Jerusalem.

B) ὅτι κατὰ τὴν ἀκριβεστάτην αἵρεσιν τῆς ἡμετέρας θρησκείας ἔζησα Φαρισαῖος

Once again Paul identifies himself with the Pharisaic party.

Paul continues his speech by restating his belief in the resurrection: "And now I stand here on trial for the hope in the promise made by God to our Fathers, ... And for this hope I am accused by Jews, O King! Why is it thought incredible by any of you that God raises the dead?" (XXVI, 6–8).

Once more the apostle draws the attention of his audience to the fact that his dispute with the Sanhedrin is doctrinal. By referring to the fathers (patriarchs), Paul is showing that his religious activity is squarely rooted in the Old Testament. Paul points out the absurdity of the Sanhedrin's prosecution of a man who believes in the resurrection and the hope of Israel, which were central Pharisaic beliefs.

The apostle goes on to talk of his early persecution of the Church: "I myself was convinced that I ought to do many things in opposing the name of Jesus of Narazeth. And I did so in Jerusalem; I not only shut up many of the saints in prison by authority from the chief priests, (τῶν ἀρχιερέων ἐξουσίαν) but when they were put to death I cast my vote against them. (ἀναιρουμένων τε αὐτῶν κατήνεγκα ψῆφον). And I punished them often in all the synagogues (καὶ κατὰ πάσας τὰς συναγωγὰς πολλάκις τιμωρῶν) and tried to make them blaspheme (αὐτοὺς ἠνάγ καζον βλασφημεῖν); and in raging fury against them, I persecuted them even to foreign cities. (ἕως καὶ εἰς τὰς ἔξω πόλεις). Thus I journeyed to Damascus with the authority and commission of the chief priests." (μετ᾽ ἐξουσίας καὶ ἐπιτροπῆς τῆς τῶν ἀρχιερέων) (XXVI,9–12).

A) ἀναιρουμένων τε αὐτῶν κατήνεγκα ψῆφον

1) ἀναιρέω – to kill, put to death, murder. The verb occurs 23 times in the NT; interestingly enough 20 of the occurrences are in Luke-Acts.

---

61 cf. Acts VII,58; VIII,1; 3; IX,1–2; XXII,19–20.
62 In 1 Cor. XV,9, Paul states that he is unfit to be called an apostle because "I persecuted the Church of God". In Gal. I,13, he notes that he "persecuted the Church of God violently and tried to destroy it".

Paul's words recall the intensity of the persecution of the Church mentioned earlier on in Acts. Paul's participation in the persecution of the Church is stressed on several occasions in the Acts-narrative[61] and the apostle mentions it himself in the epistles as well[62]. The persecution was bitter and was aimed at the destruction of Church.

2) ψῆφος — a pebble used in voting; hence, ψῆφον καταφέρω = to give one's vote. This notice raises the question as to whether Paul had been a voting member of the Sanhedrin earlier on in his career. This is rather unlikely. The members of the Sanhedrin were normally elderly men of note, who belonged to the Jerusalem aristocracy. Paul was still a young man at the time of the persecution mentioned in the narrative and moreover hailed from the Diaspora community of Tarsus. It is more plausible to understand Paul's statement in a metaphorical sense: he cast his vote in that he *approved* the murder of the martyr Stephen and the putting to death of the saints.

B) καὶ κατὰ πάσας τὰς συναγωγὰς πολλάκις τιμωρῶν αὐτοὺς ἠνάγκαζον βλασφημεῖν

1) τιμωρέω — to take vengeance on, to punish. The verb occurs only here and in an earlier account of the persecution in XXII,5. The punishment referred to here is flogging, which was used by the synagogue as a means of punishment for a number of offences including disobedience against rabbinical authority[63].

2) βλασφημέω — to calumniate, to revile; to speak of divine persons or things in impious and irrevant terms. Here the apostle is referring to a renouncing of Christ (*maledicere Christo*)[64].

C) μετ' ἐξουσίας καὶ ἐπιτροπῆς τῆς τῶν ἀρχιερέων

The passage indicates that the Sanhedrin enjoyed judicial authority, not only over the Jews in Jerusalem and in Judaea, but also over those living in the Diaspora. It also indicates that the supreme Jewish tribunal could legally prosecute Jews for breaches of religious law ἕως καὶ εἰς τὰς ἔξω πόλεις (*in exteras civitates*). Paul twice mentions that he was acting by authority (μετ' ἐξουσίας = *cum potestate*) from the chief priests and also by their commission (ἐπιτροπῆς = *et permissu*). This *potestas* did not, however, include the right to carry out the death penalty. The *ius gladii* was a power held exclusively by the Roman authorities. If Christians had in fact been legally executed in the persecution that Paul evokes in his

---

63 cf. A.J. Hultgren, "Paul's pre-Christian Persecutions of the Church", *JBL*. Vol. 95, No. 1; March 1976, pg. 104. Paul himself was a victim of this chastisement (cf. 2 Cor. XI,24).

64 cf. Pliny, *Ep.* X,96. The juridical sense of this passage is that the Christians were condemned because of their profession of faith and their refusal to renounce Christ. cf. I Cor. XII,3.

speech, then these executions were carried out by the Roman administration at the official request of the Jewish authorities[65].

After citing his role as a fierce persecutor of the saints, Paul continues by relating the events on the road to Damascus and the heavenly vision that he had. He stresses that his calling and ministry were divinely ordained. Jesus Himself spoke to Paul who was called henceforth "to serve and to bear witness to the things in which you have seen me," (XXVI,16). The Lord will not abandon his newly-chosen servant and witness: "I will appear to you, delivering you (ἐξαιρούμενός σε) from the people and from the Gentiles." (XXVI,17). The apostle was sent[66] by the Lord to proclaim the message to Jews and to Gentiles both "that they may turn from darkness to light and from the power of Satan to God, that they may receive forgiveness of sins and a place among those who are sanctified by faith in me" (XXVI,18).

A) ἐξαιρούμενός σε

A particularly appropriate promise in Paul's present predicament. But as the Acts-narrative makes abundantly clear, the people (λαός) were far bitterer foes of the apostle than the Gentiles (ἔθνη).

B) Paul makes a fundamental theological point in his discourse: the inheritance is associated henceforth with sanctification by faith in the Lord Jesus Christ.

Paul was faithful to his mission, preaching "first to those at Damascus, then at Jerusalem and throughout all the country of Judaea, and also to the Gentiles, that they should repent and turn to God and perform deeds worthy of their repentance" (XXVI,19b–20)[67]. These verses show that Paul's missionary endeavours were not atypical of the Jewish missionary who was attempting to convert the Gentiles. Apostolic exhortation was firmly rooted in the Jewish concept of repentance/conversion. Paul had

---

65 cf. *ThWb.* Vol. VII, pg. 866: "The Mishnah ordains that in towns of at least 120 adult male Israelites there is to be a Sanhedrin of 23 members, *Sanh.*, I,66. The term is attested for these lesser courts. In the case of capital crimes the Mishnah lays down that all 23 persons must pass sentence. In respect of these courts, too, the Jews clung to their claim that the *ius gladii* belonged to them even though the right of the sword was exercised only by the Roman authorities." cf. Origen, *Ep. ad Africanum* 14: "Now, for instance, that the Romans rule, and the Jews pay the half-shekel to them, how great power by the concession of Caesar the [Jewish] ethnarch has; so that we, who have had experience of it, know that he differs in little form from a true king! Private trials are held according to the law, and some are condemned to death. And though there is not full license for this, still it is not done without the knowledge of the ruler, ..."
66 ἐγὼ ἀποστέλλω σε.
67 cf. Rom. XV,19: "By the power of signs and wonders, by the power of the Holy Spirit, so that from Jerusalem and as far round as Illyricum, I have fully preached the Gospel of Christ".

now arrived at the heart of his *apologia*. He *had* to obey the Lord's order to preach to all men, Jews and Gentiles. It was utterly impossible for him to resist divine directives. In ministering to the Gentiles he was following God's will.

Paul states that it was as a consequence of fulfilling this divinely-ordained mission that he was arrested: "For this reason the Jews seized me in the temple and tried to kill me" (XXVI,21). But the apostle was not deserted by the Lord: "To this day I have had the help that comes from God" (XXVI,22a). With this divine succour — the fulfillment of the promise recorded in Acts XVI,17 — the apostle was able to continue his ministry despite the many obstacles in his way: "and so I stand here testifying both to small and great" (XXVI,22b). He then concludes his speech by a mighty proclamation of the resurrection and Messiahship of Jesus: he had never said anything "but what the prophets and Moses said would come to pass: that Christ must suffer, and that, by being the first to rise from the dead, he would proclaim light both to the people and to the Gentiles." (XXVI,22c–23). The good news preached by Paul was nothing other than the realization of Old Testament expectations. Paul was attempting to demonstrate to Agrippa that Christianity enjoyed real and genuine unity with the Old Covenant. In embracing Christianity, the apostle was not being unfaithful to Judaism; on the contrary, he was being obedient to its teachings and living its promises to their fullest according to God's plan for mankind's salvation[68].

IV. Agrippa gives his Opinion in Paul's Case

Luke concludes his relation of Paul's *apologia* by two short dialogues, the first with Festus and the second with the King. As Paul was making his defence, Luke writes that Festus shouted out: "Paul, you are mad (Μαίνη, Παῦλε); your great learning is turning you mad (εἰς μανίαν). But Paul said, I am not mad, most excellent Festus, but I am speaking the sober truth (ἀληθείας καὶ σωφροσύνης ῥήματα)." (XXVI,24–25).

Throughout his speech, the apostle's remarks had been centered on theological points which were utterly bewildering to Festus. The governor could not consider anyone having eschatological expectations as anything but mad. Paul, however, rejects this categorization, his words are words of truth and sanity. Thus σωφροσύνη is the antithesis to μανία.

---

[68] cf. Lk. XXIV,44: Rom. XVI,25–26; I Cor. XV,3.

There may be an underlying legal dimension to Festus' exclamation. The jurist Modestinus notes in his comments on the *Lex Iulia Maiestatis* that the defendant's mental condition should be taken into consideration by the judge. The judge had to evaluate if the treason were premeditated or whether the accused was in his right mind (*sanae mentis*) when the act was perpetrated[69].

Paul now concludes his remarks to Festus by bringing the King into the dialogue: "For the King knows about these things, and to him I speak freely; for I am persuaded that none of these things has escaped his notice, for this was not done in a corner. King Agrippa, do you believe the prophets? I know that you believe." (XXVI,26–27).

A) Here Paul assures the governor that his doctrinal presentation was not a product of madness, but something the King understood very well. The question of whether the King himself believed in the prophets was a well-crafted one. Had Agrippa responded negatively, he would have been denying the prophets thereby antagonizing the orthodox Jews; had he responded affirmatively, he would have brought upon his head the ridicule of the Greeks and Romans in his entourage by lending support to Paul's eschatological pronouncements. The King, however, was not to be outdone for he skirted the question quite skillfully: "And Agrippa said to Paul, 'In a short time you think to make me a Christian!'" (ἐν ὀλίγῳ με πείθεις Χριστιανὸν ποιῆσαι) (XXVI,28). The hearing was now at an end, the exchanges were becoming embarrassing and inconvenient to the King; but Luke has Paul get in a last word: "Whether short or long, I would to God that not only you but also all who hear me this day might become such as I am – except for these chains" (XXVI,29).

B) ἐν ὀλίγῳ με πείθεις Χριστιανὸν ποιῆσαι

According to Acts XI,26, it was in Antioch that the disciples were called Christians for the first time. Here the King's use of the word Christian, rather than the term Nazarene used by the Jews to designate Christ's followers, is purposeful. The exchange between Paul and Agrippa took place in a Gentile setting where the Jewish expression would not likely have been understood. Moreover as Agrippa had no intention of confessing Christianity, his use of the term Christian has to be given a negative connotation[70].

---

69 cf. *Digest* XLVIII,4.7: "*Quamquam enim temerarii digni poena sint, tamen ut insanis illis parcendum est, si non tale sit delictum, quod vel ex scriptura legis descendit vel ad exemplum legis vindicandum est*".

70 The only other NT use of the term Χριστιανός occurs in I Peter IV,16: "Yet if one suffers as a Christian, let him not be ashamed, but under that name let him glorify God".

The hearing having ended, "the King arose, and the governor and Bernice and those who were sitting with them; (οἱ συγκαθήμενοι); and when they had withdrawn, they said to one another, (ἀναχωρήσαντες ἐλάλουν πρὸς ἀλλήλους λέγοντες) 'This man is doing nothing to deserve death or imprisonment'." (οὐδὲν θανάτου ἢ δεσμῶν ἄξιον πράσσει ὁ ἄνθρωπος οὗτος) (XXVI,30–31).

A) οἱ συγκαθήμενοι

συγκαθίζω – In the Middle and Passive Voices the verb has the sense of to 'sit in conclave', to 'meet for deliberation'[71].

B) ἀναχωρήσαντες ἐλάλουν πρὸς ἀλλήλους λέγοντες

The councilors are meeting in accordance with standard Roman procedure.

C) οὐδὲν θανάτου ἢ δεσμῶν ἄξιον πράσσει ὁ ἄνθρωπος οὗτος (Vg. = *quia nihil morte aut vinculorum dignum quid facit homo iste*)

The Council's opinion was that Paul was engaged in a theological dispute with the leaders of his nation and that his missionary activity did not constitute a danger to the public weal or a threat to the Emperor's authority. For the third time in the Acts-narrative, Paul is found innocent of the political charges preferred against him.

The words used by the Council here to express Paul's innocence are very similar to those used by Lysias in XXIII,29 and Festus in XXV,25. To stress the point even more, Luke relates Agrippa's evaluation of Paul's case immediately after the Council's finding: "This man could have been set free if he had not appealed to Caesar" (ἀπολελύσθαι ἐδύνατο ὁ ἄνθρωπος οὗτος εἰ μὴ ἐπεκέκλητο Καίσαρα) (XXVI,32).

A) ἀπολελύσθαι ἐδύνατο ὁ ἄνθρωπος οὗτος εἰ μὴ ἐπεκέκλητο Καίσαρα (Vg. = *dimitti poterat homo hic si non appellasset Caesarem*)

The verb *appeal* (ἐπεκέκλητο) is in the Pluperfect tense rather than in the Aorist. Paul's appeal to Caesar "was not a mere act in the past, but had put him into a definite position in the eyes of the law"[72]. By appealing to the Emperor for protection, Paul had placed himself under imperial security. Henceforth only the Emperor could judicially dispose of Paul's case.

---

71 *LS*[9], pg. 1662.
72 Bruce, pg. 450.

B) The strong emphasis which Luke places on the fact that both Governor and King had found Paul innocent of the political charges in the indictment would imply that Festus' letters of report to the appellate jurisdiction would be favourable to the apostle's cause. Conversely the plaintiffs' case had been substantially weakened. The fact that the most important political authorities in Palestine considered Paul innocent may very well have persuaded the Sanhedrin not to pursue the case against the apostle in Rome.

Chapter IX
Rome: Paul Spends Two Years Awaiting Trial

I. Paul is transferred from Caesarea to Rome

The story of Paul's transfer from Caesarea to Rome (XXVII,1–XXVIII, 15) is one of the most exciting tales in Acts. G.B. Miles and G. Trompf call this story the "dramatic center of Acts": "It is the moving bridge between the mysterious scene of Christian origins and the awesome power of the Roman forum, and it is an adventure recounted with much more than Luke's usual amount of detail"[1]. It is outside the subject of this work to describe at length Paul's voyage, the shipwreck, the sojourn in Malta and the voyage thence to Puteoli. We shall therefore limit ourselves to the points directly touching the apostle's legal situation.

The 27th chapter of Acts opens with an account of Paul's boarding the boat: "And when it was decided that we should sail for Italy, they delivered Paul and some other prisoners (παρεδίδουν τόν τε Παῦλον καί τινας ἑτέρους δεσμώτας) to a centurion of the Augustan Cohort, (σπείρης Σεβαστῆς), named Julius." (XXVII,1). Paul was not without his companions on board. Not only does Acts specifically say that the apostle was accompanied by Aristarchus (XXVII,2); but also the *we*-narrative resumes at this point, possibly implying that the author of Acts himself boarded the vessel with Paul.

The centurion was benevolent towards his prisoner: "The next day we put in at Sidon; and Julius treated Paul kindly and gave him leave to go to his friends and be cared for." (φιλανθρώπως τε ὁ Ἰούλιος τῷ Παύλῳ χρησάμενος ἐπέτρεψεν πρὸς τοὺς φίλους πορευθέντι ἐπιμελείας τυχεῖν) (XXVII,3).

---

1 G.B. Miles & G. Trompf, "Luke and Antiphon", *HTR.* Vol. 69, No. 3–4, July–October 1976, pg. 259. This interesting article treats the theology of Acts 27–28 in the light of pagan beliefs about divine retribution, pollution and shipwreck.

A) παρεδίδουν τόν τε Παῦλον καί τινας ἑτέρους δεσμώτας

The verb παρεδίδουν has no precise subject, but it is surely the Roman authorities who are meant[2]. Here we should note three things:

1) The text states that Paul was transferred with other prisoners. The fact that Paul was a Roman citizen and was on his way to Rome to have his case heard by the Emperor set him apart from peregrine prisoners in the eyes of his captors. That Aristarchus and others[3] were able to accompany the apostle was a sign of Festus' benevolence, for the governor was under no obligation to grant this special favour.

2) The centurion was surely bearing Festus' letters of report which he was to deliver along with the prisoner to the appropriate authorities in Rome[4]. As examining magistrate he was obliged to furnish this report to the Emperor which would have contained his point of view in the case and the criteria used to justify his decision[5].

3) Insofar as the financing of the voyage was concerned, it would seem that Paul's transportation was most likely at state expense. The prisoners, however, had to pay for their own food. The fares of Paul's companions were either paid by Paul or else they travelled at their own expense. All these expenses were in addition to the prescribed deposit that Paul had to pay as part of the appellatory process. The apostle did not seem to have any financial cares at this point in his story.

B) σπείρης Σεβαστῆς

Josephus notes that there were *cohortes Sebastenorum* in the garrisons of Herod the Great at Jerusalem and Herod Agrippa I at Caesarea[6]. It is most probable, however, that the σπεῖρα Σεβαστή in this passage refers to the '*cohors Augusta* and not to the *cohors Sebastenorum*[7].

It is possible that Julius[8], a legionary centurion, was part of a group of couriers responsible for communication between the Princeps and his armies[9].

---

2 The Western Text, represented by 97 (421) h p^c sy(p) hmg, reads "And then the governor decided to send him to Caesar ..." (καὶ οὕτως ἔκρινεν αὐτὸν ὁ ἡγεμὼν ἀναπέμπεσθαι Καίσαρι).
3 614pc, sy^h read "Aristarchus and Secundus".
4 cf. I. Buti, *op.cit.*, pg. 57.
5 cf. F. de Visscher, *LES EDITS D'AUGUSTE*, Osnabrück, 1940, reprint 1965, pg. 79.
6 Josephus mentions the *cohortes Sebastenorum* quite a number of times in his writings, e.g. *Ant.* XIX, 9.2 (365); XX, 6.1 (122); *BJ.* II, 3.4 (52); 4.2 (58); 4.3 (63); 5.2 (74); 12.5 (236).
7 cf. *OGIS.* 421 for an inscription with the mention σπείρης Αὐ[γούστης].
8 The Codex Alexandrinus reads Ἰούλιανος.
9 cf. Ramsay, *SPT.*, pg. 315; Bruce, pg. 452.

C) φιλανθρώπως τε ὁ Ἰούλιος τῷ Παύλῳ χρησάμενος

1) χράομαι — to treat, to behave towards, to deal with.
2) φιλανθρώπως — humanely, benevolently, kindly, courteously.

Twice in the present narrative Julius' benevolence is underlined: here he granted Paul the privilege of going to his friends at Sidon to be cared for. Later in Acts XXVII,43 he prevented the killing of the prisoners during the shipwreck off Malta in order to save Paul's life[10].

D) ἐπέτρεψεν πρὸς τοὺς φίλους πορευθέντι ἐπιμελείας τυχεῖν (*permisit ad amicos ire et curam sui agere*)[11].

The boat docked at Sidon, no doubt for commercial reasons. Although the apostle was allowed to go into the city, he was still a prisoner. He could visit the Christians of Sidon only in the company of a soldier responsible for guarding him. The brethren at Sidon not only cared for Paul while he was among them, but most probably furnished him with supplies for the long sea voyage to Rome.

The remainder of Chapter 27 recounts the voyage across the Mediterranean Sea and the shipwreck off Malta. The narrative stresses that despite the tremendous dangers the apostle encountered during the voyage and shipwreck, it was God's will that he be miraculously saved in order to testify in Rome[12].

The beginning of Chapter 28 tells of Paul's stay on Malta. Luke notes that the apostle and his companions as well as the other passengers stayed on Malta for three months (XXVIII,11). This is the first of a series of chronological notations punctuating the account of Paul's arrival and sojourn in Italy[13]. During this time spent in Malta, Paul and his friends were received and entertained for three days by Publius, "the chief man of the island" (τῷ πρώτῳ τῆς νήσου) (XXVIII,7) whose father Paul had cured of fever and dysentery. The expression "chief man of the island" (*principis insulae*) could simply designate a leading man of the island or, as is more likely, the chief official on Malta. If so this is yet another example of

---

10 cf. the favourable description of the centurion Cornelius in Acts X,1–2: "At Caesarea there was a man named Cornelius, a centurion of what was known as the Italian cohort, a devout man who feared God with all his household, gave alms liberally to the people, and prayed constantly to God." cf. Lk. VII,1–10; XXIII,47.
11 cf. the variant reading in the *Codex Floriacensis*: "*permisit amicis qui veniebant (ad eum) ut curam eius agerent*".
12 cf. Miles & Trompf: "the theology of Acts is such that Paul's innocence was established by a divinely controlled happening *en route* to Rome which made the Emperor's judgement superfluous" (Miles & Trompf, *op.cit.*, pg. 265, note 22).
13 Acts XXVIII,12 (three days); 13 (one day); 14 (seven days); 17 (after three days); 23 (appointed a day); 30 (two years).

Luke's use of correct terminology in designating a local or provincial official[14].

When the three months in Malta were over, Paul and his companions set sail for Italy. After putting in at Syracuse and Rhegium, they landed at Puteoli where "we found brethren, and were invited to stay with them for seven days" (οὗ εὑρόντες ἀδελφοὺς παρεκλήθημεν παρ' αὐτοῖς ἐπιμεῖναι ἡμέρας ἑπτά) (XXVIII,14a). The apostle had now reached journey's end: "And so we came to Rome (καὶ οὕτως εἰς τὴν Ῥώμην ἤλθαμεν). And the brethren there when they heard of us, came as far as the Forum of Appius and Three Taverns to meet us (ἦλθαν εἰς ἀπάντησιν ἡμῖν). On seeing them Paul thanked God and took courage" (οὓς ἰδὼν ὁ Παῦλος εὐχαριστήσας τῷ Θεῷ ἔλαβε θάρσος)(XXVIII,14b—15).

A) οὗ εὑρόντες ἀδελφοὺς παρεκλήθημεν παρ' αὐτοῖς ἐπιμεῖναι ἡμέρας ἑπτά

παρακαλέω — to entreat, beseech. The verb can also have the meaning of to comfort, encourage, cheer or console[15].

There was a well-established Jewish community residing at Puteoli. Josephus mentions it when he relates the story of Pseudo-Alexander's arrival in Italy[16]. No doubt a goodly number of the brethren mentioned in the Acts-narrative were converts from that community. Seven days was a rather lengthy stay at a place so near the journey's end. It is possible that the centurion consented to so long a period of time out of esteem for his prisoner, preoccupation about his health or simply for commercial reasons.

B) καὶ οὕτως εἰς τὴν Ῥώμην ἤλθαμεν

The divine order which God had twice given Paul that he must bear witness at Rome had now come to the point of realization[17]. Clearly too, Paul's own human desire coincided with the divine command. In his epistle to the Romans, the apostle had made it clear that he wanted to come to Rome very much to preach the Gospel of Jesus Christ in the capital[18]:

> "From the beginnings of Christianity, it was easy to realize that the future of the new religion would be decided in the capital of the Empire; the meeting place of all races, the place from

---

14 cf. *IG.* XIV.601; *CIL.* X, 7495. cf. A. Brunot, "Malte, Fille de St. Paul", *Bible et Terre Sainte*, Paris, No. 89, February 1967, pg. 8—17 for an overview of the archeological discoveries made in the mid-1960's at the Church of St. Paul Milqi where a very ancient tradition localizes Publius' villa.
15 cf. the variant appearing in the *Codex Gigas:* "et inventis fratribus consolati sumus et mansimus apud eos dies septem".
16 *Ant.* XVII,12.1 (328); *BJ.* II,7.1 (104).
17 cf. Acts XXIII,11 ; XXVII, 23—24a.
18 Rm. I,15; XV,23b. cf. Acts XIX,21b.

which all doctrines radiated. Only the genius of Rome could give to Christianity that stamp and seal of universality which it needed in order to assure its diffusion and which it would acquire by shedding the Jewish particularism inherited from its origins. The apostle to the nations understood this quite clearly"[19].

C) ἦλθαν εἰς ἀπάντησιν ἡμῖν

ἡ ἀπάντησις — meeting, encounter, also an escort[20]. The word appears four times in the NT; here it means a delegation's going out to meet an arriving dignitary.

Luke's treatment of the Roman Christians is quite summary. He does indeed mention them when he says that they went out and met the apostle at the Forum of Appius and Three Taverns. He further relates Paul's grateful reaction upon meeting them: οὕς ἰδὼν ὁ Παῦλος εὐχαριστήσας τῷ Θεῷ ἔλαβε θάρσος. Nonetheless it is striking that the only recorded meeting between Paul and the Roman Christians takes place *outside* Rome; once in the city Paul seems to have no further contact with them. After their appearance at the beginning of the pericope, the Roman Christians simply disappear from the Acts-narrative[21]. It is possible that Luke gives little place in his account to the Roman Christians because of subsequent tension between them and Paul[22]. But their absence from the narrative could be simply part of Luke's literary design: the author's attention is manifestly drawn to the Jewish community residing in Rome and to the Jewish rejection of Paul's evangelical message rather than to the relationship, spiritual or psychological, between Paul and the Roman Christians.

II. Paul a Prisoner at Rome

After having been greeted by the brethren, the apostle entered the city: "And when we came to Rome (ὅτε δὲ εἰσήλθομεν εἰς Ῥώμην), Paul was allowed to stay by himself (ἐπετράπη τῷ Παύλῳ μένειν καθ' ἑαυτόν), with the soldier that guarded him" (σὺν τῷ φυλάσσοντι αὐτὸν στρατιώτῃ) (XXVIII,16).

---

19 J.B. Frey, *op.cit.*, pg. 269–270.
20 cf. Mt. XXV,6; Cicero, *Att.* XVI,11.6.
21 cf. J. Dupont, "La Conclusion des Actes et son Rapport à l'ensemble de l'Ouvrage de Luc", *LES ACTES DES APOTRES*, Louvain, 1979, pg. 362.
22 Oscar Cullmann puts forth the hypothesis that relations between Peter and Paul on the one hand and the Christian community of Rome, dominated by Judeo-Christians, on the other were very bad. He maintains that Peter and Paul were martyred late in Nero's reign quite possibly because they were denounced to the imperial authorities by members of the Roman Christian

The description of Paul's stay in Rome is very brief. It begins here at verse 16 and continues at vs. 30–31. Although replete with legal terms and juridical allusions, the three verses serve mainly as the framework against which the more important story of Paul's meetings with the Roman Jewish leadership is set. Luke's primary interest here is to reiterate for the final time in Acts the Jewish rejection of the Gospel and the parallel mission to the Gentiles; it is not to describe Paul's dealings with the imperial tribunal. The scene of the action is thus set in the apostle's lodgings, not in the *Praetorium*; his interlocutors are the city's Jewish leaders and not the Roman judicial authorities, who are strikingly absent from Luke's account.

1. *The Stratopedarch*

A) ὅτε δὲ εἰσήλθομεν εἰς 'Ρώμην

The mention of the Forum of Appius and of the Three Taverns would mean that the apostle had come up the *via Appia*, probably entering the city itself by the Porta Capena.

There is an important variant reading here which inserts the following lesson after the word *Rome*: "the Centurion handed over the prisoners to the Stratopedarch, but Paul was allowed ..." (ὁ ἑκατόνταρχος παρέδωκεν τοὺς δεσμίους τῷ στρατοπεδάρχῳ τῷ δὲ Παύλῳ ἐπετράπη ...)[23].

B) ὁ στρατοπεδάρχης

This is the 'military commander', the *praefectus castrorum*[24]. At Rome τὸ στρατόπεδον referred to the *Castra Praetoriana*. The exact identification of the Stratopedarch referred to in the Western variants has been subject to much debate.

---

community itself. This would help to explain, in Cullmann's view, why Luke speaks so little of the Roman Christians in Acts and why Clement of Rome gives so few details of the last days of the two apostles. Clement and " ... for the same reasons the author of Acts and all his contemporaries avoid recalling in too precise a way this spot which sullied the history of the Roman Church". ("Les Causes de la Mort de Pierre et Paul d'après le témoignage de Clément Romain", *RHPR*, No. 3, May–June 1930, pg. 299–300.) cf. Clement of Rome, *Cor.* V,2–7, where he notes that Peter suffered διὰ ζῆλον ἄδικον and Paul διὰ ζῆλον καὶ ἔριν.

23 δ 614, byz, g,p, vg.codd., hcl*, sah, eth.
24 *LS*[9], pg. 1653. cf. Mason, *GREEK TERMS*, pg. 87. cf. *CIL*. III,13648; 14187, where στρατοπεδάρχης = "*praefectus kastrorum*". A.C. Clark notes that the most frequent sense of Stratopedarch is "Commander of a legion, ... a rarer sense is that of *praefectus castrorum*". (Clark, *THE ACTS OF THE APOSTLES*, Oxford, 1933, pg. 386).

One hypothesis identified the Stratopedarch with the *princeps peregrinorum*[25]. This official was the commander of the *Castra Peregrina*[26], located on Mt. Caelius, which was a center for legionary officers on leave in Rome and a base for the *milites peregrini* or *frumentarii*:

> "These officials, probably originally charged with business relating to the supply of food for armies, fulfilled other functions also – the bearing of important messages, imperial secret police, etc., and were general liaison officers between the legions in the provinces and legionary centurions on furlough at Rome[27].

According to this identification, it would have been the *frumentarii* who had the care of prisoners who were to appear in Caesar's court. A.N. Sherwin-White notes, however, that although the office of *princeps peregrinorum* was known in the time of Trajan, there is no solid evidence that the *frumentarii* had assumed police duties before the 2nd Century:

> "Their original duty was to organize the supply of corn, as their name implies, and their police duties arose as a by-product of their peregrinations around the Empire. In the first century there is nothing to connect them with police functions, still less with the organization of appellate jurisdiction"[28].

Indeed Broughton himself cautions that *princeps peregrinorum* is an interpretation and not an accurate rendering of Stratopedarch which "may refer to the head of the Praetorium"[29]. Thus another possibility is to identify the Stratopedarch with the Praetorian Prefect into whose keeping prisoners from the provinces were confided:

> "As for the prisoners sent from the provinces to Rome for judgement by the imperial tribunal, their transport and their surveillance were most likely entrusted primarily to the legionary units stationed in the *castra peregrina* of the capital city. These units were under the authority of the military commanders of Rome, i.e. under the Praetorian Prefects. These prefects ... also doubtlessly directed the capital's prison system"[30].

Tacitus gives an example of the police duties entrusted to the Praetorian Prefect:

> "Claudius ... dispatched at full speed a body of soldiers under the praetorian prefect Crispinus, who found Asiaticus at Baiae, threw him into irons, and hauled him to the capital"[31].

In the Western variants, the word Stratopedarch is in the singular. A. Wikenhauser concludes that this would put Paul's arrival in Rome during the

---

25 "*Stratopedarch*" is so translated in the *Codex Gigas*.
26 cf. *CIL*. VI, 354 (reign of Septimus Severus) for the expression "*princeps castrorum peregrinorum*". cf. *BJ*, II, 19.4 (531).
27 T.R.S. Broughton, *op.cit.*, pg. 444. cf. A.C. Clark, *op.cit.*, pg. 386.
28 Sherwin-White, pg. 109. cf. *CIL*. III,433 (reign of Trajan).
29 Broughton, *op.cit.*, pg. 444.
30 Th. Mommsen, *STRAFRECHT*, pg. 316. A.C. Clark notes that the *frumentarii* were employed by the Praetorian Prefects when in Rome in the execution of sentences pronounced by them. (Clark, *op.cit.*, pg. 387).
31 Tacitus, *Ann.* XI,1 (year 47 A.D.). E.T.–J. Jackson, *Loeb*, 1963. cf. Pliny, *Ep.* X,57 where Trajan writes: "*vinctus mitti ad praefectos praetorii mei debet*".

time of Afranius Burrus (prefect from 51 to 62 A.D.), for after Burrus' death there were normally two Praetorian Prefects functioning simultaneously[32].

Finally Sherwin-White identifies the Stratopedarch with the chief administrator of the *officium* of the Praetorian Guard, the *princeps castrorum*, who was a subordinate of the Praetorian Prefect:

> "This post happens to be known at Rome only from the Trajanic period onward, but it corresponded in duties and standing to the like-named officer in the legionary army, the *princeps praetorii legionis*, the head of the organizational command of a legion. This necessary post is testified, in the legions, from the time of Claudius onwards, and there is no reason to suppose that the *princeps castrorum* of the Praetorian Guard was a later creation. This official is the personage most likely to be in executive control of prisoners awaiting trial at Rome in the Julio-Claudian period"[33].

We would have to conclude on the basis of the evidence available (notably epigraphical) that the Stratopedarch mentioned in the Western variants is to be identified with the *princeps castrorum* even though the existence of this precise post cannot be indubitably proved for so early a period as Nero's reign.

2. *In Custodia Militari*

Acts XXVIII,16 is quite clear as to the conditions of Paul's custody: he was allowed to stay by himself with the soldier who guarded him.

A) ἐπετράπη τῷ Παύλῳ μένειν καθ' ἑαυτόν

Luke conveys a very important message here. The Roman authorities felt that Paul was no danger to public order. He was thus not imprisoned in the *Castrum*, but was allowed to take his own lodgings *extra castra*[34]. Luke's purpose in stressing the lenient conditions of custody was to provide his readers with a virtual attestation that the Roman authorities considered the apostle to be innocent of the political charges preferred against him.

B) σὺν τῷ φυλάσσοντι αὐτὸν στρατιώτῃ

φυλάσσω — cf. Latin *custodio*. to guard (a prisoner), to keep watch on.

While waiting for his appeal to be heard, Paul, of course, remained in

---

32 A. Wikenhauser, *op.cit.*, pg. 286.
33 Sherwin-White, pg. 110.
34 The Western variants add the words "outside the barracks" (ἔξω τῆς παρεμβολῆς) after καθ' ἑαυτόν. cf. δ 614 1611 2147 g p vg.codd Ambst hcl*.

Roman custody. He was lightly chained with the ἅλυσις (*catena*) to a soldier detailed to guard him.

The jurist Ulpianus notes that it was the proconsul who normally determined the type of custody into which a prisoner was remanded: imprisonment, handing him over to the military, placing him under the trusteeship of a surety or putting him under his own recognizance. The proconsular decision was not only based on the nature of the charge preferred against the accused, but also on the basis of his status in society, wealth or rank[35]. Conditions of custody were thus subject to a great deal of magisterial arbitrariness.

Here we should like to distinguish between two forms of custody: *custodia militaris* and *custodia libera*. *Custodia militaris* was a creation of the Empire; "it was a relatively mild form of imprisonment and was somewhat lighter than going to jail — and contrary to the latter — was *aperta libera et in usum hominum instituta* ..."[36]. Those in *custodia militaris* were handed over to soldiers to be guarded (*militi tradere*). The guard was composed of at least two soldiers, neither of whom could be a recruit. Sometimes those in military custody were detained in the *Castrum* and were lightly chained. Others were on bail and had to promise to appear at their trials or face the penalty of even heavier fines. The defendant was under surveillance of sorts, but could go about his daily business.

Custodia libera was a middle ground between imprisonment and freedom. Under the Republican régime, *custodia libera* meant that the accused was not hauled away to prison, but was handed over to a magistrate or to a prominent citizen who would have legal charge of him. They watched over the accused in their own house and insofar as circumstances allowed, they treated him with indulgence and leniency[37]. Those accepting this charge became responsible for the defendant's appearance at his trial. With the establishment of the Principate, *custodia libera* gradually died out, giving way to new forms of preventive detention[38]. These newer forms of preventive detention gave greater arbitrary power to the magistrates.

---

35 *Digest* XLVIII,3.1: "*Hoc autem vel pro criminis quod obicitur qualitate vel propter honorem aut propter amplissimas facultates vel pro innocentia personae vel pro dignitate eius qui accusatur facere solet*".
36 Hitzig, "Custodia", *PAULYS-WISSOWA-RE*, Vol. IV,2; col. 1898. cf. Tacitus, *Ann.* XIV,60, where Poppaea is put under military supervision (*addita militari custodia*). cf. *Codex Justinianus* IX,3.1; X,19.2.1.
37 cf. Livy XXXIX,14; Sallust, *Cat.* XLVII,3–4.
38 cf. The case of Aulus Stlaccius Maximus, who while waiting for the Emperor Augustus to make an inquiry into his case, was freed from his guard, but confined to the city of Rome. (Edict II, in de Visscher, *op.cit.*, pg. 19–20).

Josephus describes Agrippa's imprisonment at the end of Tiberius' reign and this description sheds some light on what imprisonment was like for more distinguished prisoners:

> "Antonia, though distressed at the misfortune of Agrippa, saw that it would be too much of an undertaking to discuss his case with Tiberius and would besides be useless. She gained from Macro [the successor of Sejanus as Praetorian Prefect] the following concessions for him, that the soldiers who were to guard him and the centurion who would be in charge of them and would also be handcuffed to him should be of humane character, that he should be permitted to bathe every day and receive visits from his freedmen and friends, and that he should have other bodily comforts too. His friend Silas and two of his freedmen, Marsyas and Stoecheus, visited him bringing him his favourite viands and doing whatever service they could. They brought him garments that they pretended to sell, but, when night came, they made him a bed with the connivance of the soldiers, who had Macro's orders to do so. These things went on for six months. Such was the situation with regard to Agrippa"[39].

A little further on, Josephus describes the change in Agrippa's situation with the accession of Caligula to the throne:

> "Two letters then arrived from Gaius: one to the Senate informing that body fully of the death of Tiberius and of his own succession to his office, the other to Piso, the prefect of the city, containing both this statement and the order that Agrippa should be removed from the camp (ἐκ τοῦ στρατοπέδου) to the house where he had lived before his imprisonment. After that he had no hardships to fear, for though he was still guarded and watched, yet the watch on his daily activities was relaxed"[40].

Acts indicates that Paul's detention was of the most lenient sort and that he had his own lodgings and visitors when he wished. Nonetheless one has to bear in mind the legal reality of Paul's situation. He was a prisoner, unable to leave Rome; indeed under house arrest and chained to a soldier.

III. Paul and the Roman Jews

1. The Jewish Communities At Rome

Acts records two interviews between Paul and the leaders of the Roman Jewish communities, both of which took place at the apostle's lodgings. In the first interview (XXVIII,17–22), the apostle spoke of his captivity, the reason motivating his appeal and the theological nature of his dispute with the Sanhedrin. In the second interview, (XXVIII,23–28), he attempted to convince his Jewish listeners about Jesus. Disagreement and dissension ensued; Paul's attempt was thus a failure. The apostle thereupon

---

39 *Ant.* XVIII,6.7 (203–204); E.T. = L.H. Feldman, *Loeb*, 1965.
40 *Ant.* XVIII,6.10 (234–235); E.T. = L.H. Feldman, *Loeb*, 1965.

announced his intention to turn to the Gentiles, dramatically marking his break with the leadership of the Jewish communities at Rome.

By Paul's time, the Jews of Rome could already boast of a long history. The community dates from the 2nd Century B.C., although we have little definite information about the beginnings of Jewish settlement in Italy. By the first half of the 1st Century B.C., there was already a large and influential Jewish community at Rome; the community further increased in numbers when Pompey returned in 61 B.C. with numerous Jewish captives following the taking of Jerusalem[41]. During the political troubles marking the end of the Republic, the Jews opposed the Senate and Roman aristocracy[42]. It is not surprising then that with the coming of the Principate, the Jewish community at Rome became much more powerful and influential than had hitherto been the case. Indeed under Julius and Augustus Caesar, the Jewish *collegia* were maintained when many other groups were disbanded and Judaism was protected and much favoured by these two rulers[43]. Philo is full of praise for Augustus in his description of the Roman Jewish community:

> "He [Augustus] was aware that the great section of Rome on the other side of the Tiber is occupied and inhabited by Jews, most of whom were Roman citizens emancipated. For having been brought as captives to Italy they were liberated by their owners and were not forced to violate any of their native institutions. He knew therefore that they have houses of prayer and meet together in them, particularly on the sacred sabbaths when they receive as a body a training in their ancestral philosophy. He knew too that they collect money for sacred purposes from their first-fruits and send them to Jerusalem by persons who would offer the sacrifices. Yet nevertheless he neither ejected them from Rome nor deprived them of their Roman citizenship because they were careful to preserve their Jewish citizenship also, nor took any violent measures against the houses of prayer, nor prevented them from meeting to receive instructions in the laws, nor opposed their offerings of the first-fruits. (...) Yet more, in the monthly doles in his own city [i.e. Rome] when all the people each in turn receive money or corn, he never put the Jews at a disadvantage in sharing the bounty, but even if the distribution happened to come during the sabbath ... he ordered the dispensers to reserve for the Jews till the morrow the charity which fell to all"[44].

The overall impression gained from the writings of Juvenal and Tacitus is that the Roman Jews were not a particularly rich group of people, nor, judging by the quality of the inscriptions, particularly literate. According to Philo the majority were freedmen, former prisoners of war or their descendants, who had been freed in the course of time by their masters[45]. The Jewish communities were nonetheless influential in Rome, not only

---

41 cf. H.J. Leon, *THE JEWS OF ANCIENT ROME*, Philadelphia, 1960, pg. 4.
42 cf. M. Stern, *op.cit.*, pg. 161; Leon, *op.cit.*, pg. 8 ff.
43 cf. Suetonius, *Iul.* XLII,3; *Aug.* XXXII,1; Josephus, *Ant.* XIV,10.8 (213–216).
44 Philo, *Legat. ad Gaium*, XXIII,155–157a; 158. E.T. = F.H. Colson, *Loeb*, 1962..
45 Philo, *Legat. ad Gaium*, XXIII, 155–157.

due to the increased numbers of Jews living in the capital[46], but because of the attraction monotheistic Judaism and its imageless worship had on certain segments of the Roman population[47].

The infrastructure of the Roman Jewish community differed in a substantial way from that of the urban centres of the East in that the Jews of Rome were not grouped into a single community and did not form a πολίτευμα in the strict sense of the word:

> " ... [the Jews of Alexandria] had an ἐθνάρχης at their head, who governed the nation, decided the debates, dealt with contracts and with ordinances as if he were the head of an autonomous government; he could also have the title of γενάρχης. At Rome, one finds nothing akin to this. On the contrary, the Jews were spread out over different communities, some of which were very ancient as is shown by the sepulchral epigraphs. The common name for these groups, which formed parishes as it were, is always the name συναγωγή. In Rome, this term never designates the place of worship, which is in fact qualified ... as *proseucha* (prayer = place of prayer) by metonymy with the Greek noun transliterated into Latin"[48].

Even though the Jews were spread out into different synagogues in different parts of Rome, there was still a fundamental unity among the several Jewish communities there: strong unifying bonds of race, of national aspirations as well as of religious law and practice.

We thus gain the overall image of the Jewish communities in Rome as being well-organized, fairly large, enjoying the protection of the State, and having — in spite of occasional difficulties — a history of good relations with the successive Emperors[48a] and a consequent influence in their court.

---

46 R. Penna estimates that there were 20,000 Jews in Rome during Nero's reign. (R. Penna, *op.cit.*, pg. 328).

47 cf. E.M. Smallwood, *op.cit.*, pg. 129–130.

48 R. Penna, *op.cit.*, pg. 327. For the use of the word *proseucha* for the Jewish place of worship in Rome, cf. Juvenal, *Sat.* III,296: "*in qua te quaero proseucha?*" H.J. Leon lists the eleven Roman synagogues as follows: the synagogues of the Agrippesians, Augustesians, Calcaresians, Campesians, Elaea, Hebrews, Secenians, Siburesians, Tripolitans, Vernaclesians and Volumnesians. (Leon, *op.cit.*, pg. 140 ff). A goodly number of the eleven were probably functioning during Paul's stay in Rome. This is most likely the case for the Hebrews, Vernaclesians, Agrippesians, Augustesians and Volumnesians (cf. E.M. Smallwood, *op.cit.*, pg. 138). Penna notes that no ruins of any of these synagogues have as yet emerged from the soil of ancient Rome (Penna, *op.cit.*, pg. 327). The geographical distribution of the synagogues and of the Jewish catacombs would indicate that the Jews were not strictly confined to the Trastevere, but were dispersed in the different quarters of Rome. The inscriptions found in the excavations of the Jewish catacombs (i.e. the catacombs of Monteverde, Vigna Randanini, Vigna Cimarra, Via Appia Pignatelli, Via Labicana and the double catacombs of the Villa Torlonia) shed a precious light on the life and society of the Roman Jewish communities. cf. the comprehensive compendium by the great scholar J.B. Frey, the *Corpus Inscriptionum Iudaicarum* (*CII*), Vol. I, 1936; Vol. II, 1952.

48a The synagogal names, Augustesians and Agrippesians, indicate the positive relationship which existed between Augustus and Agrippa and the Roman Jews. (cf. Schürer, *op.cit.*, Vol. III, part 1; 1986, pg. 78, note 97).

2. The First Interview: Paul Explains His Case

The first interview with the Jewish leaders at Rome took place soon after Paul had arrived: "After three days he called together the local leaders of the Jews: (συγκαλέσασθαι αὐτὸν τοὺς ὄντας τῶν Ἰουδαίων πρώτους); and when they had gathered, he said to them, 'Brethren (ἄνδρες ἀδελφοί), though I had done nothing against the people or the customs of our fathers, (οὐδὲν ἐναντίον ποιήσας τῷ λαῷ ἢ τοῖς ἔθεσι τοῖς πατρῴοις), yet I was delivered prisoner from Jerusalem into the hands of the Romans." (δέσμιος ἐξ Ἱεροσολύμων παρεδόθην εἰς τὰς χεῖρας τῶν Ῥωμαίων) (XXVIII,17).

A) συγκαλέσασθαι αὐτὸν τοὺς ὄντας τῶν Ἰουδαίων πρώτους

συγκαλέω — to call together, to assemble, convoke, convene. It was the leadership of the local Jewish communities whom Paul called together. These would have included Presbyters, *Archontes*, Scribes and other leading men of the synagogues who together made up the leadership of the overall Roman Jewish community. The Presbyters were members of the *Gerousia* or Council of Elders, which administered the local synagogues; the *Archontes* were the executive board of the *Gerousia*, the Gerousiarch was its chairman[49] and the Scribe was the Doctor of the Law and clerk of the synagogue. These men would be the ones Paul most likely received at his lodgings. In view of the multiplicity of synagogues in Rome, Paul's visitors may have numbered as many as 40 to 50 persons.

B) ἄνδρες ἀδελφοί

As in Acts XXIII,1, Paul once again addresses an important group of Jewish dignitaries as *brethren*.

C) οὐδὲν ἐναντίον ποιήσας τῷ λαῷ ἢ τοῖς ἔθεσι τοῖς πατρῴοις

In this first interview, Luke has Paul recapitulate his legal history to his listeners. Paul again declares his innocence, this time on the religious charges. The political charges are not discussed as his audience is exclusively Jewish. For the final time in Acts Luke draws the image of Paul as faithful to his people and to his ancestral customs. If he is awaiting his case to be heard in a Gentile court, it is solely as a result of the misdeeds of the unpersuaded Jews grouped in and around the Sanhedrin.

---

[49] For the epitaph of Anastasius, the ἀρχιγερουσιάρχης, discovered at the Jewish catacomb of the Villa Torlonia (Via Nomentana), cf. G.H.R. Horsley, *op.cit.*, No. 73, pg. 114–115. This inscription is dated 3rd–4th Century A.D. There is no evidence that such a function or title existed during Paul's time.

D) δέσμιος ἐξ Ἱεροσολύμων παρεδόθην εἰς τὰς χεῖρας τῶν Ῥωμαίων

παραδίδωμι – to give into the hands of another, to deliver into someone's power or custody, to deliver someone to be judged. The word occurs frequently in the accounts of trials in the NT[50]. In this passage, the verb suggests treachery and injustice. What Paul is announcing here is essentially the fulfillment of Agabus' prophecy (Acts XXI,11). In both accounts the verb παραδίδωμι is used and both depict the apostle's direction as being *from* Jerusalem *into* Roman (Gentile) hands. This does not however square with Luke's account of Paul's arrest in Acts XXI,33 which puts Paul in Roman hands from the beginning. Luke's literary design in having Paul present his arrest in this way most likely aims at assimilating Paul's case to that of Jesus[51].

Paul next summarized the judicial proceedings that had taken place in Caesarea: "When they had examined me, (ἀνακρίναντές) they wished to set me at liberty, because there was no reason for the death penalty in my case. But when the Jews objected, (ἀντιλεγόντων), I was compelled to appeal to Caesar (ἠναγκάσθην ἐπικαλέσασθαι Καίσαρα) – though I had no charge to bring against my nation." (οὐχ ὡς τοῦ ἔθνους μου ἔχων τι κατηγορεῖν) (XXVIII,18–19).

A) ἀνακρίναντές

As in Tertullus' speech to Felix, the verb here means to examine, inquire into or hold an investigation. Some texts add πολλά before the verb, thereby signifying "after a long examination"[52].

Paul exculpates Felix and Festus from any procedural malfeasance in his case and places the blame for his continued imprisonment on the objections raised by the Jews.

B) ἀντιλεγόντων δὲ τῶν Ἰουδαίων

ἀντιλέγω – to speak against, to gainsay, to contradict, to speak in opposition to. After the word 'Jews', other versions add: "and shouting, Away with our enemy!" (Αἶρε τὸν ἐχθρὸν ἡμῶν)[53].

C) ἠναγκάσθην ἐπικαλέσασθαι Καίσαρα

Luke has Paul explain the reason which motivated his appeal to Caesar: the relentless opposition of the Jewish leaders to his Messianic expectations.

---

50 cf. Mt. X,17; Mk. XIV,10; XV,1;15; Lk. XXIII,25; Acts XII,4.
51 cf. Lk. XVIII,32; Acts III,13.
52 614, 1518, hcl*.
53 614, 1518, sy[h]. cf. Acts XXII,22. The expansion provides a reminiscence of Jesus' trial.

D) οὐχ ὡς τοῦ ἔθνους μου ἔχων τι κατηγορεῖν

Paul is very specific here. His appeal cannot be construed as a hostile act against his people.

Certain Western variants add the words "in order to save my soul from death" (ἀλλ'ἵνα λυτρώσωμαι τὴν ψυχήν μου ἐκ θανάτου) after the word κατηγορεῖν[54]. The Western tradition thus offers its own theological viewpoint as to the reasons for Paul's appeal to Caesar. The expansion centers around the verb λυτρόω (Middle λυτροῦσθαι). In sacrificial language this term means to cause to be released by the payment of a ransom, hence to redeem:

> "The appeal to Caesar is the λύτρον by which Paul ransoms his imperilled life from death — a death that he did not wish to receive at the hands of the Jews of Jerusalem; a premature death, inconceivable at that moment when he had received from Jesus the order to go to Rome"[55].

Paul finishes his speech by putting his dispute with the Sanhedrin back into its proper theological framework: "For this reason therefore I have asked to see you and speak with you, since it is because of the hope of Israel that I am bound with this chain" (XXVIII,20). Once again Luke centers the dispute around the Hope of Israel "a motive which could not leave his listeners indifferent"[56].

The narrative now goes on to relate the Jewish leaders' reply to the apostle: "We have received no letters (οὔτε γράμματα) from Judea about you, and none of the brethren coming here (οὔτε παραγενόμενός τις τῶν ἀδελφῶν) has reported or spoken any evil (πονηρόν) about you. But we desire to hear from you what your views are; for with regard to this sect we know that everywhere it is spoken against." (περὶ μὲν γὰρ τῆς αἱρέσεως ταύτης γνωστὸν ἡμῖν ἐστιν ὅτι πανταχοῦ ἀντιλέγεται) (XXVIII, 21–22).

A) οὔτε γράμματα ... οὔτε παραγενόμενός τις τῶν ἀδελφῶν ... πονηρόν

The Roman Jews' response was characterized by a remarkable degree of circumspection expressed by the double negative οὔτε ... οὔτε. It is antithetical to the situation in Acts XXI,21 where the Jerusalem Judeo-Christians are said by James to have been told a great deal about Paul – all bad!

It was not unusual for the Jerusalem authorities or the Diaspora Jews to ask the Roman Jews to help in the prosecution of a case which was to be heard by the highest Roman authorities. In his *Defence of Flaccus*,

---

[54] δ 614, 1518 minn c,g,p, sy^h.
[55] Delebecque, *op.cit.*, pg. 410.
[56] Dupont, "La Conclusion des Actes ... ", *op.cit.*, pg. 368. cf. Acts XXIII,6; XXIV,21; XXV,19; XXVI,6; XXVI,23.

Cicero notes how the Roman Jews attempted to use their influence against the governor and in favour of their coreligionists' interests and in what way they exerted strong pressure on the legal proceedings[57]. Josephus gives another pertinent account in his *Antiquities*. He relates that some 8000 of the Roman Jews supported the complaint to the Emperor Augustus against Archelaus made by 50 representatives of the Jerusalem Jews who had previously been given leave by the legate Varus to appear before the Emperor with their petition[58]. In the *Vita*, Josephus writes that he himself went to Rome to try to secure the acquittal by the Emperor of certain Jewish priests sent to Rome as prisoners by Felix[59]. In order to gain a favourable decision by the Emperor, Josephus relied on two influential people in Nero's immediate entourage: the Jewish actor Aliturus, Nero's special favourite with whom Josephus formed a friendship, and the Jewish sympathizer, Poppaea, Nero's consort, to whom he was introduced by Aliturus. Poppaea was influential in securing for Josephus the release of these priests[60].

According to the account Luke give us here, the Sanhedrin had neither contacted the Roman Jews officially by letter nor had they sent any delegation to Rome to press their case. Acts makes no mention of any witnesses coming from Jerusalem to testify against Paul. In view of the Sanhedrin's fierce hostility to the apostle, this seems most surprising. It is possible that the Roman Jews had already been contacted and were simply denying any knowledge of Paul's affair so as not to involve themselves in the case of a Roman citizen who had previously received rather favourable opinions from Agrippa and Festus. But the Roman Jews had not hesitated in the past to involve themselves in cases as delicate and controversial as Paul's and had defended the Sanhedrin's cause in these other litigations with vigour and zeal. With Paul out of Jerusalem, perhaps the Sanhedrin felt that the need to pursue its old enemy was less pressing than hitherto. The divisons within the Sanhedrin itself between the Sadducees and the Pharisees could very well have blocked the pursuit of the case against the apostle. Perhaps, too, the lack of cogent evidence to present against him in the Empire's highest court made the case too great a risk for the plaintiffs. There is absolutely no indication in Acts that

---

57 Cicero, *pro Flacco* XXVIII,66–69.
58 *Ant.* XVII,11.1 (300).
59 *Vita*, 3.13.
60 *Vita*, 3.16. That Poppaea was powerful especially after 62 A.D. and could be a deadly enemy is seen from a passage in Tacitus, *Ann.* XV,61: "*Ubi haec a tribuno relata sunt, Poppaea et Tigellino coram, (quod erat saevienti principi intimum consiliorum), interrogat an Seneca voluntariam mortem pararet*".

the Sanhedrin was ready to pursue the case before Nero. On the contrary, the verse suggests that the Sanhedrin had decided not to press charges against Paul in the appellate court out of fear of losing the case due to the inexistence of any substantiating evidence and the lack of previous convictions in the apostle's judicial record.

B) περὶ μὲν γὰρ τῆς αἱρέσεως ταύτης γνωστὸν ἡμῖν ἐστιν ὅτι πανταχοῦ ἀντιλέγεται

Once again the Christians are referred to as a αἵρεσις.

It would have been impossible for the Jewish leaders in Rome not to have had some first-hand knowledge of the Christians and their faith. The Christian community in Rome had existed along side the Jewish communities for some time. The foundation of the Christian community in Rome remains obscure, but may have gone back to the Roman visitors present in Jerusalem on the day of Pentecost (Acts II,10). Paul's epistle to the Romans, written shortly before his arrest, was addressed to a well-organized and well-known congregation[61]. Many of the members of the Roman Christian community were of Jewish origin. Acts says nothing of the relations between the Jewish and Christian communities of Rome, but they most likely were full of tension[62].

Luke has a very specific objective here. He portrays the Roman Jews as being ignorant of Christianity except for some depreciatory hearsay. He is thus able to put Paul in the position of being the first to announce the Good News to the Jewish leadership at Rome.

3. *The Second Interview: Paul Turns to the Gentiles*

The second interview began as a theological presentation about Jesus: "When they had appointed a day for him, they came to him at his lodging (εἰς τὴν ξυνίαν) in great numbers. And he expounded the matter to them from morning till evening (ἀπὸ πρωῒ ἕως ἑσπέρας), testifying to the Kingdom of God (διαμαρτυρόμενος τὴν βασιλείαν τοῦ Θεοῦ) and trying to convince them about Jesus (πείθων τε αὐτοὺς περὶ τοῦ Ἰησοῦ) both from the Law of Moses and from the prophets." (XXVIII,23).

---

61 cf. Romans I,8: "First I thank my God through Jesus Christ for all of you, because your faith is proclaimed in all the world".

62 H. Solin notes that the restrictive measures taken by Claudius against the Roman Jews and Christian communities at Rome may have played an important role in dividing the Jewish and Christian communities at Rome and of increasing tensions within the Christian community itself between its Gentile and Jewish members. (Solin, *op.cit.*, pg. 664).

A) εἰς τὴν ξενίαν

ἡ ξενία — cf. Latin *hospitium*. It is the hospitable reception given a guest, hospitality, entertainment. In the NT the word occurs only here and in Phm. 22 where it means a guest chamber. In this verse, it means to his lodging, to receive the hospitality of the host (ξένος).

B) ἀπὸ πρωΐ ἕως ἑσπέρας

Luke specifies that the discussion with the Roman Jews lasted the whole day, thereby showing how keen the apostle was on winning them over to Jesus Christ.

C) διαμαρτυρόμενος τῆς βασιλείαν τοῦ Θεοῦ

διαμαρτύρομαι — to testify earnestly, to bear witness to, or solemnly affirm. The verb describes the Christian proclamation: to testify to things disclosed by divine revelation. Here it means to give solemn testimony to the Kingdom of God in eschatological expectation.

D) πείθων τε αὐτοὺς περὶ τοῦ Ἰησοῦ

The use of the verb πείθω stresses the efforts that Paul the missionary made to convince his Jewish interlocutors of the Messianic dignity of Jesus.

Despite the apostle's zealousness, his fervent efforts at persuasion were not successful for the narrative states, "some were convinced (ἐπείθοντο) by what he said, while others disbelieved. (ἠπίστουν)." (XXVIII,24). The apostle got one last word in before his fractious listeners departed: "So, as they disagreed among themselves, they departed, after Paul had made one statement: 'The Holy Spirit was right in saying to your (ὑμῶν) fathers through Isaiah the prophet:

> 'Go to this people, and say,
> you shall indeed hear but never understand,
> you shall indeed see but never perceive,
> For this people's heart has grown dull,
> and their ears are heavy of hearing,
> and their eyes they have closed;
> lest they should perceive with their eyes,
> and hear with their ears,
> and understand with their heart,
> and turn for me to heal them'." (XXVIII,25–27).

A) ἐπείθοντο / ἠπίστουν

In spite of the wording in verse 24, it does not seem that many of the apostle's interlocutors were really persuaded by what he had to say:

"In ἐπείθοντο there is no thought of a real conversion any more than in a similar scene at XXIII,9. Theoretically the Jews are not at one as regards the Christian doctrine; but in practice neither of the two groups decided for Christianity"[63].

What is important for Luke is not that a few of the Jews were persuaded, but that almost the totality of them rejected the Gospel. Paul accuses all of them of obstinacy — without exception — when he terminates the meeting by quoting the prophet Isaiah[64]. The application of these devastating verses of obduracy to the Jews was meant to show that their rejection of Jesus as the Hope of Israel, as the Messiah, was a striking fulfillment of prophecy[65].

B) ὑμῶν

Your fathers, and no longer *our* fathers[66].

Paul concludes his speech by turning once again to the Gentiles: "Let it be known to you then (γνωστὸν οὖν ἔστω ὑμῖν) that this salvation of God has been sent to the Gentiles; they will listen." (ὅτι τοῖς ἔθνεσιν ἀπεστάλη τοῦτο τὸ σωτήριον τοῦ Θεοῦ αὐτοὶ καὶ ἀκούσονται)(XXVIII, 28). The Western variants add: "And when he had said these words, the Jews departed, holding much dispute among themselves." (XXVIII,29)[67].

A) γνωστὸν οὖν ἔστω ὑμῖν

This very solemn expression[68] introduces vs. 28 which is the dramatic climax to the whole story of Paul's stay in Rome and — in view of Luke's intense attention to the Gentile mission — to the whole Book of Acts itself.

B) ὅτι τοῖς ἔθνεσιν ἀπεστάλη τοῦτο τὸ σωτήριον τοῦ Θεοῦ αὐτοὶ καὶ ἀκούσονται

---

63 Haenchen, pg. 723–724.
64 cf. Isaiah VI, 9–10. cf. Mt. XIII,13–15; Mk. IV,12; Lk. VIII,10; Jn. XII,39–41; Romans XI,8.
65 S.G. Wilson notes: "This third explanation of the turning from the Jews to the Gentiles is final; it is Luke's overall assessment of the Jews' position". (Wilson, *THE GENTILES AND THE GENTILE MISSION IN LUKE-ACTS*, Cambridge, 1973. pg. 226. A. George writes: "Here the sentence appears definitive. For Luke, when the Gospel reached Rome, it reached the uttermost part of the earth. It had been announced everywhere in the synagogues and refused; everywhere the people of Israel as such had rejected the Salvation offered. It was to them that the Word had first been announced. Now this priority had ended and with it the unique situation of Israel in Salvation history". (George, *op.cit.*, pg. 521–522).
66 ὑμῶν – is attested in A Bpm p s sa bo^{pm}; R. ἡμῶν – is attested in H L P 614al lat bo(1). The Vg. reads *ad Patres nostros*.
67 H L P 614pm c g syh∫ ; Rm . The Vg. reads here: *Et cum haec dixisset, exierunt ab eo Iudaei, multam habentes inter se quaestionem.*
68 cf. Acts II,14; IV,10; XIII,38.

In Acts there is a very close relationship between the Jewish rejection of the Gospel and the Gentile attainment of God's Salvation. This climatic verse turns the reader's attention away from Paul, his legal situation and his relationship to official Judaism, to focus instead on God's plan of Salvation offered to all mankind. The mission to the Gentiles at Rome (and elsewhere) and the latter's acceptance of the Gospel had the effect of making the church aware of its independent destiny as the true and only heir of the Old Testament promises. It was another concrete sign that the church was gradually disengaging itself from organized Judaism[69].

Paul's break with the Roman Jewish community was intimately bound up with that disengagement process. It meant that he would be forced thereafter to take into account the deadly enmity of the Roman Jews. This extreme antipathy would be felt in two places. First of all it would at some point or another cause the apostle greater difficulties with the imperial tribunal since he could no longer shelter under the roof of official Judaism[70]. Secondly the break with the Roman Jews could only increase tension between the Judeo and Gentile Christian members of the Roman Christian community itself.

IV. Biennis Captivitas Romana

The Book of Acts concludes by describing Paul's sojourn at Rome: "And he lived there two whole years (ἐνέμεινεν δὲ διετίαν ὅλην) at his own expense (ἐν ἰδίῳ μισθώματι), and welcomed all who came to him (πάντας τοὺς εἰσπορευομένος πρὸς αὐτόν) preaching the Kingdom of God and teaching about the Lord Jesus Christ quite openly and unhindered" (μετὰ πάσις παρρησίας ἀκωλύτως) (XXVIII,30–31).

These verses form the last in a series of summaries which punctuate the Acts-narrative. Their literary function is that of a short epilogue comparable to the concluding verses of the Gospel of Luke.

A) ἐν ἰδίῳ μισθώματι

μίσθωμα – In this passage, μίσθωμα has the sense of *at his own expense* or *living on his own earnings*[71]. The point Luke wishes to make is that

---

69 cf. J.C. O'Neill, *THE THEOLOGY OF ACTS IN ITS HISTORICAL SETTING*, London, 1961, pg. 170.
70 cf. P. Keresztes, "Nero, the Christians and the Jews in Tacitus and Clement of Rome", *LATOMUS*, Tome 43, 1984, pg. 410.
71 H.J. Cadbury notes: "μίσθωμα means money paid, and though it probably comes to the same

Paul was not dependent for financial support on the Roman (or any other) Church. During the *biennium*, he was able to support himself either through his own labours or by private revenues.

The noun μίσθωμα can also mean the price at which something is hired, contract price or rent[72]. cf. the Latin *conductum*. It is quite clear from the text of Acts that Paul did have his own lodging. This is indicated not only here but in Acts XXVIII,16 (καθ᾽ ἑαυτόν) and XXVIII,23 (ξενία).

B) πάντας τοὺς εἰσπορευομένος πρὸς αὐτὸν

The central idea in Acts that the message of Salvation is for all men is stressed here by Luke in his use of the word πάντας which highlights the universalist application of the verse.

A certain number of texts add the precision Ἰουδαίους τε καὶ Ἕλληνας[73]. By this addition, the Western tradition aims at underlining Paul's continuing ministry to the Jews of Rome despite his break with the official community established there.

C) μετὰ πάσης παρρησίας

ἡ παρρησία — boldness of speech, frankness, freedom to speak publicly, before all. On the political level, the word indicates the right a citizen enjoyed to full freedom of speech. A characteristic word of Greek democracy, it was a very visible sign of the freedom to speak out publicly that citizens of the *polis* enjoyed[74].

The word appears over 30 times in the NT, especially in the later Epistles (5 times in Acts). In Acts, the παρρησία, bold speaking, is a virtue granted by God to his apostles to accomplish their mission of proclamation and teaching in the face of threats, imprisonment or death (cf. Acts IV,31).

D) ἀκωλύτως (Vg. = *sine prohibitione*)

ἀκώλυτος — quite openly, unimpeded[75], without hindrance[76]. The term regularly appears in legal documents especially from the 2nd. Century A.D. on[77], but this is the only time it occurs in the NT. Ἀκωλύτως is the

---

thing in the end, it may refer here to what was paid to Paul as wages for his work rather than to what was paid by Paul for food and lodging", (Cadbury, "Luke's Interest in Lodging", *JBL*, Vol. 45, 1926, pg. 321–322).

72 *IG*. XII–7, 55.15.
73 614 pc (g p) sy^h Ephr.
74 cf. Polybius I,38.6; Euripedes, *Ion*. 673.
75 Plato, *Cratylus*, 415 D.
76 Strabo, *Geo*. XVII,24.
77 cf. *P. Oxy*. III,502.31 (yr. 164 A.D.); VIII,1127.16 (183 A.D.).

last word in the text: Luke thus closes the Book of Acts with a term that is both distinctly legal and clearly apologetic. Ἀκωλύτως evokes a sense of leniency; such leniency could only be interpreted as proof that in Roman eyes Paul was innocent of the accusations lodged against him[78] The Lucan account clearly implies that the Roman authorities did not in the least object to Paul's preaching or receiving visitors, i.e. exercising a personal freedom while awaiting trial[79]. Luke's aim is unambiguous here: Rome is depicted as showing tolerance towards Paul's ministry and towards the Christian message.

E) ἐνέμεινεν δὲ διετίαν ὅλην

The mention of the *biennium* is the last chronological piece of evidence which the narrative affords us. What effect did the two years have on Paul's case? Were they of judicial significance? Were there legal provisions in Roman law which set a period of time for the accusers to appear and repeat their accusations in the court of appeals? If they failed to appear by the deadline, did the case go by default, so enabling the defendant to obtain his release?

As we have already seen, the accusers themselves had to appear in court. In Paul's particular case, this meant that a delegation from the Sanhedrin had to come from Jerusalem to Rome, repeat the accusations before the Imperial tribunal in the presence of the apostle and produce pertinent evidence to substantiate the accusation.

A widespread habit existed of plaintiffs' failing to appear at trials to repeat accusations which they had previously made in the lower courts. Emperor Claudius bestirred himself to combat this habit by promulgating concrete measures aimed at discouraging plaintiffs from not following up on charges they had previously made. An example of the Emperor's desire to see a more rapid and equitable disposal of criminal cases can be seen from a small fragment of one of his *orationes*, extant on a papyrus[80] in which the plaintiffs were exhorted to terminate the presentation of their case as quickly as possible once the time limit set for the investigation had expired. Dio Cassius notes that plaintiffs often did not put in an appearance at the trial they themselves had provoked, if they thought beforehand that they were going to lose the suit:

---

[78] A certain number of texts (m p syh Éphr.) add the following after ἀκωλύτως: *"dicens quia hic est Christus Iesus filius Dei per quem incipiet totus mundus iudicari. Amen."*, This closing is on a rather more eschatological note.

[79] cf. Jerome's account " ... *et biennium in libera manens custodia adversus Iudaeos de adventu Christi quotidie disputavit*". (de Vir. ill. V).

[80] *Orationes Claudii de decuriis iudicum et de accusatoribus coercendis* in *BGU*. II,611. The text of the *oratio* is also given in Bruns, *FIRA*, 53 and Riccobono, *FIRA*, 44.

"As the number of law-suits was now beyond all reckoning and those expected to lose their cases would no longer put in an appearance, he [Claudius] issued a proclamation announcing that he would decide the cases against them by a given day even in their absence; and he strictly enforced this rule"[81].

In 61 A.D. the Senate issued a decree condemning one Valerius Ponticus for entering a case of fraud with the intent of obstructing justice first by a legal subterfuge and then by prevarication. This decree came to be known as the *SC Turpilianum*. Tacitus notes that a clause was added to this decree providing that a person obstructing justice by preferring false charges or by prevarication was liable to the same penalties as if convicted of *calumnia*[82].

It was thus firmly rooted in Roman legal practice from the time of Claudius and Nero onwards that the prosecutor — once he had initiated the proceedings — *had to* prosecute. Pliny gives an account of the trial of one Gallitta on charges of adultery. Her husband had made the accusation in writing, but later drew back out of fondness for his wife. Pliny writes that the husband "was admonished to proceed in the suit, which he did with great reluctance: it was necessary, however, she should be condemned, even against the prosecutor's will"[83]. The jurist Marcianus notes that an accusation once made could only be annulled by the authority of the judge and not by the wish of the accuser[84] Therefore the protection of the accused essentially lay in the severity of the punishment meted out to accusers who defaulted and not in any intrinsic right of the accused to release in the event of a default[85].

The accused also had to be present in court for if he did not have the opportunity of answering his accusers face to face and of defending himself before the judge, the proceedings could not go on and the case would be *inaudita*[86]. Apuleius Madaurensis writes:

"The magistrates ... prayed the decurions and the people of the city to proceed by examination of witnesses on both sides, like good citizens and with order of justice according to the

---

81 Dio Cassius LX,28.6 (yr. 46 A.D.) — E.T. = E. Cary, *Loeb*, 1961. Suetonius, *Claud.* XV,2 writes in a similar vein: "Whenever one party to a suit was absent, he was prone to decide in favour of the one who was present, without considering whether his opponent had failed to appear through his own fault or from a necessary cause." (E.T. = J.C. Rolfe, *Loeb*, 1959). cf. Seneca, *Apocolocyntosis* XII.
82 Tacitus, *Ann.* XIV,41.
83 Pliny, *Ep.* VI,31. E.T. = W. Melmoth & W.M.L. Hutchinson, *Loeb*, 1961.
84 *Digest* XLVIII,16.1.10. In this passage the *Digest* defines calumny as the bringing forth of false charges (*false crimina intendere*), prevarication as the concealment of the true charges (*vera crimina abscondere*) and tergiversation as the total abandonment of accusations previously brought forth (*in universum ab accusatione desistere*).
85 Sherwin-White, pg. 114. In *P. Lond.* II,359.7 one reads that a fine of 200 Drachmae was levied on an accuser not appearing in court.
86 cf. Plutarch, *Caius Gracchus* III,4.

ancient custom; for the giving of any hasty sentence or judgement without hearing of the contrary part, such as the barbarous and cruel tyrants accustom to use, would give an ill example in time of peace to their successors"[87].

Thus any condemnation of the accused in his absence would go against the *aequitatis ratio*; it would be inequitous "in the precise etymological sense of the word"[88].

Not only were the parties expected to be in court, but they were also expected to appear within a certain time limit. There is some evidence for a two-year legal limit: Pliny mentions such a *biennium* in one of his letters:

> "A person was brought before me who had been sentenced to perpetual exile by the Proconsul Julius Bassus; but knowing that the decrees of Bassus had been rescinded, and that the Senate had granted a new trial to all those who had come under his sentence, provided they appealed within the space of two years (*ex integro agendi dumtaxat per biennium*), I inquired of this man whom he had banished whether he had acquainted the Proconsul with his case? He replied he had not"[89].

Trajan's response to Pliny's query was that as the man had not availed himself of the possibility of appealing within the *biennium*, he was to be sent in chains to the prefects of the Emperor's Praetorium[90].

A second mention of a two-year period occurs in Philo:

> "Lampo had been put on his trial for impiety to Tiberius Caesar and as the trial had dragged on for two years (ἐπὶ διετίαν τριβομένου) he had broken down under it. For the ill-will of his judge had concocted postponements and delays, as he wished, even if he was acquitted of the charge, to keep hanging over him as long as possible the fear of the uncertain future, and so render his life more painful than death"[91].

Finally there is a fragment of an edict extant on papyrus, the *Edictum de temporibus accusationum*, which sets time limits that plaintiffs and defendants had to respect in appellate cases heard in the imperial tribunal. The maximum delays accorded both parties in capital cases were nine months for plaintiffs and defendants living in Italy and a year and a half for those living outside the Italian peninsula[92].

---

87 Apuleius Madaurensis, *Met.* X,6. E.T. = W. Adlington/S. Gaselee, *Loeb*, 1958.
88 Dupont, "Aequitas Romana", *op.cit.*, pg. 546. cf. the inequitous treatment meted out to Apollonius by Verres, which was denounced by Cicero in *Verr.* II,v.8.18–20. Elsewhere in the *Verrine Orations*, Cicero notes that the judge or judges who had voting power in a case had to be present in person at the trial: "When Gaius Verres was presiding at a trial as City Praetor, senators were found to vote against a man whom they were condemning without having attended his trial" (*Verr.* I,13.39) – E.T. = L.H.G. Greenwood, *Loeb*, 1959.
89 Pliny, *Ep.* X,56. – E.T. = W. Melmoth/W.M.L. Hutchinson, *Loeb*, 1963.
90 Pliny, *Ep.* X,57.
91 Philo, *in Flaccum* XVI,128–129. E.T. = F.H. Colson, *Loeb*, 1960.
92 *Edict*, Col. II,4–6 in *BGU*. II,628. The text also appears in Bruns, *FIRA*, 78. The difficulty with this edict is its date. It was promulgated by an Emperor who is not named. J. Dupont

The two year period which Luke mentions does therefore seem to have a concrete judicial basis. It was the length of time normally allowed the accusers to come from the provinces to prosecute a case.

Luke breaks off his account with Paul spending a *biennium* in Rome freely preaching the message of Salvation to all who would come to hear him. The most likely conclusion that can be drawn on the basis of the judicial evidence available in Acts is that Paul was released at the end of the two-year period consequent to the Sanhedrin's failure to continue the proceedings against him within the prescribed time. The positive tone on which Acts ends strongly suggests that Paul's legal situation had improved. Nonetheless release on a legal technicality was rather far removed from a formal verdict of innocence[93]. As his case ended by default, Paul probably had little chance to make a defence in Caesar's court. He thus failed to obtain a positive evaluation by the court of his activities which the Jewish leaders found so threatening. He was not judged innocent on any of the political charges, a fact which boded ill for the future of his own personal ministry as well as for the communities he had founded. Of course he had recovered his liberty and was free to continue his apostolic ministry, but nonetheless he now had a judicial record and remained liable to re-arrest at any given moment. Luke concludes Acts in the most positive way he can, but even this apologetic consideration could not hide the fact of how fundamentally precarious Paul's judicial position really was.

---

dates it in the First Century A.D. (Dupont, *Aequitas Romana, op.cit.*, pg. 544–545). Mommsen (*STRAFRECHT*, pg. 472) and Sherwin-White, (pg. 115) both see it as a document of the later Empire.

93 cf. L. Pherigo, "Paul's Life after the Close of Acts", *JBL.*, Vol. 70; 1951, pg. 278.

Chapter X
An Afterword – The Lucan Account of Paul's Legal History

Luke's account of Paul's legal history has a basic unity of theme and purpose and is a major component in the author's overall historical programme for Acts. For Luke, Paul's legal history is not a series of disconnected judicial encounters with various Roman magistrates which happened over a considerable period of time. Rather he understands it as a consequence of the ongoing expansion of the Gentile mission and thus as one of the main events marking the Church's increasing awareness of its new, mostly Gentile, identity.

Luke constructs his story around two fundamental points:

A) *Paul's Roman citizenship*. On three occasions the apostle invoked the right to protection inherent in that citizenship and thereby dramatically altered his situation.

B) *The appeal to Rome*. By the end of the narrative the apostle was under imperial security as an appellant to Caesar's court awaiting his turn to testify.

The appeal to Caesar is the central event on which Luke's whole account of Paul's legal history turns. The appeal highlighted the importance of Paul's Roman citizenship to his case. It put Paul into a new and specific juridical situation in the eyes of the Roman authorities; thus it affected all subsequent procedure in the apostle's case. Finally the appeal to Caesar had a significant effect on the relationship between the apostle and the official Jewish authorities.

The appeal was first of all the providential giant step to Rome. The narrative twice mentions that Paul was accomplishing a divinely ordained mission in going there:

A) "The following night the Lord stood by and said, 'Take courage, for as you have testified about me at Jerusalem, so you must bear witness also at Rome'." (Acts XXIII,11).

B) "For this very night there stood by me an angel of the God to whom I belong and whom I worship, and he said, 'Do not be afraid, Paul; you must stand before Caesar';" (Acts XXVII,23–24a).

Thus one of the main points which Luke makes in his account of Paul's legal history is that God's power overcame all human injustice and natural obstacles impeding His faithful servant from reaching Rome.

Luke also notes that the apostle himself was far from recalcitrant about accepting God's directive to go to Rome. Indeed Acts portrays him as desirous as he was eager to reach the capital: "After I have been there [Jerusalem], I must also see Rome". (Acts XIX,21b). Paul himself clearly expresses his heartfelt wish to go to Rome in his epistle to the Romans. Acts then is entirely concordant with Romans on this point:

A) "For God is my witness ... that without ceasing I mention you always in my prayers, asking that somehow by God's will I may now at last succeed in coming to you". (Rm. I,9–10).
B) "So I am eager to preach the Gospel to you also who are at Rome." (Rm. I,15).
C) "I have longed for many years to come to you." (Rm. XV,23b).

Rome then was Paul's goal as well as the culminating point of his legal trajectory. It was his *patria* as a Roman citizen, the authority from which he thrice sought protection when beset by his enemies.

Paul's Roman citizenship was a crucial factor in his case. The Acts-narrative stresses how much Paul's right to personal security from magisterial abuse and to the protection of a Roman court was respected by the officials with whom he came into contact. The importance of Paul's citizenship is especially manifest in the cries for protection he made at Philippi and Jerusalem against magisterial abuse and, of course, in the appeal he made at Caesarea to have his case heard in Rome. Luke notes again and again that Paul's rights as a citizen were honoured throughout his long legal history and that standard procedure was usually adhered to in his case. Luke constantly relates the favourable attitude the Romans had toward Paul, especially once the appeal had been lodged. Festus and Agrippa both found him innocent, Julius the Centurion treated him with great deference, the Roman police allowed him to have his own lodging and to speak *sine prohibitione.* None of this would have transpired had Paul not enjoyed the status of a Roman citizen. As a peregrine he would have been treated as an inconsequential figure with no rights – one to be humiliated at every turn.

Another point which Luke makes in his narrative is that no Roman court found Paul guilty on any political charge. Delays might occur in the legal proceedings, Felix might have expected a bribe, thus showing his personal venality, but Paul's overall experiences with Roman officialdom are depicted as being generally positive. Indeed Luke took great pains, not only to show the Roman authorities' sense of justice and equity, but also to emphasize how Paul was viewed as innocent of the grave political charges lodged against him:

> A) Lysias to Felix: "'I found that he was accused about questions of their law, but charged with nothing deserving death or imprisonment", (Acts XXIII,29).
> B) Festus to Agrippa: "But I found that he had done nothing deserving death;" (Acts XXV,25a).
> C) Agrippa to Festus: "This man could have been set free if he had not appealed to Caesar", (Acts XXVI,32).

Luke has clear apologetic aims in his account of Paul's encounters with Roman justice:

> A) First of all, by his repetition of the positive opinions of the different magistrates, Luke makes a strong case for Paul's innocence to his essentially Roman readers.
> B) Luke tries hard to cast the Roman authorities in as favourable a light as possible. He can thereby demonstrate the inherent justice of the Roman system of law, which he sharply contrasts to the basic injustice and violence of Paul's Jewish foes (especially the Sadducaean wing of the Sanhedrin).
> C) Luke tries to show the basic tolerance (or at the worst indifference) which Rome had for the Christian message. Rome is nowhere depicted as an enemy or persecutor of Christians or their communities.
> D) Finally, Luke's marked pro-Roman stance is meant to counterbalance certain anti-Roman tendencies present in the Church in the wake of the savage Neronian persecution.

The question which might be raised in this context is to what extent Luke's apologetic aim and authorial bias modified the historic reality of Paul's legal situation. On the basis of the evidence in Acts itself, one readily sees that Paul's legal situation was not so positive after all. The Philippian *Duoviri* had expelled him from the Roman colony. The Politarchs had allowed him to escape furtively from Thessalonica from which he remained banished for some time thereafter. Gallio would not listen to his *apologia* although he dismissed Paul's foes from the proconsular court with disdain. Felix wanted a bribe and then left Paul in prison in order to gain favour with the Jewish authorities. Festus thought him innocent of the political charges preferred against him, but still wanted to extradite him to the Sanhedrin's juristiction where a sentence of death on the charge of profanation was inevitable. Agrippa also thought him innocent of any political charge, yet ridiculed his proclamation of Jesus Christ. At Rome, he might very well have been able to speak out boldly, but he was still confined to his lodgings and chained to a guard. Thus Paul could not have gone into his trial at Rome with the expectation that the *verdict would necessarily be favourable*. What he did do in Acts was to ask the *protection* of a Roman court from his adversaries. As a Roman citizen he could and did claim his right to be heard in a Roman court before a Roman judge especially as one of the charges in the indictment against him was the charge of sedition.

Acts states that the various Roman authorities found the apostle innocent of the *political* charges his enemies had lodged against him. They had respected and honoured the rights and privileges he enjoyed as a Roman citizen. Nonetheless some of the charges against Paul were *religious* in nature. Paul was also a Jew and a member of the Tarsian Jewish community. Rome recognized the Sanhedrin's judicial competence in Jewish religious affairs. There is thus in Acts a constant desire on the part of the Roman authorities to shift jurisdiction in the case to the Jewish authorities. Paul successfully counters this desire by his insistence that he remain in Roman custody for his case to be heard on the charge of sedition.

Finally the appeal had a significant effect on the very complex set of relations between Paul and the Jews. Throughout his account, Luke depicts the apostle as attempting to keep his dispute with the Jewish authorities within a strictly theological framework by maintaining that his argument with the Sanhedrin was on the doctrinal issues of the resurrection and the Messianic hope of Israel:

A) Paul to the Sanhedrin: "Brethren, I am a Pharisee, a son of Pharisees: with respect to the hope and the resurrection of the dead I am on trial." (Acts XXIII,6b).
B) Paul to Felix: "with respect to the resurrection of the dead, I am on trial before you this day." (Acts XXIV,21b).
C) Paul to Agrippa: "And now I stand here on trial for hope in the promise made by God to our fathers, ... And for this hope I am accused by Jews, O King! Why is it thought incredible by any of you that God raises the dead?" (Acts XXVI,6;8).
D) Paul to the Roman Jews: "it is because of the hope of Israel that I am bound with this chain". (Acts XXVIII,20b).

Acts tells the story of how the apostle's efforts to keep the quarrel on a theological plane were progressively overturned, and it blames the unpersuaded Jews for causing Paul's consequent legal difficulties. Luke stresses in most dramatic terms the sharp reaction of Paul's Jewish adversaries not only to his overall theological beliefs, but especially to his advocacy of the Gentile mission. Not only did these foes perpetrate violence on the apostle's person, but they also officially lodged political accusations which were aimed at demonstrating to the Roman authorities the seditious nature of Paul's proselytism. The very essence of the Christian confession, centered around the sovereignty of Jesus Christ, was given strong political overtones: i.e. Paul was essentially proclaiming another king, a rival to Caesar. The Jewish authorities thus laid down a political challenge to Paul as a result of their theological quarreling. The final consequence of this political challenge was to undo Paul's previous efforts to affirm his place within mainstream Judaism. Paul had finally been forced publicly and officially to reject the Sanhedrin's authority over him. The Jewish authorities could only consider the appeal to Caesar not so much as directed *to* Rome as *against* Jerusalem. Such an appeal was the right of a Roman citizen, but it was hardly the deed of an Orthodox Jew. By rejecting the Sanhedrin's political and juridical authority over him and by invoking the Emperor's exclusive legal competence in the case, the apostle had consummated the break with official Judaism at least on the political and judicial levels.

At a very decisive moment in his ministry, the apostle Paul had shown that his earthly *patria* was Rome and not Jerusalem.

Bibliography

1. Reference Works

Bibles:
   English – *The Holy Bible*, Revised Standard Version, Thomas Nelson & Sons, New York, 1952 revision.
   Greek – Η Καινή Διαθήκη, 2nd Edition with revised critical apparatus, The British and Foreign Bible Society, London, 1958; reprinted 1975.
   Latin – *Biblia Sacra*, Iuxta Vulgatam Versionem; adiuvantibus B. Fischer, I. Gribomont, H.F.D. Sparks, W. Thiele; recensuit et brevi apparatu instruxit R. Weber, Württembergische Bibelanstalt, Stuttgart, 1969, Tomus II.

Digest of Justinian:
   Digesta, Corpus Iuris Civilis, Vol. I, ed. Th. Mommsen, Berlin, 1886.

Dictionaries and Grammars:
   Bauer, Walter, Arndt, William & Gingrich, F.W. *A Greek-English Lexicon of the New Testament*, (E.T.), University of Chicago Press, 10th Impression, 1967.
   Blass, F. & Debrunner, A. *A Greek Grammar of the New Testament* (E.T.), University of Chicago Press, 3rd Impression, 1967.
   Kittel, Gerhard, et al., *Theological Dictionary of the New Testament*, (E.T.), Eerdmans, Grand Rapids, Michigan, 9 Volumes.
   Liddell, Henry George & Scott, Robert, *A Greek-English Lexicon,* Clarendon Press, Oxford, 9th Edition, 1940, reprinted 1978.
   Moulton, James Hope, *A Grammar of New Testament Greek*, Volume I = Prolegomena, T & T Clark, Edinburgh, 3rd Edition, 1908, reprinted 1957.
   Moulton, James Hope & Milligan, George, *The Vocabulary of the Greek Testament*, Hodder & Stoughton, London, 1930, impression 1963.
   Zerwick, Maximilian, *Biblical Greek*, (E.T. from the 4th Latin Edition of *Graecitas Biblica*), Rome, 1963, *reeditio* 1982.

Encyclopedias:
   Daremberg, C. & Saglio, E. (eds), *Dictionnaire des Antiquités Grecques et Romaines*, Paris, 5 Tomes, 1877–1919.
   Hastings, James (ed.), *A Dictionary of the Bible*, Edinburgh, 4 Volumes, 1898–1902.
   The Oxford Classical Dictionary, Clarendon Press, Oxford, 1949, reprint 1957.
   Paulys Real-Encyclopädie der Classischen Altertumswissenschaft, Stuttgart, 1894 – .
   de Ruggiero, Ettore, *Dizionario Epigrafico di Antichita Romane*, Rome, 1895 –.

2. Bibliography of Works cited

Abbott, Frank Frost and Johnson, Allan Chester, *Municipal Administration in the Roman Empire*, Princeton University Press, Princeton, New Jersey, 1926.
Alföldy, Géza, "Die Stellung der Ritter in der Führungsschicht des Imperium Romanum," *Chiron*, Munich, Band 11; 1981.
Allison, J.E. and Cloud, J.D., "The Lex Iulia Maiestatis", *Latomus*, Vol. 21; 1962.
Anderson, J.G.C., "Augustan Edicts from Cyrene", *JRS*, Vol. 17; 1927.
Applebaum, Shimon, "The Legal Status of the Jewish Communities in the Diaspora", *The Jewish People in the First Century*, van Gorcum & Comp. B.V., Assen, 2nd. Printing, 1974.
Applebaum, Shimon, "Judaea as a Roman Province: the Countryside as a political and economic Factor"' *ANRW*, II,8; 1977.
Badian, Ernst, *Foreign Clientelae (264–70 B.C.)*, Clarendon Press, Oxford, 1958.
Badian, Ernst, "Ancient Alexandria", *Studies in Greek and Roman History*, Basil Blackwood, Oxford, 1968.
Bauman, Richard A., *The Crimen Maiestatis in the Roman Republic and Augustan Principate*, Witwatersrand University Press, Johannesburg, 1967.
Bauman, Richard A., *Impietas In Principem* – A Study of Treason against the Roman Emperor with special Reference to the First Century A.D., Verlag C.H. Beck, Munich, 1974.
Bell, H. Idris, *Jews and Christians in Egypt*, British Museum and Oxford University Press, London, 1924.
Benko, Stephen, "The Edict of Claudius of A.D. 49 and the Instigator 'Chrestus'", *TZ*, No. 25, Heft 6, Nov–Dec. 1969.
Benoit, Pierre, "Prétoire, Lithostroton et Gabbatha", *RB*, Tome 59; 1952.
Bickerman, Elias, J., "The Warning Inscriptions of Herod's Temple", *JQR*, Vol. 37, No. 4, April 1947.
Bickerman, Elias J., "Consecratio", *Le Culte des Souverains dans l'Empire Romain*, Entretiens sur l'Antiquité Classique, Tome 19, Fondation Hardt, Vandoeuvres-Genève, 1973.
Bleicken, Jochen, "Provocatio", *Paulys-Wissowa-Re*, 26er Halbband (Nachträge), 1959.
Bleicken, Jochen, *Senatsgericht und Kaisergericht*, Vandenhoeck und Ruprecht, Göttingen, 1962.
Bleicken, Jochen, *Die Verfassung der Römischen Republik*, Ferdinand Schöningh, Paderborn, 2e Auflage, 1978.
Blinzler, Josef, *Le Procès de Jésus*, F.T. = Maison Mame, Paris, 1962.
Bovon, François, *Les Derniers Jours de Jésus*, Delachaux et Niestlé, Neuchâtel, 1974.
Brassac, A., "Une Inscription de Delphes et la Chronologie de St. Paul", *RB*, Tome 10; 1913.
Broughton, T.R.S., "The Roman Army", *BC.*, Vol. 5, London, 1933.
Bruce, F.F., *The Acts of the Apostles*, Wm. B. Eerdmans, Grand Rapids, Michigan, 8th Printing, 1975.
Bruce, F.F., "The Acts of the Apostles: Historical Record or Theological Reconstruction", *ANRW.*, II,25.3; 1985.
Brunot, Amedée, "Malte, Fille de St. Paul" *Bible et Terre Sainte*, Paris, No. 89, February 1967.
Bruns, Karl Georg, *Fontes Iuris Romani Antiqui*, Scientia Verlag Aalen, Tübingen, 2nd. New Impression, 1969.
Brunt, P.A., "Procuratorial Jurisdiction", *Latomus*, Brussels, Tome 25; 1966.
Brunt, P.A., "Lex de Imperio Vespasiani", *JRS*, Vol. 67; 1977.
Brunt, P.A., "Princeps and Equites", *JRS*, Vol. 73; 1983.
Burkill, T.A., "The Competence of the Sanhedrin", *VC*, Vol. 10; 1956.
Buti, Ignazio, "La 'Cognitio extra Ordinem'", *ANRW*, II,14; 1982.
Cadbury, Henry Joel, "Luke's Interest in Lodging", *JBL*, Vol. 45; 1926.
Cadbury, Henry Joel, "Roman Law and the Trial of Paul", *BC*, Vol. 5, London, 1933.
Cadbury, Henry Joel, *The Book of Acts in History*, Adam and Charles Black, London, 1955.
Calderone, Salvatore, "Superstitio"' *ANRW*, I,2; 1972.
Cassidy, Richard J., *Society and Politics in the Acts of the Apostles*, Orbis Books, Maryknoll, Maryland, 1987.

Cerfaux, L. and Tondriau, J., *Le Culte des Souverains dans la Civilisation Greco-Romaine*, Bibliothèque de Théologie Série III, Vol. 5, Desclée et Cie., éditeurs, Tornai, 1957.
Chilton, C.W., "The Roman Law of Treason under the Early Principate", *JRS*, Vol. 45; 1955.
Clark, Albert Curtis, *The Acts of the Apostles*, A critical Edition, Clarendon Press, Oxford, 1933.
Collart, Paul, *Philippes, Ville de Macedoine: depuis ses Origines jusqu'à la fin de l'Epoque romaine*, Thèse de l'Université de Genève, 85; 1937.
Cullmann, Oscar, "Les Causes de la Mort de Pierre et de Paul d'après le Témoignage de Clément Romain"' *RHPR*, No. 3, May–June, 1930.
Cuss, Dominique, *Imperial Cult and Honorary Terms in the New Testament*, University Press, Fribourg, 1974.
Daniel, Jerry L., "Anti-Semitism in the Hellenistic-Roman Period", *JBL*, Vol. 98, No. 1, March 1979.
Danielou, Jean, "Paul dans les Actes des Apôtres", *AXES*, Paris, May 1969.
Davies, R.W., "Cohortes Equitatae", *Historia* (Wiesbaden), Vol. 20; 1971.
Delebecque, Edouard, *Les Deux Actes des Apôtres*, Etudes Bibliques, N.S. 6, Librairie Lecoffre-J. Gabaldi, Editeurs, Paris, 1986.
Dibelius, Martin, *Studies in the Acts of the Apostles*, E.T. = SCM Press Ltd., London, 1956.
Dupont, Jacques, "Aequitas Romana", *Etudes sur les Actes des Apôtres*, Lectio Divina 45, Editions du Cerf, Paris, 1967.
Dupont, Jacques, "La Conclusion des Actes et son Rapport à l'Ensemble de l'Ouvrage de Luc", *Les Actes des Apôtres*, Bibliotheca Ephemeridum Theologicarum Lovaniensium 48, Editeurs J. Duclot S.A., University Press, Louvain, 1979.
Ehrenberg, Victor and Jones, A.H.M., *Documents Illustrating the Reigns of Augustus and Tiberius*, Clarendon Press, Oxford, 2nd. Edition, 1955.
Fascher, Erich, "Paulus (Apostel)", *Paulys-Wissowa-Re*, Supplementband 8; 1956.
Ferenczy, Endré, "Rechtshistorische Bemerkungen zur Ausdehnung des römischen Bürgerrechts und zum ius Italicum unter dem Prinzipat", *ANRW*. II,14; 1982.
Foakes-Jackson, Frederick John and Lake, Kirsopp (eds.), *The Beginnings of Christianity*, Macmillan and Co., London, in five volumes, 1920–1933.
Fougères G., "Flagellum", *DAGR*, Tome II, Part 2; 1896.
Frey, Jean-Baptiste, "Les Communautés Juives à Rome aux premiers Temps de l'Eglise", *RSR*, Tome 20; 1930.
Frova, Antonio, "L'Iscrizione di Ponzio Pilato a Cesarea", *Rendiconti*: Classe di Lettere e Scienze Morali e Storiche; Istituto Lombardo, Milan, Vol. 95; 1961.
Garnsey, Peter, "The Lex Iulia and Appeal under the Empire", *JRS*, Vol. 56; 1966.
Garnsey, Peter, "The Criminal Jurisdiction of Governors", *JRS*, Vol. 58; 1968.
Garzetti, Albino, *L'Impero da Tiberio agli Antonini*, Licinio Cappelli editore, Bologna, 1960.
Gaudemet, Jean, *Institutions de l'Antiquité*, Sirey, Paris, 1967.
George, Augustin, "Israel dans l'Oeuvre de Luc", *RB*, Vol. 75, No. 4, October 1968.
Gilchrist, J.M., "On what Charge was St. Paul brought to Rome?" *The Expository Times*, Edinburgh, Vol. 78, Oct. 1966–Sept. 1967.
Giovannini, Adalbert, *Consulare Imperium*, Schweizerische Beiträge Altertumswissenschaft, Heft 16, Friedrich Reinhardt Verlag, Basle, 1983.
Girard, Paul Frédéric, *Textes de Droit Romain*, Publiés et Annotés, Arthur Rousseau, éditeur, Paris, 4th Edition, 1913.
Goguel Maurice, "La Vision de Paul à Corinthe et sa Comparution devant Gallion", *RHPR*, No. 4–5; 1932.
Goguel, Maurice, *La Naissance du Christianisme*, Payot, Paris, 1946.
Grant, Michael, *The Jews in the Roman World*, Charles Scribner's Sons, New York, 1973.
Greenidge, A.H.J., *The Legal Procedure of Cicero's Time*, Clarendon Press, London, 1901.
Gschnitzer, Fritz, "Politarches", *Paulys-Wissowa-Re*, Supplementband 13: 1973.
Haenchen, Ernst, *The Acts of the Apostles*, A Commentary, (E.T. = Basil Blackwell, Oxford, 1971).
Hammond, Mason, "Germana Patria" *HSCP*, Vol. 60; 1951.
Hammond, Mason, *The City in the Ancient World*, Harvard University Press, Cambridge, 1972.
Hanson, R.P.C., "The Provenance of the Interpolator in the 'Western' Text of Acts and of Acts itself", *NTS*, Vol. 12, No. 3; April 1966.

Bibliography

Hengel, Martin, *Die Zeloten: Untersuchungen zur Jüdischen Freiheitsbewegung in der Zeit von Herodes I bis 70 N. Chr.*, E.J. Brill, Leiden/Köln, 1961.

Hengel, Martin, *Acts and the History of Earliest Christianity*, SCM Press, ltd., London, 1979.

Herrmann, Léon, *Chrestos*: Témoignages paiens et juifs sur le Christianisme du premier siècle, Collection Latomus 109, Brussels, 1970.

Hitzig, Hermann Ferdinand, "Custodia", *Paulys-Wissowa-Re.*, Vol. IV, 8er Halbband, 1901.

Hock, Ronald F., "Paul's Tentmaking and the Problem of his Social Class", *JBL*, Vol. 97, No. 4; December 1978.

Homo, Léon, *Les Empereurs Romains et le Christianisme*, Payot, Paris, 1931.

Horovitz, Philippe, "Essai sur les Pouvoirs des Procurateurs-Gouverneurs", *RBPH*, Tome 17; 1938.

Horsley, G.H.R. (ed), *New Documents Illustrating Early Christianity*, The Ancient History Documentary Research Centre, Macquarie University, North Ryde, N.S.W., Australia, 1981.

Hultgren, Arland J., "Paul's Pre-Christian Persecutions of the Church: Their Purpose, Locale, and Nature", *JBL*, Vol. 95, No. 1, March 1976.

Iliffe, J.H., "The 'Thanatos' Inscription from Herod's Temple: Fragment of a second Copy", *QDAP*, Vol. VI; 1938.

Jacquier, E., *Les Actes des Apôtres*, Gabalda, Paris, 1926.

Jervell, Jacob, "Paul in the Acts of the Apostles: Tradition, History, Theology", *The Unknown Paul: Essays on Luke-Acts and Early Christian History*, Augsburg Publishing House, Minneapolis, 1984.

Jewett, Robert, *A Chronology of Paul's Life*, Fortress Press, Philadelphia, 1979.

Jones, A.H.M., "I Appeal unto Caesar", *Studies in Roman Government and Law*, Basil Blackwell, Oxford, 1968.

Jones, A.H.M., "Imperial and Senatorial Jurisdiction in the Early Principate", *Studies in Roman Government and Law*, Basil Blackwell, Oxford, 1968.

Jones, A.H.M., "Procurators and Prefects in the Early Principate", *Studies in Roman Government and Law*, Basil Blackwell, Oxford, 1968.

Jones, Donald L., "Christianity and the Roman Imperial Cult", *ANRW*, II,23.2; 1980.

Jullian, Camille, "Jus Italicum", *DAGR*, Tome III, Part 1; 1900.

Juster, J., *Les Juifs dans l'Empire Romain*, Geuthner, Paris, 1914.

Kasher, Aryeh, "Les Circonstances de la Promulgation de l'Edit de l'Empereur Claude et de sa Lettre aux Alexandrins – 41 après J.C." *Semitica*, Paris, Vol. 26; 1976.

Kasher, Aryeh, *The Jews in Hellenistic and Roman Egypt*, Texte und Studien zum antiken Judentum, 7, J.C.B. Mohr (Paul Siebeck), Tübingen, Revised English Edition, 1985.

Keresztes, Paul, "Nero, the Christians and the Jews in Tacitus and Clement of Rome", *Latomus*, Brussels, Tome 43; 1984.

Klausner, Joseph, *From Jesus to Paul*, London, 2nd. Edition, 1946.

Knox, John, *Chapters in a Life of Paul*, Adam and Charles Black, London, 1954.

Kornemann, Ernst, "Coloniae", *Paulys-Wissowa-Re*, Vol. IV, Part 1; 1901.

Koukouli-Chrysanthaki, Chaido, "Politarchs in a new Inscription from Amphipolis", *Ancient Macedonian Studies in Honor of Charles F. Edson*, Institute of Balkan Studies 158, Thessalonica, 1981.

Kübler, Bernhard, "Lictor", *Paulys-Wissowa-Re*, Vol. XIII, 25er Halbband, 1926.

Lake, Kirsopp, "Paul's Controversies", *BC*, Vol. V, London, 1933.

Lemonon, Jean-Pierre, *Pilate et le Gouvernement de la Judée*, Textes et Monuments, J. Gabalda et Cie., Paris, 1981.

Lenormant, F., "Colonia", *DAGR*, Tome I, Part 2; 1887.

Leon, Harry J., *The Jews of Ancient Rome*, The Jewish Publication Society of America, Philadelphia, 1960.

Lietzmann, Hans, *Histoire de l'Eglise Ancienne*, F.T. = Payot, Paris, in four volumes, 1936–1949.

Lifshitz, Baruch, "Césarée de Palestine, son Histoire et ses Institutions", *ANRW*, II,8; 1977.

Lifshitz, Baruch, "Jerusalem sous la Domination Romaine", *ANRW*, II,8; 1977.

Lintott, Andrew W., "Provocatio: From the Struggle of the Orders to the Principate", *ANRW*, I,2; 1972.

Lohse, Edouard, *Le Milieu du Nouveau Testament*, F.T. = Editions du Cerf, Paris, 1973.

Lüdemann, Gerd, *Paulus, der Heidenapostel*, Studien zur Chronologie, Vandenhoeck & Ruprecht, Göttingen, Band I, 1980.

Lüdemann, Gerd, *Das Frühe Christentum nach den Traditionen der Apostelgeschichte*, Vandenhoeck & Ruprecht, Göttingen, 1987.

Mantel, H., "Sanhedrin", *Encyclopaedia Judaica*, Macmillan Co. Jerusalem, Vol. 14; 1971.

Marquardt, Joachim, *Römische Staatsverwaltung*, Verlag von S. Hirzel, Leipzig, 2nd Edition, in three volumes, 1881–1885.

Martini, Carlo M., *Atti degli Apostoli*, Edizione Paoline, Rome, 6th Edition, 1982.

Mason, Hugh J., *Greek Terms for Roman Institutions*, A Lexicon and Analysis, American Studies in Papyrology, Vol. 13, Hakkert, Toronto, 1974.

Meeks, Wayne A., *The First Urban Christians*: The Social World of the Apostle Paul, Yale University Press, New Haven, 1983.

Menoud, Philippe-Henri, "L'Eglise Naissante et le Judaisme", *Jésus Christ et la Foi*, Delachaux et Niestlé, Neuchâtel, 1975.

Miles, Gary B., and Trompf, Garry, "Luke and Antiphon: The Theology of Acts 27–28 in the Light of Pagan Beliefs about Divine Retribution, Pollution and Shipwreck", *HTR*, Vol. 69, No. 3–4, July–October 1976.

Millar, Fergus, "The Emperor, the Senate and the Provinces", *JRS*, Vol. 56, Parts 1 & 2; 1966.

Millar, Fergus, "The Imperial Cult and the Persecutions", *Le Culte des Souverains dans l'Empire Romain*, Entretiens sur l'Antiquité Classique, Tome 19, Fondation Hardt, Vandoeuvres-Genève, 1973.

Mommsen, Theodor, *Römisches Staatsrecht*, Verlag von S. Hirzel, Leipzig, in three volumes, 1887–1888.

Mommsen, Theodor, *Römisches Strafrecht*, Duncker & Humblot, Leipzig, 1899.

Moore, George Foot, *Judaism in the First Centuries of the Christian Era*, Harvard University Press, Cambridge, 3rd Impression, 1932.

Munck, Johannes, *The Acts of the Apostles*, Anchor Bible, 31, Doubleday and Co., Garden City, New York, 7th Printing, 1978.

Munier, Charles, *L'Eglise dans l'Empire Romain*, Eglise et Cité, Editions Cujas, Paris, 1979.

Murphy-O'Connor, Jerome, *Corinthe au Temps de St. Paul*: d'après les Textes et l'Archéologie, F.T. = Editions du Cerf, Paris, 1986.

Neil, William, *The Acts of the Apostles*, New Century Bible, Oliphants, London, 1973.

Nicolet, Claude, *Le Métier de Citoyen dans la Rome Républicaine*, Gallimard, Paris, 1976.

Oliver, James H., "Greek Applications for Roman Trials", *AJP*, Vol. 100; 1979.

O'Neill, John Cochrane, *The Theology of Acts in its Historical Setting*, SPCK, London, 1961.

Penna, Romano, "Les Juifs à Rome au Temps de l'Apôtre Paul", *NTS*, Vol. 28; 1982.

Perry, Alfred M., "Acts and the Roman Trial of Paul", *HTR*, Vol. XVII, No. 2, April 1924.

Pherigo, Lindsay P., "Paul's Life after the Close of Acts", *JBL*, Vol. 70; 1951.

la Piana, George, "Foreign Groups in Rome during the first Centuries of the Empire", *HTR*, Vol. XX, No. 4, October 1927.

Plassart, André, "L'Inscription de Delphes mentionnant le Proconsul Gallion", *REG*, Tome 80; 1967.

von Premerstein, Anton, "Ius Italicum", *Paulys-Wissowa-Re*, Vol. 10; 19er Halbband, 1917.

Prigent, Pierre, "Pourquoi les Persécutions?", *RHPR*, Vol. 55; 1975.

Rabello, Alfredo Mordechai, "The Legal Conditions of the Jews in the Roman Empire", *ANRW*, II, 13; 1980.

Rajak, Tessa, "Was there a Roman Charter for the Jews?", *JRS*, Vol. 74; 1984.

Ramsay, William Mitchell, *The Church in the Roman Empire before 170 A.D.*, Hodder and Stoughton, London, 1895.

Ramsay, William Mitchell, *St. Paul The Traveller and the Roman Citizen*, Hodder and Stoughton, London, 1896.

Ramsay, William Mitchell, "Corinth", *HDB*, Vol. I; 1898.

Riccobono, Salvator, *Fontes Iuris Romani Antejustiniani*, G. Barbera, editore, Florence, 1941.

Robert, Louis, "Recherches Epigraphiques", *REA*, Tome 62; 1960.

Ross, Robert C., "Superstitio", *CJ*, Vol. 64; 1968–1969.

Rotondi, Giovanni, *Leges Publicae Populi Romani*, Georg Olms Verlagsbuchhandlung, Hildesheim, 1966.
Ruggini, Lellia C., "Pregiudizi razziali, Ostilità politica e culturale, Intolleranza religiosa nell 'Impero Romano", *Athenaeum*, Pavia, N.S., Vol. 46; 1968.
Saddington, D.B., "The Development of the Roman Auxiliary Forces from Augustus to Trajan", *ANRW*, II,3; 1975.
Samter, Ernst, "Fasces", *Paulys-Wissowa-Re*, Vol. VI, 1909.
Sanders, Ed. Parish, "Jesus, Paul and Judaism", *ANRW* II, 25.1; 1982.
Sanders, Henry A., "Two Fragmentary Birth Certificates from the Michigan Collection", *Memoirs of the American Academy in Rome*, Rome, Vol. IX; 1931.
Saulnier, Christiane, "Lois Romaines sur les Juifs selon Flavius Josèphe", *RB*, Tome 88; 1981.
Saulnier, Christiane, "Rome et la Bible", *Supplément au Dictionnaire de la Bible*. Ed. Letouzey, Paris, 1984.
Saumagne, Charles, "St. Paul et Felix, Procurateur de Judée", *Mélanges d'Archéologie et d'Histoire offerts à André Piganiol*, S.E.V.P.E.N., Paris, Vol. III; 1966.
Scheid, John, *Le Délit Religieux dans la Rome Tardo-Républicaine*, Collection de l'Ecole Française de Rome 48, Rome, 1981.
Schubert, Paul, "The Final Cycle of Speeches in the Book of Acts", *JBL*, Vol. 87, No. 1; March 1968.
Schuler, Carl, "The Macedonian Politarchs", *CP*, Vol. 55; April 1960.
Schulz, Fritz, "Roman Registers of Births and Birth Certificates", *JRS*, Vol. 32; 1942 (Part 1); Vol. 33; 1943 (Part 2).
Schürer, Emil, *The History of the Jewish People in the Age of Jesus Christ*, Revised English Edition, G. Vermes, F. Millar & M. Goodman (eds.), T. & T. Clark, ltd., Edinburgh, in 3 volumes, 1973–1986.
Schwartz, J., "A propos du Statut personnel de l'Apôtre Paul", *RHPR*, No. 1; 1957.
Scramuzza, Vincent M., "The Policy of the early Roman Emperors towards Judaism", *BC*, Vol. 5, London, 1933.
Seston, William, "L'Empereur Claude et les Chrétiens", *RHPR*, Tome 11; 1931.
Sherwin-White, Adrian Nicolas, *The Roman Citizenship*, Clarendon Press, Oxford, 1939.
Sherwin-White, Adrian Nicolas, *Roman Society and Roman Law in the New Testament*, Clarendon Press, Oxford, 1963.
Sherwin-White, Adrian Nicolas, *Racial Prejudice in Imperial Rome*, University Press, Cambridge, 1967.
Sherwin-White, Adrian Nicolas, "The Roman Citizenship: A Survey of its Development into a world Franchise", *ANRW*, I,2; 1972.
Smallwood, E. Mary, *The Jews under Roman Rule*. E.J. Brill, Leiden, 1976.
Smith, Morton, "Zealots and Sicarii: Their Origins and Relation", *HTR*, Vol. 64, No. 1, January 1971.
Solin, Heikki, "Juden und Syrer im westlichen Teil der römischen Welt", *ANRW*, II, 29.2; 1983.
Stegemann, Wolfgang, "War der Apostel Paulus ein römischer Bürger?", *ZNW*, Band 78, Heft 3–4; 1987.
Stern, M., "The Jewish Diaspora", *The Jewish People in the First Century*, van Gorcum and Comp. B.V., Assen, Vol. 1, 2nd Printing, 1974.
Sullivan, Richard D., "The Dynasty of Judaea in the First Century", *ANRW*, II,8; 1977.
Taubenschlag, Rafael, *The Laws of Greco-Roman Egypt in the Light of the Papyri*, Panstwowe Wydawnictwo Naukowe, Warsaw, 2nd Edition, 1955.
Taubenschlag, Rafael, "Customary Law and Custom in the Papyri", *Opera Minora*, Panstwowe Wydawnictwo Naukowe, Warsaw, 1959.
Taubenschlag, Rafael, "Il Delatore e la sua Responsibilità nel Diritto dei Papiri", *Opera Minora*, Panstwowe Wydawnictwo Naukowe, Warsaw, 1959.
Taubenschlag, Rafael, "Le Procès de l'Apôtre Paul en Lumière des Papyri", *Opera Minora*, Panstwowe Wydawnictwo Naukowe, Warsaw, 1959.
Tcherikover, Victor, *Hellenistic Civilization and the Jews*, Atheneum, New York, 4th Printing, 1977.
Turner, Cuthbert Hamilton, "Philippi", *HDB*, Vol. III, 1900.

van Unnik, Willem Cornelius, "Tarsus or Jerusalem", *Sparsa Collecta*: The Collected Essays of W.C. van Unnik, Supplement to Novum Testamentum, Vol. XXIX, Part 1, E.J. Brill, Leiden 1973.
van Unnik, Willem Cornelius, "Die Anklage gegen die Apostel in Philippi", *Sparsa Collecta*: The Collected Essays of W.C. van Unnik, Supplement to Novum Testamentum, Vol. XXIX, Part 1, E.J. Brill, Leiden, 1973.
Urch, Edwin, J., "Procedure in the Courts of the Roman provincial Governors"' *CJ*, Vol. XXV, No. 2; November 1929.
Vardaman, Jerry, "A New Inscription which mentions Pilate as 'Prefect', *JBL*, Vol. 81. No. 1; March 1962.
Veltman, Fred, "The Defense Speeches of Paul in Acts", *Perspectives on Luke-Acts* (C.H. Talbert ed.), Association of Baptist Professors of Religion, T. & T. Clark, ltd., Danville, Virginia/Edinburgh, 1978.
de Visscher, Fernand, *Les Edits d'Auguste découverts à Cyrène*, Otto Zeller, Osnabrück, 1940, reprint 1965.
Walaskay, Paul W., *And So We Came to Rome: The Political Perspective of St. Luke*, NTS Monograph Series 49, Cambridge University Press, Cambridge, 1983.
Watkins, Thomas H., *A Study of the Origin and Historical Development of Ius Italicum*, Dissertation, University of North Carolina, Chapel Hill, 1973.
Wikenhauser, Alfred, *Die Apostelgeschichte*, Verlag Friedrich Pustet, Regensburg, 4th Edition, 1961.
Wikgren, Allen P., "The Problem in Acts 16:12", *New Testament Textual Criticism*, Clarendon Press, Oxford, 1981.
Williams, C.S.C., *A Commentary on the Acts of the Apostles*, Adam and Charles Black, London, 2nd Edition, 1964.
Wilson, Stephen G., *The Gentiles and the Gentile Mission in Luke-Acts*, NTS Monograph Series 23, University Press, Cambridge, 1973.
Wiseman, James, "Corinth and Rome I: 228 B.C.–A.D. 267", *ANRW*, II, 7.1; 1979.

Index of Passages

1. Holy Scripture

Genesis
  XXIII,11   79

Exodus
  XXX,13–14   16

Numbers
  XI,16   99
  XI,24–25   99

Deuteronomy
  XVII,6   100
  XIX,15   100
  XXV,3   74

2 Chronicles
  XIII,7   121
  XIX,8   98

Psalms
  I,1   121

Proverbs
  XI,9   79

Job
  XXXIII,11   26

Isaiah
  VI,9–10   190

Ezekiel
  XXIII,38–39   123

Wisdom
  XII,27   154

1 Maccabees
  VIII,23–30   22
  XIV,44   99
  XV,16–21   121

2 Maccabees
  I,10   98
  IV,44   98
  IX,19   79
  XI,27   98

3 Maccabees
  I,22   79

St. Matthew
  II,23   122
  X,17   58
                          185
  XII,5   27
                          123
  XII,7   27
  XIII,13–15   190
  XIV,3   123
  XVII,24–27   16
  XVIII,16   100
  XXII,23   96
  XXV,6   176
  XXVI,4   123
  XXVI,66   100
  XXVI,67   100
  XXVII,1   100
  XXVII,2   112
  XXVII,11   112
  XXVII,14   112
  XXVII,15   112
  XXVII,19   138
  XXVII,21   112
  XXVII,26   25
  XXVII,27   112
                          118
  XXVIII,14   112

St. Mark
  IV,12   190
  V,4   68
  VI,17–29   103
  VI,17   123
  XII,12   123
  XII,18   96
  XIII,9   58
  XIV,1   123
  XIV,10   185
  XIV,53   96
                           99
  XIV,55–56   100
  XIV,64   96
                          100
  XIV,65   100

XV,1	96	*Acts of the Apostles*	
	185	I,10	92
XV,15	25	II,10	188
	185	II,14	190
XV,15a	43	III,4	92
XV,16	118	III,13	185
		III,14–15	143
St. Luke		IV,1	10
I,3	106	IV,3	64
I,9	155		100
II,1	35	IV,5	10
	158	IV,9	124
II,42	155	IV,10	190
VII,1–10	174	IV,31	192
VIII,10	190	V,17	99
VIII,29	68		122
IX,9	153	V,18	64
XII,11–12	125		100
XV,15	79	V,24	10
XVIII,32	185	V,40	100
XIX,19	79	VI,13–14	64
XX,20	112	VI,14	155
XX,27	96	VI,15	92
XXI,11	121	VII,1	99
XXI,14–15	125	VII,54–VIII,2	101
XXII,52	10	VII,55	92
XXII,63	100	VII,57	78
XXII,66	96	VII,58	165
	99	VIII,1	165
XXIII,1	96	VIII,3	165
XXIII,2	36	VIII,40	109
XXIII,6–7	117	IX,1–2	99
XXIII,7	159		165
XXIII,8	153	IX,11	78
XXIII,10	91	IX,15	163
XXIII,11	153	IX,30	78
	159	X,1ff	109
XXIII,14	91	X,1–2	174
XXIII,15	159	X,4	92
XXIII,16	25	XI,6	92
XXIII,25	185	XI,25	78
XXIII,41	137	XI,26	169
XXIII,47	174	XII,2	103
XXIV,44	168	XII,4	185
		XII,6	68
St. John		XII,19ff	109
XI,47–48	99		124
XII,39–41	190	XII,22	33
XVIII,19–24	93	XIII,5	49
XVIII,28	118	XIII,7	46
XVIII,31	101	XIII,8	46
XVIII,33	118	XIII,9	92
XIX,1	25	XIII,12	46
	74	XIII,14	32
XIX,9	118		49
XIX,10	101	XIII,15	50
XIX,12b	36	XIII,38	190
	140	XIII,40	163
XIX,13	138	XIII,45	49
		XIII,46	49
		XIII,50	3

XIV,1	49	XVIII,11	47
XIV,2	33	XVIII,12–13	51
XIV,5–6	3	XVIII,12	46
XIV,5	10	XVIII,14–15	56
XIV,9	92	XVIII,16–17	58
XIV,19	3	XVIII,17	8
XV,1	155		50
XV,5	81	XVIII,18a	59
	122	XVIII,19	49
XVI,11–40	4	XIX,8–9	50
XVI,12	4	XIX,8	49
XVI,12b–15	8	XIX,21	48
XVI,16–18	8		62
XVI,16b	8	XIX,21b	175
XVI,17	168		198
XVI,19–21	8	XIX,24–27	8
XVI,19	9	XIX,30–31	34
XVI,19a	8	XIX,33–34	13
XVI,20	9	XIX,38	46
XVI,22–24	24	XX,3	62
XVI,22	9	XX,4–5	66
XVI,35	9	XX,4	66
	26	XX,16b	61
XVI,36	9	XXI,4	62
XVI,37	27	XXI,8–10	130
	74	XXI,8	109
XVI.38–39	28	XXI,11	62
XVI,38	9		185
	75	XXI,13	62
XVI,39	5	XXI,16	109
XVI,40	29	XXI,17	62
XVII,1	30	XXI,18	62
XVII,2	31	XXI,19	62
	49	XXI,20a	62
XVII,3	31	XXI,20b	62
XVII,4	32	XXI,21	62
XVII,5	32		155
XVII,6	121		186
XVII,6a	34	XXI,23–24a	63
XVII,6b–7	35	XXI,24b	63
XVII,8	36	XXI,27–28	63
XVII,9	43	XXI,28	116
XVII,10–15	45		123
XVII,10	49	XXI,29	66
XVII,10a	43	XXI,30–33a	66
XVII,16–34	45	XXI,30	8
XVII,17	8	XXI,31	63
	49	XXI,33	8
XVII,19	8		185
XVII,22	157	XXI,33b	69
XVIII,1	47	XXI,34a+b	69
XVIII,2	47	XXI,35–36	69
	52	XXI,37–38	69
XVIII,3	47	XXI,38	35
XVIII,4	48		70
	49	XXI,39	78
XVIII,5	48		79
XVIII,6a	49		80
XVIII,6b	49	XXI,39–40	71
XVIII,7	50	XXI,40	164
XVIII,8a	50	XXII,1	72
XVIII,8b	51		

XXII,2	72	XXIII,31	108
XXII,3	72	XXIII,32	108
	78	XXIII,33	108
	81		109
	127	XXIII,34a	116
XXII,4–5	72	XXIII,34b	116
XXII,5	99	XXIII,35a	116
	166	XXIII,35b	116
XXII,6–11	72	XXIV,1	99
XXII,12	72		104
XXII,14–15	72		118
XXII,16	72		160
XXII,17	73	XXIV,2–4	119
XXII,19–20	72	XXIV,2	91
	165		139
XXII,21	73	XXIV,5–6	116
XXII,22	185		120
XXII,22b–23	73	XXIV,5	12
XXII,24	73		35
	81		122
XXII,25	27	XXIV,6b–8a	124
	74	XXIV,6b	119
XXII,26	74	XXIV,8b–9	124
XXII,27	74	XXIV,8b	91
XXII,28	75	XXIV,10–21	116
XXII,29	28	XXIV,10	164
	75	XXIV,10a	125
XXII,30	90	XXIV,10b	125
	94	XXIV,11–13	126
	160	XXIV,13	91
XXIII,1–2	92	XXIV,14–15	126
XXIII,1	184	XXIV,14	122
XXIII,3	94	XXIV,14b	81
XXIII,6	94	XXIV,15	94
	186	XXIV,16	93
XXIII,6a	81		127
XXIII,6b	200	XXIV,17	61
XXIII,7	96	XXIV,18–21	128
XXIII,8	96	XXIV,18	127
XXIII,9	96	XXIV,19	19
	190		160
XXIII,10	97	XXIV,20	57
XXIII,11	175	XXIV,21	94
	197		186
XXIII,12ff	136	XXIV,21b	200
XXIII,12	104	XXIV,22–23	129
XXIII,13	104	XXIV,22	105
XXIII,14	104		116
XXIII,15	104	XXIV,24	130
XXIII,16–17	105	XXIV,25	131
XXIII,18	91	XXIV,26	131
XXIII,23–24	105	XXIV,27	91
XXIII,25	106		132
XXIII,26	106	XXV,1–11	98
XXIII,27	107	XXV,1	135
XXIII,28	107	XXV,2	104
XXIII,29	107		135
	162	XXV,3	136
	170	XXV,4–5	136
	199	XXV,5	91
XXIII,30	108	XXV,6	116
			137

	160		165
XXV,6a	138	XXVI,6	186
XXV,6b	138		200
XXV,7	116	XXVI,7	164
	137	XXVI,8	200
	138	XXVI,9–12	165
XXV,8	116	XXVI,16	167
	138	XXVI,17	167
	139	XXVI,18	167
XXV,9	132	XXVI,19b–20	167
	138	XXVI,21	164
	139		168
XXV,10–11	142	XXVI,22–23	94
XXV,10	138	XXVI,22a	168
	164	XXVI,22b	168
XXV,11	91	XXVI,22c–23	168
	138	XXVI,23	186
XXV,11b	143	XXVI,24–29	160
XXV,12	116	XXVI,24–25	168
	138	XXVI,26–27	169
	148	XXVI,28	153
XXV,13–22	152		169
XXV,13–14a	152	XXVI,29	160
XXV,13	130		169
XXV,14b–15	154	XXVI,30–32	160
XXV,15	104	XXVI,30–31	170
	162	XXVI,30	161
XXV,16	108	XXVI,32	170
	137		199
	155	XXVII,1–	
XXV,17	157	XXVIII,15	172
XXV,18–19	157	XXVII,1	159
XXV,18	140		172
XXV,19	141	XXVII,2	172
	186	XXVII,3	172
XXV,20–21	157	XXVII,23–24a	175
XXV,20a	141		197
XXV,21	105	XXVII,43	174
XXV,22	153	XXVIII,6	137
	159	XXVIII,7	174
	160	XXVIII,11	174
XXV,23–27	152	XXVIII,12	174
	160	XXVIII,13	174
XXV,23	160	XXVIII,14a	174
XXV24–27	161		175
XXV,24	137	XXVIII,14b–15	175
XXV,25	170	XXVIII,16	176
XXV,25a	140		177
	199		179
XXV,26–27	106		192
XXV,26	152	XXVIII,17–22	181
XXV,27	163	XXVIII,17	127
XXVI,1–23	160		155
XXVI,1a	163		174
XXVI,1b	163		184
XXVI,2–3	164	XXVIII,18–19	185
XXVI,4–5	165	XXVIII,19	91
XXVI,4	164	XXVIII,20	94
XXVI,5	122		186
XXVI,5b	81	XXVIII,20b	200
XXVI,6–8	94	XXVIII,21–22	186

XXVIII,22	122	XI,24	166
XXVIII,23–28	181	XI,25	25
XXVIII,23	174	XIII,1	100
	188		
	192	*Galatians*	
XXVIII,24	189	I,13	165
XXVIII,25–27	189	I,14	72
XXVIII,28	49		81
	190	I,21	78
XXVIII,29	190	IV,20	158
XXVIII,30–31	177	V,12	35
	191		
XXVIII,30	174	*Ephesians*	
		II,12	79
Romans		VI,20	68
I,8	188		
I,9–10	198	*Philippians*	
I,15	175	I,7	156
	198	I,13	118
II,15	125	I,16	156
III,29–31	63	I,27	93
IV,14	63	III,5	81
IV,16	63	IV,16	31
IX,3b–5a	127		
XI,1b	81	*1 Thessalonians*	
XI,8	190	I,9	32
XIII,1–7	42	II,2	29
XV,19	167	II,9	31
XV,23b	175		48
	198	II,14–16	44
XV,24	48	II,17–18	43
	62		
XV,25–27	61	*2 Thessalonians*	
	128	III,2	137
XV,28	62	III,8	48
XV,30–31	62		
XVI,1	45	*1 Timothy*	
XVI,3–5a	47	III,9	93
XVI,25–26	168	IV,19	100
1 Corinthians		*2 Timothy*	
I,1	58	I,3	93
I,14	50	I,16	68
IV,3	88	IV,16a	156
	93	IV,19	47
IV,12	48	IV,20	66
IX,3	124		
IX,20	63	*Titus*	
XII,3	166	III,1	42
XV,3	168		
XV,9	165	*Philemon*	
XV,12ff	94	22	189
XVI,1–4	128		
XVI,19	47	*Hebrews*	
		VIII,11	79
2 Corinthians		XI,36	73
I,12	93		
IV,8	158	*1 Peter*	
VIII,1ff	128	II,13–17	42
XI,7–9	88	II,13	36
XI,22	81	II,17	36
		IV,16	169

2. Epigraphical and Papyrological Publications

BGU
- II,611 — 193
- II,628 — 195

CIG
- 1967.1 — 34

CII
- II,1400 — 65

CIL
- I,198 — 129
- I,204 — 30
- I,205 — 11
- I,206 — 10, 84
- I,541 — 45
- II,1963.27 — 148
- II,3271 — 111
- III,433 — 178
- III,6078 — 11
- III,13648 — 177
- III,14187 — 177
- VI,354 — 178
- IX,652 — 40
- IX,2628 — 40
- X,7495 — 175
- X,7852 — 148
- X,8023.4 — 111
- XII,2455 — 111

IG
- VII,2233 — 159
- XII−7,55.15 — 192
- XIV,601 — 175
- XIV,1072 — 159
- XIV,1124 — 162

ILS
- 96 — 37
- 229.10 — 6
- 5350 — 111
- 8888 — 82

OGIS
- 186.8 — 162
- 219.43 — 154
- 329.42 — 10
- 415.1 — 162
- 418.1 — 162
- 419 — 153
- 420 — 153
- 421 — 173
- 441.59 — 9
- 483.181 — 26
- 598 — 65
- 598 (note 1) — 65
- 629.100 — 43
- 666.4 — 35
- 668.5 — 35

P.Amh.
- II,29.18 — 105
- II,33.6−9 — 91
- II,66.41 — 126

P.Fay
- page 33 — 106
- CXI,8 — 138

P.Flor
- I,61.24 — 119
- 296.57 — 154

P.Hib.
- I,57 — 159

P.Lille
- I,29 — 74

P.Lond.
- II,359.7 — 194
- II,422 — 69
- VI,1912 — 19, 20, 41

P.Mich.
- 2737 — 85

P.Oxy.
- I,37(I),3−4 — 119
- I,41.19 — 33
- I,97.14 — 57
- II,246.37 — 162
- II,259.29 — 43
- III,502.31 — 192
- IV,745.4 — 34
- VII,1021.5−13 — 41
- VIII,1127.16 — 192
- IX,1204.13 — 119
- XXXVII,6 — 162
- CX,2 — 162

P.Petr.
- III,43 — 105

P.Tebt.
- I,22.9 — 129
- II,286.2 — 162
- II,434 — 56
- VII,7 — 159

SIG[4]
- 599.20 — 117
- 684.3 — 46
- 684.11 — 148
- 685.29 — 117
- 801.(d) — 54
- 820.6 — 159

3. Ancient Writers and Sources

Appian
Bella Civilia
I,7   6
II,140   6
III,54   156
IV,118   30
V,7   30

Apuleius Madaurensis
Apologia
LXXXIX,2–3   84

Metamorphoseon
VIII,28   73
VIII,30   73
X,6   195
X,18   45

Aristophanes
Nubes 1218   8

Ranae 1015   45

Aulus Gellius
Noctes Atticae
X,3.1–13   25
XVI,13.6–9   7
XX,1.7   131

Cicero
de Inventione
II,17.53   37

de Lege Agraria
II,34   10
   12
II,73   6

de Legibus
II,2.5   77
II,8.19   22
III,4.11   147

de Provinciis
Consularibus
I,2   156

de Republica
II,31.54   145
II,31.55   12
II,36.61   145

Epistulae ad Atticum
XVI,11.6   176

Epistulae ad Familiaris
X,32.3   150

In Verrem
I,13.39   195
II,i.29.73   148
II,i.29.74   129
II,ii.13.32   140
   148
II,ii,17.43   28
II,ii,29.70   148
II,ii.33.81   149
II,v.8.18–20   28
   195
II,v.8.18   149
II,v.31.80   118
II,v.42.109   28
II,v.57.147   28
II,v.62.161–162   25
II.v.63.163   25
II,v.66.170   28
   150

Orationes
Philippicae
II,92   82
V,11–12   82

pro Balbo
VIII,19   82

pro Flacco
XXVIII,66–69   16
   187

pro Rabirio
IV,12   28

pro Sestio
XXX,65   147

Clement of Rome
Epistle to the
Corinthians
V,2–7   177
XXI,1   93
LXI,1–2   42

Demosthenes
XXV,80   121
XLVIII,31   124

Digesta
I,16.6   46
I,16.8   46
I,18.1   110
I,18.4   113
I,18.6.8   113
IV,4.18.1   160
XLVII,22.1–4   15
XLVIII,3.1   180
XLVIII,3.11   117

XLVIII,4.6	37	V,1.27	26
XLVIII,4.7	169	V,1.44ff	151
XLVIII,6.7	150		
XLVIII,8	70	*Herodotus*	
XLVIII,11.3.7	131	V,38	10
XLVIII,16.1.10	194		
XLVIII,19.38.2	38	*Horace*	
XLIX,6.1	106	Satires I,4.140	23
L,15.6	7		

Ignatius of Antioch
  Romans V,1   68

Dio Cassius
  XXXVI,53.2   117
  LI,4.6   6
  LIII,13.6−8   112
          113

Jerome
  de Viris illustribus
    V   78
         193

  LIII,15.1−5   111
  LIII,32.5   37
  LIII,32.6   37

John Chrysostom
  de Laudibus Pauli
  Panegyric IV,10.12   32

  LVI,46.1−5   40
  LVII,18.5a   17
  LVII,8.1−2   162
  LVII,9.2−3   38
  LVII,10.2   40
  LIX,11.4   41
  LIX,11.6   38
  LX,6.6   52
  LX,17.4   86
  LX,17.5−6   75
  LX,24.4   29
  LX,28.6   194
  LX,35.2   51
  LXI,20.1   51
  LXII,25.3   51

Josephus
  Antiquitates Iudaicae
    XII,46   79
    XII,125−128   16
    XII,145   65
    XIII,297−298   95
    XIV,91   98
    XIV,110−118   20
    XIV,110   35
    XIV,168−169   98
    XIV,172   93
    XIV,175   98
    XIV,204   16
    XIV,211−212   14
    XIV,213−216   182
    XIV,223−232   16
    XIV,226   79
    XIV,228   79

Dio Chrysostom
  Discourses
    XIII,10−13   48
    XXIV,23   75

    XIV,232   79
    XIV,234   79
    XIV,235   16
              58

Dionysius Halicarnassensis
  Antiquitates Romanae
    V,70.2   27
              145
    VII,13.1−5   6
    VII,58.1   125
    IX,39.1−2   145
    X,31   11

    XIV,237   79
    XIV,240   79
    XIV,256−261   15
    XIV,324   137
    XV,173   103
    XV,331−341   109
    XV,403−409   70
    XV,417   65
    XVI,27−65   16

Epictetus
  Arrian Discourses
    III,24.41   85

    XVI,163   16
    XVI,258   156
    XVII,127   108

Euripedes
  Ion 673   192

    XVII,300   187
    XVII,328   175
    XVII,338   154
    XVIII,2   112

Eusebius
  Historia Ecclesiastica
    II,5.1−7   18
    II,6.1−2   18
    II,23.1   102
    IV,9   156

    XVIII,17   95
    XVIII,33   112
    XVIII,55   111

XVIII,81–84	17		II,119	122
XVIII,92	70		II,162–166	96
XVIII,116–119	103		II,166	95
XVIII,203–204	181		II,169	111
XVIII,234–235	181		II,172	56
XVIII,259	156			138
XIX,15	18		II,194	41
XIX,278	18		II,217	153
XIX,280–285	19		II,220	112
XIX,281–282	19			130
XIX,285	20		II,223	153
XIX,288	21		II,236	173
XIX,289	21		II,247	110
XIX,290–291	21			112
XIX,290	158			153
XIX,354	130		II,252	153
XIX,360–366	153		II,254–256	71
XIX,363	112		II,261–263	70
XIX,365	160		II,266–270	133
	173		II,269	74
XX,2	112		II,271	113
XX,103	93			135
XX,104	153		II,273	131
XX,122	173		II,301	56
XX,130	138		II,308	114
XX,131	93		II,345–401	153
XX,132	112		II,441	94
XX,134–136	153		II,531	178
XX,137	110		II,612	74
XX,138	153		III,351	36
XX,139–143	130		III,532	56
XX,145	153		IV,317	154
XX,159	153		V,144	92
XX,160	71		V,193–194	65
XX,161–163	70		V,238–242	70
XX,162	112		V,243–245	68
XX,171	70		VI,124–126	102
XX,173–178	133		VI,300–309	100
XX,179	94		VII,407–419	71
XX,182	133			
XX,185–188	135		Contra Apionem	
XX,189–196	154		II,38–39	19
XX,193	112		II,73–77	17
XX,197–203	102		II,103	65
XX,200	95		II,170	79
XX,215	134			
XX,222	153		Vita	
XX,249–251	99		3.13	187
XX,251	99		3.16	187
Bellum Iudaicum			Justin	
I,170	98		I Apol. LXVIII	156
I,242	137			
I,408–415	109			
II,52	173		Justinian	
II,58	173		Codex	
II,63	173		IX,3.1	180
II,74	173		X,19.2.1	180
II,104	175			
II,117	111		Novellae	
	112		86.4	43
	113			

Index of Passages

Juvenal
  Satires
    III,296 — 183
    VI,155–160 — 153
    XIV,96 — 13
            23

Livy
  ab Urbe condita
    III,13.4b–5 — 28
    VIII,32.11 — 25
    XXXIX,14 — 180
    XXXIX,15.1–16.3 — 22
    XLV,28 — 45
    XLV,29.5 — 4
    XLV,29.9 — 5
    LVI,3 — 6

Lucian
  de Morte Peregrini
    12 — 130

  pro Lapsu inter Salutandem
    18 — 158

Lysias
  VII,22 — 105

midrash Sanhedrin
  I,6 — 99
  I,66 — 167
  IV,1 — 92
  XI,2 — 92

Origen
  Ep. ad Africanum
    14 — 167

Orosius
  Historiarum adversus Paganos
    VII,6.15–16 — 52

Pausanias
  II,1 — 45

Paulus
  Sententiae
    V,26.1–2 — 150

Philo
  de Legatione ad Gaium
    XXI,143 — 159
    XXIII,153–154 — 16
    XXIII,155–157a — 182
    XXIII,157b — 16
    XXIII,158 — 182
    XXIV,159–161 — 17
    XXXI,212 — 65
    XXXII,231–232 — 18
    XXXVIII,299 — 111
    XXXIX,307 — 102

  in Flaccum
    X,75 — 74
    XVI,128–129 — 195

Plato
  Apologia 35C — 143

  Cratylus 415D — 192

  Respublica 565B — 33

Pliny the Elder
  Historia Naturalis
    III,25 — 7
    III,139 — 7
    IV,4 — 45
    IV,36 — 30
    IV,38 — 30
    XXXI,62 — 51
    XXXIV,6 — 45

Pliny the Younger
  Epistulae
    IV,22 — 119
    VI,31 — 194
    X,6 — 76
    X,7 — 76
    X,56 — 195
    X,57 — 178
           195
    X,96 — 22
           151
           162
           166
    X,97 — 155

Plutarch
  Aemilius Paulus
    XXXVIII,3 — 33

  Brutus
    XLVI,1 — 30

  Caesar
    LVII,5 — 45

  Caius Gracchus
    III,4 — 194

  Coriolanus
    XIX,2 — 12
    XX,4 — 154

  Marcellus
    II,4 — 145

Polybius
  Histories
    I,7.12 — 10

I,38.6	9		Caligula	
	192		XXVI,3	74
I,39.1	9			
I,52.5	10		Claudius	
III,106.6	10		XV,2	194
VIII,18.8	123		XXV	46
XXI,45.11	154			52
XXVIII,5.6	46			85
XXXII,3.13	43		XXV,5	22
XXXIII,1.5	10		XXVIII	110
				130

Res Gestae divi Augusti
34   158

Nero
X,2   147
XII   83
XLIX,2   12

Sallust
  de Bello Catilinario
  XLVII,3–4   180

Galba
IX   114

Scriptores Historiae Augustae
  Marcus Antoninus
  IX,7–8   84

Tacitus
  Annales
  I,10   40
  I,11   40
  I,72   38
  I,78   40
  I,80   45
  II,85   17
  II,87   162
  IV,15   40
    111
  IV,37–38   41
  XI,1   178
  XII,54   110
  XII,60   111
  XII,61   30
  XIII,14   133
  XIII,44   70
  XIV,41   194
  XIV,60   180
  XV,44   111
  XV,61   187
  XV,73   51

Seneca
  Apocolocyntosis
  XII   194
  XIV,1   70

  Epistulae Morales
  V,7   68
  CIV,1   51

  Quaestiones Naturalis
  IVa (praef.)   51
  IV,9–13   51
  V,11.1   51

Strabo
  Geographikon
  V,1.6   82
  VIII,6.23   45
  XVII,3.15   45
  XVII,24   192

  Historiae
  V,4   13
  V,5   13
    23
  V,9   110
    130

Suetonius
  Iulius
  XXVIII   82
  XLII,3   182
  LXXXVIII   40

Talmud (Babylonian)
  Yoma I,19b   100

Tertullian
  adversus Marcionem
  IV,8.1   122

  Augustus
  XXXII,1   182
  LII   40
  LIII,1   162

  Apologeticum
  XXI,1   15
  XXXII,1–3   42

  Tiberius
  XXVI   40
  XXVII,1   162
  XXXVI   17
  LVIII   38

Theodosian
  Codex
    IX,35.1–2   73

Theophrastus
  Characteres
    VI,2   32
    XVI,1   158

Thucydides
    I,33   132
    V,49.1   154

Valerius Maximus
  Facta Dictaque
    memorabilia
    I,3.1–3   22
    II,7.8   25

Velleius Paterculus
  Historiae Romanae
    I.13   45

Index of Names

Abbott, F.F. & Johnson, A.C., 10ff, 30ff
Alföldy, G., 110
Allison, J.E. & Cloud, J.D., 37ff
Anderson, J.G.C., 37
Applebaum, S., 14, 71, 76ff, 80

Badian, E., 18, 82
Bauer, W., 129
Bauman, R.A., 37ff
Bell, H.I., 18, 41
Benko, S., 53ff
Benoit, P., 118
Bickerman, E.J., 39ff, 65
Blass, F. & Debrunner, A., 65, 67, 119, 164
Bleicken, J., 6, 144, 146ff
Blinzler, J., 99, 101
Bovon, F., 117
Brassac, A., 55
Broughton, T.R.S., 67, 178
Bruce, F.F., 59, 71, 96, 103, 138, 143, 173
Brunot, A., 175
Bruns, K.G., 10ff, 30, 193, 195
Brunt, P.A., 37, 111
Burkill, T.A., 103
Buti, I., 114, 146ff, 173

Cadbury, H.J., 6, 83, 100, 145, 191ff
Calderone, S., 157ff
Cassidy, R.J., 76
Cerfaux, L., & Tondriau, J., 40ff
Chilton, C.W., 38
Clark, A.C., 177ff
Collart, P., 6ff
Cullmann, O., 176ff
Cuss, D., 39

Daniel, J.L., 14
Danielou, J., 81
Davies, R.W., 67, 105
Delebecque, E., 59, 186
Dibelius, M., 26, 101
Dupont, J., 108, 115, 140ff, 155ff, 176, 186, 195ff

Ehrenberg, V., & Jones, A.H.M., 83

Fascher, E., 55, 133
Ferenczy, E., 7
Foakes-Jackson, F.J., & Lake, K. (ed), 133
Fougères, G., 73
Frey, J.B., 52, 176, 183
Frova, A., 112

Garnsey, P., 113, 149
Garzetti, A., 17
Gaudemet, J., 37, 58, 112, 146
George, A., 72, 190
Gilchrist, J.M., 125
Giovannini, A., 10, 113, 145
Girard, P.F., 10ff, 30, 148
Goguel, M., 15, 59
Grant, M., 80
Greenidge, A.H.J., 145, 149ff
Gschnitzer, F., 30, 34

Haenchen, E., 7, 33ff, 71, 190
Hammond, M., 77
Hanson, R.P.C., 26
Hengel, M., 49, 70, 130
Herrmann, L., 54
Hitzig, H.F., 180
Hock, R.F., 48
Homo, L., 42
Horovitz, P., 113
Horsley, G.H.R., 40, 184
Hultgren, A.J., 166

Iliffe, J.H., 66

Jacquier, E., 94
Jervell, J., 63, 81
Jewett, R., 53, 133
Jones, A.H.M., 111, 113, 115, 144ff, 147
Jones, D.L., 41
Jullian, C. 7
Juster, J., 102

Kasher, A., 19, 77
Keresztes, P., 141
Kittel, G. (ed), 9ff, 25, 35, 57, 161ff, 167
Klausner, J., 127
Knox, J., 47
Kornemann, E., 5ff
Koukouli-Chrysanthaki, C., 34
Kübler, B., 12

Lake, K., 96
Lemonon, J.P., 101, 111
Lenormant, F., 5ff
Leon, H.J., 182ff
Liddell, H.G. & Scott, R., 8, 33, 57, 105, 107, 123, 129, 132, 143, 154, 161, 170, 177
Lietzmann, H., 15
Lifshitz, B., 96, 101, 109
Lintott, A.W., 144ff

Index of Names

Lohse, E., 15, 95
Lüdemann, G., 21, 47, 53ff, 86ff, 91

Mantel, H., 99
Marquardt, J., 11
Martini, C.M., 8, 14, 131
Mason, H.J., 5, 9ff, 36, 46, 112, 177
Meeks, W.A., 77
Menoud, P.H., 60
Miles, G.B., & Trompf, G., 172, 174
Millar, F., 39ff, 42, 150
Mommsen, T., 12, 31, 113, 138, 146, 148, 150ff, 178, 196
Moore, G.F., 23
Moulton, J.H., 43
Moulton, J.H. & Milligan, G., 9, 105, 154
Munck, J., 33
Munier, C., 41, 115, 117
Murphy-O'Connor, J., 45, 54ff

Neil, W., 7, 81
Nicolet, C., 7, 77

Oliver, J.H., 131, 150ff
O'Neill, J.C., 191

Penna, R., 53, 183
Perry, A.M., 127
Pherigo, L.P., 196
Piana, G. la, 15
Plassart, A., 55
Premerstein, A. von, 7
Prigent, P., 24

Rabello, A.M., 15, 23
Rajak, T., 14, 18
Ramsay, W.M., 24, 27, 39, 48, 82, 131, 173
Riccobono, S., 10ff, 30, 83, 148, 193
Robert, L., 106
Ross, R.C., 158
Rotondi, G., 10
Ruggini, L.C., 13ff

Saddington, D.B., 67

Samter, E., 12
Sanders, E.P., 63
Sanders, H.A., 85
Saulnier, C., 14ff, 52, 100
Saumagne, C., 132
Scheid, J., 22, 42
Schubert, P., 97
Schuler, C., 30, 43
Schulz, F., 84ff
Schürer, E., 98, 100, 102, 110, 183
Schwartz, J., 78
Scramuzza, V.M., 17, 103
Seston, W., 18
Sherwin-White, A.N., 4ff, 11, 13, 27, 30, 46, 57, 77, 84ff, 104, 114, 129, 141, 146, 151, 178ff, 194, 196
Smallwood, E.M., 15, 18ff, 23, 183
Smith, M., 70
Solin, H., 17, 53, 188
Stegemann, W., 87ff
Stern, M., 53, 182
Sullivan, R.D., 153

Taubenschlag, R., 69, 91, 104, 144, 155
Tcherikover, V., 19ff, 77, 80
Turner, C.H., 4

Unnik, W.C. van, 13, 25, 72
Urch, E.J., 115, 150

Vardaman, J., 112
Veltman, F., 70ff
Visscher, F. de, 173, 180

Walaskay, P.W., 36, 153
Watkins, T.H., 6ff
Wikenhauser, A., 58, 119, 179
Wikgren, A.P., 4ff
Williams, C.S.C., 13, 162
Wilson, S.G., 190
Wiseman, J., 45, 55

Zerwick, M., 119, 160

Index of Subjects
(Supplement to the Table of Contents)

aequitas 108
apologia 116, 125, 156
appellatio 145ff
Augustus
— confirms Jewish privileges 15
— receives title 36

captatio benevolentiae 120, 164
civitas libera 30ff
Claudius
— combats fraudulent charges 193
— expels Jews from Rome 18, 52ff
— settles Alexandrian affair 18ff
— strengthens office of Procurator 111
— traffic in Roman citizenship 82
coercitio 11, 25, 26, 29, 46, 113
cognitio 46
— *Augusti* 159
— *extra ordinem* 114ff, 151
cohors 67, 173
colonia 5ff, 45
consilium 148
consuetudo 155
crimen maiestas 38ff, 60
custodia
— *libera* 180
— *militaris* 179ff

decretum 35
dimissoriae litterae 106ff, 163
dominus (title) 162

edictum 35
— *de temporibus accusationum* 195
emperor (*princeps*)
— divinization of 39ff
— hears appeals 147
— *maiestas* 37
— powers 37, 147
— titles 36
— worship of 41ff

Felix
— hears Paul's *apologia* 125ff
— keeps Paul in prison 129
— procurator 109ff
— seeks favour with Jews 132
Festus
— arrives in Palestine 135
— consults Agrippa 152ff
— decides change of custody 140ff
— grants Paul's appeal 148
flagrum 73
Fortress Antonia 69

Gallio
— dismisses Paul's case 56ff
— proconsul 51, 54

Herod Agrippa II
— finds Paul innocent 171
— hears Paul's speech 163
— king 152ff

imperium
— limits on 150
— *maius* 37, 46, 113, 147
— *proconsulare* 46
— right of governors 99, 103, 112
intercessio 145
ius
— *gladii* 46, 113
— *Italicum* 7

Jews
— citizenship in *polis* 20
— expulsion from Rome 52ff
— grouped in *collegia* 15, 182
— jealous of Paul 32
— Roman 181ff
Judaism
— Alexandrian 19ff
— as a legal religion 13
— forms of Emperor-worship 16, 42

king (title) 36

Latin 45, 86
Lysias
— arrests Paul 66
— brings Paul to Sanhedrin 90
— institutes police inquiry 69
— orders Paul tortured 73
— remits Paul to Felix 103

messianism (political) 71

Nazarenes (sect of) 122
Nero 194

oikoumene 35

Index of Subjects

Paul
- case ends in default 196
- is uncondemned 27, 74
- missionary programme 23
- place in Acts 3
- proclaims Roman citizenship 26ff, 74
- sufferings 25

plebs 33
polis
- citizenship in 19, 77
- free speech in 192

politarchs 34
politeuma 15, 77
praefectus
- *castrorum* 177
- provincial 110ff

praetorium 117ff, 176
proconsul
- powers of 46

procurator
- evolution of term 110ff
- powers of 112ff

proselytism 13, 21ff
provocatio 113, 144ff, 150

rhetor 118
Roman citizenship
- grant of 82
- key to Paul's case 197
- possessed by Paul 86ff
- proof of 83ff

Sanhedrin
- institution 98ff
- judicial prerogatives 100ff
- jurisdiction in capital cases 101
- parties in 95

satis accipere 43
sedens pro tribunali 89, 138
sicarii 70
Stratopedarch 177ff
superstitio 157

tribunus cohortis 67

virgis caedere 25

www.ingramcontent.com/pod-product-compliance
Lightning Source LLC
Chambersburg PA
CBHW062000220426
43662CB00011B/1759